DEVELOPING ESSENTIAL STUDY SKILLS

We work with leading authors to develop the
strongest educational materials in study skills,
bringing cutting-edge thinking and best
learning practice to a global market.

Under a range of well-known imprints, including
Financial Times Prentice Hall, we craft high quality print
and electronic publications which help readers to
understand and apply their content, whether studying
or at work.

To find out more about the complete range of our
publishing, please visit us on the World Wide Web at:
www.pearsoned.co.uk

Second Edition

DEVELOPING ESSENTIAL STUDY SKILLS

Elaine Payne and **Lesley Whittaker**

Leeds Business School, Leeds Metropolitan University

An imprint of **Pearson Education**
Harlow, England • London • New York • Boston • San Francisco • Toronto • Sydney • Singapore • Hong Kong
Tokyo • Seoul • Taipei • New Delhi • Cape Town • Madrid • Mexico City • Amsterdam • Munich • Paris • Milan

Pearson Education Limited

Edinburgh Gate
Harlow
Essex CM20 2JE
England
and Associated Companies throughout the world

Visit us on the World Wide Web at:
www.pearsoned.co.uk

© Prentice Hall Europe 1999
Second edition published 2006

© Pearson Education Limited 2006

The rights of Elaine Payne and Lesley Whittaker to be identified as authors of this work have been asserted by them in accordance with the Copyright, Designs and Patents Act 1988.

All rights reserved. No part of this publication may be reproduced, stored in a retrieval system, or transmitted in any form or by any means, electronic, mechanical, photocopying, recording or otherwise, without either the prior written permission of the publisher or a licence permitting restricted copying in the United Kingdom issued by the Copyright Licensing Agency Ltd, 90 Tottenham Court Road, London W1T 4LP.

ISBN–13: 978–0–273–68804–4
ISBN–10: 0–273–68804–9

British Library Cataloguing-in-Publication Data
A catalogue record for this book is available from the British Library

Library of Congress Cataloging-in-Publication Data
A catalogue record for this book is available from the Library of Congress

10 9 8 7 6 5 4 3 2
10 09 08 07 06

Typeset in 9.5 pt Palatino by 3
Printed and bound by Ashford Colour Press, Ltd., Gosport

The publisher's policy is to use paper manufactured from sustainable forests.

Contents

List of figures and tables   xi
List of activities and exercises   xv
Preface   xix

Part 1   DEVELOPING STUDY SKILLS

Introduction to Part 1   3

Learning opportunity   3

1   Learning to learn   5

Introduction   5
How do we learn?   6
Lifelong learning   7
University or college learning   9
Independent learning   10
Learning styles   12
Factors that influence learning   20
Building on learning strengths and overcoming blockages to learning   28
Summary   31

2   Keeping a portfolio   32

Introduction   32
What is a portfolio?   33
Skills audit   37
Reflection in your portfolio   41
Summary   47

3   Employability   48

Introduction   48
Conducting a self-analysis   50
Exploring career options   53
Understanding the job market   55
Developing a curriculum vitae (CV)   57

Covering letters	63
Interviews	65
Summary	68

4 Reading for study — 69

Introduction	69
Why are you reading?	70
What happens when you read?	71
Ways of reading	72
Which technique?	78
Selecting reading material	78
Other useful techniques	81
How to read faster	82
Critically evaluative reading	88
Summary	89

5 Communication — 90

Introduction	90
The process of interpersonal communication	91
Non-verbal communication	92
Written communication	94
Words that are often confused	95
Spelling	97
Active or passive voice?	97
Transitional words and phrases	97
Style	99
Glossary	101
Summary	102

6 Making notes — 103

Introduction	103
Why make notes?	103
Ways of making notes	104
Making notes from text	109
Making notes in lectures	109
Making notes from a group discussion	113
Abbreviations and symbols	113
Keeping notes	115
Summary	117

7 Working with numbers — 118

Introduction	118
Numerical data	119

Making data easier to handle	120
Describing the data with pictures	126
Describing the data with numerical summaries	135
Spreadsheet software	142
Summary	143
Answers to exercises	144

8 Information technology skills — 147

Introduction	147
Some terms defined	147
Organising your work	152
Windows	154
Word-processing software – Word	155
Spreadsheet software – Excel	157
Presentation software – PowerPoint	161
Summary	162
Answers to exercise	162

9 Researching and obtaining information — 163

Introduction	163
A systematic approach to information gathering	164
Secondary sources	167
Printed resources	172
Other media	178
Other sources of secondary information	180
The Internet	180
Evaluation of information	188
When to stop collecting secondary information	189
Primary data collection	191
Analysis of data	207
Summary	208
Answers to exercises	209

10 Group and team-working skills — 211

Introduction	211
Why should students know about group dynamics?	212
Small group dynamics	213
Development of norms	215
Roles	216
Cohesiveness	219
Developmental stages of groups	221
How to know more about groups	224
Differences between groups and teams	227
Team role theory	229

CONTENTS

Working in groups and teams at university or college — 231
Summary — 236

11 Time management — 237

Introduction — 237
How to manage your time effectively — 238
Essentials of time management — 239
Time wasters — 245
Personal benefits from effective time management — 247
Summary — 248

12 Managing stress — 249

Introduction — 249
What is stress? — 250
Some consequences of stress — 251
Causes of stress — 252
Life events — 255
Managing stress — 257
Coping mechanisms — 258
Specific stress associated with being a student — 262
Manage your time — 264
Summary — 264

Part 2 DEVELOPING ASSESSMENT SKILLS

Introduction to Part 2 — 267

Learning opportunity — 268
Expectations — 268
Assessment criteria — 270
Presentation of assessments — 270
Deadlines — 270
Group assessments — 271
Feedback — 273

13 Case studies — 275

Introduction — 275
The use of case studies — 276
Framework for case study analysis — 277
Presentation of answers — 289
Summary — 290

14 Presentations — 291

Introduction — 291
Purposes of presentations — 292
Preparation — 293
Structure — 294
Approach — 295
The presentation — 296
Visual aids — 301
Questions — 309
Assessed presentations — 311
Creating a presentation using PowerPoint — 311
Summary — 316

15 Essay writing — 317

Introduction — 317
Analysing the essay title — 318
Finding your material — 320
Making an essay plan or outline — 322
Producing a rough draft — 324
Writing the essay — 325
Reviewing the essay — 328
Common criticisms of essays — 330
Writing essays under examination conditions — 331
Summary — 332
Answer to exercise — 332

16 Report writing — 333

Introduction — 333
Preliminary stage — 334
Preparation stage — 336
Writing the report — 338
Presentation — 345
Review — 347
Types of report — 349
Group reports — 350
Summary — 351

17 Writing dissertations or research projects — 352

Introduction — 352
Selection of a topic — 354
Defining the research question and objective — 357
Research proposal — 358
Conducting the research — 361

CONTENTS

Writing up the research 361
Management of the dissertation or research project 363
Summary 364

18 Examinations 365

Introduction 365
Why examinations? 366
Preparing for examinations 367
Revision 369
Written examinations 372
Oral examinations (*viva voce*) 387
Practical examinations 388
What to do if you fail an examination 389
Cheating 390
Summary 391

Bibliography 393
Index 394

List of figures and tables

Figures

1.1	Lifelong learning	8
1.2	The virtuous learning cycle	10
1.3	The learning cycle	12
1.4	Memory	21
1.5	Stages in learning	25
1.6	An example of a lifeline	26
2.1	Reflection	42
2.2	How to reflect	44
4.1	Different ways of reading	73
4.2	Eye movements and fixations	84
5.1	The interpersonal communication process	91
5.2	Successful communication	91
5.3	Unsuccessful communication	92
6.1	Example of sequential outline notes for Chapter 1 of this book	106
6.2	A mind map constructed from the beginning of Chapter 1	107
6.3	Some important things to listen for	111
7.1	Data set	119
7.2	Example of tabular presentation	123
7.3	Grouped frequency distribution	125
7.4	Simple bar chart	127
7.5	Component bar chart	127
7.6	Percentage component bar chart	128
7.7	Multiple bar chart	128
7.8	Pictogram	129
7.9	Pie chart	129
7.10	Histogram	130
7.11	Axes showing broken scale	131
7.12	Line graph	132
7.13	Cumulative frequency tables	133
7.14	Ogive	133
7.15	Calculation of an arithmetic mean from a frequency distribution	135
7.16	Calculation of the mean from a grouped frequency distribution	136
7.17	Estimating the median from an ogive	138
7.18	The mode	138

xi

7.19 Estimating the mode from a histogram — 139
7.20 Calculating the standard deviation from a grouped frequency distribution — 141

8.1 Possible structure for a file directory — 153
8.2 Typical Windows screen — 154
8.3 Typical menu bar for a Windows application — 155
8.4 Example of a spreadsheet — 157

9.1 Key words and phrases — 165
9.2 Structure of a World Wide Web address — 183
9.3 Strategy for eliciting information from an interview — 204

10.1 Factors that affect groups — 213
10.2 Stages of group development — 221
10.3 Factors that influence groups — 224

11.1 Estimated use of time for a typical student — 242

12.1 Optimum stress levels — 250
12.2 The human stress curve — 251

13.1 Framework for case study analysis — 278
13.2 The fishbone diagram — 285
13.3 Presenting recommendations — 288

14.1 The process of presenting — 293
14.2 Presentation structure — 295
14.3 Different types of graphical display — 303
14.4 Projection techniques to avoid — 307

15.1 Elements of a good essay — 332

16.1 Stages of report writing — 334
16.2 Conclusions — 341
16.3 Presenting recommendations — 342
16.4 An example of a report structure — 346

17.1 Refining the research — 359

18.1 Example of short answer question — 374
18.2 Examples of different types of examination question — 373
18.3 Strategy for completing essay questions — 384
18.4 Strategy for examinations — 390

Tables

1.1 Types of learning delivery — 9
1.2 Characteristics of the dependent and the independent learner — 11
1.3 The four learning tendencies and student learning preferences — 13
1.4 Kolb's four learning styles — 17
1.5 Honey and Mumford's four learning styles — 20
1.6 Examples of positive thinking and taking responsibility — 29

5.1 Common gestures and their messages — 93
5.2 Words that are often confused — 96

5.3	Examples of passive and active voices	97
5.4	Punctuation	100
6.1	Commonly used abbreviations and symbols	114
6.2	Examples of useful abbreviations	114
7.1	Examples of qualitative and quantitative data	119
7.2	Examples of calculation of percentages	122
7.3	Frequency table	124
7.4	Constructing a grouped frequency table	125
7.5	Salary data	136
7.6	Calculating the standard deviation	141
9.1	General headings within the Dewey classification system	170
9.2	Example of subdivisions within the Dewey classification system	170
9.3	Different types of journal	174
9.4	Example using the search term 'study skills'	182
9.5	World Wide Web addresses of some useful search engines	186
9.6	Sampling chart	194
9.7	Do's and don'ts of questionnaire design	199
10.1	Differences between groups and teams	228
12.1	The rating scale for life events – student version	255
PT2	Levels of intellectual behaviour	269
13.1	Example table to record information	282
13.2	Analysis of solutions	287
14.1	Criteria used to evaluate presentations	310
15.1	Common instructional words and their definitions	319
15.2	Common linking words and phrases	326
15.3	Common criticisms of essays and their remedies	330
16.1	Constructing a bibliography	343
16.2	Questions to ask when reviewing a report	348
16.3	Guidelines for compiling reports	349
18.1	Examination format	368
18.2	Example of a revision timetable	370
18.3	Common types of question used in objective tests	373

List of Activities and Exercises

Activities

1.1	Learning experiences	7
1.2	Dependent/independent learner	12
1.3	Learning cycle	15
1.4	Learning styles	18
1.5	Factors that help or hinder learning	23
1.6	Rewards for learning	24
1.7	Creating a learning development plan	25
1.8	Blockages to learning and how to overcome them	29
2.1	Skills audit	37
2.2	SWOT analysis	43
2.3	Reflection	46
3.1	Your aspirations for a job	51
3.2	Personality traits and self-management skills	52
3.3	Your chosen career field	53
3.4	Identifying a prospective employer	56
3.5	Describe yourself positively	58
3.6	Career objective	59
3.7	Compiling your CV – education	60
3.8	Compiling your CV – work experience	60
4.1	SQ3R	78
4.2	Selecting and surveying a book	81
4.3	Assessing your reading speed	83
4.4	Testing recognition span	84
4.5	Increasing reading speed	86
5.1	Confusing words	96
5.2	Consider your writing	100
6.1	Annotating text	105
6.2	Writing summary notes	106
6.3	Producing outline notes	107
6.4	Creating a mind map	108
6.5	Making notes in lectures	112
6.6	Abbreviations and symbols	115
6.7	Experiment	117
7.1	Presentation of data	134

8.1	University/college computing facilities	151
8.2	Directories and files	153
8.3	Formatting in Word	157
8.4	PowerPoint presentations	161
9.1	Using the library catalogue	172
9.2	Abstracts and periodical indexes	176
9.3	Information held on CD-ROM	179
9.4	Retrieving information from the Internet	188
9.5	Getting to know your library	190
9.6	Gathering data	207
10.1	Group norms	215
10.2	Group stages of development	223
10.3	Groups and teams behaviour sheet	233
11.1	Time allocation	239
11.2	Weekly time log	240
11.3	Prioritising activities	241
11.4	Time inventory	243
11.5	Time wasters	247
12.1	Identifying your stressors	253
12.2	Stress rating scale	256
12.3	Diagnosing personal stressors	256
12.4	Taking 'time out'	260
13.1	Categorising information	283
14.1	Practice presentation	300
14.2	Producing graphical overhead projector slides	305
14.3	Analysis of a professional presenter	311
15.1	Identifying difficulties	318
15.2	Dealing with the difficulties of essay writing	331
16.1	Referencing	343
16.2	Bibliography	344
16.3	Reviewing reports	348
16.4	Writing reports	350
17.1	Dissertation requirements for the course	353
17.2	Ethical considerations	356
17.3	Identifying suitable topics for research	356
17.4	Determining the research question	357
17.5	Constructing the terms of reference	359
18.1	Benefits gained from examinations	366
18.2	Future benefits	370
18.3	Avoiding examination failure	387
18.4	Review of examination technique	389

LIST OF ACTIVITIES AND EXERCISES

Exercises

7.1	Terminology	120
7.2	Rounding	121
7.3	Percentages	122
7.4	Constructing tables	123
7.5	Frequency table	126
7.6	Dependent and independent variables	131
7.7	Presentation of data	134
7.8	Comparison of means	137
7.9	Measures of central tendency	139
7.10	Comparison of standard deviations	141
7.11	Working with raw data	142
8.1	Spreadsheets	158
9.1	Identifying key words and phrases	165
9.2	Categories of journal	173
9.3	Government statistical publications	177
9.4	Sampling methods	195
9.5	Problem questions	199
9.6	Postal questionnaires	201
9.7	Gathering data by questionnaire or interview	205
9.8	Collecting data by observation	206
9.9	Gathering data through experiments	207
15.1	Key and instructional words	320

This book is accompanied by a Premium Companion Website at www.pearsoned.co.uk/payne containing:

- an Online Study Guide with additional topic coverage
- interactive exercises and activities
- downloadable templates for your Personal Development Plan or Portfolio.

To access these resources simply register using the pin code on the access card that came with this book.

This book is dedicated to Geoff, Geoffrey, Robert and Rachel
Lesley

This book is dedicated to Phil, my mother and family
Elaine

Preface

This book is aimed at helping you to improve your study skills. You have enormous untapped resources within you, and the ability to develop your study skills will enable you to complete your course successfully. The time spent at university or college offers great possibilities for change. Being able to study effectively will allow you to gain more enjoyment and fulfilment from the changes that you will encounter.

Why you need this book

There is an increasing trend in universities and colleges towards students becoming independent learners. It is critical that you move towards independence in studying as quickly as possible. This is one of the keys to success. This practical book is aimed at helping you become a more independent learner, which will empower you to study more effectively and efficiently. The study skills chosen to be included are the essential ones that will help you to accomplish your study objectives and be effective on your course. When you need or wish to know about a particular study skill, there is a chapter to help you. There is a wealth of background information, but not overwhelming detail. This is a how-to-do-it book, based on years of knowledge, experience and practice, which will enable you to achieve success in your studies. You can feel confident about using the material included in the book, since it has been tried and tested by the authors with the students who have been on their courses over the years.

Who this book is for

If you are new to university or college and unsure about the demands that your course will place on you, this book is intended for you. It will guide you through the essential study skills necessary for you to become a successful student.

If you are a mature student who has taken a non-traditional route to university or college and your skills need either developing from scratch or polishing up, this book is also aimed at you because it will provide you with all the information you need about studying.

There are no instant ways to acquire study skills. Skills development of any type, be it study skills or rock climbing, takes commitment and dedication. You will need to commit your energy and time to gain and practise the study skills that you require until you reach the level of proficiency that satisfies you and meets the demands of your course. The book is designed so that you can identify and choose approaches to suit your learning style and needs now and in the future.

How to use this book

The learning outcomes at the start of each chapter are the 'maps' that you can look at to decide whether you possess a particular study skill at a sufficient level of proficiency. The rest of the chapter is effectively the route you take to develop your level of expertise in a particular skill. Within the chapters you will find activities and exercises that are designed to enable you to practise different aspects of the study skill. Acquisition of study skills is an active process, not a passive one. You will not acquire the essential study skills to help you pass your course if you do not practise them regularly.

Checklists and suggestion boxes have also been included to provide you with the essentials that enable you to know quickly 'how to' do something. Each chapter also contains prompts – 'Stop and think' and 'Remember' – that encourage reflection on your progress. The summary at the end of each chapter will enable you to identify whether you have achieved what the chapter intended.

The structure of the book

The book comprises a series of chapters about different study skills. It has been organised so that each chapter can be read without reference to the other chapters. However, reference has been made to other areas where there are links that you should be aware of and might wish to explore. You can 'dip into' the book, finding and using a particular chapter that is relevant to your needs, or you can read consecutively through the chapters, depending on your requirements. However, it is a good idea to focus on a particular chapter when you need that specific study skill. Ensure, though, that you have sufficient time to acquire and practise the study skill. It is no good reading about how to write an essay the night before you have to hand one in for an assessment.

The book is structured in two main parts in addition to the Preface.

Part 1 Developing study skills

Part 1 identifies and details the skills required by students that are essential for study and transferable into employment. It will enable you to understand the learning process, compile portfolios and develop employability skills. The chapters on reading and communication will enable you to develop further these skills which are fundamental to success. The following chapters outline the practicalities of studying, including ways of making notes and working with numbers and information technology as well as researching and obtaining information.

The chapter on group and teamworking includes information about what to expect when working in groups. Many students underestimate the skills required to work effectively in groups. At university or college it can be 'fun' to be a member of a group or team for leisure activities, but there will be times when you are working in groups to complete an assessment. If you are unaware of what happens when people work together, you may face problems on your course or even disaster if the group members do not work effectively together. The remaining chapters in Part 1 provide information on time management and what causes stress for students and how to manage it.

All these skills are essential for successful study and provide a useful toolkit to enable you to meet the assessment requirements for your course.

Part 2 Developing assessment skills

Part 2 will help you to develop the study skills that will enable you to successfully complete the assessments on your course. The chapters provide key elements to enable you to write good essays, reports and dissertations, analyse a case study, deliver effective presentations and pass examinations.

Inevitably there is a little duplication where skills apply in more than one study area. This is unavoidable because of the nature of study skills, but it has been kept to a minimum. However, study skills need practice. They are not something that can be read about or practised once, after which proficiency or competency is achieved. In the case of study skills, repetition is beneficial. Skills invariably improve with practice and experience: for example, think about the first time you learnt to ride a bicycle, then compare it with the level of skill proficiency you had acquired 5 or 10 years later. With study skills there is always room for improvement.

Skills for the future

Lifelong learning will be the only way to keep abreast of the pace of change in a technological age, requiring flexible labour markets that operate in an increasingly global economy. Lifetime careers will become a rarity in the future, and the way that people are able to deal with this is by reskilling through lifelong learning. Business can only be competitive with a highly skilled, highly educated workforce. Lifelong learning and self-development will increase an individual's employment prospects and provide business with the skills it needs. Study skills are the key that unlocks the potential for independent, lifelong learning. Some of the study skills developed from using this book will bring long-term benefits that will help you in the world of work. What you should remember is that study skills are not only used when you study, but are an essential part of everyday life. For example, employers increasingly require a wider range of skills from employees. It is important to employers that transferable skills are developed. What this means is that prospective employees must possess skills which can be transferred from one situation to another. The chapter on employability provides information on how best to present the transferable skills you have developed to employers.

Working through this book will enable you to develop many of these transferable skills. For example, by the time you have read this book you should have identified a willingness to engage in lifelong learning and development, be able to use your time effectively, be self-disciplined and have the ability to deal with stress and set priorities. You should have developed group and team skills that encourage collaborative and cooperative working. You will have developed good communication skills which include being able to give a presentation, write effective reports, interpret and present numbers, and use information technology. If you ultimately decide to enter one of the professions, you should be able to pass professional body examinations. Developing the study skills outlined in this book will enable you to display the personal and intellectual skills that employers are looking for, such as good communication skills and excellent interpersonal skills, which ultimately will enable you to perform effectively and efficiently in organisations. You will also be able to develop the attribute of flexibility, which will enable you to adapt quickly to the culture of an organisation. These skills will not only assist you to be successful on your course, but will also equip you for the world of employment in the future.

PREFACE

We hope you will be inspired to develop your study skills from the ideas, activities and suggestions presented in this book. By the time you have worked through the book, you should be making progress towards the goal of becoming an effective, efficient and successful independent learner. In compiling the book we have drawn from our experience as students when we were in higher education. We have also used our experience as tutors in identifying what we think are essential study skills as well as including the study skills that our students have specifically asked about.

Elaine Payne
Lesley Whittaker

Part 1 DEVELOPING STUDY SKILLS

1. LEARNING TO LEARN
2. KEEPING A PORTFOLIO
3. EMPLOYABILITY
4. READING FOR STUDY
5. COMMUNICATION
6. MAKING NOTES
7. WORKING WITH NUMBERS
8. INFORMATION TECHNOLOGY SKILLS
9. RESEARCHING AND OBTAINING INFORMATION
10. GROUP AND TEAM-WORKING SKILLS
11. TIME MANAGEMENT
12. MANAGING STRESS

This book is accompanied by a Premium Companion Website at **www.pearsoned.co.uk/payne** containing:

- an Online Study Guide with additional topic coverage
- interactive exercises and activities
- downloadable templates for your Personal Development Plan or Portfolio.

To access these resources simply register using the pin code on the access card that came with this book.

Introduction to Part 1

Now that you are about to start your university or college course, you will need to prepare yourself for studying. What is important to remember about skills development is that once a particular skill has been acquired, such as riding a bicycle or learning to swim, it will last for your lifetime, but it can be improved with practice. Similarly, study skills once acquired will never be forgotten, but they will deteriorate if not practised regularly. What you should remember is that writing essays, reports and dissertations, taking notes, reading, giving presentations, taking examinations, etc., are all skills that require practice. If you put increased effort into these study skills, your ability will improve, and these are the fundamental skills, or springboard, that will enable you to achieve your overall objective of passing your course. The more motivated you are to improve your study skills, the more successful you will be on your course of study.

You should approach studying in the way that you approach the acquisition of all skills – with motivation, desire and determination. The study skills in this book require preparation, perseverance and practice. Working through this book will enable you to plan and organise your studies and will provide you with the tools and techniques to manage the experiences that you face during your time at university or college. The study skills set out in this book are the foundations on which you will build and it is essential, therefore, that you do not neglect this fundamental aspect of higher education. Much of your study will involve developing and improving the skills necessary to pass your course and subsequently to gain employment.

 ## Learning opportunity

Aristotle, the learned scholar, pointed out that it is not possible to learn without pain. Acquiring study skills is not easy: you will need to work very hard, but ultimately the benefits that you accrue will far outweigh any effort that you have to expend in gaining the skills. You will have to be willing to commit yourself to using your energy and giving your time to accomplish your study objectives. Your course of study at university or college is a unique learning opportunity and one that can be exciting, demanding, liberating, challenging and rewarding, as well as hard work. You must lay the foundations well. If you do, there is no doubt that you will experience the joys of studying, not only from books and other media, but also through interactions with others in group work.

1 Learning to learn

> **Learning outcomes**
> After studying this chapter, you should be able to:
> - appreciate the main elements of the learning process
> - distinguish between different learning styles
> - identify personal learning strengths and preferred learning style
> - recognise the factors that influence learning
> - identify some of the blocks that may hinder your learning
> - identify effective learning strategies and ways to implement them.

→ Introduction

What comes to mind when you think about learning? Most people will tend to think about school, maybe a teacher, or their classroom experience. These associations indicate some of the implicit assumptions we make about the nature of the learning process. However, a moment's reflection will reveal that learning is much more than this. Whilst we do learn in structured learning environments, we also acquire a great deal of our knowledge, skills, attitudes and values in an unstructured way. In the first few years of our lives we learn more than we do in all the remainder of our life, and for the learner, at least, a great deal of this is unconscious learning. For example, we learn to speak a language, we learn how to live with others, we learn what is dangerous and what is not, and so on.

Imagine for a moment the instant when a baby is born. Immediately it has to start to learn about its new environment. Instead of being in the warm, comfortable, cosseted, dark, floating and peaceful environment that was its mother's womb, where its every need was met instantaneously, the baby finds itself in a harsh, bright, loud and possibly uncomfortable world. Suddenly the imperative is to adapt and learn in order to survive. It is self-evident that we start to learn on the day we are born and only stop learning when we reach the end of our lives. However, most of us never stop to think about something that is fundamental to our existence and that is the route to a successful career.

PART 1   DEVELOPING STUDY SKILLS

Whilst it may be very useful to learn in an unstructured way in the early stages of our lives, it is essential that we, as individuals, take control of the learning process and impose structure and order on the ways we learn. Before we are able to do this effectively, we must understand the learning process.

→ How do we learn?

There are many competing explanations about how people learn, all of which can offer something to assist us in understanding this process.

> **Stop and think**
>
> How did you learn to:
> - talk?
> - read?
> - play a sport?
> - iron?
> - walk?
> - count?
> - sew?
> - sing?

The chances are that you learned many of the skills you possess not through the formal educational system, but through your own initiative. You were motivated by desire or need. You may have learned them with the assistance and guidance of others, or possibly you learned them through your own endeavours.

Some learning is related to physical development and some is linked to intellectual development. An illustration of how learning is linked to physical development is that at a certain point a baby will stand up and take a tentative step, plopping down to the ground with a bump. However, the baby is encouraged to try and try again until it successfully walks. This is one way that individuals learn, by trial and error.

When we learn to play sport, many of us will just have a go. We see people playing tennis, borrow or acquire a tennis racquet, and start hitting the ball around. It is only later that we find out that to play properly and to improve we need coaching and to learn the rules of the game. Coaching would involve someone telling us how to hold the racquet, how to stand and how to hit the ball. We also need to read the rules so that we know how to play, what is acceptable, what the scoring system is and how to implement it. Then we need to practise so that we reinforce our acquisition of this new skill. Over time there would need to be integration of practical activities with the theoretical aspects of the game.

Of course, not everyone would learn using the sequence described – doing something and then learning the theoretical approaches. Some individuals may prefer to read all about the mechanics of playing tennis, as well as the history of the game, before even picking up a racquet. This person might prefer to observe tennis being played by professional tennis players, only then setting foot on a tennis court. For each person there is a way to learn that is more appropriate than others. It is important to find out which approach to learning you have a preference for. When you understand your learning preferences, you can match these, as far as possible, to learning experiences that you encounter. Where this is not possible, you will know what your learning strengths are and be able to act to overcome or minimise the weaker areas in the ways you learn. This will allow you to use your judgement to solve increasingly complex problems by building on previous learning.

LEARNING TO LEARN

See Activity 1.1 FINDING YOUR LEARNING STYLE in the Online Study Guide.

Activity 1.1

Learning experiences

Write about your own learning experiences using the following questions to guide you:

- Do your early learning experiences differ from the way you learn now? Distinguish and write down how they differ. If you think they do not differ, identify and write down how they are similar.
- Do you think that you learn to play sport in different ways from the ways that you learned the route(s) you travel to university/college/school? Again, distinguish and write down what makes them different. If you think they do not differ, identify and write down what the similarities are.
- Is it easier for you to learn from:
  (a) experience, actually doing something, or
  (b) reading about what you should do?
- Is it easier for you to learn:
  (a) in small steps, a little at a time, or
  (b) by observing the behaviour of others and imitating it?
- Do you prefer to learn:
  (a) by being told what to do, or
  (b) by being shown the way to do something?
- Is learning a pleasurable, relatively easy experience for you, or is it something you have to work hard at?

Note down your findings carefully and reflect upon what this information tells you about how you learn.

→ Lifelong learning

Learning is a natural process, and continues throughout life. It is usually associated with practical experience, which means actually physically doing something, usually repeatedly until learning takes place. This is one of the secrets of learning. A person who is able to read books very quickly and has a photographic memory may be someone to admire. This so-called photographic memory is not usually something that occurs without any effort. Someone who appears to have a photographic memory probably spends a great deal of time reading, which in turn broadens his or her knowledge and improves memory. What is observed is the person's ability to read quickly, and their knowledge of subjects is so great that it seems that he or she has a photographic memory.

Each person has the capability to learn and develop himself or herself as a learner. In an increasingly knowledge-based society it will become more important to develop lifelong learning skills. In the future, one subject or set of subjects will not be sufficient to keep abreast of developments in a world where the pace of change is accelerating. Lifelong learning is the key to the future and will enable the learner to achieve his or her full potential. Lifelong learning and self-development will improve employment prospects as well as providing business with the skills needed to survive in an increasingly competitive global economy. Careers that span a lifetime will become a rarity in the future and the way to deal with this is by reskilling through lifelong learning. It will be necessary to learn, unlearn and relearn new skills in order to be able to deal with the change and innovation that the future will bring. It is through learning that individuals grow and mature, and one of the most important skills to acquire is learning how to learn. In a world of continuous change the most valuable investment that can be made is in learning, self-development and self-improvement.

We all have a desire to learn in order to understand the world in which we live. Most of us know someone – friend, colleague, family member – who has spent a great deal of time and energy on an informal learning experience, for instance restoring a car, decorating a room, or learning a foreign language. A great deal of time, energy, enthusiasm and passion (and frequently money) is spent on learning because the project is of great interest. Ultimately, there will also be an enormous amount of pleasure gained from the car gleaming in the sunshine, the redecorated room, or being able to communicate in a foreign language. The compliments and admiration from others make all the hard work worthwhile.

For lifelong learning it is a question of harnessing this energy, enthusiasm and passion in pursuit of knowledge, so that the pleasure and satisfaction gained act to encourage more learning. Lifelong learning is concerned with ensuring that continuous learning takes place and is consciously pursued rather than occurring in a random and unplanned fashion. Whilst we may learn naturally, haphazard learning may lead us to learn ineffectively and inefficiently, and this is why control of the learning process is essential. Learning is a central lifelong task that provides us with the basis for personal development and a successful career (see Figure 1.1).

It is also important to remember that learning takes place over time, particularly the acquisition of skills. It is only possible to assess how much learning has taken place by reflecting upon experiences and learning that have occurred, and measuring these

Figure 1.1 **Lifelong learning**

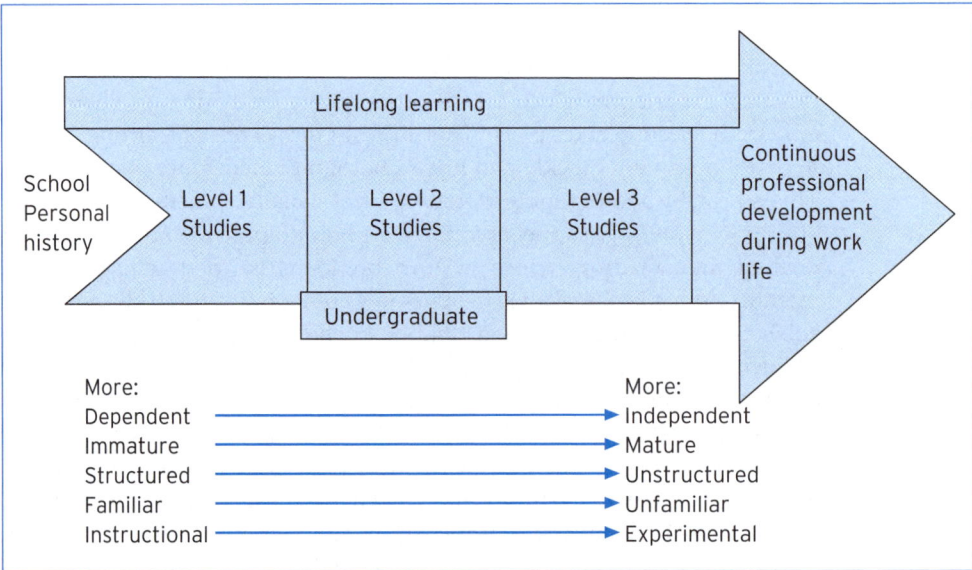

against some yardstick. If the learner does not reflect regularly, it is difficult to assess the extent of learning.

In a knowledge-based society, it is increasingly important to become effective lifelong learners. Lifelong learning should therefore be one of your primary educational goals on entry to higher education.

→ University or college learning

You enter university or college to learn, not to be taught. This is an important distinction. You cannot be taught anything. You learn in your own unique individual way and many personal factors will influence your learning. You will, of course, be given guidance in the learning process by your tutors in the form of lectures, tutorials, seminars, workshops, workbooks or handouts, booklists and specified reading for particular modules, etc. (see Table 1.1). However, being in lectures and tutorials is often a fairly passive experience, during which notes are taken from what the lecturer says in order to reproduce the material at a later date in exams or assessments. Learning is a much more active experience.

Table 1.1 Types of learning delivery

Workbook	A book provided by the tutor that contains readings, exercises, inventories, examples, etc., for you to work through.
Lecture	A talk given to a large group in a lecture theatre on a particular topic, which provides basic information. You will need to do further reading and research about the topic both before and after the lecture.
Seminar	A meeting at scheduled intervals, usually weekly, where a group of students under the guidance of a tutor discuss concepts and theories, give presentations and debate information researched since the previous meeting. You will need to study in advance of the seminar to enable you to join in the discussion.
Tutorial	Intensive tuition provided to students, either individually or in small groups. In a one-to-one discussion situation with your tutor, you will be expected to contribute to, and in some instances lead, the discussion, which will require advance preparation.
Workshop	A session where students meet as a study group to undertake exercises or simulations or some other tutor-defined activity. You may be expected to prepare for the workshop by completing set reading. However, some might involve experiential work, which may or may not require advance preparation. What happens in experiential learning is that you will take part in an activity - in other words, 'experience' a situation. When the activity is completed your tutor may lead a debriefing session in which you will explore and analyse the learning situation. During the debriefing session you will be encouraged to reflect on what you have done in order to draw out useful insights - what you have learned from the activity. Then you will be in a position to transfer that learning to other situations.

PART 1 DEVELOPING STUDY SKILLS

At university or college you must become actively engaged in the learning process by taking control of your experience. You need to read widely, thinking about, analysing and examining what you have read. Inevitably you will have to challenge your belief system, listening to alternative viewpoints and debating, discussing and probing topics in detail with student colleagues. This active learning approach will broaden your mind, stretching you intellectually, providing you with a greater understanding and expanding your capacity for thought.

→ Independent learning

In higher education today the ability to become an independent learner is crucial. While tutors and other students can provide some support and encouragement, the independent learner has to provide the inner motivation and self-discipline. When you are at university or college, you will need to assume responsibility for your own learning because increasingly there is an emphasis in the educational sector on individuals:

- taking more control over the process of learning within the framework provided
- showing initiative and persistence
- having a high level of curiosity and seeing problems as challenges rather than obstacles
- identifying their own learning needs
- finding appropriate resources to meet those needs
- evaluating progress towards the learning goal.

It is likely that university or college tutors will expect self-managed learning. Some tasks may be set, using a computer (computer-based learning), to be worked through until a certain prescribed level of competence is achieved. Alternatively, tasks such as directed reading may be set and the tasks worked through until they are completed, but within a

Figure 1.2 **The virtuous learning cycle**

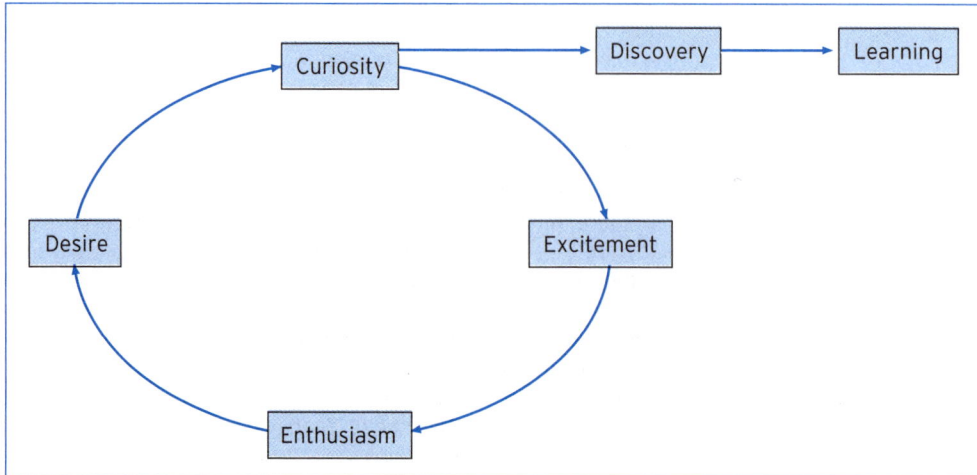

limited time scale. Tutors at university or college frequently set work for individuals or groups of students to complete without close supervision. Many universities and colleges expect students to become independent learners and it is important that you acquire the skills as quickly as possible in order to be able to function independently.

Strangely enough, many individuals do not know how to learn effectively, even though they spend most of their early years in education. Learning to learn requires an ability and willingness on your part to assume responsibility for directing and controlling the learning process. Active involvement in the learning process is empowering and engenders curiosity, enthusiasm and a thirst or desire for knowledge. The whole process becomes an end in itself through discovery, in a virtuous learning cycle as outlined in Figure 1.2.

Table 1.2 Characteristics of the dependent and the independent learner

Dependent learner	Independent learner
Learner wants: • structured learning experiences • tutor to take responsibility for the learning experience • tutor-centred approach • rewards • support • encouragement • reinforcement • esteem.	Learner anticipates: • experimentation • extensive self-paced, independent study • freedom to explore and make mistakes • complex problems for which there is no single correct solution • judgement-free support • intellectual stimulation from studies • student-centred approach.
Learner wants lecturer/tutor to be: • a subject expert • an authority figure • an instructor and to: • lecture/talk • assess/check • examine/test • design and direct the learning experience • control • lead/direct • instruct • encourage.	Learner wants lecturer/tutor to be: • a facilitator • a guide and to: • negotiate • encourage • develop • motivate • consult • listen • evaluate • act as a resource • provide feedback on request • delegate.
Learner is: • willing to learn • inexperienced – learns what is required • reliant on tutor for evaluation • in need of frequent feedback • not intellectually curious • deficient in some skills • lacking in knowledge • under instruction • in need of direction.	Learner is: • collaborator • confident in own abilities as a learner • flexible • adaptable • autonomous • self-evaluative • risk taker • independent and not reliant on tutor • knowledgeable • enterprising.

PART 1   DEVELOPING STUDY SKILLS

Figure 1.3 **The Learning Cycle** (adapted from Kolb)

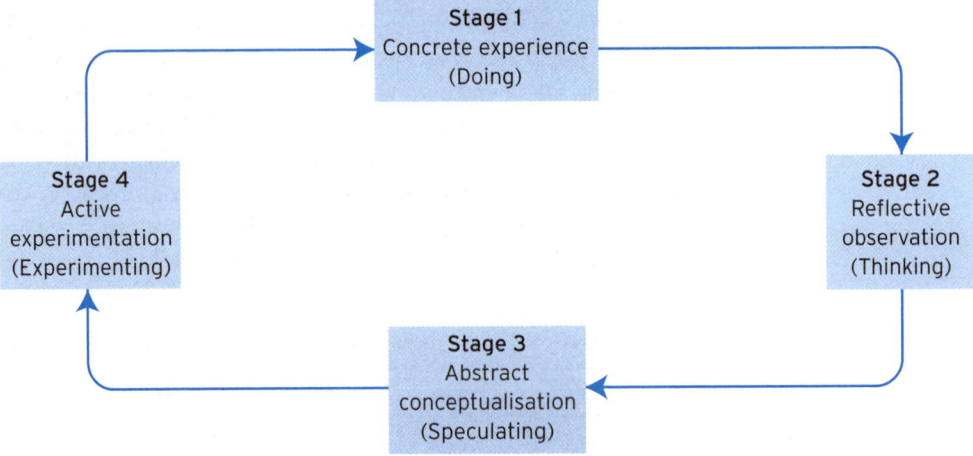

The dependent and independent learner is shown as two separate states in Table 1.2, but learning is a continuum of experience. Learners will be at different points on the continuum, and learning experiences to the present day will influence movement towards independence.

At first, at university or college students are likely to be more dependent on their tutors for guidance. As learning experience is gained, competence and confidence increase and there will be movement from dependence to independence (see Figure 1.3).

See Activity 1.2 TYPES OF LEARNERS in the Online Study Guide.

Activity 1.2

Dependent/independent learner

Look at the characteristics of the dependent/independent learner.
- Which apply to you at the moment?
- What do you need to do to become a more independent learner at university or college?

Make a list of what you need to do and review it at least each month.
- What progress are you making?
- Is there anything further you can do to become a more independent learner?

→ Learning styles

Each person learns in a unique way because individuals perceive and process experience in different preferred ways, and therefore learning is very much a matter of personal preference or style. Personal learning style will be influenced by personal history, such as parents, number of brothers and sisters, and whether first born, youngest in the family or an only son or daughter. In addition, personal life experiences, teachers and friends will all have a major influence on individual learning style.

LEARNING TO LEARN

An essential element of effective learning is developing an awareness of your own preferred learning style – the way you acquire, absorb and retain information and skills. It influences how information is collected, organised and transformed, and refers to the ways in which you learn best and how learning is approached. You can identify and examine your learning style, so that those behaviours that are effective can be built upon, whereas those that are inappropriate in a given situation can be avoided or changed.

Kolb (1984) identifies what he calls the Experiential Learning Model, in which he describes a four-stage cycle to explain learning (see Table 1.3). He says that the first stage, *Concrete experience*, is followed by *Observations and reflections*, which in turn lead to *Formation of abstract concepts and generalisations* and this is followed by *Testing implications of concepts in new situations*. What this means is that the learner:

- does something (*doing*) (concrete experience)
- reflects upon what he or she has done (*thinking*) (reflective observation)
- theorises about possible different actions (*speculating*) (abstract conceptualisation)
- tries out something else (*experimenting*) (active experimentation)

Kolb points out that this cycle recurs continuously. He says that learners test concepts through actions and modify them as a result of experiences.

Kolb suggests that each learner has a tendency towards a particular part of the cycle and that this is exhibited as a preference for specific types of learning activity that appeal to the individual's learning strengths. This tendency or inclination will shape how the learner prefers to learn and the effectiveness of the learning experience. He argues that the key to effective learning is to be able to adopt a particular approach when it is appropriate: in other words, to be able to be flexible.

> **Remember...**
> Individual learning is unique – it is a matter of personal preference or style.

Table 1.3 The four learning tendencies and student learning preferences

Learning tendency	Student preference
Kolb says that a person with a tendency towards *concrete experience*: • likes to be personally involved • emphasises feeling rather than thinking • prefers learning from specific experiences rather than from theories • is intuitive rather than using a systematic and scientific approach to problem solving • is good at relating to others • is sensitive to feelings and people • likes to work in unstructured situations • is open minded • is adaptable • believes in and enjoys their own experience.	Students with an orientation towards *concrete experience* are likely to prefer a learning experience where: • there is personalised feedback • there is a sharing of feelings • tutors are friendly helpers • class activities involve skills application to real problems • there is peer feedback • there is autonomy and self-direction • little theoretical reading is to be done.

13

Table 1.3 continued

Learning tendency	Student preference
A person with a tendency towards *reflective observation*: • likes to understand through observation and impartial description • emphasises reflection rather than action • prefers understanding to practical application • is concerned with truth • is good at thinking through situations and ideas and perceiving their implications • is good at understanding ideas and situations from different points of view • looks for the meaning of things • relies on own thoughts and feelings to form opinions • values patience, impartiality, objectivity and thoughtful judgement.	Students with an orientation towards *reflective observation* are likely to prefer a learning experience where: • the tutor is in the role of expert • the tutor guides or limits the discussions • the lecture format is used • output is evaluated against external criteria • there are few tasks to perform.
A person with a tendency towards *abstract conceptualisation*: • uses logic, ideas and concepts • emphasises thinking rather than feeling • is concerned with theories • prefers scientific rather than intuitive approaches to problem solving • is good at systematic planning • is good at manipulating abstract symbols • enjoys and is good at quantitative analysis • values precision, rigour and discipline when analysing ideas.	Students with an orientation towards *abstract conceptualisation* are likely to prefer a learning experience where: • case studies are used • theoretical readings take place • there are opportunities for thinking alone • group exercises are not used • the student is not expected to be an autonomous learner • students are not required to share feelings about subject matter • there are few instances of role play.
A person with a tendency towards *active experimentation*: • likes to experiment and initiate change • enjoys influencing people • prefers practical application rather than reflective understanding • is concerned with what works rather than absolute truth • emphasises doing rather than observing • is good at getting things done • is a risk taker to achieve objectives • likes to see results • enjoys influencing their environment.	Students with an orientation towards *active experimentation* are likely to prefer learning experiences where: • small group discussions take place • there are projects • there is peer feedback • students evaluate their own work • skills are applied to practical problems • there are few lectures • there are few instances where work is judged as right or wrong • tutors do not dictate the task.

Activity 1.3

Learning cycle

Look at the four parts of the learning cycle (Figure 1.3) and make an assessment of which one is most like the way you enjoy or prefer to learn. Carry out an analysis of your way of learning, identifying and describing the potential strengths, weaknesses, advantages and disadvantages of that approach.

Now practise moving through the stages. Think back to a learning experience that took place some time ago and was important or significant for you. It could be learning to ride a bicycle, learning a part in a play, revising for exams, overcoming the fear of flying, learning to cook, or any other you wish. Choose a learning experience that was difficult for you at the time, or one that made you aware that you did not possess certain skills.

Move through the learning stages by writing about the following.

Concrete experience – doing
Factually describe the learning experience:
- What did you do?
- When did the experience happen?
- Where did it take place?
- How long did it last?
- Were other people involved?
- Why did you undertake the learning experience?
- What did you hope to achieve?

Reflective observation – thinking
Think about the experience from different viewpoints:
- What did you notice about the learning event?
- Did any patterns emerge?
- Was the learning event different from/similar to others of your experience?
- What conclusions can you draw about the way the learning event worked for you?
- What didn't work well and why?
- Describe your feelings, thoughts and perceptions during the learning experience.
- How many different perspectives have you been able to identify?
- Use these alternative views to add to your understanding of the learning experience.

Abstract conceptualisation – speculating
Use logic and ideas to understand the learning experience you have identified:
- What does it mean?
- Can you provide explanations for what happened?
- Why do you think some things work but not others?

> **See Activity 1.3 FACTORS INFLUENCING LEARNING in the Online Study Guide.**

- What ideas did you develop about the learning experience and how were they developed?

Active experimentation – experimenting
- What will you do as a result of your reflection about and conceptualisation of your learning experience?
- How can you use your knowledge in other learning experiences to ensure a successful outcome?
- What skills have you developed which you can transfer and adapt to test in other learning situations?
- Write about what you intend to do in the future to improve your effectiveness when you encounter a similar situation.

Note down your findings carefully and reflect upon what this information tells you about how you learn. The more frequently your learning experiences mirror the learning stages, the easier and more effective your learning will become.

> **Remember...**
> It is important to reflect upon learning experiences.

If you reflect upon your learning experiences, knowledge becomes something that is within your control rather than 'out there' in the control of someone else. One way to reflect on your learning is to keep a diary in which you record learning experiences at university or college. This will enable you to track your learning over a period of time, identifying any difficulties and where you may have areas of weakness. If you have any major difficulties, you could then talk these through with the student support services at your university or college. (See Chapter 2 for more information about reflection.)

Kolb says that it is unlikely that an individual's learning style will be described in sufficient detail by just one of the approaches outlined in Table 1.3. Learning is more complex than this. He suggests that each person's style is a combination of two of the four basic learning stages. Kolb has therefore developed his model of learning by combining the dominant elements of two of the learning stages and from this he identifies four learning styles. These are outlined in detail in Table 1.4.

Whilst you may have a preferred learning style, it does not mean that you cannot operate effectively in other styles. Kolb argues that each style is no better or worse than the others and suggests that a balanced profile is not necessarily the best. His argument is that the key to effective learning is to be able to adopt a particular style when it is appropriate. So if you build up a learning repertoire and are adaptable enough to be able to move from one style to another depending upon the situation, you will have an advantage over those students who use only one dominant style of learning.

Table 1.4 Kolb's four learning styles

Converger
This learner is best at using abstract conceptualisation and active experimentation. According to Kolb, if you use the convergent learning style, you will:

- enjoy problem solving and decision making
- like the practical application of ideas, concepts and theories
- be good in situations where there is one correct answer or solution to a problem
- operate through inference based on sensory experience
- prefer technical tasks to dealing with people
- not be able to express emotions easily.

Diverger
This learner is best at using concrete experience and reflective observation. If you use the divergent learning style, you will:

- be imaginative and feeling-orientated
- have an awareness of meaning and values
- be able to view situations from many angles
- be able to see how things fit together
- like alternative ideas
- be good at brainstorming
- be people-orientated
- have broad interests
- like group discussions
- prefer to watch events rather than participate in them
- possibly experience difficulty in reaching conclusions from quantitative or technical information.

Assimilator
This learner is best at using abstract conceptualisation and reflective observation. If you use the assimilative learning style, you will:

- be able to create theoretical models
- assimilate separate observations into a logical explanation
- prefer ideas and abstract concepts to people
- be tolerant of impractical ideas
- prefer theories to be logical
- disregard or re-examine the facts if the theory does not fit them
- like precision and accuracy
- possibly be cautious about experimenting and miss opportunities for learning.

Accommodator
This learner is best at using concrete experience and active experimentation. If you use the accommodative learning style you will:

- like doing things
- be action-orientated
- learn from hands-on experience
- implement plans and tasks
- get involved in new experiences
- seek opportunities
- be a risk taker, acting on intuition
- be able to adapt easily and improvise
- discount the theory if it does not fit the facts
- solve problems through trial and error
- rely on others for information
- like people but perhaps be impatient and pushy.

PART 1   DEVELOPING STUDY SKILLS

> See downloadable template LEARNING STYLES 1.3 for your Personal Development Plan online.

Activity 1.4

Learning styles

Look at the descriptions of the four learning styles in Table 1.4 and cross out those points that do not describe you.

When you have completed this activity you will be able to determine which of the learning styles is most like yours. It is likely that this will be your preferred learning style.

You will probably have some of the points in the other styles, which will indicate that you are able to utilise that style to some extent. You can also identify the extent to which you use the other styles and you can determine how much development you need to incorporate them in your repertoire of learning styles. If you develop your learning styles, you will become more versatile at coping with changing situations.

From the activities in this chapter, note down carefully all of your findings and reflect upon what this information tells you about how you learn. This will enable you to build up a picture of how you learn best.

How can you adapt the learning experience so that it enables you to utilise your learning preferences to their fullest extent?

Look at the Suggestions to broaden your learning style and draw up an action plan (see the Suggestions box) and example action plan in Activity 1.7 to enable you to develop your learning style.

Suggestions to broaden your learning style

Converger

To develop your learning style you need to emphasise *concrete experience* and *reflective observation* by:

- placing greater value on gathering and understanding non-quantitative information
- looking at situations from various perspectives
- taking an active role in the learning process
- trying harder to listen with an open mind, non-judgementally
- working with a student who has a divergent learning style.

Diverger

To develop your learning style you need to emphasise *abstract conceptualisation* and *active experimentation* by:

- reaching conclusions and making decisions
- implementing conclusions
- volunteering to lead discussions
- setting goals
- taking risks
- working with a student who has a convergent learning style.

Assimilator
To develop your learning style you need to emphasise *concrete experience* and *active experimentation* by:

- moving to action more quickly
- becoming more aware of your own and others' feelings
- trying ideas, concepts and skills and observing what happens
- getting involved in 'people' activities, e.g. role plays, discussions, etc.
- imagining the implications of learning situations
- seeking and exploring opportunities
- working with a student who has an accommodative learning style.

Accommodator
To develop your learning style you need to emphasise *reflective observation* and *abstract conceptualisation* by:

- collecting and reflecting upon more information about learning situations
- avoiding trial and error
- using thoughtful observation and analysis
- organising information
- building conceptual models
- testing theories and ideas
- working with a student who has an assimilative learning style.

Kolb warns against stereotyping yourself and others too much with his model since these are general categorisations and you may change over time and in different situations. However, Kolb's model provides an indication of how you see yourself as a learner and it is likely that learning in your favoured style is the most comfortable and effective. For a more complete picture, it would be necessary to include information from others – feedback in terms of their observations about how you solve problems, how you behave in learning or work situations, etc.

Kolb's view is that the differing perspectives are all essential for optimal learning. If you can grasp how to learn in each of the four styles and move through the learning stages outlined earlier, you will be able to build on strengths and overcome weaknesses.

Honey and Mumford (2000) identified a model of learning styles that is similar, but not identical to that of Kolb. The learning style survey that Kolb uses asks respondents to choose descriptive words that are 'most' to 'least' like them. From this activity the respondent computes their score and identifies their learning style. Honey and Mumford use a questionnaire that has statements to which the learner responds, which identifies the learning style. The four learning styles identified by Honey and Mumford are listed in Table 1.5.

There are advantages and disadvantages to each of the learning styles, although Honey and Mumford caution that if you have a very low score in any one of the styles, it is better to concentrate your energies on strengths. They say that it will be counterproductive to spend a lot of time and energy trying to develop a style for which you have a very low preference.

You are now equipped to decide whether to develop your learning styles. The knowledge gained about yourself can enable you to become even more proficient in your

Table 1.5 Honey and Mumford's four learning styles

Activists	<ul><li>Involve themselves fully in a new experience</li><li>Are open minded</li><li>Act first and consider consequences later</li><li>Thrive on challenges</li><li>Live in the present</li><li>Like the focus of attention to be on themselves</li></ul>
Reflectors	<ul><li>Stand back and think about their experiences</li><li>Collect data before reaching conclusions</li><li>Listen carefully</li><li>Like to observe others</li><li>Live a cautious, thoughtful existence</li><li>Adopt a low profile and do not like to be the centre of attention</li></ul>
Theorists	<ul><li>Think problems through logically</li><li>Assimilate observations into complex theories</li><li>Are rational and logical</li><li>Prefer analysis and synthesis</li><li>Live in a detached, rational world</li><li>Tend to display perfectionist traits</li></ul>
Pragmatists	<ul><li>Like to apply concepts and theories to real situations</li><li>Become impatient with lengthy discussions</li><li>Prefer to solve problems through experiment</li><li>Meet deadlines</li><li>Live a down-to-earth, practical existence</li><li>Are practically minded when making decisions</li></ul>

preferred learning style, or to adapt learning that is presented to you so that it more closely matches your preferred style.

The versatility and flexibility that will be required for careers in the twenty-first century make it very important to be able to adapt to changing circumstances. It will be essential to be able to adopt an appropriate learning style that matches the situation in which you have to operate.

> **Remember...**
> The key to effective learning is to adopt the appropriate learning style for the situation.

Factors that influence learning

As well as a favoured learning style, other factors influence your learning and ability to study. It is important that you are able to identify the impact of these factors so that you can determine whether they help or hinder your learning. You can then decide what to do about those that hinder your ability to study and learn.

Memory

Memory is the ability of the brain to store thoughts and knowledge, and it enables retrieval and use of what has been stored. Memory is fundamental to learning and without it learning would be impossible. It permits recall or retrieval of information, or recognition that particular information has been encountered before. The memory enables us to recall information when it is needed.

Memory has a number of phases – immediate, short-term and long-term memory. Immediate memory is the ability to retain information for seconds, such as the scenery or streets passed in a car or on the bus when travelling to university or college. Short-term memory is the ability to retain information long enough to use it, perform a task or pursue a train of thought. An example is looking up a telephone number and remembering it long enough to dial it. However, if a distraction occurs interrupting a train of thought, the numbers will probably be confused or forgotten completely. The duration of short-term memory is fairly limited and only a small amount of information can be retained, but long-term memory is extensive and relatively permanent. Many items in short-term memory are practised or rehearsed so that they are transferred into long-term memory. Rehearsal consists of repeating information over and over until it is transferred into long-term memory. If rehearsal or practice does not take place, information will be lost or forgotten. Forgetting is linked to the limited capacity of short-term memory, in that new information seems to erase what has been temporarily stored.

Storage and retention of information over an extended period of time, at least months, possibly a lifetime, occurs in long-term memory. It is possible to improve memory by remembering information through association: for example, most people will have particular memories that are associated with songs, sights or smells from their personal history. Some of these will be extremely pleasant, such as the smell of Christmas cake being baked, which is associated with the excitement and anticipation of presents and

Figure 1.4 **Memory**

parties. Some information stored in long-term memory may be available over long periods of time, but not necessarily accessible. For example, you may meet someone again after a long period of time, but not be able to remember his or her name – in other words, you cannot access this information from your memory. A useful technique to avoid this tendency is to use association, which will improve your memory considerably when you are studying and information has to be retained for long periods, especially for examinations. Not only will the information be available in your memory, but you will be able to access it as well (see Figure 1.4).

Conditions for learning

As well as your ability to transfer information to long-term memory, the conditions in which you work will affect how effectively you study.

Whether you choose to work in your study, bedroom, lounge, kitchen or the library, you should make sure that you have sufficient space to work in. You may have to negotiate with your student colleagues or family to secure sufficient space for study. Decide which background noise is suitable for you, whether this is absolute silence, rock music, classical music, opera or the sound of the sea lapping against the shore. Hang a sign on your door that says 'Do not disturb' because it is essential that you are not interrupted while you study.

Stop and think
- Is your desk or table large enough for your books, ring binders, papers, pens, pencils, rulers, etc?
- Have you avoided lounging on the floor?
- Are all necessary materials to hand so there is no need to break off to get a different pen or ruler?
- Is your chair comfortable enough to sit on for some time and at the correct height to avoid discomfort?
- Does your chair encourage good posture by providing adequate support to the back and legs?
- Is there adequate light in the room so that the desk/working area is well lit?
- If the main light is not bright, have you got a desk lamp to provide direct light over the study area so that shadows are not cast on books and study materials?
- Is the study room well ventilated and the temperature not too hot or too cold, making it uncomfortable to study?

Activity 1.5

Factors that help or hinder learning

Identify the aspects that help you to learn better or hinder your learning. Place a tick against those aspects that help you, and add any others that you can think of. What can you do to ensure that there are more of the things that help your learning and fewer of the things that hinder it?

Factor	Help to learn better	Hinder learning
Sitting at a desk or table	☐	☐
Lounging on the floor	☐	☐
In a communal area such as a library	☐	☐
In a place reserved for study only	☐	☐
In your own bedroom	☐	☐
In small groups	☐	☐
On your own	☐	☐
With a friend	☐	☐
Working alone when it is quiet	☐	☐
In a busy place	☐	☐
In a relaxed atmosphere	☐	☐
With loud music playing	☐	☐
In front of the television	☐	☐
Reading something then trying it out	☐	☐
Trying something out then reading about it	☐	☐
At my own speed	☐	☐
Writing reflective logs or journals	☐	☐
Very late at night	☐	☐
Early in the morning	☐	☐
Before meals	☐	☐
After meals	☐	☐
At regular times each day	☐	☐
At the last minute	☐	☐
Well in advance of deadlines	☐	☐
_____	☐	☐
_____	☐	☐

Rewards for learning

Motivation to learn is usually linked in some way with rewards. Learning is more pleasurable and the effectiveness of the experience is increased if positive rewards are linked to the acquisition of a skill or knowledge.

PART 1   DEVELOPING STUDY SKILLS

> **Activity 1.6**
>
> ### Rewards for learning
>
> Think about the kinds of reward that you have received for learning. Which rewards help you to learn? Place a tick against those rewards that work for you, and add any others that you can think of.
>
> *Rewards for learning*
>
> - Admiration from others for your achievements ☐
> - Smiles and nods of approval from tutors/parents ☐
> - A ten-minute break after an hour's study ☐
> - Positive/encouraging comments on work ☐
> - Ticks on your written work ☐
> - Personal feelings of satisfaction and accomplishment ☐
> - Receipt of certificate/diploma/degree/qualification ☐
> - _____ ☐
> - _____ ☐

Whichever positive rewards work for you, try to ensure that you get sufficient to keep yourself motivated. Those rewards that come from yourself will be the most effective in keeping you motivated when you have a lot of deadlines to meet or you find the work difficult. You can always guarantee to give yourself positive rewards when you successfully complete a task. Celebrate your learning achievements with rewards that you value and this will enable you to build a record of successful learning experiences. If you rely on rewards from others, you may be disappointed because your parents, tutors or student colleagues may not provide or offer the reward when you want it most.

> **Remember...**
> Learning takes application, effort and commitment.

Blockages to learning

It is easy to construct lists of what hinders or blocks learning – not enough time, too many other important things to deal with, parents and other significant people telling us we are not as clever as our peers or our brothers and sisters. However, what stops you learning is yourself – your own mental attitude. If you want to learn, you can do so. All it takes is application, effort and commitment. Think back to a time when you wanted to learn a particular skill, possibly skiing or riding a bicycle. What did you think about? Did you identifiy that you drove yourself hard in an effort to acquire the skill? It is likely that you took lots of falls, bruising yourself in the process. However, until you had conquered the skill of skiing or riding a bicycle, you could not be deterred. Failure was not something you considered and your passion drove you to success. Figure 1.5 demonstrates how it is possible to move from inactivity in learning to become an eager, enthusiastic, passionate learner.

LEARNING TO LEARN

Figure 1.5 Stages in learning

```
                                                    Extending

                                                              Curious, enthusiastic,
                                                              eager, energised -
                          Growing/enabling                    knowledge acquisition
                                                              is exponential
   Inactivity

Doing nothing -        Progress in a positive
neutral                direction - knowledge
                       acquisition is linear

                       Movement in this direction →
```

In order to ensure that movement continues in a positive direction as shown by the model, it is important to develop personal learning plans to aid learning development.

Activity 1.7

Creating a learning development plan

Now write a learning development plan for yourself using the following:

1 Who am I?
Do not describe yourself – identify your fundamental values and beliefs that make you who you are.

To enable you to complete your studies successfully and subsequently build a fulfilling and accomplished career, you need to increase your self-awareness. This is the key to understanding and knowing yourself. It is important to explore those internal sources which make up your sense of self, self-image and personal identity – your belief system, personal values, needs, hopes and aspirations, competences and abilities. This exploration will help you make certain decisions whilst you are studying for your qualification and provide the basis for your career decisions.

You should take time to understand yourself and to reflect upon how you have become the person you are today. This is part of the process of setting personal and educational goals for yourself. Through an evaluation of your personality, future aspirations and abilities, you will be able to make career choices and investments of time, energy and commitment which will ensure that you achieve your learning and other objectives.

2 How did I get where I am today?

Your past will provide the answers to who you are today. Your personal history has shaped the person you are and significant experiences and people have shaped you as you have matured and developed. Now is the time to reflect and get some idea about how you came to be the unique person you are.

Take a piece of paper and draw on it a graph that represents your life up to the present day. Draw time along the bottom axis and feelings up the side (see Figure 1.6). Think about your life thus far and identify, examine and assess the main events and people that have affected your development. Draw representations on your lifeline of the various experiences that have influenced your life to the present time. Use pictures, symbols, colours and shapes to represent the various events. Indicate events that made you feel happy and good with peaks on the graph, and depict negative or unhappy events with troughs.

Figure 1.6 An example of a lifeline

List your major achievements and choices as well as the main influences and events that have influenced your life. You could include some or all of the following:
  (a) *events*: moving house, living abroad, changing school;
  (b) *decisions*: part-time job, starting university and college;
  (c) *achievements*: passing cycling proficiency test, winning 100 metres race, learning to swim;
  (d) *people*: changes in relationships with significant people in your life – for example, friendships at school, new brother or sister, divorce or remarriage of parents, teachers, favourite aunt/uncle, illness/death of grandparents;

(e) *things*: new bike, musical instrument, computer, books;
(f) *influences*: youth club, amateur dramatic society, music, church;
(g) *experiences*: holidays, swimming, sailing, gap year, etc.

Plot all of the events on your lifeline that you have identified to show a pictorial representation of your life.

The graph will enable you to recognise which events have made you what and who you are today. You will also be able to reflect on which events affected you in a negative way. It is important to identify the themes that are emerging. You should think about what these may mean. Have the themes always been there, just emerged recently, or crop up occasionally? It may be that you have found out that all your positive experiences are associated with older people. Armed with this information you are in a position to make choices about how to approach the situations with younger people, which you may have experienced negatively. You can then make major changes to your learning experiences.

3 Where am I now?

List your personal achievements and abilities and identify traits that have helped you meet your expectations. Have you achieved as much as or more than you expected? This analysis will enable you to achieve more in the future by identifying what makes you successful. If you have achieved less than you hoped, this will enable you to recognise where you have been less successful and allow you to identify strategies which will give you the drive to work harder in future. You should identify how your current accomplishments and aptitudes will help you in the future, and the areas you need to develop to be more successful. Remember, success generates success. Consider what you have been successful at, and try to assess how you can transfer that success to other areas of your life.

4 Where am I going?

What are your learning/skills development objectives? How do you intend to achieve them? How do the opportunities and activities on your course relate to your own preferred way of learning? What can you do actively to involve yourself in the learning process? How can you make the learning process successful for you? What kind of help will be available to you and how do you intend to make best use of it?

5 What constraints will hold me back?

It is essential to set challenging goals, though you must be honest with yourself. Achieving them requires hard work, knowledge acquisition, application, dedication and skills development as well as versatility, resilience and sacrifice. In order to be successful you need to identify what is going to get in the way of your progress. What is likely to inhibit you making headway? You might currently enjoy a rich and varied social life which takes up all of your spare time. It will therefore be necessary for you to sacrifice some of your social life to be able to give sufficient time to your studies. This is not to say that you must give up a social life altogether whilst you are a student. However, you must find the right balance so that you are successful academically but enjoy your free time.

> **6 Now commit yourself to your learning development plan**
> Write out in detail what you intend to achieve and how you will do it. You should be quite specific in detailing the time you allocate to the different areas you will study on your course. At what stage will you review what you have achieved? What contingency plans will you develop if things do not go according to your original plan?

If you are unsure about how to complete your learning development plan, think for a moment about the potential for personal change in the next few years. You have enormous personal potential and have before you the opportunity to harness and develop it. In case you need convincing of your personal potential, write as much as possible about the following:

(a) Skills I possess now but did not possess 5 years ago

(b) Skills I possessed 5 years ago but not 10

(c) Skills I possessed 10 years ago but not 15.

→ Building on learning strengths and overcoming blockages to learning

You should by now have identified your learning strengths, your learning style, factors that influence your learning and the rewards that you need, and have been able to put them to good use in your learning development plan.

You also need to have a strategy for dealing with any blockages to your learning, as these will inhibit your development. Many blockages are products of socialisation, or the conditioning and reinforcement received as children. We may have been told that we needed to be careful, not to take risks, our parents did not want anything awful to happen to us, we were a sickly child, etc. These messages are internalised deep within us as 'you cannot/must not do this, or that', 'you are not very clever', 'you will fail if you try such and such'. If messages such as these are not examined and challenged, they stay locked deep within our brains and act to hold us back.

Everyone, of course, has many messages locked inside their brains and they can be both positive and negative. Most of the messages help individuals to be successful: for example, praise when something desirable has been achieved. However, if an individual receives too many negative messages, these can encourage feelings of helplessness and inhibit achievement. In order to change these negative messages or blockages, it is necessary to use positive thinking techniques. The root of positive thinking is taking responsibility. It is easy to place blame for lack of success on anything and everything, anyone and everyone. It is frequently simply a matter of changing a point of view or description (see Table 1.6). If you think positively, you will be more successful and achieve more in your studies because you will take responsibility for your own learning.

Table 1.6 **Examples of positive thinking and taking responsibility**

Example 1. A student may say: 'It is not my fault that I didn't submit the assignment on time; my computer crashed'. However, an alternative is: 'I'm totally responsible for handing my assignment in late. I'm going to make sure I am better prepared next time. I didn't leave sufficient time to allow for problems. In future I need to plan more carefully and leave more time.'
Example 2. Another student might say: 'I'm never satisfied with my assignment. I could always do better'. However, an alternative viewpoint is: 'I want to learn and grow, so the feedback I receive about my assignment will enable me to improve next time.'
Example 3. Yet another could say: 'It's a problem tackling all of this coursework to tight deadlines.' However, he or she could say: 'Doing all this coursework to tight deadlines is an opportunity to demonstrate my organising and planning abilities and good practice for the world of work.'
Example 4. Finally, a student may say: 'It's terrible, all this work that I have to do for my course.' Alternatively, he or she could say: 'All this work I have to do for my course is a wonderful learning experience.'

Activity 1.8

Blockages to learning and how to overcome them

List your blockages to learning and develop an action plan to overcome them by using the following.

What do I want to achieve and by what date?
Write specific objectives using active verbs. 'To pass my statistics exam' is too vague. The objective should be specific and measurable and within a time scale: 'to pass the statistics exam on 21 December (year)'.

How will I achieve this objective? What do I need to do?
Detail small realistic steps such as: 'I will go to the library on Wednesday (date), and I will find six books on statistics, including how to understand the basics. I will read about measures of central tendency – mean, median and mode – on Thursday until I understand them and I will complete the exercises in the books. On Friday I will read about measures of location, normal distribution and standard deviation until I understand them and I will complete the exercises in the books.'

It is important to insert the caveat 'until I understand' because it is very easy to 'pseudo read': that is, to let the eyes roam over the work, but not make any real effort to understand.

Who will help me?
Involve student colleagues, friends and tutors at this stage. Colleagues can be very helpful if frequently you do not wish to display to the tutor that you have not understood. Invariably, whatever the topic being studied, several of the other students will understand and if approached appropriately will be only too pleased to help you. Often this helps to reinforce their own understanding and you may be able to do the same for them on another topic.

Who or what will hinder me?
Be really honest with yourself. It is amazing how riveting washing up or tidying one's bedroom becomes when a subject that one is not too fond of requires work! List all the 'essential' things that you think you must do – attending lectures, ringing parents, visiting friends, going to the pub – and then identify which of them you do not have to do until you have completed your objective.

Identify contingency plans to minimise the impact of the hindrances, e.g. cut down on the time you visit friends or ring parents for a few weeks.

When success is achieved what reward do I plan to give myself?
As soon as you are successful, you should give yourself a reward that is contingent upon that success. The reward for getting something done as planned should be something you desire and value. So, for example, when you have understood the measures of central tendency you could watch an hour of your favourite television programme, play a game of squash or whatever reward you value.

Now you have worked through this chapter, you should be ready to tackle the remaining chapters. These will give you practical guidance about the study skills you will need on your course, many of which will prove useful in employment after you have completed your qualification.

Suggestions for improving your learning experience

Write down what you have discovered about yourself as a learner. Reflect upon your learning style, make observations about how you learn, and set yourself personal learning goals for the next month, three months, six months, one year and the duration of your course, using the information about a learning development and action plan above. Review these goals periodically, in the light of your achievements, using the questions below.
Do you need to:

- do more work?
- reorganise how you work?
- work harder?
- give yourself more rewards?
- ask for more feedback on progress?
- manage your time more effectively?
- work more closely with others?

- do more individual work?

To achieve successful learning you must:
- be highly motivated and curious
- know your strengths and preferred styles of learning
- have an encouraging learning environment
- be prepared to accept constructive feedback and reflect positively on it
- remain focused on goals and organise the learning environment to achieve them.

→ Summary

This chapter has outlined that:
- learning is an ongoing process that takes place over time
- learning is not an isolated event
- learning takes place within each individual student and is influenced by personal and external factors
- a knowledge-based society requires lifelong learners who move from being more dependent to being more independent
- learning can take place through reading or watching and talking with others as well as through actual experience
- learning styles can be used to build on learning strengths and to overcome weaknesses
- factors that influence learning can be focused upon, and a learning development plan can be used to overcome any blockages to learning
- the learning process is helped if individuals set learning goals and develop action plans to achieve them.

2 Keeping a portfolio

> **Learning outcomes**
>
> After studying this chapter, you should be able to:
> - identify the essentials of a portfolio
> - start to construct a portfolio to demonstrate skills development
> - begin to reflect about learning experiences.

→ Introduction

See downloadable template 2.1 LEARNING LOG FOR PORTFOLIOS for your Personal Development Plan online.

In higher education it is now a requirement that all students keep a progress file of skills. A progress file is essentially a record of achievement. You may have started the process of keeping one at school. In future, progress files will be kept for an individual's entire life to encompass education and beyond. Whilst you are in higher education it is quite likely that your progress file will form part of the assessment for your qualification.

A progress file contains three elements:

- A transcript, which is a record of the modules studied and the grades achieved. The institution in which you study will determine the format of this.
- Personal development planning, which will encourage you to consider the skills that you possess and those that you need to develop during your studies.
- Personal development records, which consist of evidence from which you can select appropriate material to produce, for example, a CV. These will include evidence from your course and from other experiences such as paid employment, voluntary work and other extra curricular activities that might include volunteering work, playing in an orchestra or taking a 'gap' year.

In higher education, progress files are usually kept in the form of a *portfolio* which can be adapted to meet your needs. The word 'portfolio' has very positive meanings and many universities and colleges are likely to use this term in preference to 'progress file'. For this reason the progress file will be referred to as a portfolio during the remainder of the chapter.

What is a portfolio?

A portfolio is used to provide evidence about your development, learning and competence over a period of time. It enables you to convince your tutor (and importantly, yourself) what you have learned and how effectively. A portfolio may also be used to convince a prospective employer about what you have to offer and its relevance to the job for which you are applying. As well as containing evidence of your progress and development, a portfolio provides you with a focus for review, reflection and action planning, enabling you to progress towards independence in learning.

The benefits of the portfolio approach

Your portfolio will be a record of your achievement whilst you are at university and will prepare you for future personal and career development. There are other short- and long-term benefits:

- increased awareness of your level of competence and how it can be developed
- identification of your personal strengths to build upon, and weaknesses that have been minimised, to improve your self-confidence and self-esteem
- development into a reflective and reflexive practitioner through the discipline of reflecting upon what you are doing.

> **Remember...**
> One of the most important aspects of the portfolio approach is learning outcome and skills development, not the weight of evidence!

The portfolio will enable you to set challenging goals, identify support mechanisms, acquire resources needed, use ideas and concepts, reflect on and deal with past issues to find a balance, and then move forward through envisioning your future.

> **Remember...**
> Experience alone does not create learning; reflection is needed to gain real benefits.

The Quality Assurance Agency (www.qaa.ac.uk) suggests that graduates and intending managers of the future will need to utilise and develop more skills than ever before. They suggest that employers are seeking the following from graduates:

- flexibility, adaptability and the capacity to cope with and manage change
- self-motivation and drive
- analytical and decision-making ability

- communication and interpersonal skills
- teamworking ability and skills
- organisation, planning and prioritisation abilities
- ability to innovate
- leadership ability

Governments in the late twentieth century identified the need for *lifelong learning* and a portfolio is a mechanism to document skills development and demonstrate commitment to lifelong learning. The portfolio you compile during your time in higher education should show your development over time. It can also be used to prepare for employment and, if you actively engage in the process, you will be able to build a portfolio that will give you the edge over other applicants in a competitive job market. You will be able to use your portfolio to demonstrate to potential employers that you possess the skills that they desire from graduates. Your own need for skills development is continuous in that as a student you should always be actively seeking improved performance. Your development will be owned and managed by yourself and your portfolio can be used to demonstrate this.

The emphasis in higher education has moved from knowledge acquisition to skills development largely because knowledge in the twenty-first century has a shelf life of only two or three years. What this means is that the subject knowledge you acquire on your course will probably be out of date in a very short time, but the skills that you develop are transferable and, once acquired, are not likely to become obsolete. This is why employers increasingly focus on skills rather than specialist subject knowledge. It is, however, important to know where specialist subject knowledge resides and how to access it – and transferable skills facilitate this (see Chapter 9). These skills necessitate learning about self and others, working with others in team situations, oral and written communication, information technology, numeric and creative skills as well as dealing with change.

Personal transferable skills can enhance business awareness and increase personal confidence. As well as being able to demonstrate academic achievement, graduates need to be able to display a range of interpersonal skills, such as adaptability and flexibility, and to be able to work effectively in groups. Learning and skills development is your responsibility – taking this responsibility will enable you to develop your skills and ensure that you find the best alternatives to the challenges that higher education offers and subsequently to complex problems within work organisations.

Many professional institutions have recently recognised the need for what they term *continuous professional development* (CPD) to promote continuous lifelong learning and skills development. CPD is now a requirement for continued membership of many professional institutions: for example, the Chartered Institute of Personnel and Development (CIPD)* and the Chartered Management Institute both require their members to complete CPD in order to retain membership. A portfolio approach is an example of CPD, and if you get into the habit of compiling your portfolio, you will make the transition to CPD very easily in the world of work.

---

*CIPD is the professional institution for human resource managers.

Compiling the portfolio

When compiling your portfolio you should bear in mind that the more organised and better presented it is, the easier it is for you to access certain elements and ultimately present it for assessment as part of your course or to a prospective employer. It is likely that your portfolio will include the following:

- A cover containing your name, course, year and possibly the name of your personal tutor or some other person you can contact while you are at university/college.
- A contents page listing each section with a page number. The table of contents provides a clear map to the contents of the document.
- A transcript of achievements (this will normally be provided by your university or college), but in the meantime there is nothing to stop you recording your results for the modules studied.
- A personal development plan, which will enable you to plan your studies and ultimately your career.
- Personal development records, which will provide evidence of learning, experiences, skills, etc. It is a good idea to date and clearly label each piece of evidence so that it is easy to identify the reason it has been included in the portfolio.
- A curriculum vitae (CV) that you update and develop during your time at university or college. (See Chapter 3 for more information about CVs.)

All written evidence should normally be word processed because this makes the portfolio look more professional.

Sources of evidence

Evidence may be compiled from a number of different sources. The major ones are listed below:

- academic – course work, such as assignments, reflections about development, case studies and simulations
- course-related roles and responsibilities, such as course representative
- qualifications – GCSEs, NVQs, first-aid training, Duke of Edinburgh Awards, etc.
- leisure/social – voluntary work, church activities, pressure groups, club or society activities, such as president/treasurer of sub-aqua club
- paid employment
- projects undertaken, whether these are academic or social
- work experience placement.

What constitutes evidence?

Evidence may be in a variety of formats – it does not always have to be the written word. Some examples are listed below:

- reports
- certificates

- audio tapes
- video tapes of presentations, etc.
- testimonials
- peer assessments
- training courses
- appraisals
- references
- assignments – written feedback from tutors
- self-evaluation
- questionnaires
- flow charts
- computer-based material – spreadsheets, inventories, etc.
- photographs
- personal reflections
- curriculum vitae
- personal development plans
- personal learning contracts
- reflective learning journals/diaries/learning logs.

Suggestions for selecting evidence

Select work that is significant in providing evidence of learning or skill development and demonstrates:

- how your skills have developed during your course
- where or why there is a gap in your skills or understanding and the progress that you are making towards meeting future learning needs
- innovation, inventiveness and imagination
- that your understanding of the subject/course you are studying is progressing
- how you have been effective in transferring your skills to different contexts
- that you are developing skills that will bring success in higher education and employment.

> **Remember...**
> Annotate your evidence to indicate why it has been selected for inclusion.

Initially, your portfolio could be an A4 ring binder in which you keep your evidence, or your university/college may have an electronic portfolio that you have to keep as part of your course. The important thing for you to remember is that the portfolio is a reflection of your continuing skills development. You should select, present and reference items of evidence that you feel best demonstrate your competence. The choice of content is yours and you may wish to include evidence of competence taken from activities and experiences external to your course, to demonstrate expertise that you have developed over time.

You should remember that a portfolio is a dynamic document, not merely a collection of documents and other artefacts. It should demonstrate what you have learnt from experiences and situations, how you have developed and how this has impacted upon the way in which you discharge your responsibilities. You must keep your portfolio up to date so that it remains of value to you while you are at university or college and also during job search activities.

> **Remember...**
> Keep your portfolio up to date – this will ultimately save you time.

Skills audit

A useful starting point for a portfolio is an audit of your current skills, from which you can develop a personal development plan or personal learning contract. Essentially, this means identifying your starting point in skills development. This will enable you to set realistic goals for your development, and then you can 'contract' with yourself to achieve them. This contract can take the form of a personal development plan. Your development goals should be achievable in the timescale that you set. When you have set yourself goals for your development, it is a useful technique to set a 'stretch goal' to encourage you to strive for a higher level of achievement. This 'stretch goal' should be used to motivate you to work harder; it must not be at such a level as to be unachievable, otherwise this could be demotivating.

See Activity 2.1 FROM A PILE OF PAPER TO PORTFOLIO in the Online Study Guide.

Activity 2.1

Skills audit

Consider your level of skill development for each of the skills and assess your level of competence from 1 (low) to 8 (high), providing at least three reasons for your decision. In the first instance you should complete your assessment privately. When you have assessed your level of proficiency, it is a good idea to ask others to rate your skill levels. Choose people who will give you an objective and fair indication of your skill level. It is not helpful to have either an inflated idea of your skills or an unfairly negative view of your proficiency. If there are any discrepancies between your own assessment and that of others you should reflect about why this might have occurred. If you identify any areas of weakness, what can you do to overcome them?

PART 1   DEVELOPING STUDY SKILLS

Skill	Proficiency							
	1 low	2	3	4	5	6	7	8 high
1. Communication skills – I am able to:								
Verbal and non-verbal: ● speak clearly ● listen actively ● clarify ● question appropriately ● argue, i.e. put alternative viewpoints ● debate knowledgeably ● respond appropriately to others ● use reflective skills ● understand non-verbal communication.								
Writing skills: ● write clearly, concisely and grammatically correctly ● spell accurately ● express myself effectively ● use appropriate formats ● use logic and creativity as necessary.								
Presentation skills: ● structure presentations ● deliver presentations effectively ● meet the needs of a large/small audience ● present ideas clearly ● be aware of audience feedback.								
2. Personal and interpersonal skills – I am able to:								
Learning skills: ● learn new information quickly ● use knowledge to deal with new situations ● transfer learning from one context to another ● use feedback to increase effectiveness								

Skill	Proficiency							
	1 low	2	3	4	5	6	7	8 high
• understand and use my preferred learning style • reflect on learning in order to improve • learn from mistakes by self and others • be an independent learner • set my own goals, plans and priorities • action plan • identify, create, recognise and seize opportunities • be flexible and adaptable when dealing with change • meet deadlines • use time management and stress management skills appropriately • organise and plan – sequencing activities and dealing with them effectively • deal with diversity – gender, disability and other cultures.								
Self-motivation and drive: • manage career and personal development • build self-confidence, promote and sell my strengths • develop self-awareness • deal with and overcome personal limitations • maintain a personal sense of self-worth • maintain humour in the face of adversity.								
3. Working with information and data – I am able to:								
• process and manipulate information and numbers with accuracy and conviction								

PART 1   DEVELOPING STUDY SKILLS

Skill	Proficiency							
	1 low	2	3	4	5	6	7	8 high
• interpret and present data accurately • interrogate business financial data confidently • manage my personal budget • use research skills to identify potential sources of information, help and support • use library and research skills effectively – including e-journals.								
4. Working with technology – I am able to:								
Demonstrate IT skills: • word processing • databases • spreadsheets • graphics • e-mail • Internet Use effectively: • OHPs • video/DVD recorders/ players • camcorders • mobile phone/telephone.								
5. Teamworking ability and skills – I am able to:								
• work effectively as a team member • lead or follow as necessary • delegate effectively • motivate self and others • agree goals and priorities with others • help others • encourage and guide • influence with integrity • act ethically • counsel others appropriately								

KEEPING A PORTFOLIO

> See downloadable template 2.2 NEW SKILLS AND ATTRIBUTES GAINED for your Personal Development Plan online.

Skill	Proficiency								
	1 low	2	3	4	5	6	7	8 high
• be innovative and creative • demonstrate skills or explain ideas • deal with conflict • accept responsibility for my role in conflict situations • confront and negotiate with others • contribute constructively • work cooperatively and collaboratively.								
6. Decision-making skills – I am able to:								
• take routine decisions • develop creative solutions • make ethical choices • identify and diagnose simple problems • make judgements and take responsibility for the consequences • use analytical skills to compare, evaluate and examine progressively more complex problems.								

→ Reflection in your portfolio

Reflection enables you to 'stand back' and critically examine your beliefs, assumptions, inferences, interpretations, evaluations, judgements, purposes, etc. Through the process of reflection you will be able to improve your skills and competences and be more accepting of diversity because, as well as considering your own viewpoint, you will also be able to appreciate the perspective of other participants. By viewing behaviour in a wider context and examining it carefully, you will be able to make sense of the situation and understand it from the point of view of others. Reflection will also lead to self-understanding and enable you to change your behaviour if necessary. As you become more proficient at reflecting, you should progress through many loops as a learner, which will raise your awareness of yourself and of other perspectives (see Figure 2.1).

Figure 2.1 Reflection

Behaviour → Reflect → Theories → Reflect → Adjust → Reflect → Experiment → Reflect → New behaviour → Feedback

An important part of your portfolio is the reflection on your development and learning, and how it may affect your future personal and career development. This should be the result of a period of deliberation on your experiences and how you have progressed. It is important when reflecting that the processes (how and why) are analysed as well as the outcomes achieved (what). The ability to review and reflect on your progress and achievements will enable you to plan your next steps in learning and is the route to independent study.

Why Reflection?

Reflection encourages you to think about why certain things happen. It is also concerned with a search for knowledge about yourself and will allow you to monitor and keep track of your learning. Another aspect of reflection is to consider why other people behave the way they do and this will enable you to see situations from alternative perspectives.

Once you have carried out a skills audit (see Activity 2.1) and reflected on your skill levels another useful technique is to complete a *SWOT analysis*. This entails identifying your:

Strengths
Weaknesses
Opportunities available to you
Threats which may hinder you.

> See Activity 2.2 WHAT TO INCLUDE IN A PORTFOLIO in the Online Study Guide.

Activity 2.2

SWOT analysis

List your strengths, weaknesses, opportunities and threats in the grid.

Strengths	Weaknesses
Opportunities	Threats

Your portfolio should contain an honest initial assessment of your current skills because this will provide the basis for your development. It is not helpful to have a harsh assessment of your skills; neither should you have an over-optimistic view of them.

Stop and think
- How can you build upon your strengths?
- What can you do to overcome your weaknesses?
- What do you need to do to grasp the opportunities that will be presented to you within the next year? The next three years?
- Can you turn the threats into opportunities?

In the early stages of your course you should reflect about what works, or does not work, for you. If, for example, you find that you cannot understand lectures and you question why this does not work for you, you might decide that the way to make lectures a more positive experience is to read about the topic in the recommended text before you go to the lecture. In this way you are taking responsibility for your learning and you have learned through reflection to find a solution to a problem situation. The outcome of this reflection is that lectures become a satisfying experience for you rather than an unsatisfying one. The process of reflection will enable you to assess your own progress, which will facilitate self-reliance skills. During and subsequent to your course you will be able to use these techniques and tools to assess and pursue professional development to achieve your career goals.

PART 1   DEVELOPING STUDY SKILLS

Figure 2.2 How to reflect

Reflection is a continuous process similar to Kolb's learning cycle (see Chapter 1), in which you:

- do something, e.g. a current skills analysis
- reflect about strengths and weaknesses
- choose to do something different, such as develop particular skill areas
- experiment by trying out the behaviour associated with the skills (see Figure 2.2).

This may involve you taking risks to move forward, followed by self-evaluation to determine the progress made. You may wish to include feedback from other trusted people because sometimes we are too hard on ourselves, assessing our skills too negatively. On the other hand, some students may be too optimistic or unrealistic about skills development, believing in competence where little or none exists! Many students actually find it easier to identify weaknesses than strengths. If you list more weaknesses than strengths, do not be overwhelmed, but use the list as an impetus to overcome them. It is also useful to check out with others what you perceive to be your weaknesses because sometimes other people will see them as your strengths. Other people may also point to strengths that you did not know you possessed, and you could add them to your list.

When choosing learning experiences to reflect upon, it is a good idea to choose events that are meaningful or significant to you as this will increase your motivation to look at

> **Remember...**
> Learning takes place over time – it is not a once-and-for-all experience.

the various issues and engage with them in a constructive way. It is not advisable to consider the learning experience in isolation because there will be connections, associations and relationships to other aspects of your life and learning.

How to reflect

Boud et al. (1985) proposes that there are three elements to reflection:

- *Returning to experience.* After the event you should think about it in detail.
- *Attending to feelings.* Think about your feelings at the time and identify positive and negative emotions
- *Re-evaluating the experience.* At a later time or date you can be more dispassionate about the experience and learn from it.

Donald Schön (1983) has also written about this type of reflection. He terms it 'reflection-on-action' because it entails revisiting an experience from the safety of the present in order to learn from that experience. By doing this it is possible to be more objective and to separate oneself from the emotions that might have been influencing the situation.

How to get started

See Activity 2.3 MAKING A PORTFOLIO in the Online Study Guide.

When you start to reflect, identify critical incidents relating to your skills development which can be subjected to detailed reflection. In order to do this it is a good idea to keep a diary. At first you may think that there is nothing really significant in your writing for you to reflect about. However, when you read your diary entries after an interval of time, it may be that certain themes or patterns of behaviour that you were not aware of are affecting you positively, or detrimentally. Identifying these aspects of behaviour will enable you to build upon and utilise your strengths, or develop strategies for dealing with and overcoming weaknesses.

Once you have written about several incidents, you could choose situations to reflect about where you were less effective than you had hoped or the outcome was not very satisfactory. The identification and evaluation of strengths and weaknesses will provide you with the opportunity to adopt behaviour that will lead to more effective performance in future studies and ultimately in the workplace.

You can keep handwritten notes in your diary, or you could use word-processing software on a computer. Word processing is very versatile and may aid with reflection, as it will enable you to change your mind about what you have written, modify, delete, insert or move sections of your diary.

> ### Activity 2.3
>
> #### Reflection
> Choose an event to reflect upon which was challenging in some way. Be as objective as possible in your description. Think about the incident in detail:
> - where it took place
> - the participants
> - your part in it
> - your feelings – apprehension, pleasure, disquiet, etc.
>
> Now write about the event. Describe:
> - what happened
> - the setting
> - others involved and their behaviour or actions
> - your behaviour or actions
> - any other relevant information.
>
> What did you do and say at the time? What did you expect as a result of your behaviour or actions and words?
>
> You are now in a position to analyse the incident. This will enable you to develop a deeper understanding of your behaviour or actions and thoughts.

When you have completed this activity, ask yourself the following:

- Was the outcome what you expected?
- What would someone else understand from the situation you have described?
- What interpretations can you offer to explain the situation?
- What can you learn from analysing the situation using the questions why, what and how?
- What can you learn from this analysis – did misinterpretations, misunderstandings or inaccurate inferences occur?
- From your analysis are there any changes in your behaviour or thinking patterns that would lead to a more effective outcome?
- Would the situation be different if you adopted a new/different role?
- Would the outcome be different in the future if you change your behaviour?

The process of reflection

The reflective process needs time, practice and a supportive environment. You should identify a process that suits you: for example,

- when to compile evidence and subsequently to reflect on it
- where to write up your description and subsequent analysis
- how to do it, e.g. on a computer, keep a reflective diary, tape record, etc.

As you develop intellectually at university or college you will find that something that seemed impossible in one semester is straightforward by the next. If you keep diagnosing your learning experiences, monitoring what happens and evaluating the experience through reflection, you will be able to build upon your strengths and learn from any failures. At first this may seem to be hard work, but ultimately you will improve your learning experience and become a self-directed, responsible, independent learner. As you become more proficient at reflecting upon your learning experiences, you will become more self-aware and that will lead to personal and intellectual growth, enabling you to choose which are the appropriate actions for future use. Your portfolio will capture this development over time because you will select what to include and what to present to the various audiences who may need to access your evidence, such as a tutor or a prospective employer. This process of selecting, diagnosing, monitoring, refining and evaluating your work and other evidence will prove to be an enriching and rewarding learning experience and will enable you to identify new and exciting learning opportunities. As your confidence builds, you will discover possibilities for self-development that stretch your abilities, and this will become self-perpetuating. These possibilities might include new roles, new ways of thinking or risk-taking behaviour that takes you out of your comfort zone, all of which might provide you with further insights that will transform the learning experience for you.

Summary

This chapter has outlined:
- what a portfolio constitutes
- how to compile a portfolio to demonstrate skills development
- the kinds of evidence that could be included in a portfolio
- the importance of reflection in learning
- the process and essential elements of reflection.

3 Employability

> **Learning outcomes**
>
> After studying this chapter, you should be able to:
> - conduct an effective job search
> - develop a curriculum vitae (CV)
> - write a covering letter
> - apply confidently for employment.

→ Introduction

Many if not all of the skills developed during your time at university will be valuable in the workplace. For example, the communication skills developed in writing essays and reports as well as oral skills developed when giving presentations and engaging in discussions should be easily transferred to the workplace. You will also learn to analyse problems, seek and implement solutions, reach informed decisions, search for information, manage stress and time, work as part of a team and so on. All of these skills and more will be critical to your success in employment.

Lifelong learning will be the hallmark of the 'Learning Society' of the twenty-first century, and employers of graduates will be looking for employees who can manage their own learning. You will find that throughout your course you become increasingly independent or self-reliant and are encouraged to manage your learning through personal critical reflection and a planned programme of study that will progressively develop your skills. As you progress, you will acquire more knowledge and be able to deal with increasingly complex problems. This will enable you to refine and develop a repertoire of skills that will then be available to you in the workplace.

Employers are looking for recruits who have developed a range of personal and intellectual skills which equip them for the world of work. The things that employers attach greatest weight to when recruiting graduates are:

- self-motivation and self-awareness
- willingness to engage in continuous learning and development

- quickness to learn
- enthusiasm and a commitment to get results
- teamworking, working cooperatively and collaboratively
- effective use of time, timekeeping, self-discipline, ability to deal with stress and set priorities
- reliability
- initiative
- creativity and innovation
- enterprise and entrepreneurship
- integrity, through open and honest dealings with others
- leadership skills and the ability to motivate others
- problem-solving skills
- critical and reflective ability
- good communication skills, which include the ability to listen, coach and give clear direction to others
- flexibility and adaptability
- risk taking
- ability to deal with change.

Sources: Compiled from Chartered Institute of Personnel and Development; Chartered Management Institute; Quality Assurance Agency; Harvey et al. (2002).

All of these attributes are precisely the ones that you have the opportunity to develop on your course of study at university. They will enable you to engage effectively in the modern business organisation. Students who develop flexibility and the ability to adapt quickly to the culture of an organisation, work effectively in teams, communicate well, exhibit good interpersonal skills, and perform effectively and efficiently are exactly the type of recruits that employers want.

To be successful in seeking a job you must have both good information and well-developed job search skills. It is important that the job you finally end up with is compatible with your skills, knowledge, personality and interests, and provides the right balance for you in terms of work, family and leisure. Therefore you need to develop your self-awareness whilst at university or college. It is also important to understand the job market if you are to conduct a well-planned and structured job search campaign.

There are several steps to a successful job search:

- Conducting a self-analysis.
- Exploring the career options.
- Understanding the job market.
- Targeting employers.
- Preparing materials for your job search.
- Developing a job search strategy.

It is important to start thinking about a career when you enter higher education so that you can become aware of the possibilities as you progress through your course of study.

This will enable you to refine your options as you progress, so that when you achieve your qualification you are able to look forward to a successful career.

→ Conducting a self-analysis

In order to begin your search for employment you need to consider what you want from a job, what you do not want and what it is you have to offer prospective employers. Carrying out a self-analysis will help you to identify what you value, your strengths and weaknesses, etc. (see Chapter 2 for more information). This will enable you to plan what is required to overcome anything that may hinder you in getting a job that you value and which fits your skills. The information you generate will be particularly helpful if you have no real idea about what you wish to do.

To do the self-analysis you need to identify and list your values, skills and interests, and have some idea of your personality traits.

Values

Values are the qualities that are important and desirable to you in life and a career. Identifying your work values is an important aspect of developing your career aspirations. Work values may be divided into two categories:

- *Intrinsic values.* These arise within the individual from internal sources. They relate to the importance to you of the work activities themselves or to the benefits that the work contributes to society: for example, helping people, influencing government policy decisions, etc.
- *Extrinsic values.* These are from external sources. They are the factors linked with an occupational choice such as the physical setting, material rewards and other external features. The presence of extrinsic values is usually not enough to satisfy most people over a long period of time – they must also find some personal intrinsic value in the work.

Interests

See Activity 3.1 PREPARE TO WRITE A CV in the Online Study Guide.

The interests you have are the things that you find appealing and which arouse your enthusiasm. They are often closely related to your values and may encourage you to develop skills in a particular area. For example, an interest in politics may tempt you to join a particular political party and help in an election campaign. This would develop your communication and influencing skills.

Personality

In order to find and apply for a job that suits you, you need to evaluate your personality – who you are now.

Activity 3.1

Your aspirations for a job

In the following table, list the factors that you want/do not want from a job.

Things that are essential to me in a job	Things I would like in a job	Things I do not want in a job

The sort of things that you may include are: teamworking, job security, financial reward, responsibility, varied tasks, challenge, recognition, creativity, achievement/promotion opportunities, contact with members of the public, making decisions, working to deadlines, influencing people, managing others, good working conditions, overseas travel, independence, etc.

List the five most important factors.

1 _____
2 _____
3 _____
4 _____
5 _____

Look at your list of the five most important factors and identify any themes that emerge. How can you use this self-knowledge to help you choose a career? Check with the careers service to find out if there are any careers that match your factors.

PART 1   DEVELOPING STUDY SKILLS

Activity 3.2

Personality traits and self-management skills

Listed below are a mixture of personality descriptors and self-management skills. Cross out the ones that do not apply to you. Add in any others that are not on the list but apply to you.

Able	Conscientious	Inquisitive	Persistent	Sensible
Accurate	Conservative	Imaginative	Persuasive	Sensitive
Active	Consistent	Independent	Poised	Sincere
Adaptable	Creative	Intelligent	Practical	Sociable
Adventurous	Critical	Inventive	Pragmatic	Stable
Aggressive	Curious	Kind	Precise	Studious
Ambitious	Diplomatic	Knowledgeable	Progressive	Supportive
Analytical	Discreet	Likeable	Professional	Tactful
Artistic	Easy-going	Logical	Punctual	Teachable
Assertive	Efficient	Loyal	Quick	Tenacious
Attentive to detail	Emotional	Mature	Quiet	Thorough
Calm	Empathetic	Mechanistic	Rational	Thoughtful
Capable	Energetic	Methodical	Realistic	Tough
Caring	Enthusiastic	Meticulous	Reflective	Trusting
Careful	Evaluative	Modest	Reliable	Trustworthy
Cautious	Flexible	Motivated	Reserved	Understanding
Cheerful	Friendly	Open-minded	Resourceful	Versatile
Clear-thinking	Good-natured	Optimistic	Responsible	Witty
Communicative	Hardworking	Organised	Risk-averse	_____
Competent	Helpful	Outgoing	Risk-taking	_____
Competitive	Honest	Patient	Self-confident	_____
Confident	Humorous	Persevering	Self-controlled	_____

Choose six that you think fundamentally describe you and provide examples that demonstrate this:

Trait/skill	Examples to demonstrate
1	
2	
3	
4	
5	
6	

Are you able to draw any conclusions from this? Does it tell you anything about yourself?

Exploring career options

The next step in the job search is to match your skills and interests with different career fields. During your research, you may identify a number of career fields/jobs that are attractive to you. At this stage, it is important that you are realistic in deciding which of these are practical. It is unlikely that one single career field will match 100% with your skills, interests and values, so you need to select the ones that most closely match and satisfy the factors you have identified in previous activities. The career fields or jobs you have identified should become your career goals.

Note that part-time or summer jobs, work experience placements or voluntary activities provide excellent opportunities to try out jobs and explore career options. It is also useful to get information from people who are already working in the areas you have identified as being of interest.

Activity 3.3

Your chosen career field

For one of the occupations/jobs identified in your chosen career field, complete the following table. In the second column, insert the details for your chosen occupation or field and then make a list of your own personal details. Compare what is required for a particular occupation with your own skills and abilities. This will enable you to match your details against those of your chosen occupation/job and highlight what you need to do in order to be able to gain employment in a particular occupation.

Note that not all the rows will be appropriate for everyone.

About the occupation/job	Details
Occupation/job	
Major duties and responsibilities involved	
Specialisation within the field	
Personal traits/qualities required, e.g. 'highly motivated'	
Opportunities for advancement	
Societal status of the occupation	
Academic qualifications required	
Skills and abilities required – intellectual, physical	
Experience required	

PART 1   DEVELOPING STUDY SKILLS

About the occupation/job	Details
Training provided	
Length of time to qualify fully	
Continuous professional development	
Professional body or association	
Average age range	
Salary range	
Non-financial benefits, e.g. holidays, training	
Special requirements, e.g. foreign language, IT skills	
Physical working environment, e.g. office, factory, inside/outside	
Work schedule, e.g. daytime, night-time, shift work, seasonal	
Benefits provided by employer, e.g. car, mobile telephone, health insurance	
Dress requirements	
Travel requirements – local, regional, national, international	
Geographical location of employment	
Types of organisation in which work of this nature is to be found, e.g. multinational	
Employment trends	
Stability of employment	
Prospects for employment in the next 25 years, e.g. implications of technological advances	
Sources of information about this occupation	

About the occupation/job	Details
Sources of part-time/volunteer work or other experience to help to obtain a job in the field	
Name of contact(s) in the occupation who could supply more information	
Other occupations similar to this	

Source: Adapted from R. D. Lock (1999)

→ Understanding the job market

When conducting a job search it is important that you have an understanding of the changing nature of jobs and careers – there is little point in focusing your attention on a job or career that will offer few opportunities in the future world of work.

It is also important to consider the changing nature of the workplace (flexible working, hot desking, etc.) and work patterns (increase in short-term contracts, stable and secure positions disappearing, etc.). The nature of some jobs has changed dramatically over the last few years, not least because of advances in technology. This usually requires a change in the skills as, for example, jobs in manufacturing are replaced with jobs in the service sector.

No one can guarantee a job for life. Whereas your parents may have been fortunate enough to have a career or job for their whole working lifetime, increasingly you may expect to change careers several times during your working life. This may necessitate retraining or a further period in higher education – hence lifelong learning.

> **Remember...**
> You are in charge of your own career. Managing it will be a lifelong process – be proactive.

Target Employers

Once you have identified your career goals, you need to identify the employing organisations in that/those fields. You should undertake rigorous research about these organisations through as many sources as practicable. Annual reports, industry analyses, local and national newspapers, professional journals, university placement units, libraries and personal contacts can provide a wealth of information. You could even attempt to secure part-time or vacation employment at your preferred company which will provide you with a great deal of inside information and will enable you to assess whether you feel there will be a good fit between yourself and the organisation.

Thorough research on employers not only provides you with a competitive edge in your job search, but will also help you to decide which organisations you wish to contact and the strategies you will use to do this.

> ### Activity 3.4
> #### Identifying a prospective employer
> Identify the largest employing organisation in the sector you are interested in and find out the following:
> - Name of organisation.
> - Location of the head office.
> - Are there other sites/locations and if so where are they?
> - How many people are employed by the organisation?
> - Does the organisation have a graduate recruitment programme?
> - If so, what are the entry requirements?
> - Do they have a website? (Many organisations have websites that can provide invaluable information.)
> - What information is available about their recruitment process?
> - What can you learn from their latest published reports and accounts?
>
> Identify the small and medium-sized employers in the sector and repeat this research.

Prepare materials for your job search

Once you have identified your goals and the employers you wish to target, you can begin to compile your CV and covering letters so that they reflect your qualifications and experience as they apply to the needs of prospective employers.

Develop a job search strategy

Job search is a time consuming activity. Some students say they are unable to free up time from studies or a current job to search for a (new) job. Others procrastinate. However, unless you are prepared to free up the time required, you will miss job opportunities or the annual recruitment cycles.

To carry out the job search successfully, you must first establish the target date for getting a job, marking the date on a calendar or in your diary. Once you have established your target date, you can decide how much time to allocate to the task of finding a job. You could devote a certain amount of time each week to your job search activities. The more contacts and interviews you have during your job search, the greater the chance of being successful.

EMPLOYABILITY

Developing a curriculum vitae (CV)

A useful way to start a self-analysis and to identify your skills and abilities whilst you are at university is to put together a curriculum vitae (CV) and keep it up to date. A CV is a resumé or outline of your educational and professional history, containing details of your skills and experience, and it is usually prepared for job applications. It is basically a way of 'selling' yourself to a prospective employer; it can help you paint a clear and accurate picture of your education, skills and experience. When compiling your CV it is essential that you conduct a careful self-analysis and are as honest as possible in order to ensure a good match with the organisation.

If during your time at university you wish to send out speculative applications to organisations, you will be able to do so quickly and easily with your completed CV. When you apply for part-time, vacation, voluntary or full-time employment, your CV will prove very useful. If an organisation requires you to fill in its own application form, your CV will be a prompt to providing the essential details.

Competition in the job market is fierce and recruiters face many CVs for each vacancy. It is suggested that the attention span of the recruiters who have to sift through mountains of forms is between 3 and 20 seconds in the first instance, and therefore any CV that does not have an immediate impact is likely to be discarded. So, how can you make sure that your CV grabs the recruiter's attention? Recruitment experts say that you should:

- keep the layout simple
- focus the content on the needs of the company
- detail the contribution you made to meeting the needs of previous employers
- ensure that you understand the nature of the job you are applying for so that you can mould your CV according to the job you are aiming for.

Quality and simplicity are the hallmarks of a good CV. The most effective CVs are two pages long, make an impact, are business focused and contain relevant information about the applicant's personal, educational and employment life. It is best to avoid the use of a computer graphics package, so do not include pictures of houses at the side of the address and mortar boards at the side of educational achievements. These add nothing to an information document, the purpose of which is to demonstrate to a prospective employer whether someone is a suitable candidate. If you can demonstrate that you meet the essential requirements for the job and that you possess the appropriate experience and qualifications, you will be in with a chance.

See Activity 3.2 WORDS TO AVOID IN A CV in the Online Study Guide.

Remember...
Your CV should be designed to grab attention and get that interview for you. Once your have an interview, you are probably down to the last six candidates or so and are in with a real chance of landing the job.

57

PART 1   DEVELOPING STUDY SKILLS

> See Activity 3.3 WORDS TO INCLUDE IN A CV in the Online Study Guide.

Activity 3.5

Describe yourself positively

Write in the space provided all the positive adjectives or phrases that may be used to describe you and which would interest an employer.

[   ]

How many did you manage? Often students and other job applicants are not very good at identifying their positive attributes. If you came up with only five or six, consider the following and add to your list all those that apply to you:

adaptable, acts with integrity, a leader, analytical, able to work on own initiative, able to work well with others, competent, confident, conscientious, copes well with the unexpected, courteous, creative, dedicated, eager to learn, effective communicator, efficient, energetic, enthusiastic, flexible, good at meeting deadlines, good negotiator, hard working, honest, innovative, loyal, methodical, numerate, organised, outgoing, persuasive, principled, problem solver, punctual, thrives on challenges, reliable, resourceful, results oriented, self-motivated, teamworker

Component parts of a CV

The components of a CV are fairly standard, but how you present them will differ according to which particular parts you are trying to emphasise.

Basic information

> See Activity 3.4 CV SECTIONS AND HEADINGS in the Online Study Guide.

This section should contain basic information about yourself such as:

- Name.
- Address (permanent and term time if appropriate), including the postcode.
- Telephone number (home, mobile and work where appropriate, but make sure it is evident which is which), including the national and possibly the international dialling code.
- E-mail address (if you include this, remember to check your e-mail regularly).

> **Remember...**
> Only include personal information that is relevant to your objective or application.

In most cases there is no need to include data such as age, sex, marital status, national origin, health, etc. unless it is of relevance to the job for which you are applying.

Career objective

This section is optional, although many employers now expect a statement about your career goals. The objective is a one- or two-sentence statement about your career goals and should describe the focus of your job search. A well-written objective will indicate the type of work, the level at which you wish to work, the sort of organisation in which you are seeking work, and the skills and abilities you wish to utilise. The objective should provide a sense of direction, indicating that you know what you want and where you are going.

Beware of making your objective too broad, as this will reflect indecision. On the other hand, if it is too narrow you may exclude yourself from jobs for which you may otherwise have been considered.

Activity 3.6

Career objective

Consider your ideal job. Write a two-sentence objective that embraces your aspirations.

_____
_____
_____

Education

This section details your education and should be presented with the highest academic qualification first. Ensure that you present your qualifications in the most positive way, so if you went to Oxford University and achieved an unclassified degree, you would emphasise Oxford University. If, on the other hand, you achieved a first-class honours in Business Studies at Leeds Metropolitan University, you would probably want to emphasise the fact that you achieved a first-class degree because only a very small proportion of the population achieve one.

The more qualifications you possess, the less detail you will be able to include or need on your CV. If, for example, you achieved four A-grade A-level GCEs and eight GCSEs at school, you would not list them separately, but simply include the dates you attended the school, the name of the school and the number of GCEs and GCSEs that you obtained.

Details to include:

- The name of the educational institution attended.
- Dates of attendance.
- Qualification gained.
- Field in which qualification achieved (e.g. Business Studies).
- The year in which the qualification was confirmed

A brief summary of any short courses you have attended and any study abroad programmes may also be included here.

PART 1   DEVELOPING STUDY SKILLS

Example:

Educational institution	Dates	Qualification	Field	Date awarded
Leeds Metropolitan University	September 2006–June 2007	MSc	Information Systems	2007
Leeds Metropolitan University	September 2002–June 2006	BA (Hons) – upper second	Business Studies	2006
Whilst doing my first degree I took the opportunity to study for one semester at the University of Illinois in Chicago.				

If your education relates to your objective and is within the last three years, it should be the first section; if not, it should follow the work experience section.

Activity 3.7

Compiling your CV – education
Compile the education section for your CV.

Employment history/work experience

This section details all your work experience, including full-time paid jobs, part-time paid jobs, summer jobs and work experience placements. Start with the most recent first, allocating more space to this. Include any voluntary unpaid work, but there is no need to mention that it was unpaid. You may wish to outline the scope of your duties, but do not give too much detail.

Details to include:

- The dates of employment.
- Job title or position.
- Name of the employer.
- Location of the employer.
- Responsibilities or major duties. Keep these brief and put them in order of relative value to a future employer. You could also highlight any transferable skills that you used or developed.

Activity 3.8

Compiling your CV – work experience

A CV may be brought to life by the use of action verbs such as analysed, created and established. In the space provided, write down 10 action verbs relating to your work experience that may be useful to you in constructing your CV.

> See Activity 3.7 DESCRIBING YOUR ABILITIES in the Online Study Guide.

Skills

This section provides an opportunity to highlight any special skills that you possess which may be relevant to your application – for example, foreign language proficiency or information technology skills.

Achievements

This section should highlight any special awards or achievements you have, for example:

- Academic, e.g. winner of Student of the Year prize.
- Professional, e.g. chair of local Women in Management group.
- Community, e.g. scout leader.
- Sporting, e.g. represent the county at tennis.

Interests and activities

If you have not yet worked in paid employment, then your interests take on special significance. They will indicate to employers that you have the qualities and skills that they are looking for. Include details of any professional or community organisations of which you are currently a member or in which you hold office, and any voluntary activities in which you participate.

Do not be afraid to include things such as contemporary music or novels, but do not include items that are not interests of yours. If you do and the prospective employer asks you a question about your interests, he or she is likely to infer that you are not being very honest.

Organisation of your CV

See Activity 3.5 CV FORMAT in the Online Study Guide.

A CV is difficult to write unless you know how you are going to use it – for example, which field of employment are you looking at, what type of employer, etc. This will influence the way in which you present your CV. The sections of your CV should therefore be organised according to what is most important to the prospective employer and/or your career objective.

If you have been in education in the last three years, are a recent graduate or if academic qualifications are a qualifying requirement (for medicine, law, teaching, etc.), the education section should be presented first. However, if you want to emphasise significant work or leadership experience then the employment section should be presented first.

The traditional way of presenting a CV is in chronological order – employment history and education are presented in reverse order, with the most recent first. This is easy to read. Duties and accomplishments are described in detail, thus emphasising a career path. However, it can draw attention to a lack of experience in a single profession. After the basic information, the order of presentation is usually: employment history, education, achievements, skills and interests and activities.

Note that if you are applying for an academic position, it is necessary to include all published works, presentations at conferences, professional achievements and much greater detail about your education.

PART 1   DEVELOPING STUDY SKILLS

See Activity 3.6 FIND THE CV MISTAKES in the Online Study Guide.

Suggestions for preparing a CV

- Be concise – do not use more than two pages.
- Focus on your strongest assets, especially those relevant to the job.
- Do not expect prospective employers to read your mind. If you want them to know something, tell them.
- Critical information should go on the first page.
- Emphasise achievements rather than responsibilities.
- Be honest: you should represent accurately what you are able to do. Do not exaggerate your qualifications.
- Keep it active and positive to create a strong favourable image.
- Consider your choice of words carefully – remember, they should accurately describe you.
- Use good-quality, white paper.
- Type or word process your CV.
- Extensive education and employment records should appear on the second page.
- Do not put curriculum vitae or CV as a heading to the document.
- Do not list references but offer to supply them if requested.
- Do not reveal any personal circumstances, such as divorce or disabilities, or personal statistics, such as height and weight, unless the job requires it.
- Avoid the use of 'I'.
- Use correct grammar, spelling and punctuation. Ensure there are no typographical errors.
- Do not include pictures.
- Wherever possible be specific.
- Exclude irrelevant information and experiences.
- Submit an original rather than a photocopy.
- Just include the facts.

Using the sections you have already developed in previous activities, construct your CV. Use the following checklist to evaluate your CV. Assess it carefully, using the criteria given in the table. If you consider that your CV is average or poor in any area, identify the ways in which you can improve it.

See downloadable template 3.1 CHECKLIST TO ASSESS CV for your Personal Development Plan online.

Checklist: how to prepare a good CV

Is the CV clear?	☐
Will the reader be able to get a complete picture of the writer?	☐
Is irrelevant personal information excluded?	☐
Does it emphasise the benefits of employing the writer to the potential employer?	☐
Is it well structured and logical?	☐
Is the language used understandable and appropriate?	☐
Is it set out to invite attention?	☐
Does it sell the writer to the potential employer?	☐
Do the writer's accomplishments, skills and abilities stand out?	☐
Is it clearly printed, on good-quality, white paper?	☐

Covering letters

Your application for employment will usually involve the production of two documents – a curriculum vitae (CV) and a covering letter. Whilst a CV is a generic advertisement about yourself, which you may send to many different organisations without changing the content, a covering letter enables you to tailor your application to the specific job for which you are applying.

You should always include a covering letter with your CV – many employers will not even look at a CV that is not accompanied by one. An unaccompanied CV gives the impression that you are not interested enough to make the effort to write a letter. It may also indicate to a prospective employer that you are mass mailing your CV – even if this is the case, you do not want to publicise it.

The covering letter must therefore arouse a potential employer's interest by reflecting your personality, enthusiasm and intellect. Regard it as a marketing tool, providing you with an opportunity to sell yourself and persuade the employer to look more closely at your CV and invite you for an interview.

The CV and covering letter provide the first indication to an employer of your communication skills. It is therefore vital that you take great care and time in the preparation of your CV and the accompanying covering letter.

What to include in a covering letter

A covering letter should be three or four paragraphs long, single-spaced and on one side of paper. Begin with:

- Your name and address.
- The employer's name and title.
- The company name and address.
- The date.
- An appropriate salutation. It is a good idea to find out the name of the person who will process the application so that you can address the person by name.

First paragraph

It is important to begin with a strong statement to create impact. Employers receive many letters of application and you need to be sure that yours attracts their attention. This is sometimes referred to as an 'elevator pitch' – in other words, imagine that you get into an elevator/lift with the person and you have, at most, three minutes to speak with them before they get out. What would you say? Explain why you are writing, where you saw the advert, which job you are applying for, etc. Within this paragraph you could briefly state your general qualifications for the job.

Middle paragraphs

Use the middle paragraphs to help you stand out from the rest of the applicants by arousing the employer's curiosity. Explain how your qualifications are a good match for the organisation's needs and demonstrate how your background and experience qualify you for the job. Highlight your strengths and any special accomplishments that are relevant. Wherever possible, provide specific examples to support your statements.

Do not fall into the trap of repeating the information within your CV, but highlight the parts that really identify you as a good candidate for the job. Refer the reader to your CV if they require further details.

Final paragraph

In your final paragraph, make a specific request for an interview. Give an indication of when you are available and how you may be contacted. It is also useful to indicate that further background information about yourself and your interests can be supplied on request. Finally, end your letter by thanking the employer for their time and consideration, and finish with an appropriate closing signature.

See downloadable template 3.2 ASSESSMENT OF CVS for your Personal Development Plan online.

Types of covering letter

There are different types of covering letter – an *application* letter and a *prospecting* letter.

An *application letter* is written in response to an advertisement for a job. The purpose of the application letter is to get a potential employer to read your CV and invite you for an interview. In an application letter you should show how your qualifications, skills and experience match the requirements of the job advertised by emphasising the appropriate parts of your CV. You should also quote the reference on the advertisement and the source (the newspaper, journal, etc.) in which you saw the advertisement.

A *prospecting letter* is written to search for possible vacancies in your area of work, rather than as a response to a specific job advertisement. These letters are usually targeted at specific organisations and should be addressed to the appropriate contact person. The letter should focus on the organisation's needs, products, trends or problems, and describe how your qualifications, skills and experience might meet their requirements.

Suggestions for covering letters

- Check carefully for spelling or grammatical errors.
- Organise the information you are communicating, ensuring a logical presentation.
- Make it interesting from line 1.
- Make it brief but informative.
- Try to convey your enthusiasm for working in the organisation.
- Be positive and persuasive.
- Use a polite, formal style.
- Provide specific facts or examples to demonstrate observations about yourself.
- Avoid jargon and clichés, such as 'excellent interpersonal skills' and 'self-starter'.
- Be truthful – do not overstate your qualifications, experience or skills.
- Emphasise your strengths.
- Make specific reference to the organisation to which you are applying.
- Keep a copy.

Employee specifications

Many employers now include employee specifications with the details about a job. These provide you with some information about the knowledge and skills that an employer is looking for. It is important, when completing your application form, that you target the skills identified in the employee specification, providing examples to demonstrate that you have the skills required. This will enable your application to grab the attention of the recruiter.

> **Remember...**
> Ensure that your application form or CV has significant, relevant and user-friendly information that is high impact.

Online applications

An increasing number of employers will now only accept online applications from prospective employees. Be sure to find out if this is the case with the employer(s) that you wish to target.

→ Interviews

Once your CV or application form has been successful in gaining an interview, the next step of the process is to ensure that you perform well. Find out all you can about the job and organisation before your interview. You will be able to gather information from the careers service, the university library, the local library and online from the Internet.

There are a number of points to bear in mind when preparing for and attending an interview.

Do

- Prepare for the interview by finding out as much as you can about the prospective employer: for example, the main area of business; what the product range is and/or what services are provided; financial situation; culture; mission statement; stance on corporate social responsibility. Many of these are available in the annual report or via the company website. This will enable you to speak knowledgeably about the organisation.
- Make sure that you know the time and the place, and ensure that you know how to get there and plan for any traffic or transport delays. It is a good idea to have a trial run at the same time of day, on the same day of the week, as your interview. This will alert you to any difficulties (e.g. parking, road works or public transport delays).
- Be on time for your interview appointment – do not arrive too early and certainly not late.
- Try to find out who will be interviewing you and their role in the organisation.

- When you ring to confirm that you will be attending the interview, ask if there will be any tests because advance information of these will give you chance to prepare. This will improve your confidence, as you will not face an unanticipated test.
- Look your best, well groomed and appropriately dressed for the post that you have applied for.
- Prepare yourself mentally for the interview by visualising yourself giving a professional performance.
- Stress your accomplishments and ability to do the job. Emphasise your past experience, training and skills. If you do not have the experience required, turn the question round to match your skills and competences to the employer's requirements, so that they understand what you are offering them in terms of your ability to achieve results.
- Talk about your successes, but do not overdo it. If you are probed about any failures, be honest, but also emphasise what you have learned from the experience.
- Be enthusiastic, convincing, confident and positive. If it is possible to have practice interviews with the careers service at university or college, take advantage of this type of opportunity until you feel comfortable in an interview situation.
- Answer questions honestly. Be fairly brief but focused on what was asked to demonstrate that you have grasped the facts, and if possible provide illustrations from your experience.

Do not

- Be disheartened if the first interview is unfavourable. Assess what went well and what you can do to improve next time.
- Be afraid to sell your qualities. Evidence suggests that interviewers make up their minds in the first few minutes, so it is a good idea to get your pitch in early and aim for maximum impact.
- Get flustered if the interviewer asks a difficult or awkward question. They may be probing your weaknesses to see how you handle pressure.
- Volunteer information about your weaknesses,
- Argue with the interviewer, become aggressive or appear arrogant.
- Answer in monosyllables. Whether the interviewer asks open or closed questions, you should provide a sufficiently detailed response.
- Ask immediately about the salary.
- Say how much you need a job.

It is impossible to predict what questions the interviewer will ask. They may have a number of questions that they will ask each applicant, but may ask different supplementary questions depending on the answers. Often interviewers will start by asking why you want the job or by making small talk to put you at ease. Prepare in advance responses to issues such as:

- the relevance of your experience to the job

- your major achievements in paid employment and at university or college – but be careful not to overstate your achievements
- your core skills and abilities and how these would make you effective in the organisation
- any challenges that you have faced in your life and/or at university/college and how you have dealt with them
- why you have chosen that particular career field
- what you think you could contribute to the organisation

It is likely that the interview will follow a set format. It might take place with one individual, two people or a panel of three or four. The structure is likely to be:

- Arrival at a designated place where you wait to be called into the interview room.
- Welcome and introduction(s) to interviewer(s). You may want to shake their hand(s) if this is possible. Try to make eye contact with each interviewer when you shake hands.
- Explanation of the process by the main interviewer, or chairperson if it is a panel.
- The interviewer may provide details about the organisation and the job, or this may be towards the end of the interview.
- Questions from the interviewer(s).
- Time for you to ask any questions.
- The interviewer may ask if there is anything further that you wish to say to support your application, and to check whether you have any final questions.
- The interview will close with information about when you are likely to hear the outcome. You may be thanked for attending and you should ensure that you thank the interviewer(s).

> **Remember...**
> In a panel interview, look at each person in turn. Avoid looking only at the person who asked the question.

During the interview

The first impression you make on the interviewer(s) is very important and lasting. You should be smartly dressed, and if you shake hands make sure that it is a firm handshake. Smile and appear confident and relaxed even if you are very nervous. At this stage it is useful to take several deep breaths and make yourself comfortable in the chair. This will calm your nerves and help you to relax. Do not be afraid to pause slightly in order to collect your thoughts. Throughout the interview you should try to remain genuine, positive and enthusiastic. Be aware of your body language – maintain eye contact, sit upright, smile, look interested and nod appropriately. Ensure that your voice is loud enough for the interviewer(s) to hear, and add emphasis, intonation and inflection appropriately. Avoid speaking in a monotone. Speak clearly and not too fast, taking your pace from the interviewer(s). (See Chapters 5 and 14 for more information.)

After the interview

Afterwards, think about all the positive aspects of the interview. Think about how you answered the questions. What types of question could you have answered better and how can you bring about this improvement for next time? Do not dwell on all the things that you now remember but didn't say at the time. Analyse your performance carefully so that, if you have been unsuccessful, you have learned what to do and what not to do next time. If the interviewer gives you the opportunity for feedback, take it. You may learn valuable lessons for the future. If you are successful, well done. Congratulate yourself and celebrate the culmination of your course and the start of your career.

→ Summary

This chapter has outlined:
- that employers are looking for graduates who possess personal and academic skills
- how to undertake various job search activities, such as analysing career options and understanding the job market
- the essentials of a CV and how to prepare one
- how to write a covering letter
- what to do and what not to do in preparation for an interview.

4 Reading for study

Learning outcomes
After studying this chapter, you should be able to:
- identify a strategy to read systematically and effectively
- describe ways of reading
- select the most appropriate way to read for different reading materials
- define and use the SQ3R method
- know the techniques to increase reading speed.

→ Introduction

Reading is a fundamental aspect of academic work. It is likely to be the major way to gather information about the discipline(s) you are studying and it is a very valuable skill to enhance and develop at university or college. One of the ways to develop the ability to think about and describe the world in terms of a particular approach is through reading. Reading will provide an understanding of the academic discipline being studied. Ultimately it will be one of the keys that unlock the door to a career as a business manager, psychologist, engineer, chemist, teacher, scientist or whatever. As well as guiding you through your course, it will be an invaluable learning tool in the world of employment. Reading opens up the possibility of gaining access to and an understanding of the thinking of all the people who have developed models and theories or written about a particular discipline or subject.

One of the principal objectives of reading for study is to gather ideas and information and to assimilate them into your own view of the world, and then to be able to express that view through the assessment programme or in seminars. Only by doing this can you understand a subject. During your time at university or college you will need to approach your reading very intelligently and diligently by putting considerable effort into it.

As a student it is important to recognise that reading may be the most demanding work you do at university or college and that a huge volume of reading will be required to pass a course. Almost certainly, reading strategies need to be developed in order to get through the amount of reading to be done. For some people it may be a matter of changing perceptions about reading. For example, on entering a library some students will think, 'Oh no, look at all these books to read!', while others will think, 'Oh wow, look at all these books to read! Where shall I start? Let me get going!'

Over the years, authors have identified, described and analysed the issues relevant to a particular area of study, such as business, philosophy, botany, education or psychology. Within each discipline, theorists examine a subject from a number of viewpoints, identifying key themes and issues, and embodying certain assumptions. One of the particular advantages of reading is that in many instances it is possible, through books, to read the original works of an author, such as Sigmund Freud, Karl Marx, F. W. Taylor or B. F. Skinner. The written word is still the main way of accessing academic debate in all fields of study. Through reading, it is possible to discover the fundamentals of a subject, its basic assumptions, the facts upon which it is built and how these are examined and approached. For instance, organisations can be described and interpreted very differently from the point of view of a psychologist, a sociologist, an anthropologist, a theologian or an historian.

This chapter will help you to make the best possible use of your reading and enable you to approach it in the most effective way during your studies.

Why are you reading?

A student will read for many different reasons, and it is important to remember that the way reading is approached should change depending on the purpose. Glancing through a newspaper to pick out the main news items is quicker than and different from reading for study, and both involve a variety of skills. A newspaper often gives only a cursory coverage of a topic, ignoring the details. A textbook may require detailed study to extract the essential knowledge it contains. When reading, for example, it is possible to:

(a) read an instruction book with the intention of immediately applying the information in order to play a new MP3 player, use the cooker or repair a car;

(b) read an enjoyable, exciting novel for escapism, as quickly as possible, with no need to worry about remembering any of the story afterwards;

(c) skim through the pages of a computer magazine for the latest developments; or

(d) scan the pages of a newspaper to absorb the main headlines that day, disregarding the advertisements altogether.

There are, of course, different ways of tackling reading, which will vary according to both the reading material and the particular task and focus. Reading is, after all, one of the basic tools of work for students. It is crucial that reading skills are developed so that you are able to get the most out of reading and importantly to make the best use of it. Many techniques can be used to gain a detailed understanding from a textbook or article, to identify the main themes or issues, or to get a general overview.

The reading skills that you have already developed can be put to good use in academic study. New students may neglect to use the abilities that they have developed in their everyday lives, and which are often overlooked as important skills. Reading is a skill that is often taken for granted. It is easy to believe that it no longer requires any thought or effort. However, the fact is that reading is concerned with understanding the meaning that the author is trying to communicate, not just a matter of recognising words on a page. When you are studying it is important to think about *why* you are reading and to realise your need for a variety of approaches. It can be only too easy to read without thinking about it, because a tutor has provided a reading list or because you think that reading is a requirement of your course.

> **Stop and think**
> Consider the different kinds of reading you have used over the last few days.
> - What was the purpose of your reading?
> - Make a list of the different approaches you used from (a), (b), (c) and (d) above.
> - Did you realise that you had used these approaches?
> - How can you use this knowledge to help you improve your reading skills?

Most people tend to feel that the way to read a book, an article, an abstract or information on a CD-ROM or personal computer is to start at the beginning and read through to the end. At first this tends to be the approach that many students adopt with books, opening the textbook and starting to read from Chapter 1 until they lose interest, find it too difficult, fall asleep or, in some cases, finish the book with relief. This method is unlikely to be the approach that brings the most benefit whilst studying at university or college.

→ What happens when you read?

It can be quite informative and revealing to consider what you are trying to achieve when you read.

- Is it to remember factual information?
- Is it to gather information and an understanding of a particular theoretical perspective for an assignment?
- Is it to build up an overview of the work of different authors?

Two different approaches to reading can be adopted – the 'surface' and the 'deep' approach. There are occasions when each approach is necessary and it is a good idea to develop skills in both approaches. The reader using the 'surface' technique tends simply to memorise the facts presented without taking time to understand the significance of what has been learned. The reader who adopts the 'deep' technique tends to be less interested in factual details and tries to understand the underlying principles, the connections between them and the assumptions that underpin the material. With practice it is possible to change your approach to reading depending on the requirements. In some instances, if there is to be a test based simply on the facts, it may be acceptable to adopt the surface approach. However, if the assessment requires a more comprehensive knowledge of the underlying principles, it would be necessary to use a different way of reading, which provides for understanding and making sense of the material.

On the whole, students who take a detailed and critical approach to their reading usually have a deep and abiding interest in their work, and study for longer periods of time because of their fundamental interest in the subject. The student who takes the deep approach frequently does better in assessments because he or she possesses a better understanding of the subject matter and can use the knowledge gained to complete the assessment comprehensively. If energy is used to understand what has to be learned, a more active approach to reading and study will be adopted. As a consequence, details will be remembered more easily. For example, we remember a series of numbers more readily than numbers presented in a random fashion because we have developed an underlying understanding of sequence in the numbering. Thus, 4, 8, 12, 16, 20, 24 is relatively easy to memorise, whereas 16, 24, 4, 20, 12, 8 would be much more difficult to recall. We utilise a similar principle with words: the word 'tongue' can be remembered more easily than 'ngetuo' because we have a concept that these six letters in a particular sequence refer to an object. In other words, they have a certain meaning for us. In the examples given, it is much easier to remember the individual numbers and letters if they form part of a meaningful whole. This principle also applies to reading. It is much easier to learn the details of a particular approach if the fundamental ideas have been understood or an overview of the subject matter to which they belong has been obtained.

The main objective should be to read academic work thoughtfully and actively. In this way it will be much easier to learn and remember the theorist's or author's main argument, proposition or ideas, and the detailed information that supports his or her research.

If you make the effort to understand clearly the underlying meanings of what the author is arguing, this provides the foundations for the next stage in making use of reading. Once the fundamentals of a particular approach have been grasped, the author's ideas can be evaluated. It will be possible to compare a particular author's ideas with the arguments of others and to consider whether the perspective put forward is based on sound reasoning and the argument is clearly and explicitly stated. Ultimately you will be able to evaluate the author's perspective and to develop your own intellectual stance on his or her viewpoint.

Ways of reading

It can be useful to think in terms of different ways, or styles, of reading:

- background reading
- skimming
- scanning
- detailed and critical reading.

All of these reading styles will be useful at some stage during your course and you should practise them frequently until you can adopt them at will.

Figure 4.1 Different ways of reading

- Big picture
- Overview
- Pre-course reading

Background

- Gain general impression
- Use cues
- Superficial knowledge

Skimming

Reading

Detailed and Critical

- Thorough
- Essential
- Analytical
- Evaluative

Scanning

- Look for specific parts
- Read only what is necessary
- Moderate level of information

Background reading

Background reading is an essential element in any course of study. It provides an overview of the topic area and may identify a framework to which more detail is added later. It is, in effect, the skeleton upon which the flesh is added through more detailed reading. Some books on course reading lists are recommended for background reading and a general reading of these texts would enable the central ideas to be quickly understood. Thus you will be able to receive the new ideas or concepts readily, easily and quickly, assimilating them into your thoughts. From this you will get a feel for the subject as well as a context into which more detailed information can be added. Normally background reading is done quite quickly at a steady, easy pace and in a fairly relaxed and receptive frame of mind. General views and background information are identified rather than detailed and specific arguments, theories, models and perspectives. If a course provides a pre-course reading list for use before you enter university or college, background reading would be appropriate.

> **Remember...**
> Background reading enables you to grasp the 'big picture'.

Skimming

Skimming through a text, running your eyes down the page very rapidly, can provide a good general impression of what the material is about. Skimming involves searching through a text or article very quickly by reading the first and last paragraphs and noting other cues such as introduction, findings or summaries. It is appropriate to skim a text when only the most superficial knowledge of a subject is needed.

> See Activity 4.3 SKIMMING PRACTICE in the Online Study Guide.

Normally the reader does not know exactly what he or she is looking for when skimming reading material and in fact may not be searching for anything in particular. As a consequence, when skimming it is useful to prepare by reading the title, source and author and then to question the text using the Who, Why, When, Where, What and How questions that are relevant. Using this questioning technique, you can direct your eyes down the column of print, or alternatively a zig-zag can be used if the lines are long.

Skimming is a technique that should always be used before reading any article or textbook in detail. Initially it will be the headings, bold type, highlighting, capitalised words, italics and underlining that draw attention. As proficiency in skim reading is developed, you will be able to detect the more important facts, unusual vocabulary, concepts and words that are clues to focus on. When you become more efficient at skim reading, look for certain things that should claim attention. For example, look for:

- names of people
- places
- models
- graphs
- numbers

and words such as:

although	consequently	furthermore	moreover	until
advantages	despite	in addition	results	versus
because	disadvantages	instead	therefore	whenever
causes	effects	in summary	thus	

Terms such as these are identifiers of the main ideas and issues, or will show that the author is indicating a change of direction or something new in the text or article. Always remember that authors of textbooks want the reader to identify the important concepts, issues, models and theories. The author will also use major headings and subheadings, lists preceded by bullet points or numbers, words and phrases in italics, bold or underlined, or possibly repetition to alert the reader to important points or to add emphasis.

> **Remember…**
> When you pick up a text or article in the library, always skim it before you make a final decision to read it thoroughly, discard it or use it for assessments.

Scanning

> See Activity 4.4 SCANNING in the Online Study Guide.

Scanning also involves running the eyes over a text, looking for particular facts or key words and phrases. When texts are scanned they are read very rapidly, searching the material and looking for specific points. It is advisable to read the chapter introduction and conclusion in detail and to speed-read the remainder of the chapter. Scanning a text means that no more is read than is absolutely necessary to find the essential details sought. When scanning a chapter take particular note of any graphs or diagrams, as these are likely to summarise important points. Scanning a text will provide a moderate level of information about a subject.

Scanning is a valuable tool in the repertoire of reading skills, as it enables the reader to identify any new terms introduced in a chapter. When a new term or concept is identified, try to find its definition. If the meaning of the new term is not evident from the text, it is a good idea to look it up in a dictionary or a glossary. A glossary is an alphabetical list of terms that are special to a particular field of knowledge, with definition or explanations. If the text does not have a glossary, it is a good idea to start one of your own by recording the term and its definition as well as the page number where the term first appears. When revising for examinations or preparing an assessment, your glossary will be a convenient and comprehensive outline of the subject being studied. It may also prove very useful if you are looking for answers to particular questions or for specific references for an assessment.

Detailed and critical reading

Detailed and critical reading is essential when you need to be very thorough about what you are reading – to analyse, to compare, to evaluate the material. When critical reading is required:

- Skim the material to gain an overview of the article, chapter or book.
- Then read it in detail, ensuring that you understand the information as well as how it relates to the subject overall.
- Pause frequently to think about what has been read. At the end of critical reading, all the main facts and arguments presented in the material should have been absorbed and understood.

Detailed and critical reading is particularly necessary in academic work, for articles, books and other material that is categorised by tutors as 'essential reading'. Developing critical reading skills is a much slower process, a task more suitable to a time of day when plenty of time, energy and attention can be devoted to it. Detailed and critical reading requires a formal method of reading such as SQ3R, a technique that provides the deepest level of understanding possible.

SQ3R

SQ3R is a very well-known and successful reading technique. It is a reading method that has stood the test of time and has proven useful to the majority of students. It is an active approach and is a very systematic way of reading a textbook.

(S) Survey

This will help you to gather the information necessary and to decide upon objectives. It is possible to survey a single chapter or the book as a whole, surveying the material for content and organisation. Flick through the book or chapter, looking at the first and last paragraphs and at the major headings for each section. This will provide a general impression of the material. Note any graphs, illustrations, charts, diagrams, maps, glossaries, chapter reviews, summaries or appendices, as these usually contain important information. Look for reading aids such as learning outcomes, bold print, italics, subheadings and end of chapter questions, as these will be included to help you comprehend and remember the material.

(Q) Question

When surveying the chapter or material, think about who, what, when, where, why and how, as this will reveal a great deal of information. Survey the chapter, marking anything you consider important plus any terms that are new or that you do not understand. If you do this, it will help your mind engage and concentrate. For instance, what does the author say about a particular theoretical perspective? Does the chapter or section explain certain concepts? Continue reading and think up more detailed questions by turning the headings and subheadings into questions. Comprehensive questions will lead to a better understanding of the material. Use any study guides provided by your tutor, or chapter questions provided by the author.

If you have never used this approach of developing questions about the chapter, it might be a little difficult initially. One way to start is to formulate questions from what is contained in the textbook. To give you an example, if the textbook is entitled *Organisational Behaviour*, the following questions could be posed:

- What is it about?
- What are the main ideas?
- From what standpoint is the author approaching this vast subject?
- Is the author presenting fact or opinion?
- How are the main perspectives presented?
- Are conclusions supported from the material presented?

These are fairly typical questions, but finding their answers through reading requires some thought. More questions may be developed as you proceed through the chapter or book.

Becoming a questioning reader is an essential skill to develop because it will enable you to read in a purposeful, focused manner. A questioning approach means that you actively engage with the reading material, and as you search for answers to your questions, this will enhance learning. Adopting this questioning technique when reading is useful for various reasons: for example, it will enable you to keep your mind and attention concentrated on what is being read. By linking reading to what you know already, this will identify the gaps in your knowledge so that you know specifically what you need to find out. If you actively engage in reading in this way, you will be able to build a framework on which you can place details later, as well as identifying, formulating and questioning the author's argument in your mind as you read.

(R) Read

When you begin to read the material actively, search for answers to the questions identified initially. Try to read the whole of the chapter if it is a manageable size. Read fairly quickly and fluently, underlining key words and trying to get an overall grasp of the contents. Do not underline whole paragraphs or make notes at this stage because this encourages concentration on details rather than on an overview. It is not possible to identify the main ideas until a whole chapter has been read.

Having read the material through once, divide it into smaller sections and re-read each section carefully and thoroughly. Note all the underlined words, reduce reading speed for difficult sections, and stop to re-read anything that is not clear. It is advisable to avoid taking notes at this stage. This second reading will allow you to fill in the details around the framework you have built.

(R) Recite or Recall

When you have read a section, look away from the material and try briefly to recall or recite answers to questions or summarise what has been read. Make sure you know what the section is about and that you understand it. Once you are confident that you have understood the section, make notes about it in your own words. Identify the main issues and the supporting themes and ideas. Make sure your notes are not too detailed. (See Chapter 6 for specific information about how to make notes.) Repeat this for each of the sections in the chapter or material.

> **Remember...**
> The more of your senses that you use, the more likely it is that you will remember what has been read.

It is essential to write notes in your own words as it will ensure that you understand the text or article. You will be able to use your notes more readily in assignments, and it will be easier to work from them when you need to revise before examinations. If the notes are in your own words, this avoids the problem of *plagiarism*, which is the inclusion of unacknowledged material in an assessment. (See Part 2 for more information about plagiarism.)

(R) Review

When you have completed the whole of the chapter or material using the preceding steps, the next stage is review. Go back over it again, skimming through it, checking that you can still answer all of your questions. The review stage is the time to consolidate and integrate the information gathered. For example, ask yourself the following questions:

- Have you identified the main issues and do you understand the concepts?
- Have you managed to answer all your questions?
- Are you able to make sense of your notes?
- Have you now grasped what the chapter is about?

If you cannot answer your questions, look back at the chapter and refresh your memory, then continue with the review. Try covering up your notes and attempt to recall the notes you have made under a subheading. Test yourself regularly and decide if there is anything else that you need to know. Repeating the review process with all the chapters you read will help you to improve your memory.

PART 1   DEVELOPING STUDY SKILLS

> ### Activity 4.1
>
> ### SQ3R
>
> The *SQ3R* approach is a very useful approach that will help you to read purposefully and methodically.
>
> - Select an article or a chapter from a textbook to try out this technique. It is probably a good idea to choose something that will be useful to you on your course, so one of the recommended texts or pre-course reading is ideal.
> - Assume that you need to take notes from it that will be useful to you at a later date.
> - Focus on understanding rather than memorisation, as this will be much more productive in the long term.
> - Use each of the steps detailed in the SQ3R method.
> - How has this improved your understanding of the selected reading?

→ Which technique?

A skilled reader varies the method and speed of reading to suit the material and the reason for reading it. Whichever technique is used, it is important to remember to engage in active reading. Try active reading by annotating the text in the margins, underlining and/or highlighting important points, because this will emphasise and draw attention to information during re-reading or review. If you develop the skill of active reading, it will keep you focused on the text or article and stop your mind wandering.

One reason for reading may be to find ideas and information for a particular assessment. In this case it is not necessary to read whole books; indeed, to do so would take up too much time. Instead, it is important to select carefully, both between books and within them.

See Activity 4.5 PRACTISING YOUR READING TECHNIQUES in the Online Study Guide.

It is usually a good idea to *skim* through parts of a book to get a general idea of its content, or to *scan* particular chapters or sections to gather information for a specific assessment. It can be difficult at first to approach reading in this very selective way. It may be uncomfortable and your reaction might be to think that you are likely to miss something important or that it is a strange way to read a book. However, being selective is necessary to enable you to get through all the reading required and to get your assessments and seminar work completed in the time available. You will be able to deal with a broad spectrum of material, rather than being overcome by a mass of reading that is impossible to digest. If you practise the skimming and scanning techniques outlined, not only will reading take much less time, but retention of the important details will greatly improve.

→ Selecting reading material

When you receive a reading list from a tutor, or you are faced with a row of books or journals on the library shelf, how do you decide which book or article to read? Many journals are now available electronically through a university or college library, which makes the choice wider than ever. Fortunately the electronic journals can be searched to identify relevant reading material. Books and journals on library shelves have to be searched manually, but it is, in fact, relatively easy to pick up the essence of a book or article very quickly, so choosing an appropriate text or journal is fairly straightforward and not too time consuming. Next time you visit the library to search for books to enable you to complete assessments, you will find it helpful to practise looking at the following.

Title/author

Some books and articles have a subtitle which is often more descriptive than the title and may provide just the information you need. The author's name is obviously critical. Tutors will initially recommend certain books, journals, articles or authors. Eventually you will be able to make your own mind up about a particular author. If the name is a familiar one, you should be able to assess how useful the book will be.

The publication date is given on the back of the title page of a book, or frequently on the front cover of a journal, and can be very important. If it is not a recent publication, a book may be a classic text, possibly the original theorist presenting his or her fundamental, influential and important contribution to the field of knowledge. Alternatively, if the text is more than a few years old, it may have been replaced by a newer updated edition and is probably out of date. Journals are usually much more up to date, and it would be unlikely for a tutor to recommend a journal article more than a few years old. The tutor frequently will advise students about previous editions of books, whether they are still useful or not. Some subjects, such as information technology and microelectronics, require the most up-to-date books because technological developments mean that the field of study is changing very quickly.

Index

Once you have looked at the title, author and date of publication of a book, it is necessary to consider the index next. This will show immediately whether the topic you are searching for is in the book, and how detailed the coverage is likely to be. One or two sections you locate from the index may be all that you need to read in a specific book. If the topic required appears in a footnote, there is unlikely to be sufficient detail to make it worth reading a section of a book. If the author has devoted 50 pages to the topic, it is worth a closer look. If the topic you are interested in does not appear in the index, return the book to the library or bookshop shelves. Whilst at university or college it is important to remain focused on the particular area you are studying; do not be tempted to spend a lot of time reading material that does not achieve your current objectives.

Contents

The contents page generally provides a list of the topics included in the book or journal. It enables the reader to see how the author(s) present and sequence the subject matter. Usually the contents page in a book includes the chapter headings and the various subsections of each chapter. You will also be able to identify the importance that the author gives to different topics. A good indication of this is the number of pages an author devotes to the topic or subsection.

Introduction

This should provide an indication of the scope of the book or article and how it is organised. The introduction of a book may suggest that ideally it should be read sequentially as one section builds upon another, or it may indicate that each chapter can be read independently of any of the other chapters. The introduction will also outline the author's particular approach and may signal to the reader essential pointers to watch out for. Scanning the introduction will help you decide whether to reject the book or article, or in what order or how much of the text it is necessary to read.

Publisher's comments

These normally appear on the back cover of a book and give a short and helpful explanation of the content. They are likely to include notes about the author(s) and frequently the comments will describe the readership that the book is aimed at. For example, the comments may say that the book is written for final-year business undergraduates. In this case, a first-year student should look for alternative texts. If, on the other hand, the text states that it is aimed at level one undergraduate students, first-year students should have no hesitation in looking at it, providing it covers the necessary topics.

Bibliography

This is a list of the books and journals that the author has used for reference during the research, and which provide some of the basis for ideas and arguments. The author's sources are normally very useful. They may provide specific suggestions for further reading and examination of the topic. The bibliography will enable you to identify other texts that will prove useful in your information search. It may also reveal, for example, the kind of approach taken, the parameters of the approach and the breadth and depth of coverage of the topic.

Skim through the book

After considering the above, if the book has not been rejected, a quick skim through it will provide a general impression about whether it is likely to be useful or not. For example, if you skim one or two chapters, looking at the first and last paragraphs, you will get a general impression of the topics included and how clearly the author has presented the material. Focus immediately on summaries, as well as diagrams, graphs and figures, because they often contain essential information. A quick look at these can be a useful time saver because they present the author's perspective very concisely.

After a few minutes, which is all it takes to complete the steps necessary to select a book, you will be in a position to make a decision about whether to buy it from the bookshop or borrow it from the library. Do not spend time reading a book unless it specifically covers the particular topics that you need to know about for your course. If you adopt the strategy outlined, you can quickly discover whether you need to read a specific part of one particular chapter, or whether the book is useful only for background information and it is only necessary to skim through it.

> **Activity 4.2**
>
> **Selecting and surveying a book**
> - Go to a library and take a book from the shelf in your subject study area.
> - Survey the book in the ways suggested.
> - Identify and note how much you can find out in a very short time.
> - Identify the usefulness of the book to your specific study needs.

Other useful techniques

Readers

Look for 'readers'. These are textbooks that contain chapters that encapsulate the essence of the work of a number of authors on a particular topic or subject area. Each chapter, article or reading will offer concise, interesting and authoritative work containing the contemporary debates in the field of study and the main points of leading theorists' arguments. They will usually elaborate on the main features of the most recent thinking on a particular subject area, in some cases synthesising the arguments of current thinking, comparing it with traditional theory and possibly demonstrating the links to the wider literature.

Summaries

A useful technique to assist learning from reading is to write a summary or précis of a part of a book. When writing a summary it is important to ensure that the most relevant information is extracted to get a clear picture of the author's perspective. The material should be modified by changing it into your own words. It is a good idea to do this as concisely as possible. This technique will help you to understand the material or will highlight any areas that you have not understood clearly. The summaries will later be useful for your revision or when you are completing written work for your course. It is important to remember that material you have produced yourself is always easier to recall.

Discussion

Make use of your colleague students when you are studying. Students frequently do not help each other as much as they could. Discussing the reading with other students in a small group can be a very effective way of demonstrating an understanding of the material. In some cases, this may lead to new ideas being formulated. It is often much easier to admit to not understanding a particular concept or theory with peers in an informal setting. Joining a discussion group of like-minded students will facilitate independent learning and may avoid a lack of understanding becoming apparent in a seminar or, worse still, in assessed work. These types of discussion, when the tutor is not present, may take place informally and in an unstructured fashion. Alternatively, students may feel more comfortable if the discussion group is conducted in a structured and organised environment.

→ How to read faster

The focus of this chapter has been on enabling you to develop a more active, purposeful and methodical approach to your reading. Some students will, however, be interested in learning how to read more quickly. The following section provides advice on how reading speed may be improved, although it is important to point out that to increase the speed of reading at the expense of understanding can be counterproductive. Different types of reading require different reading rates, and speed should be adjusted as appropriate for a particular reading assignment.

In some instances, slow reading speed may be due to uncorrected eye defects. So before embarking on any attempt to increase reading speed, it is a good idea to have your eyes tested by an optician or optometrist so that any eyesight difficulties are corrected with spectacles or contact lenses.

Stop and think
- What do you think causes slow reading speeds?
- What can you do to increase your reading speed?
- Is this desirable?

Reading speeds

You will read for many different reasons and the key is to have not one but several different reading speeds. Each one is appropriate for particular tasks. For example, reading an exciting, fast-paced novel is a quicker process than reading a business textbook. Textbooks vary in how well they are written and as a result some are more difficult to read than others. Flexibility of approach is something to aim for, because reading everything at the same speed will handicap you in your role as a student.

Evidence suggests that most people can increase their reading speed considerably and that many students would benefit from reading faster. If you are able to increase your reading speed, it will get you through the material more quickly and can also help concentration. Usually most people can double their speed of reading while maintaining the same level of comprehension.

> **Remember...**
> Most people can increase their reading speed.

READING FOR STUDY

> **Activity 4.3**
>
> ## Assessing your reading speed
>
> - Assess your reading speed on something that you read for pleasure by selecting a passage from a newspaper, magazine or novel. Read a section or a page and time yourself accurately. Then count the number of words in the section or page to find out the number of words you read per minute.
> - When you have practised some of the ideas below, test your reading speed again and see if there is any improvement.
> - The average speed for reading fiction and non-technical material is probably 250–300 words per minute. However, it can range from 100 to 650 w.p.m. What speed can you achieve?
> - Each semester, time yourself reading a chapter in your textbook. Practise reading one chapter for each module or subject you are studying. See how many pages you are able to read in 10 minutes. Once you have an accurate indication of your reading speed, you can plan your reading and studying time with more precision.

Improving your reading speed

There are three main things that can encourage you to improve reading speeds. These are:

- the personal motivation to practise
- a desire to improve
- the willingness to experiment and try new techniques.

Do not be afraid to try to speed up the pace at which you read. Usually an increase in speed is accompanied by an increase in comprehension and a decrease in speed leads to a decrease in comprehension. Surprisingly, reading word for word tends to inhibit understanding. Frequently it is the brain rather than the eyes that limits reading speed: the eyes are able to absorb many more words than the brain is used to processing. But with practice the brain will deal with an increased number of words, and this will, in turn, increase reading speed.

Fixations and recognition span

Notice how you are reading this text. You will find that when you read your eye moves across a line of print and it makes transient, fleeting stops. These last only a fraction of a second. The eye does not move smoothly in a continuous flowing movement, but jumps from one fixation point in the line of print to the next. You are not actually reading a word at a time, but blocks of words. Your eyes will move from one block of words to the next in what is called a *fixation* (see Figure 4.2). It is during these fixations or pauses that reading takes place because a few words are in sharp focus and therefore information can be absorbed. A reader who takes less time for each fixation and who can include several words in a fixation will obviously read faster than a reader who includes only one word in each fixation and pauses for a longer period of time.

Figure 4.2 Eye movements and fixations

Short fixation

Eye movements

the   cat   sat   on   the   mat

Regression and rereading

Longer fixation

Eye movements

the | cat sat | on the mat | by the warm fireside

The number of words recognised at each fixation is called a *recognition span*. The recognition span varies considerably between the slow and fast reader. A slow reader will read only one or two words in each recognition span, whereas a skilled reader may read between five words and an entire line at each fixation. As well as improving your recognition span, you should attempt to lessen the time between fixations. Try to develop quick, rhythmic eye movements, but at the same time keep the head and shoulders still.

Activity 4.4

Testing recognition span

Test your recognition span by looking at a line of print in a book. Retain your fixation in the middle of the line and see how many words you can see to the right and left of it without moving your eye. You will probably see two or three words clearly and have a rough idea of one or two more.

Your objective is to increase this recognition span to five or six words. If you practise by stopping on every *fourth* word in the line you will make fewer fixations per line and speed up your reading.

If you are a relatively slow reader, at first you can practise fixing on two words at a time, then three words and four words. You will read faster if you can include more words in each fixation. Try to minimise the amount of time needed for each fixation and you will, with practice, improve your reading speed considerably. The more you practise, the more confident you will become and the faster you will read.

Another effective way to increase reading speed is to consciously make yourself read faster. You can use a finger or a pencil as a guide and move this down the text, gradually speeding up, making the eyes move more quickly down the lines of print. Scan a full page at a time with a general left–right movement of the eyes, but 'pushing' down the centre of the page with a finger or a pencil leading the eyes. This focuses the eyes and leads them to move more quickly and more smoothly. If you try this, make sure that your finger or pencil is used to encourage you to read faster, pushing rather than following the eyes.

The only way to improve reading speed is to practise regularly. It is a good idea to allocate between 10 and 15 minutes a day for this activity and start off with fairly easy reading such as a magazine. Once you have started to improve, check your understanding of what has been read. When reading speed has increased and you have extracted the main ideas from the article, move on to more difficult, longer and more complex articles in journals such as *The Economist*, or quality newspapers like the *Financial Times*. After a week or so, move on to textbook material. If you learn to concentrate on *why* you are reading – for example, to find specific ideas and details – you will find that both your speed and comprehension improve. You should be concerned about not simply how quickly you can get through a particular chapter or book, but how fast you can identify the specific ideas and details that you are searching for.

It is usually the case that improved reading speed leads to reading being a much more enjoyable experience. Students who acquire the skills associated with increased reading speed normally understand more of what they are reading and absorb it in less time.

Avoid vocalising

Many people pronounce the words as they read, albeit under their breath, and this is called *vocalisation*. If you do this, it is left over from when you learned to read as a child and had to read out loud to your teacher or parent. Whispering the words to yourself, or pronouncing the words in your head, will reduce your reading speed to speaking speed and it is advisable to overcome this habit as quickly as possible.

If a reader vocalises as he or she reads, they will read very slowly until this habit is broken – roughly 120–200 words per minute. Reading speed increases by at least two or three times, if reading occurs silently. Breaking the habit of vocalisation will invariably increase reading speed considerably. If you have been in the habit of saying the words to yourself when studying, concentrate on keeping your mouth closed and not sounding the words. In this way you will soon overcome this tendency.

Avoid regression (re-reading)

This is the habit of going back over words or groups of words to check your understanding, or to re-read them. Regression considerably reduces the speed at which you read and may mean that you lose much of the meaning of a sentence or paragraph (see Figure 4.2). If, however, you are reading material that is very difficult, it may be necessary to go back and check on the meaning of something. Even so, a better strategy may be to read the whole section through twice quickly rather than once at a much slower speed.

Extend your vocabulary

You will only be able to improve your reading speed if you possess the necessary vocabulary and comprehension skills. Take every opportunity to extend your vocabulary at university or college by reading widely, not only the subject you are studying, but also the 'quality' press, possibly biographies, dictionaries, thesauruses and encyclopedias. Use new words as often as is practicable and look up words you do not understand in a dictionary or by using a software package on the computer.

> ### Activity 4.5
>
> ### Increasing reading speed
>
> Spend 10-15 minutes a day practising reading more quickly. Over three or four weeks this is likely to bring about a significant improvement. Choose your own material, or use recommended textbooks, but keep them similar in nature. Read as fast as you can without losing comprehension.
>
> At the end of this period, test your reading speed again and see what improvements you have made.
>
> Bearing in mind the points made in this chapter about eye fixations, recognition span, regression and vocalisation, try a systematic approach to improving your own reading speed. Usually students who practise the techniques outlined make a significant improvement in their reading speed and this brings positive benefits in their course of study.
>
> Use the following table to record your reading speeds:
>
> | Date | Number of words | Time taken |
> | --- | --- | --- |
> | | | |
> | | | |
> | | | |
> | | | |

Reading flexibility

Finally, remember that it is necessary to adopt a flexible approach to reading. In essence it is useful to consider reading as a kind of dialogue with the theorist. The author presents his or her research and you consider and evaluate it; in some cases your thoughts are perhaps modified or stimulated, or they may be inspired by it. At the very least you should find it interesting and thought provoking, and it should encourage you to read more widely about the subject you are studying.

The material you read may reinforce, add to, modify or even dramatically challenge your own ideas. During your time at university or college, you are likely to encounter some topics which encourage you to re-evaluate the way that you have perceived a particular approach. It may be that through reading you will completely change your view about certain topics. What you should remember when you read is that reading should be a dynamic, active process, providing new insights into aspects of the subject you are

READING FOR STUDY

studying. Even if all of your academic reading is not as thought provoking as this, it is much more likely to be so when you approach it with curiosity and an open frame of mind. Always remember that the information acquired from reading is important. If reading is approached as a necessary evil, you will learn much less than you could and you will waste a lot of time. However, if you approach reading as something that will enhance and enrich your life, and are willing to take risks and to change your worldview, you will ensure that you learn something every time you read. Train your mind to be receptive and to learn as much as possible from reading.

Suggestions for improving reading

- Engage in active reading, as this will ensure that you stay focused on the material. Ask yourself questions about the content of what you are reading.

- Read appropriately – background, skim, scan, detailed and critical, using SQ3R when necessary.

- Look at contents and index pages first to identify whether to skim the book.

- Check headings, illustrations, tables, italics, bold type, lists and underlining for clues about content.

- Use the opening of paragraphs as clues to significant information being presented.

- Practise speed reading so that you can still extract the appropriate information for your needs.

- Look for phrases that indicate where important points, conclusions or summary statements are being made: 'The basic idea ...'; 'The consequences of these ...'; 'In summary ...'; 'Therefore we believe ...'; 'In contrast to ...' and so on.

- Make notes because this also facilitates active reading. When you take notes, read a section of the chapter, evaluate what you are reading, and decide what the main ideas are. Paraphrase the author's ideas in your notes in your own words, but do not copy information straight from the textbook. You should review your notes to ensure that they make sense. Are there any gaps? Is there something you still do not understand? You will need to re-read certain sections to resolve these problems. You should write your notes on a separate piece of paper – taking a photocopy is no substitute for reading, note taking and understanding.

- Many of us have been taught that it is wrong to write in books. However, providing it is your *own* textbook (or photocopy of a chapter), write and scribble comments in pencil in the margins; if you have questions, note them in the text. Number important points or sequential ideas in the margins. Use highlighter pens selectively to highlight the main ideas or special vocabulary. Whilst you are at university or college you should remember that textbooks are the implements that help you to understand your course and you should use them according to your needs.

See downloadable template 4.5 READING LOG for your Personal Development Plan online.

Critically evaluative reading

When you have developed your reading skills using the techniques outlined in this chapter and as you progress on your course of study, it will be necessary to become increasingly evaluative when reading. Critically evaluative or critically analytical reading is an essential skill. To facilitate the development of critically evaluative reading skills, try to identify the paradoxes, contradictions and discrepancies in the arguments presented by the author(s). It is necessary to interrogate, examine, probe, check, scrutinise, explore, challenge and be generally sceptical of the material. It is useful to try to identify the assumptions upon which the author's argument is based – are these complementary or in conflict? Many authors will not explicitly identify the assumptions underpinning the work, but it is possible for the critically evaluative reader to identify them. If the assumptions are identified through critically evaluative reading, it is often possible to offer alternative perspectives that explain the data more clearly or match more of the variables cited. Check that the evidence presented by the author is up to date, factually correct, complete and not biased in favour of a particular perspective. Judge whether the author has presented conclusions that are not convincingly supported by logical arguments and facts – re-examine them carefully. For example, could an alternative conclusion be reached that is equally valid? Do not be afraid to challenge conclusions reached, providing that the author's evidence has been carefully reinterpreted. Look for alternative perspectives that can be used to refute or redefine a particular argument.

As your experience increases, you will find that authors critique each other's work, challenging and questioning the assumptions made and the conclusions reached. Reinterpretation of data and questioning of assumptions and conclusions often further academic research. Authors regularly disagree with each other and argue that a particular perspective explains a particular phenomenon more than another one does. Conceptual and theoretical discussions clarify particular approaches and examine the ways in which the theorists have solved or dealt with the results of their research. It may be that, whilst a subject is broad and diversified, the discipline may have an underlying unity because different strands of research integrate and link together through common interests and overarching research questions. The critically evaluative reader will unearth many of these intricacies during what is likely to be a fascinating and challenging search. For example, numerous approaches have been developed within the subject of psychology, such as psychoanalysis, behaviourism and cognitive psychology, and there are many other subcategories such as developmental psychology, abnormal psychology, occupational psychology and social psychology, to name but a few. All of these attempt to explain the human mind and behaviour, and inevitably there are differences in the explanations offered, the methodologies used and the conclusions reached. This is not to say that any one approach is less valuable than another, but each seeks to explain from certain assumptions, approaches and methodologies that a critically evaluative reader can exploit to full advantage in assessments.

Learning to read in a critically evaluative and analytical way will enable you to gain a great deal more from study. Questioning, interrogating and challenging what is read rather than simply accepting a particular author's viewpoint, will broaden and deepen your understanding.

→ Summary

This chapter has identified:

- that reading is one of the keys to successful study
- the different ways of reading that will be necessary on a course - background, skimming, scanning, detailed and critical - and has outlined the differences between them
- the benefit of learning from reading using the SQ3R (survey, question, read, recite/recall and review) techniques
- how to select a book and assess it quickly for relevance to study needs through consideration of the various parts of the book
- effective techniques for speed reading, which will enable you to take steps to improve your reading performance.

5 Communication

> **Learning outcomes**
>
> After studying this chapter, you should be able to:
> - identify the main aspects of business communication
> - assess your spelling and written English
> - choose the most appropriate words for your assessed work
> - identify commonly confused words
> - write clearly and concisely.

→ Introduction

When you are at university or college, you will need to be able to communicate effectively with your tutors and colleague students. You may have to present orally in tutorials and seminars and/or write essays, reports and possibly dissertations in order to achieve your qualification. It is important to develop your communication skills while you are in higher education because employers want employees who are able to communicate effectively. Good communication skills will enable you to find employment and also enhance your career prospects.

Communication has a number of elements: for example, verbal, written and non-verbal. Verbal communication always has the advantage that it is face to face or via telephone, or possibly a webcam on the Internet, and this allows the individuals involved to be able to check immediately if there are any misunderstandings. In face-to-face communication, if there is a misunderstanding or confusion, the parties involved can clarify what is meant. If confusing or ambiguous words are used, clarification can be sought immediately if necessary.

It is argued by some writers (Mehrabian 1970, Pease 1981) that non-verbal communication is very powerful indeed and that, if it is in conflict with what is said, the verbal communication will not be believed.

This chapter will outline the interpersonal communication process, consider non-verbal communication and describe some of the conventions for written communication. You should read this chapter in conjunction with Chapters 14–17.

COMMUNICATION

→ The process of interpersonal communication

Interpersonal communication is a two-way process. The sender sends his or her message to the receiver, and the receiver will normally respond in some way. This can be seen in Figure 5.1.

Figure 5.1 The interpersonal communication process

Noise is anything that interferes with the process, e.g. stereotypes, emotions, semantics, time pressures

Figure 5.2 Successful communication

Message: Hello. How are you today?

Feedback: I am very well, thank you. How are you?

Sender — Receiver

Figure 5.3 Unsuccessful communication

Message
This licence will run out at the end of the month.

Sender

Noise

Feedback
Run out of what?

Receiver

Figure 5.2 depicts successful communication because the 'noise' indicated in Figure 5.1 would not have affected it. However, if the conversation runs something like that in Figure 5.3 we can see that 'noise' has interfered with the message sent. 'Noise' frequently interferes with the message in oral communication because each individual has a different set of codes that influences the process. What happens is that the message is received by the receiver's senses (hearing, sight, touch, smell, taste). The receiver then interprets the message, but this is affected by the senses, possibly associated with particular words. Thus 'noise' affects the interpretation and may interfere with the receiver's understanding. An example of this is if the sender of the message is highly computer literate, whereas the receiver may have only basic skills. The receiver may not be able to understand the technical code used by the sender and may therefore completely misunderstand the message. The reason that the codes are different in each individual is because of each person's cultural background, education, family influences, interests, friends, etc. Bearing in mind that these codes are often very different, it is amazing that people manage to communicate at all!

→ Non-verbal communication

Non-verbal communication covers such things as gestures, gaze, touch and space (Pease 1981). An important thing to remember about non-verbal communication is that it is culturally bound and the meanings attributed can be totally different in different countries. A gesture may be a sign of approval in one country but a rude gesture in another.

Table 5.1 **Common gestures and their messages**

Gesture	Likely interpretation
Crossed arms and legs	Leave me alone.
Crossed legs and kicking foot in direction of other person	A negative gesture that will be interpreted as impatience or metaphorically 'kicking' the other person.
Open palm-hand gesture	Non-confrontational, e.g. wave, swearing the oath in court.
Head nods	Indicate agreement and also encourage conversation. If you wish to terminate a conversation, keep your head still and adopt a 'poker' face – the other person will stop talking and go away very quickly!
Head on one side	Listening intently.

Gestures

The gestures that we use convey messages to other people, whether we are aware of it or not. Some examples of commonly used gestures are given in Table 5.1.

Gaze or eye contact

There are unwritten rules about gaze. Eye contact, or gaze, is maintained in a conversation between people. The speaker will generally make less eye contact than the listener. The speaker will look at the listener's face fairly frequently, which is a check that they are listening. The listener, on the other hand, tries to maintain eye contact to indicate that they are listening. When the listener is unable to look the speaker in the eye, they will look in the vicinity of the eyes so that, when the speaker looks back, their interest is assured. It is particularly important for students, when giving presentations, to maintain sufficient eye contact with the audience. If eye contact is not maintained, the audience may make judgements that the presenter is uninteresting or being untruthful, and they will lose interest quickly.

Touch

Touch is also rule-bound. We receive contact from our parents when we are children, but as we grow up and become adults, this tends to become less frequent. Touch is largely reserved for friends and lovers, although touch is acceptable between relative strangers in handshakes, back pats or in a medical situation with doctors or dentists. Touch is culturally bound and some cultures touch frequently, such as Arab and southern European societies, whereas other countries, such as the USA and the UK, have low-touch cultures. Most people have a social network of people whom they touch and are touched by, such as friends, work colleagues and sports teams. When you attend university or college, you may find at first that you feel starved of touch until you get to know other students fairly well.

Space

In terms of space, each person has a personal 'bubble' of space around them that they normally do not let others enter without certain conditions being met. For example, we do not normally let people within what is called our *'close intimate space'*, that is, about 15 centimetres around our body, unless they are going to touch us. There are exceptions to this, but these are bound by 'rules'. When we sit next to someone in a lecture theatre, on a bus or on a train, our bodies may touch slightly – for example, the upper arm or possibly the leg. In order to make this acceptable, we will not make eye contact with the other person, and as far as possible we will normally try to avoid contact except when the bus or train motion makes this impossible. When we are in social gatherings, we will normally stand at about arm's length (50–80 centimetres) from others when we are in conversation, but if we are conversing with a delivery person at the door, we will usually stand at least 1 metre away from him or her. When tutors or students are delivering a formal presentation to others, it is normal to have at least 2 metres and possibly up to 4 metres between the audience and presenter.

Appearance

Our appearance sends non-verbal messages about us. The clothes a person wears sends messages about them, as does whether he or she wears jewellery; colours their hair; shaves their head; has tattoos or body piercing; wears a baseball cap or other headwear. All of these and more will be interpreted positively or negatively by others. It may be that a hairstyle or clothes will be interpreted as non-conformist, or that an individual is a trendsetter, or a follower of fashion. You will need to bear this in mind when delivering assessed presentations to tutors. It is not a good idea, for example, to wear a baseball cap or other informal headwear, nor to dress too casually, as this sends the wrong message to the tutor.

> **Stop and think**
> - What messages do your gestures send to others?
> - Are you able to maintain sufficient eye contact with other students, lecturers/tutors, older people, shopkeepers, your boss, etc?
> - Are you able to satisfy your needs to touch and be touched with your friends?
> - Have you experienced a negative reaction overseas when you thought you had made a positive gesture?
> - What impression do you think your clothes/hair style/jewellery make?

→ Written communication

During the course of your studies you will have to write essays, reports, dissertations, notes and bibliographies, and it is essential that you are able to communicate your ideas to your lecturers/tutors as well as other students. One of the major mistakes that new students make is to try to write in ways that they think are required in higher education, and this often means that they are unable to communicate adequately with their audience. It is vital that initially you use words that you are familiar with. In addition, it is also much better to use short words that you understand rather than trying to use long words to impress the tutor. It will be very obvious to the tutor if you use words incorrectly. If you have any problem with reading or writing, it is wise to approach the university/college student services for a check to ensure you are not dyslexic or have some other difficulty.

Initially try to write in simple, short sentences and check your work regularly. A laptop or personal computer can be very helpful, as it will check your spelling and grammar and offer suggestions that may improve your work. However, you do need to be careful, as some suggestions made by the computer may not make sense. If you complete your work on a computer, you can set it up either to automatically correct spelling or to highlight words that are incorrect. However, you should bear in mind that a computer has to be set up to check English (UK) and not English (US). If the computer is set for English (US), this will mean that your work will contain American English spelling, which would not be acceptable in a British university or college. Note that it will *not* pick up words spelt correctly but used in the wrong context (for example, 'there' and 'their').

Whether or not you use a computer, it is a good idea to invest in a conventional dictionary to assist with spelling. In addition, a dictionary provides pronunciation for the word; provides a meaning, or several meanings; indicates the type of word (e.g. verb, adjective, noun); and sometimes provides examples of usage and origins of the word. A thesaurus is also a useful tool for finding synonyms (words that mean the same).

See Activity 5.1 CLEARER WRITING in the Online Study Guide.

Remember...
Make sure any spelling/grammar software is set for the correct language.

Words that are often confused

The words listed in Table 5.2 are frequently confused in student assignments. You should try to ensure that you know the difference between them. It will enable you to produce accurate work if you are able to use the right word.

If you have the occasional word that you frequently misspell, it would be a good idea to develop a strategy to help you overcome the difficulty, but if you misspell many of these words, it would be worth seeking assistance from the student support services at your university or college to check for dyslexia.

Stop and think
○ Are there any words in Table 5.2 that you confuse?
○ What steps can you take to ensure that you learn the appropriate word?

PART 1   DEVELOPING STUDY SKILLS

Table 5.2 **Words that are often confused**

Word	Often confused with
It's (a contraction of 'it is')	Its (possessive pronoun)
Accept (to take or receive something, agree to)	Except (other than, to exclude)
Their (of, belonging to)	There (in that place)
Council (an assembly of people)	Counsel (to advise)
Lose (to be without something either through accident or negligence)	Loose (not confined)
Advice (recommendation of an appropriate course of action)	Advise (to offer advice to a person)
Morale (a state of mind)	Moral (an ethical principle)
Stationary (at a standstill, not moving)	Stationery (writing material, e.g. paper)
Your (a pronoun)	You're (a contraction of 'you are')
Been (the past participle of 'be')	Being (self, human being)
A lot (many, a great number)	Allot (allocate, apportion)
Effect (to bring about)	Affect (to influence)
Amount (quantity, not countable)	Number (countable units)
Are (the plural form of the present tense of 'be')	Our (belonging to us)
Sight (the ability to see)	Site (the land on which a building is located)
Complement (adds to, or supplements)	Compliment (flattery or praise)
Confidant (someone to confide in)	Confident (positive)
Dependent (depending upon)	Dependant (a person who depends on another for financial and other support)
Discreet (prudent, diplomatic)	Discrete (separate, distinct)
Fewer (a smaller number)	Less (smaller quantity)
i.e. (that is)	e.g. (for example)
Rational (using logic for problem solving)	Rationale (reasoned argument, justification)
Principle (a guiding belief)	Principal (first in importance, head of a college)
Quiet (silent)	Quite (very, extremely)
Whether (introduces first of two alternatives)	Weather (climate)
To (towards)	Too (as well, in addition to)
Role (a part in a play)	Roll (move by rolling over)

Activity 5.1

Confusing words

Create sentences that use both words so that you can differentiate between the two. For example:
   The Principal believes in the principle of equality of opportunity.

Spelling

The following list contains words that students frequently spell incorrectly. In order to get your message across to your tutor, you should practice spelling if you know you have any difficulties.

accommodation	concede	gauge	medicine	psychological
bureaucratic	definite	hierarchy	occurred	separate
business	dependent	independent	privilege	unnecessary
competent	embarrassment	liaise	professional	

Active or passive voice?

Try to use the *active voice* rather than the *passive voice*. The active voice is a much more powerful mode of communication than the passive. Examples are given in Table 5.3.

The passive voice is not incorrect and you will need to decide if it is preferable to the active voice on some occasions. It can be quite helpful to use the passive voice when it is not desirable to attribute responsibility: for example, 'The number of items required is not stated' rather than 'You did not state how many items are required'.

Table 5.3 **Examples of the passive and active voices**

Passive voice	Active voice
The results were reported at the exam board.	I reported the results at the exam board.
A complete restructure was effected by the Dean.	The Dean restructured the department.
An increase of 20% was reported by the administrator.	Student numbers increased by 20%.
The regulations were enforced by the academic board.	The academic board enforced the regulations.
The subject group will be reviewed by the Quality Assurance Agency.	The Quality Assurance Agency will review the subject group.
The pay claim is supported by the union.	The union supports the pay claim.

Transitional words and phrases

When you are writing assignments, it will be necessary to connect together ideas, thoughts or parts of your work. In conversation you will do this quite naturally and it is necessary to develop this skill for assignment writing, otherwise your writing will be quite abrupt. When you write a draft of your work, look for aspects that can be connected together. If you use the phrase 'In addition', this means that you will build on your discussion. 'On the other hand' indicates that you are going to contrast ideas. Your work should flow smoothly and transition words will help you do this. The following words can be used to make transitions or links in your work:

and	similarly	however
thus	finally	for this reason
also	for example	in order to illustrate
first, second, third, etc	indeed	because of
in addition	on the other hand	therefore
likewise	but	

(See Chapter 15 for more transitional words.)

Suggestions for improving your business writing skills

Unless you are expressly asked to do otherwise, avoid the use of the following.

Aspect of poor writing	Suggestion
'I' – the first person	Avoid writing your assignments in the first person. It is much better to write in an impersonal style, as 'the author', 'the researcher'. It is possible to write assignments in such a way that personal pronouns are avoided completely. For example, 'I have researched the recruitment and selection process in this company and I found that it does not conform to the procedures set out in the regulations' could be written: 'The recruitment and selection process in the company was investigated and it was found that it does not conform to the procedures set out in the regulations.'
Slang	Informal expressions or colloquialisms may be acceptable and suitable for conversation, but they are not appropriate for formal academic work or business communication. Slang frequently contains metaphorical elements that others may not necessarily understand, especially if English is their second language (e.g. 'He's opened a can of worms'; 'She's got a bee in her bonnet').
Clichés	These are words and phrases that have lost much of their impact through overuse, e.g. bottom line; it goes without saying; hook, line and sinker; burn the candle at both ends; last but not least; to add insult to injury; it's got to get worse before it gets better; it's not rocket science.
Discriminatory language	When writing academic work, and subsequently in employment, you should avoid language that may offend particular groups because it is gender specific or may exclude some people unnecessarily. Think carefully about whether it is relevant to your work to indicate the gender of a role.

COMMUNICATION

	Avoid using:	Change to:
	Chairman	Chair or chairperson
	Fireman	Firefighter
	Policeman	Police officer
	Salesman	Sales person or sales representative
Vagueness	In academic work you should avoid being imprecise. It is important to demonstrate to your tutors that you can construct an academic argument with precision.	
	Be precise and avoid:	*Change to:*
	The company made a significant loss in the last financial year.	The company made a £2m loss in the last financial year.
	The students had a good attendance record.	95% of the students attended all five sessions.
	The majority of students used the sports facilities.	70% of the students used the sports facilities.
	The report is due to be submitted in the near future.	The report is due to be submitted before 16.00 hours on Friday.

→ Style

See downloadable template 5.1 CHECKLIST FOR WRITTEN ASSIGNMENTS for your Personal Development Plan online.

When you write academic essays or other work, you will need to consider the style in which your work is written. The style adopted will have a bearing on the effectiveness of what is written. In most assessed work, tutors may judge style and therefore it is important that you consider your writing style. This means choosing an appropriate style for the assignment and it is essential that while you are at university or college you are able to choose from a variety of different styles of writing. It is likely that for academic work you will have to write in a formal style, adopting various conventions – see Chapters 15, 16 and 17. If you are sending an e-mail it can be less formal and a text message (SMS) can be very informal.

Before starting to write, you need to consider the needs of the audience (readers) of the work, what you have to convey to the audience and the appropriate way to structure what you wish to communicate. Initially you should read widely about the topic that you will write about. When reading you should look for major themes that emerge. This will enable you tentatively to plan your assignment. Once you have drawn up a plan, you should write a draft and then subsequently revise and review it until you are satisfied that it meets the criteria outlined by your assignment brief. Obviously you will choose different styles depending on the requirements of the assignment. For example, if you are asked to adopt the role of a human resources manager and you are required to write a

PART 1   DEVELOPING STUDY SKILLS

> See Activities 5.2–5.5 in the Online Study Guide.

Activity 5.2

Consider your writing

Look at something you have written recently. Do you use:

- short or long sentences?
- jargon without a good reason?
- paragraphs that contain only one idea?
- a questioning approach?
- lots of exclamation marks?
- many hyphens/dashes?

What can you learn from this?

letter to employees, this would require a different style from an assignment in which you are asked to adopt the role of a chief executive officer and to write a report to shareholders for the annual general meeting.

Table 5.4 Punctuation

Punctuation	Symbol	Indicates
A full stop	.	The end of a sentence.
A comma	,	The sentence is continuing, but there is an interruption or pause in the sentence.
A colon	:	A list or quote will follow.
A semi-colon	;	A pause greater than a comma but less than a full stop. A semi-colon also sometimes separates items in a list after a colon.
An apostrophe	'	Something has been omitted: for example, 'We're working on the assignment.' The apostrophe can also be used to indicate possession: for example, 'Rachel's dog'. The apostrophe is frequently misused and you should learn how to use it correctly.
A hyphen	-	A word has been split, often at the end of a line of text.
The dash (slightly longer than a hyphen)	–	Singly, it is used in place of a colon. In pairs, it shows that a remark is in parentheses (brackets).
Brackets (parentheses)	( )	A phrase has been inserted into a sentence to which it is not grammatically connected.
Question mark	?	The sentence is a question.
Exclamation mark	!	An exclamation, e.g. shouting or commands.

Factors that influence style

Style is influenced by the following factors.

Punctuation

You should ensure that you use full stops, commas, semi-colons, colons, question marks, quotation marks, exclamation marks and apostrophes appropriately to enable the reader to understand the essence of the message in your assignment. See Table 5.4, which provides an outline of each form of punctuation.

Paragraphs

A written piece of work should generally be subdivided into paragraphs. These should be used to separate one idea or topic from another. All the discussion in a paragraph should be related to that proposition or idea, giving the paragraph coherence. Each new idea is introduced in a new paragraph. It is not a good idea to have very long paragraphs, but similarly single-sentence paragraphs will mean that your work is abrupt and is likely to lack coherence and flow.

Sentence length

You should try not to use very long sentences. The reader may lose the point being made because the sentence is convoluted and complex. Try to ensure that you write in simple sentences.

Jargon

There are times when it is appropriate to use jargon because it is specialist language relating to a specific subject. However, if you use jargon that you do not understand, this will be very evident to the tutor.

Glossary

It is a good idea when studying at university or college to create and build a glossary of the terms that are in use on your module/course. It may be that you have studied the subject before going to university or college and have some knowledge of the terms used, but you may be completely new to the subject. Either way, a glossary of terms will help you build your vocabulary in the subject. At first you might have to use a dictionary to help you to understand what the term means, but try to explain it in your own words because this will aid your understanding. Once you understand the term, take every opportunity in seminars or tutorials to use it in discussion. In this way you will become more familiar with the technical language in use on your course. Each time you encounter a new word or technical term used on your module/course, add it to your glossary and very quickly you will develop your knowledge of the essential elements of your chosen subject.

PART 1   DEVELOPING STUDY SKILLS

→ **Summary**

This chapter has outlined:
- the process of interpersonal communication, including the non-verbal communication aspects of gestures, gaze, touch, space and appearance
- aspects of written communication, such as words that are confused and that students frequently misspell
- suggestions that will improve business writing skills for assessments.
- the factors that influence style.

6 Making notes

> ### Learning outcomes
> After studying this chapter, you should be able to:
> - use different techniques for making notes
> - develop effective note-making strategies that are appropriate to the study task
> - make notes from different situations
> - produce notes that are relevant, accurate and understandable
> - produce notes that are legible, structured and well organised for retrieval.

→ Introduction

During the course of your studies you will receive and read much information. It will be impossible to remember all that you are told or read, so you will find it beneficial to develop skills in making notes. You may have to make notes in lectures, from books and journals and perhaps from videos, radio or television. Making notes does not mean that you must write down every word that a lecturer says or copy out lengthy pieces of text from books and journals. The key is to decide when to make notes, how to make notes and how much detail should be recorded. The ability to make good notes takes practice but will eventually save you time and help you to study more successfully. The aim of this chapter is to help you to adopt effective note-making strategies so that your notes will be organised and you will be able to understand them weeks or months later.

→ Why make notes?

The main objective of making notes whilst at university or college is so that they can be used to help you through your studies. Whilst studying you will find you need to reuse a great deal of the material you read or receive in lectures and seminars for the preparation of essays, reports, presentations, examinations, etc. It is therefore important to keep some notes as a permanent record that can be referred to quickly rather than having to go back to the original text or trying to remember what that lecture was about.

Making notes serves two purposes:

> See Activity 6.2 BENEFITS OF NOTE TAKING in the Online Study Guide.

- *To aid understanding and learning*. We cannot remember much of what we read unless we recall and review regularly – this is crucial to our long-term memory. Making notes in your own words aids retention of the material in your memory. By summarising theoretical approaches, arguments and ideas in note form, you will also gain a better understanding of their strengths and weaknesses. When making notes it is important that you aim to understand the material rather than taking down word for word what is said or written.

- *To aid concentration*. More concentration and effort is required for making notes than for reading or listening. Making notes can help your concentration if you find the lecture you are listening to or the text you are reading does not capture your imagination. Note making forces you to pay attention.

→ Ways of making notes

There is no 'best method' of making notes. It is a matter of individual preference and is often a reflection of learning style, how the mind works, the time available to make the notes and the situation. When making notes it is important to bear in mind their source and what you are hoping to achieve. This may also influence the way you make notes, what to include and how to arrange them. Different sources will require different approaches – the way you make notes in a lecture may be different from the way you make notes from an academic textbook. The more complex the material that the source covers, the more detailed your notes may have to be to aid your comprehension.

Stop and think
- Do you need to make notes?
- Why do you need to make notes?
- Are you able to make notes effectively?

Annotation

One way of making notes is to annotate the text you are reading. Many people feel uncomfortable about writing in books. However, most academic textbooks are not going to become valuable antiques in the future and therefore do not need to be preserved in pristine condition. So, as long as the book is your *own copy*, you may choose to annotate it as you read. This will, of course, reduce the book's second-hand value if you are intending to sell it to another student when you have finished with it.

Common ways of annotating text are:

- *Underlining* the main points.
- *Using the margins* to make notes, e.g. question marks (?) if you do not understand; 'agree' or 'disagree'; ticks and crosses, etc.

- *Highlighting* the main points using a fluorescent marker. This can make learning easier and quicker because on returning to the book or article only the highlighted text needs to be reviewed. However, this method does not require rephrasing the text into your own words and therefore may not aid your understanding. If this is the case, you may have to study the whole text again when you return to it. Be sure that you understand what you are reading and highlight sufficient to enable understanding without reading the whole text again. This method needs practice in identifying what to highlight.

If you are uncomfortable annotating text (or if the text does not belong to you), identify important sections or pages by using Post-it notes to indicate the important sections.

> **Remember...**
> Do not highlight the whole text, only the main points.

Activity 6.1

Annotating text

See Activity 6.1 NOTE TAKING in the Online Study Guide.

- Choose a chapter or section from one of your own textbooks and make notes in the margins. If you are concerned about writing in a book, use a pencil and you can erase your notes later.
- Look back at the notes a week later and see if you can still understand the material without reading the whole chapter or section.

Written notes

There are essentially two different ways to write notes: sequential and pattern.

Sequential or linear notes

Sequential notes are the most common way of presenting notes. Taking sequential notes involves listening or reading and then recording, in your own words, the relevant information in the same sequence as the original material is presented. The notes are therefore sequential or linear.

Sequential notes may be made as a summary or an outline.

Summary notes

These are a summary of what has been read or listened to, but in your own words. They are merely a shorter version, or précis, of the original. To make summary notes you need to write, in note form, the essential facts and ideas from your reading or listening. One advantage of this method is that, because the notes are in your own words, understanding will be greater and the notes can be used verbatim for essay or report writing.

It can be time consuming to formulate the author's thoughts and arguments into your own words, but sequential or linear notes will help to retain the flow of the lecture or text.

PART 1   DEVELOPING STUDY SKILLS

> **! Remember...**
> Summary notes aid understanding, but they can be time consuming.

Activity 6.2

Writing summary notes

- Find an article from one of your reading lists and write summary notes for it.
- Ask a friend to write summary notes of another article on your reading list and exchange summary notes.
- Check each other's understanding of the notes.
- What differences or similarities can you identify?

Figure 6.1 Example of sequential outline notes for Chapter 1 of this book

---

Chapter 1 Developing Essential Study Skills

LEARNING

1. How
   Unstructured - trial and error
   Structured - instruction, practice
   Individual - tailor learning experience to preferences

2. Life long learning
   Devpmt of skills impt
      accelerating rate of change
      interest
      development - personal, career
   Continuous learning
   Importance of reflection

3. Uni./college learning
   Taught =   passive
              directed, repro of material

   Independent Learning = Active
                          Take control
                          Organise

              broaden mind
              intellectually stretched
              greater understanding
              capacity for thought

Outline notes

This is a popular way of making notes. Only the key words and phrases used should be noted. The notes may be sequentially numbered or use headings, subheadings and indentation for clarification (see Figure 6.1). This makes outline notes easy to follow and remember, although they may take longer to write than summary notes.

> **Remember...**
> Outline notes are easy to follow, but they can be time consuming.

Activity 6.3

Producing outline notes

- Select a textbook on the reading list for a module that you are studying. Make outline notes from a chapter which covers a topic studied in the lecture or seminar.
- Look back at the notes a week later and see if you can still understand the material without reading the whole chapter or section.

Figure 6.2 A mind map constructed from the beginning of Chapter 1

Pattern notes
Mind maps

Mind maps do not follow a linear sequence but are free-form (see Figure 6.2). When making mind maps the main subject or topic is placed in the centre of the page with the main ideas and concepts branching out from it. Mind maps clearly indicate the relationships between ideas and concepts by using lines to identify the links. Only the key words and phrases characterising the topic and the associated ideas and concepts are recorded.

Many people claim that these are the most useful form of notes and that, once you are proficient in this technique, you will never use another method. Enthusiasts of the technique argue that whilst other methods are linear, this approach is creative, using image and colour, which makes things easier to remember. It relies on laws of association rather than logic.

To make a mind map:

- It is usual to use the page landscape-fashion. Begin by putting the name of the topic in the centre of the page and draw a circle around it.
- Extend a line out from the circle and write the first main heading for the topic on this line. The line may go out in any direction.
- For each subheading, draw lines radiating from the associated heading, labelling each one.
- Use only single words, a short phrase or an image to capture the ideas and concepts in the text or lecture. Each word or image should be on a line, with each line connected to another.
- Use only one unit of thought per line to facilitate flexibility.
- Avoid very straight lines to discourage linear thinking.
- It is useful to use different colours for different ideas or sections.

The result is a diagram that looks like a spider with many legs, or a seed with many shoots growing from it. The mind map takes the central topic and then has the main ideas sprouting from it. The most important ideas will be near the centre; the further away from the centre the ideas are, the less important they become. A mind map enables the origins or development of a theme to be traced, and the connections to be identified.

An advantage of this method is that it shows the relative importance of the central themes and displays them clearly. The brain is able to make the necessary associations and therefore, it is claimed, this method makes recall easier. A disadvantage is that it can take a long time and considerable practice to get used to making mind maps.

> **Remember...**
> Mind maps clearly indicate important concepts, but they take time and practice to perfect.

Activity 6.4

Creating a mind map

- Create a mind map about yourself as a student. Put your first name and family name in a circle in the centre of the page and write 'Student' underneath your name. Use your imagination. Compare your mind map with that of a friend in your class and see where there are similarities and differences. How much can you remember about your friend now you have seen their mind map?
- Now try out this method with notes you have to make from a textbook.
- Consider the different ways of making notes. Which is the most effective for you?

Making notes from text

To make notes from text:

i First skim read the text to gain an appreciation of what it is about (see Chapter 4 for advice on skim reading). This will help to avoid the temptation to copy everything down rather than just the relevant points.

ii Record the bibliographic details of the text: that is, the title of the book or journal, chapter or article name, author, publisher, place and date of publication.

iii Read the whole chapter or article and then try to sum it up in a few sentences, using your own words. Avoid the temptation to make notes whilst reading, as you are likely to write too much.

iv Leave plenty of space in your notes, as this will allow additions or changes later.

v Re-read the chapter or article and then make notes that are more detailed. Decide what the main ideas are and paraphrase them *using your own words*. Aim to condense and rephrase rather than copy large sections from the text. The process of converting to your own words helps you become actively involved in and understand the material.

    If you think that the author has been particularly incisive and you could not put it better yourself, use the exact words but make sure that you put quotation marks at the beginning and end of the quote. Any quotes you write must be correctly referenced and succinct – probably no more than one sentence, and possibly only a phrase. Ensure that you make a note of the page number in case you wish to use the quote in an assessment.

vi When you have completed your notes, re-read them immediately. If they do not make sense now, you can be sure that they will not do so in a few months' time.

Suggestions for making notes from a text

- Aim for understanding, not voluminous notes.
- Look for meaning, patterns and connections.
- Identify key words and themes.
- Be selective.
- Do not write continuous prose.

Making notes in lectures

It can be quite difficult and frustrating making notes in lectures. The spoken language is diffuse and transient. Unlike reading, you do not control the pace and it is usually not possible to ask the lecturer to go back, repeat a point or stop for a while. Each lecturer will have his or her own style, speed and method. Some lecturers will present well-organised material, whilst others may ramble or present anecdotes, leaving you to determine their significance. It is important to determine a lecturer's style and how they convey ideas, and to adapt your note making to suit the style. You may be able to persuade a lecturer to slow down or repeat things, but you have to find a way to make notes that satisfies you and the style of the lecture.

Before the lecture

Prepare yourself in advance for the lecture. If a lecture programme is provided before the lectures start, try to read about the subject before attending the lecture. This will aid your understanding and it will be easier to make notes during the lecture, as you will be able to recognise the most relevant information. Review your notes from any previous lectures to help you put the prospective lecture topic in context.

During the lecture

Sit as near to the front of the room as possible, where there are fewer distractions. This will help your concentration and it will also be easier to see and hear. Look at the speaker – this will help to focus your attention and their mannerisms may provide clues to what is to follow or the importance of what is being said. However, do not let the personality or mannerisms of the individual lecturer put you off!

The lecturer may use overhead projector slides or a computer-based presentation, and elaborate on the information outlined on the screen. As a note maker you will need to analyse what is said and select the appropriate points to note, whilst at the same time continuing to listen (see Figure 6.3).

Some lecturers may provide handouts at the beginning or summaries at the end of the lecture. These will help you to organise your own notes.

> **Stop and think**
> - How can you prepare for a lecture?
> - What does the tutor provide?
> - What should you write?
> - Have you reviewed your notes after the lecture?

What to write down

There is no template that indicates what to include in lecture notes – it depends on your purpose and ability to select and summarise. Some students write lengthy notes during lectures whilst others will make brief notes covering the important points.

Listen carefully to the introduction to the lecture, as this may give an indication of the structure and thus help you to organise your notes.

Essential information

Make a note of the module/subject name, topic, lecturer and date. This helps you if you lend your notes to a friend, and your friend returns them a month later. If your file unexpectedly opens and all your papers fall out, sorting them out afterwards can be almost impossible unless you know the topic and date.

Identify themes

Listen carefully. You should be able to work out the important themes of the lecture. Often lecturers will outline the important points and then provide examples to aid understanding. Record the key words and concepts. Jot down details or examples that support the main ideas, rather than trying to write down exactly what the lecturer is saying.

Look for cues from the lecturer

Look and listen for cues from the lecturer as to what is important and most relevant. This may be picked up from the tone, voice inflection or gestures used by the lecturer. Frequently, lecturers will repeat the main points for emphasis. The lecturer may also use diagrams to illustrate important points, or indicate specific texts or references.

Figure 6.3 **Some important things to listen for**

Listen for

Cue words such as:
remember
most
first
then
thus
therefore
there are 3 main ...

Qualifying words such as:
sometimes
usually
rarely
never
only
always
must

Signals

Change of direction:
but
however
on the other hand
although

Support:
for example
in contrast
for instance

Emphasis:
Repetition of words or phrases
Hand gestures
Pauses
Words stressing importance, e.g.
primary
major
focal
significant
crucial
influential
foremost
dominant
leading

Be selective

Do not try to write down every word the lecturer says. You will not be able to write at speaking speed, and if you try to record everything, the likely result will be incomprehensible notes. Spend time listening and attempt to record the main points and illustrations. If you are writing as fast as you can, you cannot be a discriminating listener.

Often the lecturer will summarise the main points of the lecture before finishing. It is very tempting to start gathering your things together while this is happening, but you may miss something that will aid your understanding.

PART 1   DEVELOPING STUDY SKILLS

After the lecture

As soon as possible after the lecture, review your notes while they are still fresh in your mind, rewriting them where necessary.

- Identify any gaps from examples and facts that you did not have time to write down during the lecture and see if you can complete them.
- Follow up anything that is unclear whilst your memory is still fairly fresh.
- Read the recommended texts and references to help to fill any gaps in your notes.
- Check for accuracy. It is very easy in a lecture to make a mistake in what you write down, draw a diagram upside down, or put a word in the wrong box. This means that the information you have noted will mislead you later. Mistakes need to be corrected quickly – any delay in reviewing your notes may mean that a basic error is overlooked, which could be very costly in an examination.

Generally, it is not worth completely rewriting lecture notes unless you are going to add value to them. It is better to spend the time reading and reflecting on them. Rewriting notes may add value if it changes them to a format that better suits your learning style: for example, word processing your notes may add value if you learn better from typed notes rather than handwritten ones.

Many students fall into the habit of making notes and not reading them until they are required for an assessment or examination. Read and reread the notes until you become familiar with the material. Reading your notes will provide reinforcement and aid retention. If you do not look at them again until just before an examination or assessment, you will have to relearn the material rather than review it.

> **Stop and think**
> ○ Will rewriting your lecture notes add value to them? If not, spend time reading and reflecting on them.
> ○ Do you need to make your lecture notes clearer?
> ○ How can you make your lecture notes more useful?

Activity 6.5

Making notes in lectures

1. (a) Make notes during a lecture. After the lecture, compare your notes with those of a friend.
   (b) Identify the similarities and differences between the two sets of notes.
   (c) What is better about your notes?
   (d) What is better about the notes made by your friend?
2. If you have never made notes in the form of a mind map, attend a lecture and draw a mind map of the topic. Compare your mind map with the sequential or linear notes of a friend.

> **Suggestions** for improving note making in lectures
>
> - Aim for a skeleton outline rather than the full script.
> - Do not rush – be attentive and listen carefully and critically.
> - If you take down quotations, be sure to get the exact source so that you can reference them properly.
> - Note down any references that are made to a specific text in case you need to follow them up.
> - Spend time reading and reflecting on your notes as soon as possible after the lecture.
> - Do not make notes at the expense of listening to the lecture.
> - Avoid the temptation to read a handout instead of listening to the lecturer.
> - Avoid the temptation to copy down all the information on an OHP or PowerPoint slide.

There may be occasions when you need to make notes in other situations, such as from television, video or radio. This is similar to making notes in lectures, although the delivery may be faster and you are not able to ask the speaker to slow down. However, there may be an opportunity to see or hear the appropriate material again if it is not a live performance.

Making notes from a group discussion

See downloadable template 6.1 COMPARING NOTES for your Personal Development Plan online.

Sometimes you may have to make notes from group discussions. This is a very demanding situation in which to make notes, so make sure that you are very well prepared. Sit in a position where you will be able to hear everything but which will not inhibit any discussion. Remember, it is not always possible to stop the discussion to ask someone to repeat his or her comments. If you do interject, this will interrupt the free flow of the discussion.

In this situation, it is generally easiest to make notes in the form of a mind map, as the discussion within the group will be free flowing. Using mind maps will enable you to add points easily using loops, lines and linkages.

Abbreviations and symbols

Wherever possible, use abbreviations and symbols when making notes. These can save a great deal of time. Some commonly used abbreviations are shown in Table 6.1.

You can develop your own list of abbreviations and, as long as you are consistent, you will soon remember them. Try to make them intuitively obvious. At first it is probably useful to write a key for new ones that you use. Table 6.2 shows some more examples of useful abbreviations.

PART 1   DEVELOPING STUDY SKILLS

Table 6.1 Commonly used abbreviations and symbols

i.e.	that is	imp.	important
e.g.	for example	no.	number
NB	note well	esp.	especially
&	and	approx./c.	approximately/*circa*
∵	because	≠	is not equal to
∴	therefore	=	equals
K	kilogram, kilometre, thousand*	<	is less than
fig.	figure	>	is greater than
tog.	together	ref.	reference
et al.	and others	cf.	compare
ibid.	In the same place (a quotation cited is from the same source as the last given reference)	op. cit.	in the work cited

* In informal use only; the official abbreviations for kilogram and kilometre are kg and km. K (thousand, strictly 1024) is used mainly in computing and is often kb for kilobyte.

Table 6.2 Examples of useful abbreviations

orgn	Organisation	gp	group
pop	Population	intro	introduction
econ	Economy	lrng	learning
govt	Government	comms	communications
cttee	Committee	nvc	non-verbal communication
mgt	Management	raw mats	raw materials
beh	Behaviour	lab	labour

Many English words have the same endings, such as *-tion*, *-ism*, *-al*, *-ist* and *-er*. A useful way of creating your own abbreviations is to use the stem of the word and a letter which signals the ending of the word. For example, *comm-* is the stem of a number of words with different endings: *communication, communicational, communicator, communicated,* etc. These words would be indicated by the following abbreviations: *commn, comml, commr* and *commd*. Thus *n* represents *-tion*, *l* represents *-al*, etc. Similarly:

beh	behaviour
behm	behaviourism
behl	behavioural
beht	behaviourist

Of course, you have to be careful where there are two very similar words that could be represented in the same way, e.g. *communicational* and *communal*.

You could also use mnemonics or acronyms (aids to memory) such as:

SWOT (strengths, weaknesses, opportunities and threats)

PEST (political, economic, social, technical)

MAKING NOTES

The use of these will depend upon the topic for which you are making notes.

When making notes about a particular theorist or approach, you could write the name or approach in full the first time and thereafter use the capital letter underlined. This will save a lot of time. For example:

behaviourism	becomes	B
psychoanalysis	becomes	P
Freud	becomes	F
Marxism	becomes	M
Keynesian	becomes	K
Weber	becomes	W

However, use common sense when adopting this short cut. If, for example, the topic and one or more of the theorists have the same first initial, confusion could easily arise. For instance, economists could lecture about *monetarism* and *Marxism*. If you used the initial letter and underlined it (M), you might have difficulty in knowing which perspective your notes referred to. Any confusion could be avoided in the first place if, for example, different-coloured pens were used to make notes about each approach.

It is also useful to develop a code for marking your notes. For example, the following symbols may be used:

?	Something you do not understand and need to investigate
! or *	Something important
C	Your own comments or thoughts
Q	Question
→	Lecturer's opinion
‡	Lecturer thinks this is important

See Activity 6.3 USING ABBREVIATIONS in the Online Study Guide.

Activity 6.6

Abbreviations and symbols

Construct a list of abbreviations, symbols and mnemonics that are appropriate for a topic you are studying. Try using them when making notes from texts or in lectures.

Keeping notes

You will need to decide how you are going to keep the notes that you make. A loose-leaf ring binder is very flexible, allowing the organisation and reorganisation of material and the insertion of any supplementary material in the appropriate place. All the notes on one particular topic should be kept together.

Some students use different-coloured paper so that the source of the notes can be quickly identified: for example, white paper for lecture notes, yellow paper for notes taken from essential reading texts, and green paper for reading identified from browsing the library shelves. Dividers are useful to keep the different subjects or topics separated.

If your notes are to be used for open-book examinations, create an index for them. This will save time finding the appropriate topics or pages during the examination.

See Activity 6.4 NOTE TAKING PRACTICE in the Online Study Guide.

Suggestions for making notes

- Develop a standard method of note making, including abbreviations and symbols.
- Write in your own words except for quotations, definitions and formulae.
- Make them memorable – the more distinctive the notes, the more easily remembered. Use different-coloured pens and include doodles, etc.
- Distinctly mark ideas and concepts that the tutor (or author) emphasises.
- Do not duplicate notes from different sources, but aim to add new examples.
- Group your notes into topic areas so that all material on a topic is together when you come to review or revise your notes.
- Do not destroy your notes at the end of the module or course – they may be useful for subsequent study.
- Put your name, the date and page numbers on your notes – this is helpful if you lose or lend them.
- After making notes, find answers to any questions they raise.
- If you can afford it, make notes only on one side of the page. It is easier to see exactly what you have if you can spread out the pages without having to keep turning them over. It also allows you to add extra notes or comments on the reverse when you review them.
- Always record the source of your notes.
- Make your notes legible – but remember that neatness does not necessarily increase learning.
- Small writing may save paper but can be tiresome to read.
- Do not cram in extra lines at the top and bottom of the page – leave plenty of space around your notes so you can add comments later.
- Do not carry all your notes around with you – not only are they heavy, but they may get lost.
- Be discriminating and selective, picking out the key concepts, principles or facts. Do not write everything down.
- Keep notes brief.

Stop and think
Look back over the notes you have made so far.
○ Are you able to recall the topics in detail?
○ Do you need to review the way you make notes?

Remember...
The notes you make are for you!

See Activity 6.5 FROM NOTES TO A SUMMARY in the Online Study Guide.

Activity 6.7

Experiment

Get used to listening and writing at the same time. Practise this by watching a television programme with a friend and making notes. Compare your notes. Are they better or worse? Why?

Repeat this activity, experimenting with different forms of note making.

→ Summary

This chapter has outlined that:

- good notes are brief, clear, understandable, relevant and organised in a way that suits your learning style
- there are different ways of making notes and it is important that you find a way that is effective for both you and the situation in which you are making the notes
- it is more important to gain an understanding of the material that you are reading or listening to than to capture every word and make detailed notes
- reading through your notes as soon as possible after making them is essential so that any omissions and areas of difficulty can be dealt with. Reading notes after completing them also improves the remembering process
- making notes requires practice. Experimenting with the different ways of making notes from different situations will improve your proficiency.

7 Working with numbers

> **Learning outcomes**
> After studying this chapter, you should be able to:
> - select and use an appropriate method of organising and presenting numerical data
> - select and use appropriate summary measures
> - interpret summary measures of data.

→ Introduction

Few people are mathematicians or statisticians, but all of us have to make some sense of the numbers presented to us as part of our everyday lives. Most people go on shopping expeditions and manage their income and expenditure, both of which involve calculations to varying degrees of complexity. For example, buying a newspaper involves counting money and checking change. Making a larger purchase such as a car involves the comparison of prices, consideration of interest rates (percentages) and budgeting. Some of these numbers are often so familiar to us that we do not think about them. The weatherman or woman provides daily temperatures, and we absorb these without a second thought. We understand if a temperature is hot or cold and thus whether to take our coat. The weekend's football scores usually present no problem; we can easily decide whether our favourite team has won and where they are placed in the division. Nevertheless, some students have a great fear of being asked to do anything during their course of study that involves numbers and calculations. The problems occur for many people when numbers are presented in a new and unfamiliar way and they are asked to use or manipulate the numbers to gain more information about a situation.

Whilst not all jobs involve calculations, it is likely that at some stage you will have to use some numeracy skills in your work – not least to work out how much you should be paid. The ability to work with numbers is an essential skill, particularly in a world of increasingly powerful computer and communications technology. Computers may now be linked, not just to a near neighbour but across the world, allowing access to vast amounts of data and information. Although computers and calculators can help in the

WORKING WITH NUMBERS

processing of these data, it is increasingly important that organisations have people with the skills to understand and analyse the data so they may be communicated and used in an effective way. Numeracy skills can be the key to unlocking the valuable resource of data in organisations. The aim of this chapter is to develop the skills of communicating and analysing numerical data.

→ Numerical data

See Activity 7.1 QUANTITATIVE OR QUALITATIVE DATA? in the Online Study Guide.

Items about which data are collected are known as *elements* (or units of analysis). Numerical data result from either measuring or counting the characteristics of elements. *Variable* is the term used for a characteristic that varies from one element to another. Some of the characteristics (variables) may be measurable on a scale: for example, height, age, income, turnover and temperature. This results in *quantitative* data. Other characteristics are not measurable but are descriptive, for example, gender (male or female), marital status (single, married, widowed, divorced) and nationality. These are *qualitative* data. Table 7.1 shows examples of qualitative and quantitative data.

Figure 7.1 represents a *data set*, providing data that have been collected about employees (elements). Each employee has a name, gender, etc. Thus the first element in the data set has the following values for each variable: Joe Ashton, male, computer operator, salary of £17,500, etc.

Table 7.1 **Examples of qualitative and quantitative data**

Elements	*Examples*	*Variables*	*Example values*
Persons	Employee	Gender	Male
		Age	36
Entities	Town	Population	54,666
Objects	House	Type	Detached
Time periods	Month	Sales	10,654
		Production	15,892

Figure 7.1 **Data set**

Employee Name	Gender	Job Title	Salary	Age	Days Absent
Joe Ashton	M	Computer operator	17,500	25	10
Mary Baker	F	HR Manager	25,000	34	0
Clive Brown	M	Salesperson	21,000	42	24
etc.					

PART 1   DEVELOPING STUDY SKILLS

> **Remember...**
> Always identify your data set, elements and variables before doing anything to the data.

Exercise 7.1

Terminology

For the following investigations, identify the elements and variables, and indicate whether the data are qualitative or quantitative.

(a) The amount of money spent by students on textbooks, food and travel during an academic year.

(b) The destination of people flying out of Heathrow airport during May.

(c) The amount of water used each year by industrial organisations.

(d) The number and gender of children in families in a town.

(e) The attitude of employees towards health and safety procedures.

→ Making data easier to handle

The compilation and presentation of data has become an essential aspect of everyday life for organisations. It is important to be able to reduce, arrange and present data in a form that can be easily appreciated and interpreted. There are a number of different ways of doing this – the method selected will depend on the type of data and what you are trying to demonstrate or the points to be highlighted.

Rounding

See Activity 7.2 ROUND UP NUMBERS in the Online Study Guide.

Raw data are often presented accurately to a number of decimal places, which can be very confusing to the reader. Whereas long strings of digits may be important for scientific or technical purposes, often such accuracy is inconvenient and not always necessary (unless you are an engineer or technical expert). A figure to the nearest thousand or hundred may suffice. Data may be made more manageable and easier to read by rounding the data.

How to round

Example: round 247.36791

1 Decide how many decimal places are appropriate to round the number. If the numbers represent money, it is usual to round to two decimal places. For this example, assume that the number 247.36791 represents money.

2 Look at the digit immediately to the right of the last digit you wish to keep. In this example, two decimal places are required, thus the digit we need to look at is the third one to the right of the decimal point (7).

WORKING WITH NUMBERS

3 Ignore all digits to the right of this digit, i.e. the 9 and the 1.

4 If the digit is 5 or above then the previous digit is raised by 1, otherwise it remains unchanged. In this case, the digit is 7 and the previous digit must therefore be raised by 1. The number 247.36791 rounded to two decimal places is therefore 247.37.

> **Stop and think**
> ○ Do you need to round your data?
> ○ How accurate do your data need to be?

Recognising rounded data

In calculations it is important not to claim a higher degree of accuracy in the solution than is warranted, by including an unnecessary number of digits or decimal places. For example, a series of figures representing takings in a shop during a series of weeks may be shown as £2120, £3060, £1870 and £1700. It is unlikely that the revenue for week 1 was exactly £2120 and therefore it is natural to assume that each of the figures has been rounded to the nearest £10. However, a series of lengths of wood may be given as 1.356 metres, 1.875 metres, 2.150 metres, etc. In this case, it would be correct to assume that the figures are accurate to the number of decimal places given.

> **Remember...**
> Remember that if the original data upon which calculations are based are rounded, it is not possible to give an answer that is any more accurate than the original data.

Exercise 7.2

Rounding

Round the following numbers to the number of decimal places indicated.

	Decimal places	*Rounded number*
36.7846	3	
213.45824	4	
25.675	2	
16.786	1	
2386	Nearest hundred	
11571	Nearest thousand	

Percentages

Percentages are used frequently in both business and everyday life: for example, in salary negotiations, price rises in shops, and interest calculations for money borrowed or saved. A percentage shows the *relative* size of a given value compared with the total,

PART 1   DEVELOPING STUDY SKILLS

Table 7.2 Examples of calculation of percentages

	Total number	Number who smoke (absolute)	Percentage who smoke (relative)
Women	15	10	$(10 \div 15) \times 100 = 67\%$ (to the nearest whole number)
Men	35	15	$(15 \div 35) \times 100 = 43\%$ (to the nearest whole number)
Total	50	25	$(25 \div 50) \times 100 = 50\%$

rather than the *absolute* size. Percentage means per hundred, thus the whole or total is 100%. For example, 15% means 15 per hundred. If you share a chocolate bar equally with three friends, the whole of the chocolate bar is 100% and you would each get 25% $(100 \div 4)$. If the chocolate bar were divided into 100 equal parts, you would get 25 of them.

As percentages are relative, it is sometimes useful to convert data to percentages. This enables comparisons to be made. For example, in a group of 50 people, 15 are women and 35 are men; 10 of the women are smokers and 15 of the men. Because there are different totals of men and women, it is difficult to compare the number of female smokers with that of men. By calculating percentages, a comparison can be made: 67% of the women are smokers compared with only 43% of the men (see Table 7.2).

Exercise 7.3

Percentages

(a) You are due to receive a pay increase of 3% on your hourly pay of £8.50 per hour. How much is the new hourly rate?

(b) The following figures represent the number of visits to a website during the first three months of its operation. Calculate the percentage of visitors in each month.

Month	Number of visitors	Percentage
1	559	
2	743	
3	1266	
Total		

See Activity 7.3 PRESENTING DATA in the Online Study Guide.

What is the percentage increase of visitors from month 1 to month 3?

Tables

A convenient way of facilitating the understanding of numerical data is to present them in a table. A table is a matrix in rows and columns, with each column and row having a label, thus providing an ordered pattern to the data. Tables may be built up in many different ways, but an example of a table is given in Figure 7.2.

WORKING WITH NUMBERS

Figure 7.2 Example of tabular presentation

Column headings						
Row headings			ABC Ltd			Title explaining clearly what the data represent
		Monthly Sales Analysis by Product				
			(£000s)			Units of measurement
Derived statistic - calculate totals where relevant		X	Y	Z	Total	%
	Jan	10	12	13	35	30
	Feb	6	10	8	24	20
	Mar	11	20	11	42	35
	Apr	3	5	10	18	15
	Total	30	47	42	119	100
Source - always indicate where the data has come from	Source: Sales ledger, ABC Ltd.					Derived statistic where appropriate, e.g. percentages calculated from the original data $(42 \div 119) \times 100$

Suggestions for the construction of tables

- Tables should not be so large as to confuse the reader.
- Tabulation should be vertical rather than horizontal wherever possible.
- Sets of data that are likely to be compared should be close together.
- Lines should be used to distinguish between different parts of the table.
- Provide derived statistics such as totals, percentages, etc., where appropriate.
- Use footnotes for explanations.
- Always show the source of the data.

Exercise 7.4

Constructing tables

Present the following data in a table, including any derived statistics (e.g. totals, percentages) where appropriate.

The numbers of students on courses in the different faculties within a university are: Faculty A 675, Faculty B 543, Faculty C 750.

Faculty A has 315 male students, Faculty B 475 and Faculty C 300.

Stop and think
- Will a table help the reader to understand the data?
- Which data should be presented in rows?
- Which data should be presented in columns?
- Would the calculation of totals and/or percentages aid understanding?

PART 1   DEVELOPING STUDY SKILLS

Frequency distributions

An investigation may result in so much data that it overwhelms our ability to deduce anything from it. In order to try to understand what the data are indicating, it is necessary to sift through them, amalgamating and condensing them into a more manageable form. Putting the data into a simple table may not be sufficient; it may be necessary to condense them further by constructing a frequency distribution. A frequency distribution indicates the number of times (frequency) that a variable has a particular value or characteristic.

For example, the following data represent the value of the weekly orders (to the nearest £5) taken at the local florist for the last 50 weeks:

210	110	95	80	75	150	170	60	70	195
200	95	60	45	45	75	75	45	55	140
45	65	75	70	95	160	70	50	65	85
60	140	105	80	80	95	105	65	70	70
70	190	170	65	140	90	190	120	45	65

Looking at the data in this form, it is difficult to deduce anything. Constructing a frequency distribution of the data will help to make them more manageable and enable an insight to be gained. To construct a frequency distribution, the number of times a value occurs (frequency) is counted. These frequencies are then recorded in a table, as in Table 7.3.

It can be seen from Table 7.3 that the most frequent value of orders taken is £70, which occurred in six of the weeks. Although constructing a frequency distribution for these data has condensed the amount of data because of the number of different values that 'orders' can have, it may be more helpful to condense it even further by constructing a *grouped frequency distribution*.

Table 7.3 Frequency table

Value	Frequency	Value	Frequency	Value	Frequency	Value	Frequency
45	5	75	4	110	1	190	2
50	1	80	3	120	1	195	1
55	1	85	1	140	3	200	1
60	3	90	1	150	1	210	1
65	5	95	4	160	1		
70	6	105	2	170	2	Total	50

Grouped frequency distributions

For very large sets of data, a simple frequency table will not reduce the data sufficiently to make it manageable. Grouping the data into contiguous (joined in order), but not overlapping, *groups* (or classes) can reduce data further. Each group has a *lower class boundary* (i.e. the lowest value that the group contains) and an *upper class boundary* (the highest value that the group or class contains). The number of items falling into each class is known as the *class frequency*.

A grouped frequency table is an arrangement of the data showing the frequency of occurrence of values in a particular group or class. Table 7.4 indicates the steps required to construct a frequency table.

WORKING WITH NUMBERS

Table 7.4 Constructing a grouped frequency table

Step		Example using data from the local florist
1	Identify the lowest and highest values in the set of data.	The lowest value of orders is £45 and the highest is £210.
2	Find the range (the difference between the lowest value and the highest value).	The range is £165 (210−45).
3	Decide how many classes are required (this is normally between 5 and 12) and divide the range by this number – this will give you the class interval. It is helpful to round this to an easy number to work with, such as 5, 10 or 15.	165 divided by 9 (number of classes) = 18.3 and the nearest 'easy' number is 20. The data will be grouped into nine classes with a class interval of 20.
4	Determine the class boundaries.	Determine the class boundaries by starting at or near the lowest figure. The lower class boundary of the first class will be £45 and the upper class boundary will be 45 + 20 = £65.
5	Construct a tally chart to count the number of observations in each class.	Class Tally 45 but less than 65 𝟙𝟙𝟙𝟙 𝟙𝟙𝟙𝟙 65 but less than 85 𝟙𝟙𝟙𝟙 𝟙𝟙𝟙𝟙 𝟙𝟙𝟙𝟙 III etc.
6	Construct the frequency table.	

Although a grouped frequency distribution can make the data easier to handle, some of the detail is lost. If the original data are not available, the exact value of the individual values in each class is not known. For example, in Figure 7.3 all the orders in the first class

Figure 7.3 Grouped frequency distribution

Grouped frequency distribution for the value of weekly orders

Class (£)	Frequency
45 but less than 65	10
65 but less than 85	18
85 but less than 105	6
105 but less than 125	4
125 but less than 145	3
145 but less than 165	2
165 but less than 185	2
185 but less than 205	4
205 and over	1
Total	50

Lower class boundary

Upper class boundary

Open-ended class

Number of observations in the class, i.e. there were 10 days on which the value of orders was at least £45 but less than £65

Total number of observations

125

or group (45 but less than 65) could have a value of £45 or they could all have a value of £65. It is more likely that there is a mixture of values between £45 and £64.99, but the exact mix may not be known.

Note that the last class in this example is '£205 and over' – this is known as an *open-ended class*, as there is no upper limit. The observations in this class may have any value of £205 or more. If the highest value observed were £295, it would be unwieldy to show classes of 205 but less than 225, 225 but less than 245, etc., all the way up to 300. It is easier to use an open-ended class. Open-ended classes may also be found at the beginning of the frequency table – for example, the first class could have been 'under £65'.

> See downloadable template 7.1 NUMERICAL PROBLEMS for your Personal Development Plan online.

Exercise 7.5

Frequency table

The following data relates to the marks a class of 30 students gained for a module of study. The marks are out of 100. Draw up a frequency table for these marks.

65	43	56	64	68	46	43	56	58	51
44	40	35	55	61	30	44	72	37	61
55	38	56	41	51	48	64	58	60	50

→ Describing the data with pictures

Some people find numbers difficult to interpret and managers may not have the time to study the numbers presented to them in any detail. It is often easier to appreciate the data if a visual form of presentation is used. There are a number of different formats that may be appropriate, depending on the type of data. Some of these are outlined below.

Bar charts

Bar charts are a simple and effective way of representing data. The data are shown by a series of bars representing the value of the variables. The bars may be drawn vertically or horizontally. There are a number of different types of bar chart.

Simple bar charts

Simple bar charts are used to indicate the total number of items with a particular characteristic or value at any one time. The height (or length) of each bar is proportional to the size of the group having the characteristic being measured or counted. For example, the height of each bar in Figure 7.4 represents the value of sales for each month. The width of the bars should be constant, as should the distance between the bars.

WORKING WITH NUMBERS

Figure 7.4 Simple bar chart

Total monthly sales for ABC Ltd

Compound or component bar charts

Compound bar charts are similar to simple bar charts, but the bars are subdivided into component parts, thus indicating the way the total breaks down into its constituent parts. This enables the component parts to be compared as well as the totals.

Figure 7.5 shows ABC's total sales for each month with each bar subdivided into sales for each of the products X, Y and Z.

Figure 7.5 Component bar chart

Monthly sales of ABC Ltd analysed by product

Percentage component bar charts

These are similar to component bar charts, but each bar is the same length, representing 100%. The actual magnitudes (absolute figures) are not represented, but the component parts of the total are shown as percentages of the whole. A percentage component bar chart (Figure 7.6) is used if it is important to indicate the changing proportions of the totals.

Figure 7.6 Percentage component bar chart

Multiple bar charts

Multiple bar charts consist of two or more adjoining bars, each of which represents a component of the data. A multiple bar chart makes the comparison of several component parts easy, but the comparison of totals is essentially lost.

Figure 7.7 shows monthly sales for each product X, Y and Z as a group for each month.

Figure 7.7 Multiple bar chart

Pictograms/pictographs

A pictogram is a chart that uses easily recognisable pictures to represent the data – for example, a brewery may use a barrel to represent the number of gallons of beer it brews each month. The size of the picture (or number of pictures) is proportional to the quantity it represents.

A pictogram (Figure 7.8) presents the data in a simple way and conveys the message to the reader at a glance. Pictograms are often used in newspapers and magazines to present data to the general public or when detail and accuracy are less important.

Figure 7.8 **Pictogram**

Pie charts

A pie chart is a circular diagram divided into a number of segments, so that the area of each segment is proportional to the component part it represents. This enables a comparison of the relative size of the component parts to be made, in a similar way to the percentage component bar chart. However, a comparison may be difficult if the corresponding figures are not also shown. Pie charts should not normally be used for data with more than six categories, as they can look cluttered.

Figure 7.9 **Pie chart**

PART 1   DEVELOPING STUDY SKILLS

To construct a pie chart, the angle at the centre of each segment must be calculated. This is done by dividing the total number of degrees in the full circle (360) by the percentage of the total for the segment. In Figure 7.9, February sales are 20% of the total, therefore the angle required is 72 degrees ((360 ÷ 100) × 20). A protractor will be required to draw accurate angles.

It is possible to compare the composition of two totals by drawing two pie charts. However, if the totals are significantly different in size, the area of the circles should be in proportion to the totals. For example, if the totals were £500 and £1000, the latter circle should be twice the area of the former.

Histograms

Histograms look like bar charts but are used to present grouped frequency data. There should be no gaps between the bars of a histogram. Figure 7.10 is a histogram for the data in Figure 7.3 (weekly orders for the florist shop). Note that the last class for these data is open ended (205 and over). In order to draw the bar for this class, an assumption must be made about the upper class boundary. A reasonable assumption is that the class width will be the same as the other classes. Thus in this example the last bar will finish at 225.

Figure 7.10 **Histogram**

Distribution of weekly orders (histogram with Frequency on y-axis and Value (£) on x-axis)

The number of items or observations in a class (frequency) is represented by the area of the bar rather than the height. It is therefore important, if there are unequal class widths, to ensure that the frequencies are in proportion. For example, if a class has twice the 'normal' class width, the frequency (height) must be halved in order to ensure that the area of the bar remains in proportion to the frequency. For example, if the last two classes in the previous example were combined (185 but less than 205, 205 and over), giving a class of '185 and over', the total frequency would have to be halved to ensure the area of the bar is proportional to the frequency, i.e. total frequency is 5 (4 + 1) so the height of the bar would be 2.5 (5 ÷ 2).

Line graphs

Line graphs are a very common method of presenting data. A line graph shows the relationship between two sets of numbers by either a straight line or a curve. It shows how the value of one variable changes, given changes in the value of the other variable.

WORKING WITH NUMBERS

The variable whose value is influenced by changes in the value of another is known as the *dependent variable* and is usually placed on the vertical axis. The variable that affects the value of the other is known as the *independent variable* and is usually shown on the horizontal axis. For example, data indicating attendance at a cinema and the number of ice creams sold would be graphed with the number of ice creams sold on the vertical axis – the number of ice creams sold may be dependent on attendance at the cinema. Attendance (the independent variable) would be on the horizontal axis. Graphs are particularly useful for showing changes in data over a period of time. Time is always treated as an independent variable.

Exercise 7.6

Dependent and independent variables

Identify the dependent and independent variable in each situation:

(a) Advertising and sales

(b) Demand for a product and price

(c) Top speed produced by an engine and the power of the engine.

Rules for drawing graphs

- A graph has two axes – horizontal (used to represent the independent variable) and vertical (used to represent the dependent variable). If time is on the horizontal axis, it is referred to as a time series.
- Clearly label the axes and indicate the unit of measurement.
- Always mark the origin (the point at which the two axes intersect).
- Choose the scale carefully – make it as large as possible so that it may be read clearly. If necessary, do not start the scale at zero, but show a broken scale (see Figure 7.11).
- Include a title – always provide a clear explanatory title for a graph.
- Show the source of the data and footnotes where appropriate. Footnotes may be used to explain some of the features of the graph.

Figure 7.11 **Axes showing broken scale**

PART 1   DEVELOPING STUDY SKILLS

A point represents each item of data, and a line is used to join the points. An advantage of using graphs is that a number of different lines may be superimposed on the same axes, thus enabling comparisons to be made.

The graph in Figure 7.12 shows a relationship between sales and time, and indicates how the value of sales changes as the other variable (time) changes. The value of sales is the dependent variable and the independent variable is time.

Figure 7.12 Line graph

Ogives

Ogives are usually associated with frequency distributions. An ogive is a cumulative frequency curve and indicates the cumulative number of items or observations with a value less than the upper class boundaries of the classes. To find the cumulative frequencies, the individual frequencies for each class are added up as we progress down the table.

For example, Figure 7.13 shows that there are 10 weeks in which the value of orders taken was less than £65 (the upper class boundary of the first class), 28 weeks with orders less than £85, 34 weeks with orders less than £105, etc. The cumulative frequencies may also be converted to percentages of the total frequency (see the last column of the table in Figure 7.13). This is particularly useful if two or more frequency distributions are to be compared and the total frequencies for each are different.

WORKING WITH NUMBERS

Figure 7.13 **Cumulative frequency tables**

Weekly Order Values – Florist Shop			
Value of orders (£)	Frequency	Cumulative frequency	% Cumulative frequency
45 but less than 65	10	10	20
65 but less than 85	18	28	56
85 but less than 105	6	34	68
105 but less than 125	4	38	76
125 but less than 145	3	41	82
145 but less than 165	2	43	86
165 but less than 185	2	45	90
185 but less than 205	4	49	98
205 and over	1	50	100
Total	50		

Cumulative frequency as a percentage of total frequency $(10 \div 50) \times 100 = 20$

$(28 \div 50) \times 100 = 56$

Frequency of first class (10) + frequency of second class (18)

Cumulative frequency of previous class (28) + frequency of third class (6)

If the cumulative frequencies are plotted on a graph, a curve called an *ogive* is formed (Figure 7.14). The cumulative frequencies must be plotted against the upper class boundary for a 'less than' cumulative frequency distribution.

See Activity 7.4 PRACTISE PRESENTING DATA in the Online Study Guide.

Figure 7.14 **Ogive**

The ogive is a useful graph as it may be used to determine the proportion of the observations that fall into a range of values.

133

> **Stop and think**
> - Which form of visual presentation will effectively communicate the message you wish to convey with the data?
> - Does the chart or diagram highlight the important features of the data?
> - Does the chart or diagram have a clear, unambiguous title?
> - Are the axes (where appropriate) clearly labelled?
> - Are the units of measurement clearly identified?
> - Is the scale of the diagram appropriate?
> - Is the source of the data clearly identified?
> - Is there sufficient detail to get the message across?

Exercise 7.7

Presentation of data

1. The numbers of workers employed on various jobs in an organisation are as follows:

Machinists	110
Finishers	50
Clerical staff	65
Managers	12

   Represent this information in (a) a pie chart, (b) a simple bar chart.

2. A smallholder has produced the following crops for the last four years:

	2003	2004	2005	2006
Cabbages	34	43	38	24
Cauliflowers	18	20	14	12
Marrows	24	27	20	25

   (a) Construct a component bar chart to illustrate this.

   (b) For each year calculate the figure for each vegetable as a percentage of the annual total and construct a percentage component bar chart.

Activity 7.1

Presentation of data

1. Find suitable data from a newspaper and construct a line graph.
2. Find an example of a pictogram or pictograph in a newspaper or journal. What are the problems of using this form of data presentation? Is it an appropriate form for the data presented and the audience? Why or why not? If not, what would you recommend?

WORKING WITH NUMBERS

→ Describing the data with numerical summaries

Sometimes it is not appropriate or sufficient to describe or summarise the data with pictures. If so, then it is possible to derive some numbers that are representative of the complete set of data and may therefore be used to summarise or describe the data set. They fall broadly into two kinds:

- Measures of *central tendency*, which measure where the centre of the data is located. They are sometimes referred to as measures of location, but are more commonly known as *averages*.
- Measures of *dispersion*, which measure how spread out the values are within the data set.

Measures of central tendency (averages)

The average of a set of data is a value that is representative of those data and indicates the value around which the data are centred. There are different types of average but this section will concentrate on the three most commonly used: the arithmetic mean, the median and the mode.

The arithmetic mean

See Activity 7.5 MEAN, MEDIAN AND MODE in the Online Study Guide.

The arithmetic mean of a set of data is the total of all the values divided by the number of values. For example, a student has gained the following marks for the modules that he or she has studied: 65, 58, 55, 62, 52. The arithmetic mean of the marks attained is therefore:

$(65 + 58 + 55 + 62 + 52) \div 5 = 58.4.$

In some circumstances a number of items may have the same value – for example, if six students score 52, eight score 65 and three score 45 (frequency distribution), it would be incorrect to add up the marks of 52, 65 and 45 and divide by 3 to find the average. Some of the marks occur more frequently than others and this needs to be taken into account. In other words, the frequency with which the mark occurs will affect the calculation of

Figure 7.15 Calculation of an arithmetic mean from a frequency distribution

Mark	Number of students (frequency)	Total
52	6	312
65	8	520
45	3	135
Total	17	967
The average is therefore: 967 ÷ 17 = 56.9		

Note: this is a frequency distribution. The calculation of the arithmetic mean involves multiplying the mark by the number of students achieving that mark and dividing by the total number of students.

$45 \times 3 = 135$

135

Table 7.5 Salary data

Position	Number of staff (frequency)	Salary (£)	Total of salaries at each grade
Managing director	1	110,000	110,000
Director	1	65,000	65,000
Managers	3	30,000	90,000
Clerical staff	20	13,000	260,000
Total	25		525,000

the average. The average mark is found by multiplying each mark by the number of people scoring the mark (frequency), summing the total marks and dividing by the total number of people (see Figure 7.15).

Although the mean is easy to understand and calculate, sometimes it can lead to a value that is not very representative of the set of data. Consider the data shown in Table 7.5 about salaries within an organisation.

The arithmetic mean is £21,000 (525,000 ÷ 25). However, five employees receive a salary above this and 20 receive salaries below this figure. An arithmetic mean of £21,000 is therefore not very representative of the set of data. The value is affected by the extreme value of the salary of the managing director. Other types of average, such as the median or mode, may be more meaningful or representative if the data contain extreme high (or low) values.

In a grouped frequency distribution, the individual values of the items are lost, i.e. it is impossible to determine the value of each individual item within a class. This means that it is impossible to calculate the mean exactly. However, it is possible to *estimate* the value of the mean. To estimate the mean of a grouped frequency distribution, you need to determine a point within each class that represents the observations within that class. The midpoints of each class are used to represent the data within each class. The midpoint of each class is found by adding together the lower class boundary and the upper class boundary and dividing by 2. For example, in Figure 7.16 the midpoint of the first

Figure 7.16 Calculation of the mean from a grouped frequency distribution

Florist data			
Class (£)	Frequency (f)	Mid-point (x)	fx
45 but less than 65	10	55	550
65 but less than 85	18	75	1350
85 but less than 105	6	95	570
105 but less than 125	4	115	460
125 but less than 145	3	135	405
145 but less than 165	2	155	310
165 but less than 185	2	175	350
185 but less than 205	4	195	780
205 and over	1	215	215
Total	50		4990

The mean = 4990 ÷ 50 = 99.80 or £100 (rounded)

(45 + 65) ÷ 2

The frequency multiplied by the midpoint

10 × 55 = 550

class (45 but less than 65) is 55 ((45 + 65) ÷ 2). Each of the midpoints is then multiplied by the frequency of the class. The resulting figures are totalled and divided by the total frequency to arrive at an estimate of the mean.

> ### Exercise 7.8
>
> #### Comparison of means
> Calculate the arithmetic mean for the original weekly data from the florist shop and compare your answer with the estimate in Figure 7.16.
>
> How would you account for the difference?

The median

The median is the middle point of a set of data when the data are placed in either ascending or descending order. It divides the data set into two, with an equal number of values on either side of the median. Because it is in the middle of the set of data, it is not influenced by extreme values at either end of the data.

The median is easy to determine for a simple set of data, though the method is slightly different depending on whether there are an odd or an even number of values in the data set.

For an odd number of values in the data set:

Arrange the data in order of magnitude.

Example

    5   8   8   9   11   13   13

Find the position of the median by dividing the number of values (n) plus 1 by 2, i.e.

$(n + 1) \div 2$.

The position of the median is therefore $(7 + 1) \div 2$, i.e. the fourth value.
The value of the median in this example is therefore the fourth value, i.e. 9.

For an even number of values in the data set

Arrange the data in order of magnitude.

Example

    5   8   9   11   13   18

Find the position of the median by dividing the number of values (n) plus 1 by 2, i.e.

$(n + 1) \div 2$.

The position of the median is therefore $(6 + 1) \div 2$, i.e. the '3½th' value, which means that the median is located midway between the third and fourth values.

The value of the median is determined by calculating the arithmetic mean, or average, of the two values around the median.

In this example the median is therefore the mean (average) of the third and fourth values in the set of data, 9 and 11. The median is $(9 + 11) \div 2 = 10$.

Figure 7.17 Estimating the median from an ogive

The median of grouped data is difficult to find by calculation, but it may be estimated from an ogive of the data (see Figure 7.17). The median position is found in the same way – dividing the number of values (n) plus 1 by 2, i.e. $(n + 1) \div 2$. The median value may then be read from the graph. Using the example of the florist's weekly order (Table 7.4), which is illustrated in Figure 7.17, the median position is $(n + 1) \div 2$, which equals $(50 + 1) \div 2 = 25½$.

The median value is estimated by drawing a horizontal line from the 25½ mark on the cumulative frequency axis. From where this cuts the ogive, draw a vertical line to the horizontal axis. The value of the median is where this line cuts the horizontal axis. (This result is approximate, since the ogive is not a smooth curve and the original data values were grouped.)

The mode

Sometimes it is more appropriate for the representative value of a set of data to be a

Figure 7.18 The mode

The following data represent the local shoe shop's sales of shoes by size:

Shoe size	Number of pairs sold per day
1	4
2	6
3	3
4	11
5	15
6	5
7	6
8	12

The modal value is 5, i.e. the most popular shoe size.

WORKING WITH NUMBERS

Figure 7.19 Estimating the mode from a histogram

Distribution of weekly orders

Modal class – the class containing the most observations

The mode of a grouped frequency distribution is difficult to calculate but may be estimated graphically from a histogram of the data. It is easy to determine the modal class or group (the class that contains the mode) – it is the group having the highest frequency, indicated by the tallest bar in the histogram. To estimate the mode, a diagonal line should be drawn from the top right corner of the bar immediately preceding the modal bar to the top right corner of the modal bar. Another diagonal line is drawn from the top left corner of the bar immediately following the modal bar to the top left corner of the modal bar. A perpendicular line is then drawn from the point at which the two lines cross to the horizontal axis, and the modal value is the point where the perpendicular line crosses this axis (see Figure 7.19).

Measures of central tendency are useful figures for organisations to know, as they indicate the value around which the data are gathered, but it is important that the correct measure is used for the data that have been collected.

> measure of popularity. The mode is the most popular value in the data set – the value that occurs most frequently (see Figure 7.18).

Exercise 7.9

Measures of central tendency

Indicate which of the measures of central tendency would be most useful for the following sets of data and indicate what this measure may be used for.

(a) A supermarket collects data about the number of customers it handles each day over a few months.

(b) The government collects data about the number of children in each household in the UK.

(c) A manufacturing firm records the weight of a can of beans coming off its production line each day.

(d) A suit hire shop records the size of top hats they hire out over the year.

Measures of dispersion or spread

Averages provide information about where the data are centred or located, but they do not indicate anything about how the data are spread over the whole range of values of

139

the data. Measures of *dispersion* are used to describe the spread or variability of the data. Consider the following data relating to the test scores of two classes, A and B:

| Class A | 10 | 12 | 12 | 9 | 11 | 12 | 13 | 9 | 10 | 12 |
| Class B | 14 | 12 | 9 | 6 | 15 | 7 | 11 | 10 | 16 | 10 |

The mean score for class A is 11. The mean score for class B is also 11. However, the scores for class B are much more widely spread – the lowest value is 6 and the highest value is 16. In class A the lowest value is 9 and the highest is 13. Class A is therefore producing a much less variable set of results.

Two measures of dispersion that are commonly used to provide an indication of the spread or variability of data are the range and the standard deviation.

Range

The simplest way of calculating a measure of spread (variability or dispersion) of a set of data is to look at the range of values that the data cover. The range is the difference between the lowest and highest values within the set of data. Consider the following two sets of data:

| Data set A | 1 | 4 | 5 | 10 | 16 | 19 | 20 |
| Data set B | 1 | 10 | 10 | 11 | 11 | 12 | 20 |

Both sets have a range of 19 but the second set contains values that are much more central than the first. Although the range gives an indication of the extent of the spread of the data, it does not indicate how the data are distributed within that range.

Table 7.6 Calculating the standard deviation

Step	Calculation	Answer
1 Find the arithmetic mean of the set of data.	(1 + 4 + 5 + 10 + 16 + 19 + 20) ÷ 7	10.7143
2 Find the deviation of each item of data from the mean (observation − mean). For a grouped frequency distribution, the observation is the class midpoint	1 − 10.7143 4 − 10.7143 etc.	−9.7143 −6.7143 etc.
3 Square the deviations (all squares are positive quantities).	−9.7143 × −9.7143 −6.7143 × −6.7143 etc.	+94.3676 +45.0818 etc.
4 Find the arithmetic mean of the squared deviations (this is called the *variance*). Remember with a grouped frequency distribution to multiply the squared deviations by the frequency of the group.	Total of squared deviations = 355.4285 Mean = 355.4285 ÷ 7	50.7755
5 Find the square root of the variance. This is the standard deviation.	√50.7755	7.1257

WORKING WITH NUMBERS

The range is quick to calculate and easy to understand but does not use all the data available – it involves only two of the items of the set of data, the largest and the smallest. This also means that, like the arithmetic mean, the range is affected by any extreme values within the set of data.

Standard deviation

The standard deviation is the most commonly used measure of dispersion and is often used in more advanced statistical calculations. The smaller the standard deviation, the less variable the data.

The standard deviation considers the deviations of the values from the arithmetic mean of the data. Unlike the range, it therefore takes all the data values into account in its calculation, and thus may be regarded as truly representative of the data. However, remember that, because of its relationship with the mean, the standard deviation will have the disadvantages associated with the mean. Table 7.6 shows the procedure for calculating the standard deviation of a set of data.

Exercise 7.10

Comparison of standard deviations

Calculate the standard deviation from the raw data from the florist. Compare your answer with the standard deviation estimated in Figure 7.20.

Figure 7.20 Calculating the standard deviation from a grouped frequency distribution

Step 1: The mean is 99.8, as estimated in Figure 7.16

Step 2: Deviation from the mean

Step 3: Deviation from the mean squared

Frequency multiplied by the squared deviation

Class (£)	Frequency (f)	Mid-point (x)	fx	$(x-\bar{x})$	$(x-\bar{x})^2$	$f(x-\bar{x})^2$
45 but less than 65	10	55	550	−44.8	2007.04	20070.4
65 but less than 85	18	75	1350	−24.8	615.04	11070.72
85 but less than 105	6	95	570	−4.8	23.04	138.24
105 but less than 125	4	115	460	15.2	231.04	924.16
125 but less than 145	3	135	405	35.2	1239.04	3717.12
145 but less than 165	2	155	310	55.2	3047.04	6094.08
165 but less than 185	2	175	350	75.2	5655.04	11310.08
185 but less than 205	4	195	780	95.2	9063.04	36252.16
205 and over	1	215	215	115.2	13271.04	13271.04
Total	50		4990			102848

Step 4: 102848 ÷ 50 = 2056.96
Step 5: √2056.96 = 45.35
The standard deviation of the data is £45
Note: $\bar{x}$ represents the mean

PART 1   DEVELOPING STUDY SKILLS

→ Spreadsheet software

Whilst it can be rather laborious to draw graphs and charts and calculate some of these statistics, most spreadsheet software now has the facility to draw charts and graphs and perform statistical functions. See Chapter 8 for more information.

> **Remember...**
> Investigate the spreadsheet software package used by the university or college.
>
> Practise using it to help you describe and manage data.

Exercise 7.11

Working with raw data

The following represent raw data on the number of miles travelled to work by employees of an organisation:

12.5	9.2	5.0	25.3	15.8	11.6	2.8	3.1	9.3	20.0
18.6	14.3	16.6	19.4	1.2	1.8	7.6	12.9	17.1	5.4
15.7	11.3	12.0	21.6	4.2	6.1	5.3	5.2	12.4	8.9
9.0	11.9	21.0	12.0	10.7	13.5	11.6	2.5	12.5	11.8

(a) Construct a frequency distribution.
(b) Construct a histogram.
(c) Estimate the mean using the frequency distribution.
(d) Construct an ogive.
(e) Estimate the median from the ogive.
(f) Estimate the mode from the histogram.
(g) Estimate the standard deviation.
(h) Comment on your results.

Use spreadsheet software to check your answers.

See downloadable template 7.2 EVALUATING STUDENTS for your Personal Development Plan online.

→ Summary

This chapter has outlined that:

- it is impossible to avoid numerical data, not least because of the increasing use of computers in generating such data
- it is important that you to be able to understand, organise and represent numerical data in an appropriate format which allows analysis and interpretation
- there are a number of ways of representing simple numerical data. The amount and type of data and the message to be conveyed will determine how the data is to be presented
- numerical data may also be represented by summary measures such as measures of central tendency (averages) and dispersion (spread). In choosing an appropriate summary measure, it is important to pay regard to the limitations of those measures.

PART 1   DEVELOPING STUDY SKILLS

→ Answers to exercises

7.1

Element	Variable(s)	Data type
(a) Students	Money spent on textbooks	Quantitative
	Money spent on food, etc.	Quantitative
(b) People	Destination	Qualitative
(c) Industrial organisations	Amount of water used	Quantitative
(d) Family	Number of children	Quantitative
	Gender of children	Qualitative
(e) Employees	Attitudes	Qualitative

7.2
36.785, 213.4582, 25.68, 16.8, 2400, 12000

7.3
(a) £8.76
(b)

Month	Number of visitors	%
1	559	21.8
2	743	28.9
3	1266	49.3
Total	2568	100.0

Percentage increases of visitors from month 1 to month 3 = 126.5%

7.4

	Faculty A		Faculty B		Faculty C	
	Number	%	Number	%	Number	%
Male	315	46.7	475	87.5	300	40.0
Female	360	53.3	68	12.5	450	60.0
Total	675	100.0	543	100.0	750	100.0

7.5

Marks	Frequency
30-39	4
40-49	8
50-59	10
60-69	7
70-79	1
Total	30

7.6
(a) Advertising = independent, Sales = dependent
(b) Price = independent, Demand = dependent
(c) Power of engine = independent, Speed = dependent

WORKING WITH NUMBERS

7.7

1 (a) Pie chart: Employee jobs (Finishers, Clerical, Machinists, Managers)

(b) Bar chart: Employee jobs — Machinists ~110, Finishers ~50, Clerical ~65, Managers ~10

2 (a) Stacked bar chart: Vegetable production 2003–2006 (Marrows, Cauliflowers, Cabbages)

(b) 100% stacked bar chart: Vegetable production (%) 2003–2006

7.8

£4845 + 50 = £96.90 compared with £99.80 calculated from the grouped frequency distribution. The difference between the two figures arises because the calculation using the grouped frequency data requires the midpoint of the class to be used as an estimate of each observation.

7.9

(a) Median – used to estimate the number of checkout operators required on each day.
(b) Mean – used to estimate demand for services, e.g. schools.
(c) Mean – used to check the performance of the production lines.
(d) Mode – used to ensure adequate stocks of the popular sizes of hats.

7.10

Standard deviation = £47 compared with £45 calculated from the grouped frequency distribution.

7.11 (a)

Class	Frequency (f)	Cumulative Frequency	Cumulative Frequency (%)	Mid-point (x)	fx	$(x-\bar{x})$	$(x-\bar{x})^2$	$f(x-\bar{x})^2$
0 but less than 5	6	6	15.0	2.5	15.0	−9.13	83.36	500.16
5 but less than 10	10	16	40.0	7.5	75.0	−4.13	17.06	170.60
10 but less than 15	14	30	75.0	12.5	175.0	0.87	0.76	10.64
15 but less than 20	6	36	90.0	17.5	105.0	5.87	34.46	206.76
20 but less than 25	3	39	97.5	22.5	67.5	10.87	118.16	354.48
25 but less than 30	1	40	100.0	27.5	27.5	15.87	251.86	251.86
Total	40				465			1494.50

Mean = 465/40 = 11.63
Std. Deviation = $\sqrt{1494.50/465}$ = $\sqrt{3.214}$ = 1.79

(b)

Histogram showing miles travelled to work by employees

(Frequency vs Miles travelled; Mode indicated near 9.9)

(d)

Cumulative frequency curve (ogive)

(Cumulative % vs Miles travelled; Median indicated near 9.9)

8 Information technology skills

> **Learning outcomes**
> After studying this chapter, you should be able to:
> - explain some of the terminology associated with information technology
> - store data on an appropriate medium using an appropriate filing system
> - create simple Word documents, spreadsheets and PowerPoint presentations.

→ Introduction

The decreasing price of technology has meant that most organisations incorporate technology as part of their everyday life and many homes now also have computers. This is also true of universities and colleges, not only for administration and research, but also increasingly for teaching, learning and assessment. As a student you will be expected to use information technology (IT) to prepare your assessments, research topics, communicate with your tutors or peers, and perhaps explore particular aspects of some modules. It is therefore important that you develop the skills required to use IT effectively to support your studies.

There are a variety of tasks that you may be asked to do using IT, but the most likely applications you will need to use at university or college are word-processing, spreadsheet and presentation software. This software is now also commonplace in many business organisations, so the skills you develop will be valuable in gaining employment. This chapter will introduce you to some of the basic concepts for using IT to help you with your studies.

→ Some terms defined

Many students will have used computers before entering higher education, but for some the university or college computers will be their first introduction to this technology.

Even if you have used computers before, you need to be able to use them effectively and understand what they can do. Much of the world of technology is shrouded in jargon, but an understanding of some of these terms this will increase your confidence in using IT.

Computers are now available in many different sizes, shapes and forms, ranging from small hand-held computers to large complex computer systems used to manage data and communications in large organisations. However, even the smallest computer may have the facility to be connected (networked) to other computer systems either within the same room or across the globe. Networked computers enable the exchange of data and information between computers. The world's largest computer network is the Internet (see Chapter 9). Organisations often have their own internal network, referred to as an intranet. This allows easy communication and sharing of data between computers within an organisation. Your university or college will probably have a system to which you will be able to gain access and, through that, access the Internet.

Computers enable us to manipulate data, whether the data are letters, numbers, sounds or images. To this end, we must be able to put data into the computer (input), manipulate it (process) and retrieve the finished product (output). This forms the basic computer system.

Hardware

Hardware refers to the physical equipment, media and attached devices in a computer system. If you can switch it on, it is hardware! Together you and the hardware form the human–computer interface across which data and information are transferred.

Input

Data are transferred into the computer by means of an input device. The most common means of input are the keyboard and the computer mouse.

The keyboard

Most computer keyboards have the same arrangement as the keys on a typewriter – the QWERTY layout. However, there are some important keys on a computer keyboard that do not appear on a typewriter:

Enter or ↵   This key should be pressed after typing an instruction. It is the signal to the computer that the instruction is complete and should be carried out.

Esc   This key will allow you to exit some operations. It is usually at the top left of the keyboard.

F1 ... F10   There are usually 10 or 12 function keys on a keyboard which perform different functions depending on which software you are using. Very often F1 is a help key.

Ctrl   This key is used in combination with other keys in order to perform special operations. When using this key you should hold it down and then press the other key(s) required.

Alt   This key is also used in conjunction with other keys in order to perform special operations.

The mouse

The computer mouse may require some practice if you have never used one before. As the mouse is moved, a pointer will move around the computer screen enabling you to select commands from menus or select areas of the screen to work with. The pointer changes shape depending on which operation you are performing. A mouse usually has two buttons. To select an item or icon, the left-hand button is clicked (pressed). Clicking the right-hand button will reveal a drop-down menu for the application you are working in. Some mice have a centre wheel between the two buttons which enables you to scroll up and down the screen as you turn the wheel.

Dragging is an operation that is performed easily with a mouse. To drag, click the left-hand mouse button over highlighted text or icons and, whilst holding this button down, move the pointer to another location before releasing the button. In this way, you can move words, numbers and objects around the screen.

Processing unit/memory

The central processing unit (cpu) is the hub of the computer system and controls all the activities that the computer performs. In a personal computer (PC), the processor would be a single chip (e.g. Intel Pentium), known as a *microprocessor*.

Data and programs (instructions) dwell in the computer's memory until required. Part of the memory is Read Only Memory (ROM) and cannot be erased. This is where the essential instructions reside – normally there is no need to access this area directly. Data or programs that you are working with are transferred into Random Access Memory (RAM), a volatile temporary storage area. Data and programs only reside there whilst they are being used.

Storage devices

Data and information that you wish to store or transfer to another computer should be transferred from the computer memory to a storage medium. Most colleges and universities require students to save their work on their own storage media, such as the following:

Disk storage

Disk storage may be either fixed or portable. A fixed hard disk is a sealed unit that is generally not transferable between computers. Some universities and colleges now provide an area of 'fixed' storage for each student within the computer system. If so, you will need 'log on' information, which usually consists of a user name and password.

Floppy disks are portable, enabling the data or programs stored on them to be transferred easily between computers. Many of the disks available are already formatted (prepared to receive data). If not, you will have to format them before you can store anything on them. It is worth noting that, although relatively cheap, floppy disks are likely to become obsolete in the near future as their capacity is limited compared to some of the media currently being developed.

CD (compact disk)

A common storage medium is a CD, which will hold more data than a floppy disk – important if you want to store images or sound. In order to read from or write to CDs, you need to ensure that the computer has a CD read/write capability.

Flash drives or memory sticks

Flash drives come in many different shapes and sizes. They plug into a USB (Universal Serial Bus) and allow the storage of vast quantities of data.

Output

An output device translates computer-coded information into a format we can understand. Information from a computer system may be displayed on screen, printed or audio. As a student, the output devices you are most likely to use for retrieving your work are the screen display and the printer.

The computer screen will not provide a permanent record of your work (*soft copy*), but is vital for checking work before printing it. If you require a permanent record of your work, you will need to obtain a printout (*hard copy*) from a printer. There are many different types of printer, varying in speed and quality. Most universities and colleges provide printing facilities for students but may charge for this.

> **Suggestions for using information technology**
>
> - Spend some time familiarising yourself with the use of the keyboard and mouse - this will save you time and frustration.
> - Ensure you clearly label your disks or other storage devices.
> - Look after your disks or other storage devices - keep them out of sunlight and dust free.
> - Beware of lending your storage media to anyone - they are easy to copy and someone may inadvertently (or knowingly) transfer a virus to them.
> - Always check your output on the screen before printing your work - this will save time, paper and money.

> **Remember...**
> There may be specific rules governing the use of the university or college facilities. If there are, make sure you know what they are and how they apply to you.

Software

Software is the term used for programs, or lists of instructions, which tell the hardware what to do. The computer hardware will not function without software. Software broadly falls into two categories.

INFORMATION TECHNOLOGY SKILLS

Systems software

These are the programs that control and support the computer system. The operating system is the main component of the systems software. This supervises the overall operation of the computer, including the communication with the input, output and storage devices and the organisation of the memory and file system. It also provides an interface with the user and the hardware, thus making it easier for the user to use the system.

> **Stop and think**
> - Which operating system is used in your university/college?
> - If you have a computer at home, which operating system does it have?
> - Are they compatible?
> - Which versions of software do you use at home? At university? Are they compatible?

Applications software

These are the programs that enable the user to perform specific tasks, such as manipulating words (word-processing software) or numbers (spreadsheet software).

See Activity 8.3 PRACTISE USING THE INTERNET in the Online Study Guide.

Activity 8.1

University/college computing facilities

Make a visit to the university or college computer facilities to find the answer to the following questions:

1. Does the university or college operate a booking system for students to use the facilities? If so, does this apply to all facilities, or are there some facilities that are available on open access?
2. Do you need an identification number and/or password to use the university or college computer facilities?
3. What sort of computer system is available – stand-alone PCs, terminals, networked facilities, etc?
4. Which methods of input are available?
5. Can you use CDs to read and write?
6. Can you use flash drives?
7. Where can you print out your work?
8. Does the university or college charge for printing facilities?
9. What is the procedure for printing out your work using the university or college facilities?
10. Is there a help desk which answers student queries? If so, when is it open? What sort of help will it provide for you?
11. Which operating environment is used on the university or college facilities?
12. Can you gain access to the Internet through the university/college facilities? If so, what do you need to be able to do this?

PART 1   DEVELOPING STUDY SKILLS

→ Organising your work

All work produced on computers is held in *files*. A file may contain data or software and should have an appropriate name. A file name usually consists of two parts separated by a full stop (e.g. myfile.doc). The second part of a filename, which is optional, is known as the file name *extension*. Some applications create these automatically. Extensions may be overwritten but keeping them does help to identify what kind of data the file contains.

Examples:

filename.doc   indicates a WORD document/file
filename.xls   indicates an EXCEL file
filename.ppt   indicates a POWERPOINT file

Examples of valid filenames are: economics.doc maths.xls and smith_1.ppt. Note also that some software automatically creates back-up copies of your files – these are denoted by the extension .bak.

> **! Remember...**
> You may choose the names of your files but there are file-naming conventions:
>
> - Letters, numbers and some symbols may be used in file names.
> - Some file management systems may restrict the number of characters you may use.
> - File names should not include a space – many people use an underscore instead, e.g. my_file.
> - Upper- or lower-case letters may be used for file names.

Get into the habit of giving your files meaningful names that you will easily recognise. You could, for example, begin each filename for a particular subject with the first letter of the subject. For example, messay1.doc may denote your first marketing essay, whereas ahomewk1.xls would indicate your first piece of accounts homework. However, it is not always sufficient to rely on this sort of coding system. You should also try to keep different types of file on different disks or areas of the storage medium you are using.

Stop and think   ○ Have you devised a system for naming your files so that you can easily recognise what the files contain from their file names?

● Managing your files

You may have a number of files on your disk or storage medium. In order to make it easier to find particular files, the storage medium may be divided into named areas called *directories*. They are similar to partitions in a filing cabinet drawer. Directories have

Figure 8.1 Possible structure for a file directory

```
                    Root (\)                    Root directory e.g. c:
            ┌──────────┼──────────┐
        Economic      Mktg      Accounts       Sub-directories
                   ┌───┴───┐
                 Notes   Assessmt              Sub-directories
              ┌────┴────┐
          Topic1.doc  Topic2.doc               File names
                          ↑
                  This is the file   c:\Mktg\Notes\Topic2.doc
```

names and naming conventions as for files. You should group like files together in directories – for example, you may choose to keep all your files for a particular module together in one directory.

Directories may contain other directories (*sub-directories*) and/or *files*. They may be thought of as being created and used in a tree-like structure (see Figure 8.1).

Suggestions on managing your files

- Give your directories and files meaningful names so that you can easily recognise them when searching your disk.
- Keep your files of a manageable size.
- Always back up your files on another storage medium.

Activity 8.2

Directories and files

For the computer system/operating environment you will be using find the following information:

1. How do you select a directory?
2. How is the selected directory represented?
3. When a directory is selected, what information is given in the status bar (usually at the bottom of the computer screen)?
4. How is a file selected?
5. When a file is selected, what information is given in the status bar?
6. How do you select more than one file?
7. How can you see more information about directories and files?
8. Create a directory on your storage device called *coursework*.

PART 1   DEVELOPING STUDY SKILLS

→ **Windows**

> See downloadable template 8.1 PERSONAL ICT SKILLS ASSESSMENT for your Personal Development Plan online.

Many organisations use the Windows operating environment and Windows applications. Windows is a Graphical User Interface (GUI) environment – in other words, the user can communicate with the computer using windows, icons (pictures), pull-down menus and a mouse. This software allows more than one application to be running at a time and you can thus easily transfer data and images between the applications that are running. Software, like hardware, is continually under development and being updated. The result is that there are now many versions of Windows (95, 98, Me, NT, 2000, XP, etc). The rest of this chapter will concentrate on Windows and Windows applications.

In Windows the computer screen emulates the top of a desk – referred to as the *desktop* (see Figure 8.2). You can work on the Windows desktop and perform tasks that you would normally do at a conventional desktop. The names of any applications that are running appear in the *title bar* of the window. All Windows applications use the same icons and have similar menus. The icons, if selected, will perform the same operations, whichever application is running. For example, the top right of the screen in any Windows application will display the following icons:

- ⊟ Selection of this icon will make the application or document inactive. This does not mean it is closed, it is still open but remains temporarily suspended in the background. The name of the application will appear on the task bar at the bottom of the screen.

Figure 8.2 **Typical Windows screen**

INFORMATION TECHNOLOGY SKILLS

Figure 8.3 Typical menu bar for a Windows application

File	Edit	View	Insert	Format	Tools	Window	Help

⊠ Selecting this icon will close the application you are working in.

⊟ Clicking on this icon will reduce the size of the application Window. After this has been done the following icon will appear.

☐ Clicking on this icon will restore a window to its full size

Other useful icons:

▼ If this icon appears next to a box, it is an indication that there is a pull-down menu. Clicking on it will reveal the options available.

? This icon indicates that there is a help facility.

Menus

All Windows applications have similar options on the menu bar (see Figure 8.3). Clicking on any of these (left-hand mouse button) will reveal further menus from which you may select the operation you need. Some selections may lead you to further menus. Note that each item has one letter underlined. This provides an indication of the short-cut to accessing the functions. For example, if you want to go to the Format menu you may use the **Alt** and **o** keys together as a short cut.

Useful key combinations in Windows are:

Ctrl	**Esc**		This provides a menu of Windows applications.
Alt	**Tab**		Where you are working on more than one application, this key combination allows you to switch between applications.
Ctrl	**Alt**	**Del**	This combination will allow you to exit from all the applications.
Ctrl	**P**		This takes you straight to the print menu.

The Windows applications that you are most likely to be required to use during your studies are Word (word-processing software), Excel (spreadsheet software) and PowerPoint (presentation software).

→ Word-processing software – Word

Word-processing software enables you to manipulate words and create documents. The easiest way to create a document in Word is to input the text and then format it. There are three different levels of formatting in Word.

Page formatting

Page formatting enables you to provide instructions to indicate how you wish the page to be laid out. The commands to do this are found in: *File   Page set up*

For example this enables the following to be set:

Page orientation	portrait or landscape
Margins	both horizontal and vertical
Gutter	the vertical column of space between two facing pages of the document
Paper	size

Paragraph formatting

Paragraph formatting may be done either before or after the paragraph is typed. The commands to do this are found in either: *Format   Paragraph* or click the right mouse button when placed within the paragraph (this pulls up a short-cut menu) and select *Paragraph*.

Paragraph formatting enables you to set up paragraph indents, alignments, styles, headings, etc.

Character formatting

Character formatting deals with the way characters appear on the screen (known as attributes), such as bold, italic, underline and font. This may be done either before or after the characters are typed.

Note some of the icons that may be seen in the formatting toolbar, for example:

B | *I* | U

Highlighting the text and clicking in these boxes will change text to **bold**, *italics* and underline respectively. It is also possible to use **Ctrl B** to start bold and then **Ctrl B** to return to normal. Similarly **Ctrl I** can be used for italics and **Ctrl U** for underline.

Selection of text

In order to format text after it has been input, the text must first be selected. There are three different methods of selecting text.

Using the mouse

Word	Point to the middle of the word and double click.
Sentence	**Ctrl** key and click anywhere in the sentence.
Paragraph	Triple click anywhere in the paragraph.
Line	Arrow pointer to the very left of the line and click; a number of lines may be highlighted in this way by dragging the pointer down.
General	Click and drag to highlight all the text to be formatted, or click at the beginning of the required text, hold the shift key down and click at the end of the text required.

INFORMATION TECHNOLOGY SKILLS

Using the Shift key

To the end of a line	**Shift** and the down arrow
To the end of the document	**Shift** and **Ctrl** and **End**
To the end of the screen	**Shift** and **PgDn**

The extended selection key (F8)

Press **F8** repeatedly in order to select the text required. The **Esc** key will cancel this. To deselect any text, you must click the mouse anywhere outside the selection.

> See Activity 8.1 PRACTISING USING MICROSOFT WORD in the Online Study Guide.

Activity 8.3

Formatting in Word

Using Word or another word-processing package, type a cover letter to accompany a CV for application for a job of your choice (see Chapter 3). Use the appropriate formatting tools to make the letter look professional and easy to read.

→ Spreadsheet software – Excel

Spreadsheet software allows you to manipulate numbers and perform sophisticated calculations. Developing skill with this software is important, as it is a powerful tool. The real power of this software is its capacity to calculate certain values in the grid automatically. For example, instead of the user adding up a column of figures manually, a formula may be inserted, which automatically produces a total for the column of figures. Numbers in the spreadsheet may be altered and the software will automatically recalculate them.

In Excel each individual screen is a page or worksheet in a workbook. A *worksheet* (see Figure 8.4) is composed of columns (identified by letters) and rows (identified by

Figure 8.4 **Example of a spreadsheet**

PART 1   DEVELOPING STUDY SKILLS

numbers). A *cell* is the point where the rows and columns meet. Cells are identified by the letter of the column and the number of the row – for example, B6 is located in column B, row 6 and K25 is located in column K and row 25. The cell that you are working in is described as *active* – a bold outline and a small box at the bottom right-hand corner will identify this.

Exercise 8.1

Spreadsheets

Set up the outline spreadsheet as shown below by highlighting the appropriate cell and typing in the data indicated. For example, highlight cell A1 and type in Wine Sales.

	A	B	C	D	E	F	G
1	Wine Sales						
2							
3			Jan 06				
4		Red	White	Total			
5	Shop 1	321	89		275	16	
6							
7		208	873		199	26	
8							
9		78	136		100	43	
10							
11		45	56		204	45	
12							
13	Total						

Now complete the spreadsheet following the instructions below.

	Cell Ref.	Actions
1	E3:J4	Repeat the column headings across the spreadsheet Select cells B3:D4. Place the cursor at the bottom right-hand corner of the selection so that a plain + appears. Hold down the left mouse button and drag to J4. Release the button.
2	L3	Type in Total.
3	K4:M4	Use the process in step 1 to put headings Red, White, Total in the appropriate cells.

INFORMATION TECHNOLOGY SKILLS

	Cell Ref.	Actions
4	Column A	*Column width* Column A is not wide enough to display the contents. Select column A (click at the top of the column, next to the A). Move the cursor to the right-hand edge of the column (note the change in the pointer). Double click.
5	A7:A12	*Copying row titles* Select A5:A6. Place cursor on the bottom right-hand corner (+) and drag to A12.
6	B13	*Adding up columns of figures* Cell B13 should show the total of red wine sold in Jan 06. Ensure B13 is the active cell. Click on the sum button (Σ). Select the cells to be totalled. Press enter or the √. Note the formula in the formula bar.
7	C13:M13	*Copying a formula* Select B13. Click and drag to M13.
8	D5	Cell D5 should show the total wine sold in outlet 1 in Jan 2006 (see step 6).
9	D7:D12	Use click and drag (see step 7).
10	G5	*Copying a formula* Another way of copying a formula is: Select D5. Position the cursor so the arrow is visible. Hold down the **Ctrl** key, hold down the left-hand mouse button. Move the cursor to G5. Release the mouse button and then the **Ctrl** key.
11	G7:G12	These cells should show totals for February.
12	J5:J13	A whole column of formulae may be copied in one go. Select column G (click on the G at the top of the column). Use the **Ctrl** key to copy the column to column J.
13	K5	This should show the total of red wine sales for the three months. Highlight K5. Point to the Σ. Click on B5. Ctrl click on E5. Ctrl click on H5. Enter.
14	Columns K, L and M	Complete the columns K, L and M.

PART 1   DEVELOPING STUDY SKILLS

> Note that no numbers have been included for columns H, I and J (sales figures for March). However, if you now type in some figures the totals will automatically recalculate.
>
> Save the spreadsheet as WINE1:   File   Save   (ensure that an appropriate directory is selected on your storage medium)
> WINE1.xls
> OK
>
> Close the spreadsheet: File   Close
>
> Load the spreadsheet: File   Open
> Select WINE1 from the storage device
> OK
>
> Format the spreadsheet to give it a more user-friendly appearance. Suggestions:
>
> (a) Centre the titles in row 3
> (b) Right justify titles in row 4
> (c) Make all the titles Bold characters
> (d) Put lines around the total row
> (e) Separate the months with vertical lines
> (f) Separate the final total column with vertical lines.

Steps in designing a spreadsheet

1. Determine the purpose of the spreadsheet – this will determine the content and structure of the model.
2. Devise a title – this should reflect the content, subject matter and focus of the worksheet.
3. Determine the independent variables and dependent variables. Independent variables are constant values. Dependent variables are those defined by formulae.
4. Lay out the worksheet on paper – this may be time consuming but worth it! Indicate the position of labels, formulae, etc. and which entries may be copied.
5. Enter labels into the spreadsheet.
6. Enter the base formulae and copy into successive rows or columns as necessary.
7. Adjust the format and column widths – how should numbers be displayed (with or without £), how many decimal places, should headings be right or left justified?
8. Verify and validate the worksheet.
   Verification = check to ensure the worksheet model is correct.
   Validation = check to ensure the right model was formulated.
9. Document the worksheet – describe how the model works and how to use it.
10. Perform 'what if' analyses where appropriate – systematically adjust the independent variables over the appropriate ranges to observe the effects.
11. Print out the required reports.

Note: if required, prepare appropriate graphs, charts, etc. using the graphics facility.

INFORMATION TECHNOLOGY SKILLS

→ Presentation software – PowerPoint

During your studies you may find that some of your assessments involve presentations. It is a good idea to become familiar with presentation software in order to ensure that your assessed presentations are effective and professional. PowerPoint is a complete presentation graphics package enabling the creation of professional presentations with powerful graphics- and text-handling capabilities. PowerPoint may be used to produce presentation slides, speaker notes, audience notes, handouts and outlines. Chapter 14 provides some guidance on how to create an effective presentation using PowerPoint. Some of the basic features of the Powerpoint software are as follows:

- To create a presentation quickly, use the Autocontent wizard and answer the questions that appear in a series of dialogue boxes.
- Use templates to define the general appearance of the slides in the presentation, e.g. colour scheme and initial text formatting.
- Text objects may be created by either pointing to the text tool and typing the required text or using the WordArt facility (*Insert Object WordArt*)
- Graphic objects may be created by either *freehand drawing* (drawing and auto shapes are on the toolbar at the bottom left-hand side of the screen) or inserted from *clip-art*, a range of graphic images within PowerPoint (*Insert Object Clip-art*)
- Objects (text or graphics) inserted on the slides may be moved, resized, edited, coloured, formatted, etc.
- Some versions of presentation software enable you to animate your presentation and most allow you to set up transitions from one slide to the next.

Suggestions for creating a presentation

- Create the presentation in outline
- Decide on a template master and apply to the slides
- Edit the slides, inserting text and graphics as required (see Autolayout)
- Save the presentation
- View the master slide
- Put a logo onto the master slide. Note that you can insert text in an 'art form' by the use of Word Art
- Save the presentation.

See Activity 8.2 PRACTISE USING POWERPOINT in the Online Study Guide.

Activity 8.4

PowerPoint presentations

Create a short presentation (five or six slides) about your life as a student.

PART 1   DEVELOPING STUDY SKILLS

→ Summary

This chapter has:

- identified that information technology is omnipresent – it is therefore important to learn the associated terminology and to develop skills in using the software
- outlined the need to organise computer files effectively so that they can be found quickly and easily
- detailed how word-processing skills might be used to create professional documents
- illustrated how spreadsheet software manipulates numbers without the need to do manual calculations
- demonstrates that presentation software provides the tools for creating professional and effective presentations.

→ Answers to exercise

8.1 Wine Sales

| | Jan-06 | | | Feb-06 | | | Mar-06 | | | Total | | |
	Red	White	Total	Red	White	Total	Red	White	Total	Red	White	Total
Shop 1	321	89	410	275	16	291	–	–	0	596	105	701
Shop 2	208	873	1081	199	26	225	–	–	0	407	899	1306
Shop 3	78	136	214	100	43	143	–	–	0	178	179	357
Shop 4	45	56	101	204	45	249	–	–	0	249	101	350
Total	652	1154	1806	778	130	908	0	0	0	1430	1284	2714

9 Researching and obtaining information

> **Learning outcomes**
>
> After studying this chapter, you should be able to:
> - gather information with a purpose
> - identify appropriate sources of information relevant to and sufficient for the purpose
> - locate and retrieve information efficiently and effectively using different media
> - evaluate sources of information
> - identify and use an appropriate method for primary data collection.

→ Introduction

It is unlikely that lecture and seminar/tutorial notes and handouts will provide all the information required to get you successfully through your studies. In fact, much of your study time will be spent gathering information – not just for the assessments you have to complete but also to support lectures, seminars, tutorials and examinations. One of the most important study skills to develop is that of gathering appropriate and relevant information. This will be a critical factor in the success of your studies.

There is now a wide range of resources available on a variety of different media other than the traditional printed word, for example, CD-ROMs, microfilm, videos and DVDs. The information technology revolution has resulted in a huge expansion in the quantity of information available by making it easier and quicker to search and access. It is important to familiarise yourself with gathering information from a range of different media at an early stage in your studies.

The quality of the information available can vary from an uninformed opinion to thoroughly researched facts. When gathering material for your studies, aim to obtain the most relevant, accurate and reliable information possible, within the limits imposed by time, cost and your own research ability. Unreliable and inaccurate information leads to faulty judgement and decisions.

The vast amount of information and resources available can be very bewildering. You can spend a lot of valuable time floundering unless you adopt a systematic and orderly approach. The aim of this chapter is to help you find your way through this sea of information.

→ A systematic approach to information gathering

Why do you want the information?

Before beginning to collect information, you need to be sure why you need it. Consider the purpose of gathering the information – is it to enable you to complete an assessment, prepare for a lecture or tutorial, further your understanding of a subject or simply for interest? The purpose behind your information gathering will determine the nature, focus and depth of the information you need and how you record it.

> **Stop and think**
> ○ Why do you need the information?

What do you need to know?

You need to define precisely the topic area and any related subject matter that may be relevant to the topic. This means analysing the topic. What is it about? What are the supporting ideas and concepts? If there are words or ideas you do not understand, use a dictionary, encyclopedia or thesaurus for clarification.

Make notes on what you already know about the topic and identify any information you already have. Look at the lecture/tutorial notes and reading lists you have been given. Reading lists will provide references that the tutor considers relevant to the subject. If you are at all unclear about what is required, ask your tutor for guidance, particularly if the information is for an assessment. This will avoid you making a time-consuming search for information that may turn out to be irrelevant.

> **! Remember...**
> Brainstorm the topic – think about the what, why, when, how, where and who of the topic to provide you with a basic framework.

See downloadable template 9.2 DEFINING ESSAY TITLES for your Personal Development Plan online.

At this stage, it is useful to identify the main concepts, key words and phrases associated with the topic under investigation. *Key words or phrases* are the words that identify and are related to the subject area. This is an important part of gathering information – key words and phrases are required to locate appropriate resources, so it is worth spending some time thinking about these. Using the wrong key words may mean that relevant material is missed. Key words that are too broad will result in too much information, and those that are too narrow will lead to limited information. Figure 9.1 provides an example of how key words and phrases for an essay title may be broadened or narrowed.

RESEARCHING AND OBTAINING INFORMATION

Figure 9.1 Key words and phrases

Example: Pressure groups are an essential feature of democracy. Discuss.

Key words
pressure groups
democracy

Narrower
voting systems
Greenpeace
trade unions etc.
petition
influence
consultation
etc. etc.

Related/Synonyms
representation
lobbying
participation
etc. etc.

Broader
political systems
power
political parties
government
philosophies
etc. etc.

Exercise 9.1

Identifying key words and phrases

Examine the question below and determine the key words and phrases that could be used to search for information.

'The value of information derives from its effect on decision behaviour.' Discuss.

Key words/phrases: _____

Related terms/synonyms: _____

Narrower terms: _____

Broader terms: _____

When do you need to know the information?

Ensure that you know when you must have the information. Gathering information can be a very time-consuming activity, so it is essential to plan. The time you have available will influence how you collect the information and also in what depth. (See also Chapter 11.)

Stop and think
○ What is your deadline for completing the work?

Where will you get the information?

When embarking on the search for information, first consider whether the search may be based solely on information that has already been published by someone else (*secondary information*) or whether you need to add to this by generating it yourself (*primary research*).

Secondary information sources

Secondary sources provide information that has already been collected and issued by somebody. Examples are all the journals, newspapers, official statistics, books and other material that have been published. Investigating the material already available in a topic area should be the first step in finding information. In fact, some tasks will not require you to go beyond this.

Primary data

If information is not available or appropriate from secondary sources then it may have to be collected first hand. This can be done using a variety of different methods, such as observation, experimentation and surveys, which are covered in detail later in this chapter.

Gathering primary data can be an extremely time-consuming and expensive activity so be sure that it is necessary before embarking on such a quest. Essays and tutorials or seminars will rely mainly on secondary information but a dissertation or project may require the collection of primary data.

> **Stop and think**
> ○ Does the work you are doing require primary research?

How will you gather and record the data/information?

The method used is particularly important for primary data, which may be collected in a number of different ways, such as surveys, observation or experimentation. Refer to the section on primary data collection for more detail on this.

Chapter 6 provides advice on recording information from secondary sources, but it is vital that sources are correctly referenced and any sources used are listed in a bibliography (see Chapter 16 for advice on references and bibliographies).

Who will be able to help?

See Activity 9.1 NARROWING YOUR SEARCH in the Online Study Guide.

Make a list of the people and organisations that may be able to help in your search for information. This may include librarians, organisations external to the academic institution, other students, etc.

RESEARCHING AND OBTAINING INFORMATION

→ Secondary sources

The obvious place to start the search for secondary sources is a library.

Libraries

Libraries will be an invaluable resource during your studies. Traditionally, libraries have been a source of printed and audio-visual material, but now many libraries, especially academic ones, offer access to information stored on other media, such as CD-ROMs and the Internet. It is important to make a determined effort at an early stage of your studies to get to know the organisation, operation and facilities of the library you intend to use regularly for study.

There are a number of different types of library in the UK, which are outlined below.

Public libraries

A public library provides a service for the community in which it is situated. Many of the readers using a public library are primarily interested in fiction, but the librarian will try to meet the demands of all types of reader. It is unlikely that the subject coverage of books on a particular topic will reach a great depth, although occasionally a public library may house a special collection of information that is pertinent to the area in which the library is situated.

Academic libraries

Your university or college library will have been stocked to meet the specialised needs of the academic community it serves. The stock will include journals, periodicals, reports and professional magazines, as well as academic texts. The library may also allow access to e-journals and databases. The material provided may embrace fewer subjects than in a public library, but the depth of provision will be greater. The librarians may even be specialists in a particular subject area.

Company libraries

Some organisations have their own library, which houses material on every aspect of the firm's business in order to support all the organisation's activities. These libraries are particularly useful if you have to research a particular industry or organisation. For example, British Gas plc has a library at its headquarters in London that contains books, reports and other material relating to the gas industry and energy in general. Many hospitals house specialist library collections for their staff that in some cases may be available to students.

Specialist libraries

The Association for Information Management (formerly ASLIB, the Association of Special Libraries and Information Bureaux) publishes a *Directory of Information Sources in the UK* which lists specialist libraries with specific subject collections in the UK. An example of a specialist library is the British Film Institute National Library in London.

Using the library

You may feel apprehensive about asking the library staff where to find information – many people do, particularly in a large academic library. Do not be afraid to ask the library staff for their help – asking for help is an indication of your desire to learn and extend your knowledge. Library staff are highly trained and well-qualified people, dedicated to the task of helping people to use the facilities that the libraries offer. They build up a wide knowledge of books and other learning resources, and are generally happy to share this knowledge with anyone who asks.

It is a good idea to establish a rapport with a member of the university or college library staff, particularly one who is responsible for the subject area you are studying. Time invested in this could yield valuable time savings later on, as they become a friendly link between you and the vast range of resources available in the library. Specialist subject librarians in university and college libraries may have a bibliography already prepared on a subject you are researching. If not, they will be able to indicate the location of appropriate resources within the library.

To help their users, some libraries issue their own publications, such as lists of resources and how to use them. These are useful, but remember that such lists are out of date from the moment they are printed, as they will not contain the latest additions to the library. A very useful publication is a map of the library indicating where all the different resources are located.

There are two main categories of resources held in libraries: those for *reference* purposes and those for *lending*. The category is usually determined by usage. Reference material will generally only need to be consulted for some particular piece of information, whereas lending material will be required for periods of continuous use. Sometimes expensive resources, although they are not strictly reference, are added to the reference section because of their cost. You may also find that, if a lending resource is in great demand, there will be multiple copies and a copy will be placed in the reference section so that one copy is always available.

Some libraries, particularly academic libraries, operate a short-term loan section. This allows lenders to borrow the resources for shorter periods of time than the usual lending period. Recommended materials for courses are often placed on short-term loan so that all students have the opportunity to use them.

> **Remember...**
> Get to know the librarian for your subject area – they will have invaluable information.

Inter-library loans

One of the great benefits of the library system is the cooperation between the different libraries through the inter-library loan system. If you request a resource from your local or university/college library and they are unable to supply it, they are likely to have the facility to search the catalogues of other libraries to determine whether the item is stocked elsewhere. If so, your library may be able to make a request for this item on your behalf. The holding library will then send the item to your library for you to use if it is in stock. Note that there may be a charge for this service, and inevitably there will be a time delay whilst the material makes the journey between libraries.

If you need to use the inter-library loan system, make sure you provide the librarian with full details of the material you wish to see:

Author

Publication title

Article title (if applicable)

Publisher

Date of publication

Page number (if applicable)

ISBN (International Standard Book Number) (if known)

Many universities have reciprocal arrangements with other universities so that students may use a restricted range of their facilities.

Organisation of the library

Information is held in libraries on a variety of different media, all of which can appear very perplexing at first. However, the material is carefully organised so that information on a particular subject is readily accessible. Usually similar media are held in the same area of the library: for example, all books in one area, magazines and periodicals in another, videos in another, etc. Within these areas, material will be grouped together by subject.

The Dewey Decimal System

> See Activity 9.2 THE DEWEY CLASSIFICATION SYSTEM in the Online Study Guide.

Most libraries use the Dewey Decimal System to classify the majority of the non-electronic media within the library. This system, developed by Melvil Dewey, librarian of Amherst College, Massachusetts, in 1873, uses the decimal principle to divide the whole of human knowledge into ten broad subject areas called classes (see Table 9.1). Each class is subdivided into ten subclasses and each of these into a further ten. Dewey classification numbers are used to represent the subjects, and thus the numbers become a shorthand symbol for the subject. Material within the same classification is grouped together, usually arranged in alphabetical order of author's name. All material is arranged on the library shelves according to this system, in a progressive manner around the library.

With constant use you will quickly become familiar with the classification numbers associated with the subjects you are studying.

When looking for books, remember that many important subjects are included under a general heading – for example, the 500 class contains subjects ranging from mathematics to pure science. Each class is broken down into more precise subject headings, which become more detailed and precise at each level (Table 9.2). If there are a lot of books on the same subject with the same classification number, three letters may be added to the number. This represents the author's *last name*.

Table 9.1 General headings within the Dewey classification system

Class	Category	
000	Generalities	This includes encyclopaedias, bibliographies, periodicals, etc. – anything that ranges over the whole field of human knowledge.
100	Philosophy and related disciplines	This class includes psychology.
200	Religion	
300	Social sciences	This class includes statistics, economics, public administration, social welfare and education.
400	Philology	This includes language and linguistics.
500	Pure sciences	This includes mathematics, physics, chemistry, biology and botany.
600	Applied science (technology)	Books on medicine, agriculture, business and management are in this class.
700	The arts	This covers books on recreation as well as architecture, photography, music, and fine and decorative arts.
800	Literature	The study of the literature of the world's languages will be found in this class, whereas the study of the grammar is found in the 400 class. Using this system, fiction would be placed in this class but most libraries have a separate fiction area because of the space required.
900	Geography and history	This class also includes biography.

Note: titles of each category may change slightly depending on the library you use.

Table 9.2 Example of subdivisions within the Dewey classification system

300	Social sciences
310	Collection of general statistics
320	Political sciences
330	Economics
331	Labour economics
332	Financial economics
332.1	Banks
332.2	Specialised banking institutions
332.21	Savings banks

Another classification system that you may come across in large universities or research libraries is the Library of Congress Classification System. This system uses letters and numbers.

Library catalogues

The key to a library is the catalogue. Most libraries now hold their catalogues on a computer system, which means that searching for the information you need is fast and flexible. The library catalogue allows access to resources through a number of different routes.

Subject

The subject index lists all the subjects covered by the library in alphabetical order. This is a quick and easy way to find related subject areas, or alternative terms for the key words identified for your topic. It will also provide a rough guide to the volume of resources covering a subject area.

The Dewey classification number is provided for each subject. For example, looking up *Marketing* in the subject catalogue will identify the Dewey classification number for this topic area as 658.8.

Title

This is a list of all the books held in the library in alphabetical order by title.

Author

The author index is a list of all the books held in the library alphabetically by author's name. If the author of a book is known, this index may be used to find the classification number and thus locate it. However, this can be more time consuming than the title index, as there will be many authors with the same or similar names who may each have written a number of books, whereas most titles are unique.

Classified catalogue

The classified catalogue provides a list of all the resources that are held under a particular classification.

The *British National Bibliography* (*BNB*) is a useful publication that can usually be found in the reference section of the library. It contains an up-to-date list of books and journals in print and may be referenced by subject, author or title.

Suggestions for using the library catalogue

If you cannot find your reference in the catalogues, before asking the library staff for their help check the following:

- *Spelling*. Are the words correctly spelt? Note that US spellings may differ, e.g. colour (UK), color (USA).
- *Terminology*. Are you using the correct terminology? Beware of jargon and also the differences between languages, e.g. cars (UK), automobiles (USA).
- *Abbreviations*. Are you using the correct abbreviations? Also try the words in full.

An incorrect input will cause the search in the catalogue to be misdirected.

> ### Activity 9.1
>
> #### Using the library catalogue
>
> Look up a subject you are studying on the library catalogue system. Identify five books, three videos and two journals of interest in the subject area and locate them on the library shelves.
>
> Identify several reference books in your area of study. Are they all together in the one reference section of the library or located on the shelves with the lending resources?

Printed resources

The traditional method of publishing information is through the printed word, but there are many formats in which the information may be presented.

Books

Books contain material that has been previously written on subjects that have been investigated by other people. They therefore provide a convenient starting point in a quest for information. However, when using books, remember that they take a long time to get into print, so some information may be out of date before they appear on the library shelves. This is important in some disciplines such as technical subjects where information changes rapidly.

Before deciding to borrow a book, you need to assess its usefulness to you. Some of the things by which this may be judged are listed below:

- *Title page*. This may not be particularly useful, though it should indicate the subject matter of the book.
- *Author's name*. You may recognise the author as an expert in the particular subject. If you do not know the author, see whether their qualifications and experience are given – if so, this may provide a clue as to whether they are equipped to write such a book.
- *Publisher's name*. Some publishers specialise in particular types of book. The publisher's name can therefore be an indication of the quality of the work.
- *Copyright date*. This is usually found on the back of the title page and will indicate how up-to-date the book is, e.g. © 2006. In many subjects it is necessary and important to have the latest edition. Many printings or editions of a text may indicate that the work has become a standard source in the area and is therefore reliable.
- *Preface/foreword*. This states why the author has written the book and will often mention the level of study or type of person for whom it is written.
- *Contents list*. This will indicate the subject matter of the book and the major topic areas.
- *Index*. When searching for information, avoid books that do not have an index. Indexes save time by enabling information to be found quickly within the text.

Periodicals and journals

Periodicals and journals (also referred to as *magazines* and *serials*) are published on a regular basis and thus are an important source of up-to-date information in a subject area. Some periodicals cover very broad subject areas: for example, *New Statesman*. Others cover very specific subject areas, such as the *European Journal of Information Systems*.

Copies of periodicals and journals for the current year will be in the periodical section of the library, whilst those for previous years are usually bound in volumes and found in a different section.

With so many journals being published, it is often difficult to determine the different levels of knowledge contained in each. Table 9.3 divides journals into three categories: scholarly, substantive and popular. For most of your academic work you will need to refer to the scholarly or substantive journals for information.

Exercise 9.2

Categories of journal

In your university or college library, find examples of two (or more) journals in each category for the subject you are studying.

Scholarly: 1

                2

Substantive: 1

                2

Popular: 1

                2

Libraries subscribe to as many periodicals and journals as they can afford, but there are many thousands of journals published throughout the world and it would be very expensive to purchase them all. Abstracting and indexing services provide a very useful and convenient way of finding information, especially in those journals and periodicals to which your library does not subscribe. Increasingly, libraries subscribe to e-journals, so check whether your library has this resource.

Table 9.3 Different types of journal

	Scholarly	Substantive	Popular
Examples	Journal of Applied Psychology Harvard Business Review Long Range Planning	The Economist National Geographic People Management Management Today	Reader's Digest Vogue
Authors	Respected academics or people who have carried out some research in the subject area.	Freelance writers, members of the editorial staff or academics.	Freelance writers, editorial staff and contributions from the general public.
Sources	Sources are always cited using footnotes and/or bibliographies.	Sometimes sources are cited but often they are not.	The information is often second or third hand with the original source indeterminate.
Language	Uses the language of the discipline, assuming some scholarly background of the reader.	Uses language that is suited to any 'educated' audience.	Uses simple language, assuming a minimum level of intelligence.
Appearance	Generally sober, serious look with few glossy pages or exciting pictures.	May be attractive in appearance though some are in newspaper format. Articles may be heavily illustrated.	Glossy, attractive and eye-catching appearance using many photographs and other graphics.
Content	Substantial articles with specialist content. Many refereed articles, i.e. approved by academics other than the author.	A mixture of articles – some specialist and some broad issues. Factually based.	Short articles with little depth to the content. Often include fictional material.
Purpose	To extend the boundaries of knowledge and promote academic debate.	To provide information in a general way to a wide audience of interested people.	To entertain and sell products.

> **! Remember...**
> Use scholarly or substantive journals if you are doing scholarly research or to find bibliographies that lead you to other research in the area.

Abstracts

Abstract journals are reference sources that provide summaries (abstracts) of articles published in a given time period covering a particular field of knowledge. The abstracts should provide sufficient information to enable you to decide whether or not it is necessary to refer to the original article. A full bibliographical reference to the original article should be included to enable the source article to be traced.

Examples of general abstract journals are:

- *Emerald Reviews* (formerly *ANBAR*). This lists abstracts of articles published in a range of quality business journals and magazines. They are broken down into subject areas: for example, Personnel and Training abstracts, and Information Management and Technology abstracts. This is available electronically as well as in hard copy journal format.
- *ABI/INFORM*. This is similar to *Emerald Reviews* but includes a larger proportion of material from the USA.

Many libraries now provide abstracts on CD-ROMs, which offer a fast and easy way of searching. However, whilst more time consuming to search, the printed abstracts tend to be more current than the CD-ROM versions, as they are issued more regularly.

Periodical indexes

Periodical indexes complement the abstracting journals. They are lists of articles giving details of where the articles can be found, so that information published in numerous periodicals and newspapers can be easily traced. Some indexing services cover a single journal or newspaper. Others are published to cover a large number of periodicals dealing with one particular subject. Examples include the British Education Index, Engineering Index, Business Periodicals Index (USA), Current Technology Index (for scientific and technical subjects), and British Humanities Index (for the arts and social sciences). Indexes may be searched using author or broad subject heading. These may be available online if your library subscribes to the service.

When using indexes, take time to ensure that you understand the layout and terminology of the index, as this will differ between indexes. Most indexes will include the following information:

Author(s)

Date of publication

Title of article

Title of periodical or journal

Volume and part number of the publication issue

Page numbers of the article

> **Remember...**
> Use a periodical index when you want to find relevant articles for your topic in journals or newspapers.

> **Activity 9.2**
>
> **Abstracts and periodical indexes**
>
> Locate the abstracts in your library. Identify an abstract that is relevant to a topic you are studying. See if you can locate the original article.
>
> Repeat the activity using the periodical indexes.
>
> Note that you will only be able to locate the original article if the library stocks the particular journal to which the abstract or index refers.

Newspapers

Most libraries subscribe to a number of quality newspapers. These are useful for keeping abreast of current events and developments. Libraries may also keep back copies of newspapers on microfilm or microfiche. CD-ROMs are now available which provide indexes of the contents of back issues (for example, the *Times* index provides an index to all materials contained in the newspapers of the Times Group) and some also include the full text of the articles. Most newspapers now have websites where you can access current editions and search for articles, etc., on particular subjects. Examples include:

The Times	www.timesonline.co.uk
The Financial Times	www.ft.com
The Independent	www.independent.co.uk

It is a good idea to read the quality newspapers regularly to keep abreast of current issues and examples that could be included in your assessments.

> **Remember...**
> Use quality newspapers to find current information on issues and events internationally, nationally and locally.

Government publications and statistics

The Government Statistical Service (GSS) provides most of the official statistics for the UK. The reports and statistics it publishes cover many aspects of national life such as the economy, education, health and the environment. Official statistics are an important reference and a library will usually hold a collection of them. A useful publication is the Central Statistical Office's *Guide to Official Statistics*, which indicates all the statistics and reports that are available. Some of the statistics are also available on its website: www.statistics.gov.uk.

RESEARCHING AND OBTAINING INFORMATION

> **Exercise 9.3**
>
> ### Government statistical publications
>
> Locate the section in the library that houses government statistical publications. In which government statistical publications would you find the following information?
>
> (a) The value of exports from and imports to the UK.
>
> (b) Index numbers of producer prices.
>
> (c) Building society mortgages: balances, arrears and repossessions.
>
> (d) Road and rail passenger transport use.
>
> (e) Spectator attendance at selected sporting events.
>
> (f) Government expenditure on the National Health Service.

Special reports

Some private sector organisations specialise in collecting information and publishing it in report form. Libraries may stock a selection of these. Examples are:

- Mintel, which is one of the best-known publishers of market intelligence information on UK and European consumer and industrial products and services
- the *Jordan Report*, which analyses the financial performance of organisations.

Professional body publications

Many professional bodies have their own publication, which reports recent developments relevant to the members of the profession. Examples of professional body publications are:

The Lancet	British Medical Association
Management Today	Chartered Management Institute
People Management	Chartered Institute of Personnel and Development

Directories

Libraries may hold large reference directories containing factual information. There are a large number of directories and, although each may contain slightly different information, there will be some overlap. It is important to read the introduction to the directory, as it will provide you with information about how the data are arranged and how they were collected. This will help enable you to establish the integrity of the information and to judge whether or you can use it for comparison. Examples of directories are:

- the *Kompass Register*, which lists companies situated in the different regions and counties of the UK
- *Extel*, which provides up-to-date information, mainly financial, on all quoted British companies and some of the major European companies.

Problems associated with printed resources

The printed word has, until recently, been the most popular medium for publishing information. However, when using the printed word as a source of information, you need to be aware of the problems that may be associated with it.

Currency

Books take a long time to get into print; periodicals and journals tend to contain the more up-to-date information. However, some texts are seminal texts, laying the foundations for and influencing more current works. These texts are often worth searching for.

Time

Searching the catalogues and abstracts can be very time consuming unless you use the electronic search mechanisms. Even then, it is still time consuming to search the shelves of libraries to find the exact reference.

Other media

Developments in technology have meant that information may be published on media other than paper.

Audio-visual media

There is now a wealth of information available on all sorts of audio-visual media, such as audiotapes, videotapes, DVDs, slides, photographs and films. All these may be classified and stored in the library according to the Dewey classification system.

Microfilm/microfiche

Some libraries keep some microfilm and/or microfiche on which back issues of newspapers and journals may be held. You will need to familiarise yourself with the equipment for reading the microfilm and microfiche – it can be rather tricky, but worth the effort.

Electronic media

The computer has become an increasingly valuable tool for accessing information. It is unlikely that you will avoid using a computer to search and retrieve information during your studies. Electronic information is becoming a major source within academia, particularly with the use of e-journals and many libraries are now replacing hard copy journals with electronic versions.

CD-ROM

CD-ROMs are now a popular way of publishing information. Some libraries have computers available to access the information held in databases on CD-ROMs.

CD-ROMs are very useful when searching for specific key words or phrases, as the search facilities allow instant access to the topics and/or phrases for which you are searching. The search process may be:

- *'free text'*: a search for the occurrence of particular words or phrases
- *indexed*: words or phrases are selected from the index or thesaurus compiled to describe the contents of the database.

The information available on CD-ROM may be one of the following.

Full text

When the search has found a match for the word or phrase required, it may be possible to display the full text of the article, although diagrams or tabular data may not be included. Examples of these are *The Times*, *Guardian* and *McCarthy*.

Indexing and abstracting

These CD-ROMs provide references and a brief abstract rather than the full text: for example, ABI/INFORM, ERIC (educational and training topics) and INSPEC (information technology related topics). However, remember that the printed indexes may be more up-to-date than the CD-ROM version, as they appear more frequently.

Statistical or figure based

These CD-ROMs hold data of a financial or statistical nature: for example, Extel MicroEXTSTAT (mainly UK companies but with some continental European, US and ASEAN) and Extel MicroVIEW (company database including share prices and official company news items).

When using the CD-ROM facilities, you will probably be expected to do the search yourself. This may be rather daunting if you are doing it for the first time. Libraries may provide printed guidelines, but there is usually a fairly user-friendly search interface.

Some systems allow text and/or data to be transferred directly from the CD-ROM to a word-processing package. However, it is important to remember that this material may be subject to copyright. Remember also that CD-ROMs are a fairly recent phenomenon and therefore you may not be able to search too far back historically.

Activity 9.3

Information held on CD-ROM

Visit the library and identify a CD-ROM that holds information appropriate to your studies.

Determine where the facilities are that enable you to access the information held on the CD-ROM and look at the information on the CD-ROM.

Comment on the usefulness of the information and the way in which it is presented, and compare it with similar information found in books or journals.

PART 1   DEVELOPING STUDY SKILLS

Online databases

New technology means that some libraries now offer facilities for undertaking 'online' searches, which can enable a range of national and international databases to be accessed. An online database enables the user to search for and retrieve current information on a subject of interest. Commercial databases provide information on such things as business performance statistics, company accounts and market information. Searches are performed using a key word or a combination of key words.

Datastream is an example of an online database, which also includes analysis and graphics capabilities. It contains some of the latest accounting and financial information on individual companies and sectors: for example, share prices, balance sheets and accounting ratios. It may also be used to access data such as economic time series for all the major economies of the world.

Although academic libraries will undoubtedly have access to some of the online databases, you may find that access is restricted because of the cost of using them. They can also be very difficult to use and thus may require some training to use effectively.

Often the computer-based facilities in a library are restricted and it is therefore necessary to book time to use them. If this is the case, it is likely that there are also time restrictions, so be sure to know exactly what you want to find and have your key words and phrases prepared in advance.

→ Other sources of secondary information

See Activity 9.3 PRIMARY AND SECONDARY INFORMATION in the Online Study Guide.

There are many other sources of information available, some of which are listed below:

- Local authorities – they collect information on the local environment.
- Public bodies, e.g. national and regional tourist boards, the Civil Aviation Authority.
- Professional associations – they collect information pertinent to their membership e.g. the Chartered Management Institute, trade unions.
- Trade associations – they collect and publish information about activities within a particular industry, e.g. the Federation of Motor Traders, the Glass Manufacturers' Federation.
- Banks, building societies and other financial institutions – they publish reports and special journals, some of which are available to members of the public.
- Commercial research organisations – they tend to be expensive, e.g. British Market Research Bureau.
- The Internet.

→ The Internet

The Internet is often referred to as the world's largest computer network. However, it is actually a collaborative collection of networks enabling the exchange of information between computers across the globe. The exact size of the Internet is difficult to estimate because there is no central ownership and it is growing rapidly as more and more organisations and individuals connect in order to take advantage of the range of facilities it offers.

Each constituent network is owned by some organisation (academic, government or commercial), and each of these will have its own separate management, rules and policies. However, there is no single body that controls, manages or organises the Internet centrally and thus, importantly, no one polices the information or how it is used.

The Internet offers access to a body of global information unparalleled by the largest library imaginable. Much of this information would be too difficult or too expensive to acquire by traditional means. Through the Internet information can be retrieved on almost any topic by browsing newspapers or books, wandering electronically around libraries and museums all over the world, or entering into discussions with people on a whole host of subjects via the chat rooms.

Because there is no central body governing the way in which data are stored and accessed, retrieving information via the Internet can be a difficult and time-consuming process, yielding much irrelevant information. Imagine walking into a huge darkened warehouse with books strewn all over the floor. There is no cataloguing system, no floor plan and a hidden light switch – it would be very difficult to find anything, not to mention a specific reference. This is similar to the Internet – vast amounts of valuable material available, but with no central catalogue to help. Fortunately, however, there are organisations that are continuously developing search tools and techniques to help navigate and reach the resources of the Internet.

Just as you have to become familiar with the techniques of accessing bibliographic information, you will now also need to become accustomed to electronic information retrieval techniques. Once you have become familiar with these, you will be able to access new sources of information from across the world.

Accessing information via the Internet

Because there is so much information available through the Internet, finding what you want is not easy. A number of different search services have been developed and one of the first decisions to be made is which of these to use. The one you ultimately choose will be a matter of preference and depend on the purpose of the search.

For most users, accessing the Internet now means accessing a page on the World Wide Web.

World Wide Web

The World Wide Web (the Web or WWW) is the fastest-growing area of the Internet and was developed to give a more graphic way of finding information on the Internet. The WWW can be thought of as a collection of documents residing on thousands of computers around the world. Information is structured into pages, which may contain text, images, sound, videos (multimedia) and links to documents held on other computers accessible through the Internet. The links create a complicated 'web' of individual pages connected to one or more other pages.

Table 9.4 **Example using the search term 'study skills'**

Search method	Operation
An exact phrase match	The search would look for the specific phrase 'study skills'.
Matches on all words (AND)	The search would look for both 'study' and 'skills' on a page.
Matches on any word (OR)	The search would look for either the word 'study' or the word 'skills' on a page.

The World Wide Web is accessed by using browser software such as Netscape Navigator or Microsoft's Internet Explorer. This software enables you to read documents, view images and carry out most activities with the click of a computer mouse.

There are two main ways of finding information on the Web: search engines and network directories.

Search engines

The browser software provides links to the search engines. These are Web hosts (computers) that hold large databases of the millions of Web pages accessible to them. The search engine host will regularly explore the Web pages and update the databases. Some of the search engines provide an index of the material and may even provide comment on the quality of the site.

Search engines are generally easy to use. Most allow you to type in a key word or phrase (referred to as the *search term*). The search engine will then look for all the pages containing this key word or phrase (see Table 9.4). After extracting the detail from the database, the search engine will present a summary indicating how many documents were found that matched the search terms and rank them according to how many references to the search terms they contain. Paradoxically, the more thorough the search engine is at searching the Web, the more likely it is to yield a daunting tangle of hundreds of links, many of which will be of little value. It is therefore important to refine the search term as much as possible. (See the section on key words and phrases earlier in the chapter.)

Search engines vary in the degree of sophistication they offer for the search. Some allow searches using a single word; others allow several words and the facility to combine the search words in different ways. It may also be possible to select a search area: for example, to search the whole of the Web, UK sites only, sites in English, look for information added in the last three years, etc.

None of the search engines searches every single page of the Web. If you are unable to find the information required using one search engine, it may be useful to try the others.

Examples of popular search engines are Google, Lycos and Excite. See Table 9.5 for some addresses of search engines.

> **Remember...**
> There is no perfect search engine. Use the one which best meets your needs.

Network directories

Network directories or *subject trees* arrange pages under broad subject headings. These link to subheadings, which become more precise as you move down the tree, and eventually to individual pages. Examples of subject directories covering all subject areas are World Wide Web Virtual Library and Yahoo.

More specialised directories are also available, which concentrate on specific subject areas or are aimed at particular users. They do not cover as many Web pages as the general directories but may be more relevant, as they are usually compiled by someone with a specialist interest in the field. Examples of specialist directories are:

- *SOSIG*: the Social Science Information Gateway. This provides a reasonably structured access to information relevant to social scientists. The address is http://www.sosig.ac.uk.

- *HERO: Higher Education and Research Opportunities* (formerly NISS: the National Information on Services and Software). This provides access to information that is relevant to the UK education and research communities. The address is http://www.hero.ac.uk.

Figure 9.2 **Structure of a World Wide Web address**

http://www.campuslife.utoronto.ca/Handbook/learning/studyskills.html

The address can be broken down as follows:

How	Where	What	Format
http://	www.campuslife.utoronto.ca	Handbook/learning/studyskills	.html

www indicates the page is on a Web server. The next part of the address refers to the address of the computer on which the page is stored, in this case the University of Toronto's (*utoronto*) computer in Canada (*ca*). If there is no two-letter code, the address is in the USA. In the UK it is common to find *.ac* indicating an academic organisation or *.co* indicating a commercial organisation.

This part of the filename indicates the format in which the pages are described – in this case hypertext mark-up language.

The *http* refers to the mechanism by which the files are transferred to the local computer. This is usually http (Hypertext Transfer Protocol) or ftp (File Transfer Protocol).

This part refers to the location of the file in that computer system – this address refers to a file called *studyskills* in a subdirectory (*learning*) of the directory *Handbook*.

Addresses

Each page of the Web has its own address or Uniform Resource Locator (URL). The address of any page of the Web is shown in a box towards the top of the computer screen. Sometimes other sources will provide an Internet or WWW address, which enables you to access more information from the Internet.

If you know the exact address of the page of information you require, the browser software has a location box near the top of the computer screen into which you can type the address. However, it must be exact, including punctuation and capitalisation, otherwise the page will not be found.

The addresses look complicated but with use you will be able to recognise the component parts (see Figure 9.2). However, it is worth noting that WWW addresses frequently change as sites are developed and moved or removed.

Moving around

Links between pages are usually indicated by an underline on a particular word. If you move the cursor over the words that are underlined, the pointer should change to a hand, indicating that there is a link to another page containing further information. If you click on this link, the linked page will be accessed.

In the top-left area of the computer screen there are some useful buttons (icons) marked BACK (←) and FORWARD (→) that simplify moving around. Using the computer mouse to point and click on these will allow you to retrace your steps, one step at a time.

Bookmarks

When you have found a site or address that contains useful information, the browser software allows you to mark it with a *bookmark*. This is used like a traditional bookmark and marks any pages you may wish to return to. This facility enables you to return quickly to the site without having to type in the address or go through the search procedures you completed to get there initially.

It is essential to make a note of any addresses from which information has been retrieved so that the information may be referenced correctly when including it in your work.

Saving files

It is possible to save some Web pages as files on a computer disk. These files may then be transferred into a word-processing package for later reference. To do this it is advisable to save the information from the Web in text format – this makes the transfer to a word-processing package easier. One way of saving files in text format is as follows:

1 Select *File* from the menu at the top of the screen.
2 Select *Save As*.
3 Click on *Save file as type*: and select PLAIN TEXT (.TXT).
4 Type in the filename, ensuring it has the extension .txt (for example, MYFILE.TXT).
5 Select OK.

However, copyright laws also apply to electronic information and much of the material on the Web will 'belong' to someone. You must not publish information from the Web without obtaining the permission of the owner.

> **Remember...**
> Any information downloaded from the Internet and used in an assignment must be referenced appropriately.

Information from the Internet

Although the Internet offers access to a wide variety of information from across the globe, the information received must be used with caution. Some search engines attempt to provide some comment on the quality of the websites they access, but generally it is up to you to decide whether the information you retrieve is reliable and valid.

Things to look for are as follows:

- *Quality.* Because the Internet is not controlled and anyone can publish almost anything on it, it can be difficult and time consuming to establish the accuracy, reliability and comprehensiveness of the information.
- *Currency.* It can be difficult to ascertain if a host organisation offering statistical data is taking the responsibility for providing the most up-to-date version of the data, or is simply providing a single snapshot of the data.
- *Source.* Examine closely the source of the information – look at the address and in particular the domain part of the address. There are two types of domain:
    - two- or three-letter designations which identify the type of organisation. For example:

Domain	Likely source
.ac	An academic institution in the UK
.edu	An educational institution in the USA
.com or .co	A commercial organisation
.org	A non-profit organisation
.gov	A governmental body
.net	A network such as an Internet service provider

    - A geographic designation ending in a two-letter country code. For example sites in the UK are generally designated with .uk; US sites have .us and Australian sites .au.

    If the site is based in the UK and the address contains .ac.uk the information is from an academic site and may be used with some confidence. Check the last date the site was maintained (usually found at the bottom of the page) – this will give an indication whether the site is updated and maintained on a regular basis.

- *Focus.* Be aware that a lot of information on the Web is North American in focus rather than European.
- *Interface.* Some users may find that the interface is not very user-friendly and therefore difficult to use.
- *Security.* Although perhaps not an issue for information retrieval, it should be noted that the Internet is liable to unauthorised access from computer hackers.

Some important issues when using the Internet to retrieve information are outlined below.

Time

It can be very time consuming to search the Internet because of the lack of organisational structure. Finding a relevant resource is often achieved by luck and considerable perseverance. Experiment with the different search services until you find those you are comfortable with, but wherever possible use specialised directories for the subject area. It is important to stick to what you are doing and resist the urge to retrieve that vital piece of information that might come in handy for some uncertain thing in the future.

To speed up the transfer of information from the Internet it is possible to request text only. Graphic images slow the transfer down, so retrieve these only when you are certain the file is exactly what you want.

Table 9.5 World Wide Web addresses of some useful search engines

Address (URL)	Description
http://google.com	Google is one of the most popular and comprehensive search engines.
http://scholar.google.com	A relatively new development by Google that enables information suitable for academic work to be retrieved.
http://askjeeves.com	A natural language search engine, i.e. this may be searched by asking questions.
http://www.yahoo.com	Yahoo! Search – a simple-to-use selective subject-based approach with a useful menu-driven facility for refining a basic search. The results page links to sites that match the query and also to subject areas where sites were found.
http://www.elib.com	The Electric Library – a selective catalogue resembling the reference section of a local library.
http://www.excite.com	Excite – a fast and friendly tool for searching the full text of millions of Web pages and thousands of newsgroups. Subject-oriented approach.
http://lycos.co.uk	Lycos – a huge database of websites providing everything from constantly updated stock market share prices to downloadable road maps, a subject guide to sites and a useful multimedia index which can be searched for picture and sound files.
http://hotbot.com	This provides easy access to the Web's three major crawler-based search engines: Google, Yahoo and Teoma (used by Ask Jeeves). It does not blend the results, but it does offer a fast and easy way to get different Web search results in one place.
http://webcrawler.com	Webcrawler – a database of Web pages, indexed by content, which supports natural language searching, i.e. can be searched using plain English. Input search criteria or select a subject area, e.g. arts, education, entertainment, etc.

RESEARCHING AND OBTAINING INFORMATION

> **Stop and think**
> ○ Have you spelt your search term correctly? A search for an incorrect term is time consuming!

Access time

Unless access is via broadband, searching and retrieving information from the Internet can be slow at certain times of the day. It is advisable to use off-peak times (before 11 a.m. and after 11 p.m. UK time). Access may also be speeded up if you take the option not to download the images but concentrate on the text only.

Use bookmarks, wherever possible, to go directly to the sites you use regularly; this removes the need for complex and time-consuming search processes.

Information overload

Be specific with the search terms you use. The network is so large that searches often lead to more responses than you can handle. If you are retrieving hundreds of pages when using search terms, refine your search criteria by using the 'and' and 'or' operators. Most of the search engines offer the facility to 'refine your search'.

A search may retrieve many pages of results. If so, do not look past the first page. It is generally better and quicker to try another search using different search words.

See Activity 9.4 FINDING INFORMATION ON THE WEB in the Online Study Guide.

Suggestions for improving your web search techniques

- *Know where to go.* Use specialist directories where possible. This will reduce the search time.
- *Think small.* Look out for smaller, specialist search engines that are appropriate for your topic. For example www.ancestry.co.uk is a specialist site suitable for those researching genealogy.
- *Be specific.* Avoid using common words or general terms. Try to think of words that are very distinctive to the topic you are researching.
- *Pay attention to your spelling.* It can be very frustrating to wait for a search to be completed only to find that you typed in an incorrect spelling.
- *Learn the language of searching.* Ensure that you know how to express search terms correctly.
- *Stick to the first page.* Don't be tempted to look beyond the first page of results. It is usually better and faster to try another search using alternative key words.
- *Bookmark it.* When you find a site that is interesting and/or provides the information you need, mark it using the bookmark facility or print out the first page. This means you can carry on with the search, returning to the 'marked' sites later.
- *Check the address (URL).* This helps to identify the source and thus reliability of the information contained on the site (see Table 9.3).
- *Ask for help.* Different sites will have different rules and procedures, which can be confusing. You can always ask for help from the search engine's help area.

→ Evaluation of information

See downloadable template 9.1 ANALYSIS OF INFORMATION COLLECTED in the Online Study Guide

It is important to evaluate the information retrieved from secondary sources. Do not just accept the information, but use your powers of reason to ensure the information has the following attributes:

- *Objectivity*. What is the objective of the information provider/publisher – to inform, explain, persuade or 'sell'? Information that is being used to sell something is often biased.
- *Authority*. Check the credentials of the originator of the information. Do they have the credibility to publish the information?
- *Currency*. Check the date of publication or compilation of the source. The information may be out of date and not reflect the current position.
- *Reliability and validity*. The information should not be anecdotal, but should be supported by facts. Any data on which the information is based should have been collected using method(s) that provide reliable and valid results. The way in which the information was gathered – the research methods and sample sizes used – may distort the results. In this case, the information should be treated with caution.
- *Suitability for purpose*. The information may not meet your requirements exactly – it may have been collected with a different purpose or objective in mind. Different definitions, terminology or measurements may have been used. For example, many different definitions and measurements of unemployment are used by the different bodies that publish information in this topic area. Thus it is important to be aware of how the data you choose to use are defined or measured.
- *User friendly*. You must be comfortable with the format of the material you are intending to use. Is it easy to follow and interpret?

Activity 9.4

Retrieving information from the Internet

Find out where you are able to gain access to the Internet in your university or college. Identify a search term for a topic you are studying. Log on to the Internet and use one of the search engines to find any appropriate Web pages.

Look at the first two pages that are identified by the search engine and evaluate the information contained on them using the criteria listed above.

Try a different search engine using the same search term. Evaluate the information displayed on the first three pages.

How does the information compare using the different search engines?

When to stop collecting secondary information

It is difficult to decide when you have sufficient information to complete the piece of work you are researching. There can be a tendency to collect that little bit more, which you are convinced will gain you a better grade. However, there are diminishing returns.

Some useful guidelines to help you decide when to stop gathering information are outlined in the checklist below. If your answers are mostly 'No', you should consider continuing your search for information.

Checklist: when to stop collecting information

Does the new information repeat what I already have?	Yes/No
Does the information I have cover the core material required?	Yes/No
Is the information I am finding now irrelevant?	Yes/No
Am I becoming overwhelmed with the amount of information I have?	Yes/No
Have I run out of time?	Yes/No
Have I picked up all obvious omissions?	Yes/No
Is the information I have of the right depth and level?	Yes/No
Is the information retrieved as up-to-date as possible?	Yes/No
Do I have quality information?	Yes/No
Will the information I have allow me to complete the task?	Yes/No

Suggestions to help improve your search for secondary information

- Define precisely the purpose of gathering the information.
- Plan carefully for the time that it will take to collect the data/information required.
- Take time in defining key words and phrases, ensuring the correct terminology is used.
- Do not be afraid to change your ideas – it is not unusual to find a valuable piece of information that causes you to reflect on what you are doing and prompts you to change direction.
- Get to know the library and librarians.
- Learn how to use the library catalogues.
- Learn how to use all the facilities the library has to offer.
- Have a well-defined subject area.
- Formulate the right questions, key words and/or phrases for searches.
- Work from the general to the specific – find background sources first, then use more specific sources.
- If you are having difficulty finding information, use broader headings and revise your key words (use synonyms).

PART 1 — DEVELOPING STUDY SKILLS

- If your search produces too much information, refine your key words so that they are more specific.
- Exploit bibliographies in texts and journals – they can provide useful sources.
- Use current material where possible.
- Do not be distracted by bits of interesting, though irrelevant, information.
- Ask the librarians for help if you need it.
- Look outside the library.
- Record what you find and where you found it.
- Find a few search engines on the Web that you are comfortable with and bookmark them.

Activity 9.5

Getting to know your library

Visit the library you will use regularly during your studies and obtain a map of the facilities if there is one available.

Collect all the appropriate leaflets that the library issues to help their readers and find the answers to the following questions:

- How many items can be borrowed at any one time?
- How long may the items normally be borrowed for?
- What are the opening times of the library? Normal/weekend/holiday periods?
- Which classification system does the library use?
- What is/are the classification number(s) for the broad subject area you are studying?
- What media are used for the catalogue?
- How does the inter-library loan system operate?
- Where are the audio-visual materials located?
- Where are the abstracts? Are they held in print or on CD-ROM or both?
- What is the name of the librarian who specialises in your field of study?
- How much is charged for overdue books?
- Is there a short-term loan facility?
- Can you gain access to the Internet in the library?
- If so, what do you need? Do you have to book time?
- Which facilities, if any, do you have to book to use?
- Which facilities, if any, do you have to pay for?

RESEARCHING AND OBTAINING INFORMATION

→ **Primary data collection**

For some academic work, it is a requirement that primary data are included. For example, some academic institutions often require students to conduct some primary research for their dissertations. Primary data are data relevant to your research which you collect yourself. The collection of primary data can be very costly and time consuming, so it is essential that all secondary sources are consulted before embarking on primary data collection. This will help to determine what, from whom and how the primary data should be collected.

> **Stop and think** ○ Do you need to collect primary data?

There are many books available covering research methods. This section of this book provides an overview of some of the skills required, but students who need to conduct primary research are advised to seek out a specialist text.

Consideration of objectives and resources

The aims and objectives of the research need to be considered carefully before deciding which is the most appropriate method of primary data collection for the investigation. The objectives must be precisely defined, together with the data required to achieve them. If they are vague at this stage then you may collect irrelevant data or miss something essential.

The results of the search for secondary information will help to determine what primary data need to be collected, but the following issues regarding the primary data you may wish to collect also need to be considered.

- *Accessibility and availability*. You must be certain that the data required can be obtained, given the time and resources available.
- *Sensitivity*. People and organisations are often uncomfortable revealing information that they regard as personal or sensitive. For example, some people may not want to divulge how much they earn, or even how old they are. Organisations tend to be particularly sensitive about issues surrounding employee relations.
- *Confidentiality*. Sometimes the issue of sensitivity may be overcome by assuring confidentiality. If this is the case, confidentiality must be honoured and the confidential nature of the data must be brought to the attention of the reader(s).
- *Moral and ethical issues*. You should not attempt to collect data that will bring you or your institution into disrepute or involve you in breaking the law.

When gathering primary data it is important that the data are reliable, valid and unbiased. If not, the work that they support will not be meaningful or have credibility in the eyes of the reader. These concepts could be expressed more precisely as follows:

- *Reliability.* This is the extent to which a repetition of the research would result in the same data and conclusions – in other words, if the research were to be repeated, by you or another researcher, the same results would be achieved, assuming that nothing has changed.
- *Validity.* This is the extent to which the observations recorded are appropriate to the investigation – do they measure what they are supposed to measure? If the data suggest that A is better than B, you should have confidence that A *is* better than B and that an alternative method of measurement would arrive at the same answer.
- *Unbiased.* Eliminate any systematic errors in the data that may cause bias.

Data coverage

The next decision to be made is where to collect the data. This may be, for example, a single organisation, a number of organisations, the general public, a section of the general public, etc. In other words, the *research population* (also referred to as the *target population*) must be defined.

Research population (target population)

The research population is any complete group of people, objects or entities that share some common characteristic and from which data may be collected. For example, if data about the leisure activities of UK students are required, the research population may be defined as all UK students. The common characteristic is that all members of this population are students in the UK. However, this definition may need to be refined further. For example, the general population 'UK students' consists of a number of different populations, such as full-time students, part-time students, students of a particular discipline, students at a particular level of education (for example, higher education and further education), etc., not all of whom may be appropriate for the investigation. Note that the defined population does not necessarily have to be human in origin – the population could be objects, such as items coming off a production line, or events such as the number of cars passing a particular road junction.

If data are collected from all members of the research population, this is known as a *census*. An example of a census is the collection of data about people living in the UK, which are collected by the government every 10 years.

Often it is impossible to gather data from every member of the defined population because of the impracticalities of doing this, such as the time and cost involved. It is more likely that primary data will be collected from a *sample*.

Sampling

A *sample* is a group of items taken from the population for data collection. The basic idea of sampling is that the sample should be as representative of the population as possible. This is because the data collected from the sample are generally used to predict things about the population from which they were drawn.

> ### Suggestions for deciding when to sample
>
> Take a sample in the following circumstances.
>
> - You have limited time available for the collection and analysis of data.
> - You have limited finances available for the collection of data.
> - Data are not readily available from the population. For example, a population such as homeless people may be difficult to locate.
> - The defined population is large – smaller numbers are easier to deal with and often more checks can be done on the data, which will give a higher level of accuracy.
> - The time taken to collect and analyse data from the whole population means that the results will be out of date by the time the analysis is complete.
> - Collecting data destroys the population (destructive testing). For example, when collecting data about the life of light bulbs coming off a production line, if all the light bulbs produced were tested this would result in no light bulbs being available for sale. Clearly, this is a case where a sample must be taken.
> - There are problems of confidentiality – it may be difficult for organisations to keep their activities from their competitors if they attempt to collect data from the whole population.

When sampling there are two important issues that need to be carefully considered if the reader is to be convinced of the validity of the data collected. First, how large should the sample be? The size of the sample will depend upon the degree of confidence that you need to have in the data collected, and how much error is acceptable when making estimates about the population from the sample data. In other words, how certain do you need to be that the data collected from the sample will reflect the characteristics of the population from which they were collected? The sample needs to be large enough to ensure that it is representative of the population, but not so large that the benefits of sampling are lost. Many research methods texts provide mathematical formulae for determining sample size.

Second, consider how the sample should be selected so that there is adequate representation of the population but bias is not introduced. In some cases it can be difficult, if not impossible, to get a list of all the population members (known as the *sampling frame*). This can cause problems in selecting the sample.

Table 9.6 indicates the different methods by which samples may be selected from their populations and highlights the associated advantages and disadvantages of each method.

To decide which sampling method is most appropriate for your investigation, consider the following factors:

- The resources available to you, particularly time and money.
- The availability of the sampling frame. Some of the sampling methods outlined require you to have a complete list of all the population members.
- Your knowledge of the population. Some sampling methods require a detailed knowledge of the target population.
- The geographical spread of the population.
- The analysis of the data you collect. If non-probability-sampling techniques are used, you cannot use the sample data to project beyond the sample.

Table 9.6 Sampling chart

Types of sampling	Characteristics	Examples	Advantages	Disadvantages
Probability sampling (based on chance selection procedures, every element of the population having an equal and known probability of being selected)					
Simple random sample (SRS)	Each member of the population has the same possibility of being selected. Selection of one item does not affect selection of another.	Drawing names out of a hat; monthly draw of premium bond numbers.	Requires minimum knowledge of the population in advance; no classification errors as it does not make use of any knowledge of the population; simple to use.	Cannot guarantee the sample is free from bias; does not make use of any knowledge of the population.
Systematic	The sample is taken according to a systematic plan - the population is ordered in some way and every *n*th item is taken from the ordered list.	Every tenth customer is interviewed as they leave a shop.	If the population is ordered, it gives a stratification effect and hence reduces variability; easy to conduct.	Fluctuations/variations may coincide with the sampling intervals and thus introduce bias; a sampling frame may not exist.
Multi-stage random sampling	The sample is selected in stages, the sampling units at each stage being selected from the larger units chosen at the previous stage. The number of units selected at each stage should be proportionate to the size of the larger group from which it is selected.	To obtain the views of students at university about the student union, take a random sample of courses, and then take a random sample of students on these courses. The number of students sampled from each of the courses selected is proportionate to the number of students on the course.	Can keep costs down if geographically defined; only a list of the subgroups is needed.	Errors will increase as the number of subgroups selected decreases; errors are likely to be larger than with systematic or random sampling for the same sample size; need to know the size of each subgroup.
Stratified random sampling	The population is divided into strata so that individuals within each stratum are as alike as possible in terms of the stratification factor (e.g. age, sex, occupation), while the strata themselves are as different as possible (this is the reverse of the requirement for clusters). A random sample is selected from each stratum depending on the size.	To survey people affected by a new runway at an airport, stratify the population around the airport based on noise levels experienced, so those individuals in the same stratum experience approximately the same levels of noise. Take a random sample from within each stratum.	A comparison can be made of the stratum; ensures all sections of the population are represented; removes some of the bias of SRS, e.g. if there are equal numbers of male and female but an SRS produces 60:40; uses knowledge of the population to increase the representativeness and precision of the sample.	Need accurate information on the size of the different strata.

Table 9.6 continued

Types of sampling	Characteristics	Examples	Advantages	Disadvantages
Cluster	Items are selected in clusters – a random sample of groups is taken and all members of those groups are sampled. The clusters must be defined in such a way that each cluster is as fully representative of the whole population as possible.	Take a random sample of courses within a university and sample *all* students on these courses.	Low costs if the population is geographically spread; detailed information is required only for the groups selected; characteristics of the groups may be analysed and compared; do not need a complete list of the sample population available – can use a list of groups or clusters	Each member of the population must be assigned uniquely to a group.
Non-probability sampling (The sampler has direct or indirect control over the items selected for the sample. The sample is selected on the basis of a judgement about some appropriate characteristic required of the sample members.)					
Quota	Each member of the population must be assigned uniquely to a group.	Sampling shoppers in the town centre – it may be necessary to have certain numbers (quotas) of people in particular age groups and/or of a particular gender.	Quick, economical, easy to administer; convenient.	May fail to get the required quota; haphazard selection may introduce bias (easily found, willingness to complete, etc.); can only be used for interview surveys.
Convenience sampling	A sample is drawn from the most conveniently available population members.	Students in the coffee bar at the time the researcher goes in are asked their opinions of the college.	Data for large numbers may be gathered quickly and economically; best used for exploratory research when additional research will subsequently be conducted with a probability sample.	Cannot use the results to predict beyond the sample.

Exercise 9.4

Sampling methods

Suggest how you would sample for the following situations, giving reasons for your choice:

(a) An investigation into the resources that are used by people using the university or college library.

(b) A survey of the opinions of people in a town with regard to the development of an out-of-town shopping site.

(c) A survey of residents' opinions of the facilities in the halls of residence of the university.

(d) A study to determine whether there is any difference in the rates of absenteeism in the different age groups of employees.

Data collection

There are three basic methods of collecting primary data, whether the survey is conducted using a sample or the whole population – survey, observation and experimentation.

Surveys

A survey is the collection of standardised data from a specific population or sample. This may be done by the use of questionnaires and/or interviews.

Surveys are a quick and relatively cheap way of gathering data, especially from a large population. However, response rates can be quite low, particularly if the survey is conducted by post. You may also find that respondents do not give answers that reflect their way of life, beliefs and attitudes, but give the answers that they think you want to hear.

Questionnaires

Questionnaires are a popular method of gathering data, particularly for students who are on a tight budget. Great care must be taken in constructing a questionnaire – often, appropriate data are not collected because of a poorly structured questionnaire or an overestimation of the willingness of respondents to complete it. Wherever possible a *pilot study* should be carried out to test the questionnaire. This involves constructing the questionnaire and asking a few members of the sample or population to complete it to determine whether the answers will provide the information required.

A pilot study will also highlight any ambiguities or other such difficulties in the wording of the questions. After the pilot study, questions can be amended in the light of the data obtained, before completing the full study. It may be a good idea to include a few open-ended questions in the pilot study in order to ascertain other areas of information that are relevant, but which have not been covered by questions in the initial draft of the questionnaire.

Questionnaire design

The design of a questionnaire will depend on the following factors:

- The type of data to be collected. This may be factual (for example, the number of hours spent watching TV in a day, the number of children per family) or may include or primarily be opinions and attitudes. This will affect the type of questions used.
- The target population or sample. It is important to recognise the ability of respondents to answer the questions you intend to pose and the time they have available to complete them.
- How the questionnaire is to be administered – personally, by post or telephone.
- How the data collected is to be analysed.

There are a number of different types of question that can be considered when designing a questionnaire. The basic distinction is between questions that are open-ended and those that have pre-defined answers (closed).

Open-ended questions

Open-ended questions give the respondent the opportunity to answer the question in their own words. Using open-ended questions will provide a wide variety of responses in both content and level. Some answers may be only a word or sentence, whereas other respondents may provide lengthy answers.

Although open-ended questions are a valuable way of gathering data, the responses can prove difficult to analyse, so think carefully before including too many of them. They are also reliant on the respondent having an awareness of the subject and being able to articulate their answers. This sort of question is useful for exploratory purposes: for example, to determine what the major issues are before constructing a more detailed questionnaire.

Examples of open-ended questions are as follows:

- What is your opinion of the way in which your organisation has implemented its staff development policy?
- Identify three things that you enjoy about the course you are studying.

Closed questions

Closed questions have pre-defined answers from which the respondent is required to select the most appropriate. They are quick and easy to complete and have the advantage of focusing the respondent on the specific area of interest. The analysis of the data obtained is also somewhat easier than that for open-ended questions.

When choosing the pre-defined answers from which the respondent has to select, ensure that there are sufficient and appropriate responses so that answers are not inhibited. It is useful to include an 'Other' category, which gives the respondent the opportunity to provide a different answer if an appropriate one is not offered. Sometimes you may wish to give the respondent the opportunity to supply more than one answer – if so, provide instructions in the question to indicate this.

There are a number of different formats for the design of pre-defined answer questions depending on the type of answer required. These are described below.

DICHOTOMOUS

The question offers two answers from which the respondents select, for example: 'Yes/No', 'Agree/Disagree'.

Example: Do you own a car?   Yes/No

There is a wide choice of food in the refectory.   Agree/Disagree

TICK BOX

Respondents are asked to select one or more items from a list by ticking the appropriate box or boxes.

Example:

Which of the following do you consider when selecting a holiday destination? (Tick the appropriate box/es)

Weather   ☐
Cost   ☐
Travelling time   ☐
Mode of travel   ☐
Other – please state: _____

PART 1   DEVELOPING STUDY SKILLS

SCALING

The question is designed so that respondents place their answer on a scale. This allows an insight into the respondent's evaluation of the particular aspect under investigation. A number of different types of scale that may be used. For example:

- **Verbal** – the respondent evaluates the aspect against a verbal continuum such as:

    Never ☐   Seldom ☐   Sometimes ☐   Usually ☐   Always ☐

    Strongly ☐   Agree ☐   Neither agree ☐   Disagree ☐   Strongly ☐
    agree   nor disagree   disagree

    This type of scaling is often used to determine people's attitudes or beliefs about things. However, note that there may be a problem with respondents always selecting the middle box.

    Example:

    The choice of food in the refectory is:

    Excellent ☐   Good ☐   Reasonable ☐   Poor ☐   Very poor ☐

- **Semantic differential** The respondent answers by putting a tick or cross on a scale that has a statement at either end. These statements are polar opposites. For example:

    Good 1____2____3____4____5____6____7___ Bad

    Low morale 1____2____3____4____5____6____7___ High morale

    Example:

    What is your preferred style of working?

    Use own initiative 1____2____3____4____5____ Follow set procedures

RANKING

The respondent is asked to place things in order. This is useful if you need to establish the relative importance of the things listed to the respondent. However, there is a limit to the number of items that can be put on the list without causing the respondent some difficulty.

Example:

Rank the following factors in order of importance to you when choosing a hotel to stay in

(1 = most important, 6 = least important):

Cost per night	☐
Quality of food	☐
Service	☐
Leisure facilities	☐
Number of rooms	☐
Cleanliness	☐

RESEARCHING AND OBTAINING INFORMATION

When designing a questionnaire it is important to be perfectly clear in your own mind what you wish to find out and thus why each question is included.

Filter questions

Sometimes you may wish a person who responds to a question in a particular way to skip a question or series of questions. This is known as a *filter question*. If a filter question is used, clear and precise instructions should be included for the respondent. If not, you may confuse them, causing them to answer irrelevant questions. They may also answer the filter question in such a way that they avoid any further questions.

> See Activity 9.5 DESIGNING QUESTION-NAIRES in the Online Study Guide.

Exercise 9.5

Problem questions

Identify the problems with the following questions and suggest suitable alternative wording and/or formats.

(a) How often do you use the library?

(b) Do you have a garden?

(c) Does your university or college library have an open access policy? Yes/No

(d) When do you plan to go on holiday?

(e) Do you not agree that the union representatives are troublemakers?

(f) Do you think that, in academic terms, the module aims to incorporate the theoretical aspects of group behaviour using the perceived realities of pertinent situations?

(g) Do you agree that the refectory offers a wide range of menus?

Table 9.7 Do's and don'ts of questionnaire design

Do	Don't
Use simple, clear and unambiguous questions. There is often no opportunity for the respondent to ask for clarification of the question (postal)	Use leading questions – for example, 'Do you not agree that ...?' Respondents will usually answer 'Yes'. Leading questions make assumptions and often contain elements of approval or disapproval towards the subject.
Arrange questions in a logical sequence	
Tackle only a single issue or aspect in each question.	Use emotive words or phrases.
Use simple language.	Use catch-all questions that ask for information about too many things in one question.
Keep the questionnaire short and to the point.	Use over-personal questions
Be discreet in seeking information on sensitive issues.	Use long questions.
	Use ambiguous questions.
Use pre-printed answers where possible.	Use generalisations and abstractions.
Provide clear instructions.	Use negatives, and particularly double negatives.
Avoid giving the respondent the impression that they should know the answer – include a 'don't know' category if appropriate.	Use hypothetical questions.

Administering the questionnaire

Questionnaires may be administered in a number of different ways. The method you decide to use will depend on the resources available. It will also influence the design of the questionnaire. Questionnaires may be distributed by mail (traditionally or electronically), by telephone or personally.

Postal/mail

This involves sending a questionnaire by post for respondents to complete. Although this is an inexpensive way of gathering data, particularly if the respondents are geographically spread, the response rate is generally quite low.

> **Suggestions for improving the response rate of postal questionnaires**
>
> - Send the questionnaire to a named individual. This may involve some investigative work initially, but you are more likely to get an answer from someone you approach by name.
> - Ask permission before sending the questionnaire.
> - Ensure the instructions for completing the questionnaire are clear and unambiguous.
> - Keep the questionnaire brief and simple. Busy people do not have time to complete lengthy questionnaires and will not struggle to try to understand something if it is not clear. Often questionnaires are completed unsatisfactorily because respondents have misunderstood the question. Remember that there is no opportunity to explain the questions in person to your recipient; the questions must be clear and precise.
> - Collect the completed questionnaires personally. Some people find it more difficult not to do something if they have to face the person making the request. If this is not possible, an alternative is to include a stamped addressed envelope for the return of the questionnaire.
> - If questionnaires are not returned by the due date, send a follow-up letter gently reminding the respondents about the reply and how valuable their response is.

When dealing with questionnaires in this way, include a covering letter. This should be kept as brief as possible but include the following information:

- A full explanation of who you are, what you are doing, what you require and why, and what you intend to do with the data you collect.
- A statement about confidentiality. If the data you are requesting is of a confidential nature, you should acknowledge it and respect this confidentiality.
- If the questionnaire appears long, a statement that the questionnaire has been designed to be quick and easy to complete.
- A date by which the questionnaire must be completed and returned. If the respondent is aware of a deadline, they can assess how much time they have to complete it.
- A contact address or telephone number so that if the respondents have any queries they are able to contact you (if appropriate).

The letter needs to persuade the recipient to answer the questionnaire, so indicate how important their response is to the research. A good response rate may be achieved if they can see some benefit for themselves in completing the questionnaire – for example, you could offer to send them a copy of the results of your analysis. If appropriate, you could invite the involvement of the respondent – for example, if they disagree with any aspect of the survey, invite them to say so and why.

If possible and appropriate, it is a good idea to use headed notepaper, as this establishes your authenticity. Finally, remember to thank the respondent in advance for their time and effort.

> **Exercise 9.6**
>
> **Postal questionnaires**
> List the advantages and disadvantages of collecting data by using a postal questionnaire.

Internet or e-mail

It is also possible to distribute questionnaires over the Internet or using electronic mail. The same issues are relevant for this method as for the traditional postal method. However, be aware that by using electronic media you are immediately introducing bias (by including only those people or organisations that have access to this technology) and this may cause problems in analysing the data you collect.

Telephone

Some questionnaires may be conducted using the telephone. Whilst this does provide two-way communication, it is an expensive and time-consuming way of administering questionnaires. Because data are collected only from those people who are accessible by telephone, this may introduce bias into the sample. This method is often used if an on-the-spot response is required, but it is not a good method for gathering detailed information.

To improve the response rate, find out the name of the person you wish to question and make contact at times when the respondent is available but not busy.

Personally administered questionnaires

Questionnaires may also be completed by a process of interview, i.e. conducted by an interviewer. This means that there is two-way communication (questions may be clarified and elaborated upon if necessary) and visual aids may be used. Although these are time consuming, the response rate tends to be quite high. Using this method enables data to be gathered from a more structured sample: for example, if you are interested in the age of respondents, you can control the number of people you approach in a particular age group.

However, you need to ensure that you (or the interviewer) minimise the influence of your own personal opinions, as there is a tendency for the respondent to offer the answers they think the interviewer wants to hear, rather than giving their own answers and opinions.

> **Checklist: how to prepare a questionnaire**
>
> Will the questionnaire yield all the data required? ☐
> Will the target respondents understand the language used in the questionnaire? ☐
> Are the questions in a logical sequence? ☐
> Are the questions requiring sensitive or controversial responses at a suitable point in the questionnaire? ☐
> Will the layout of the questionnaire encourage the respondents to complete it? ☐
> Will it be easy to analyse the data from the responses given? ☐
>
> *For each question:*
> Is it necessary? ☐
> Will the question provide an appropriate response? ☐
> Will the respondent answer the question correctly? ☐
> Will the meaning of the question be the same to all respondents (no ambiguity)? ☐
> Are there unstated assumptions behind the question? ☐
> Is it a leading question? ☐
> Is the format of the question appropriate for the information required? ☐
> Are the pre-defined choices of answers appropriate? ☐
> Is there sufficient choice of pre-defined answers? ☐

Interviews

Interviews for the collection of data may be structured, unstructured or a combination of both.

Structured interviews are rather like a postal questionnaire in that the questions are pre-prepared. They are a good method to use where factual information is required and are quite common for opinion polls or audience research surveys. Many of the things highlighted in the section on questionnaire design are appropriate for composing questions to be used in a structured interview.

Unstructured interviews are more difficult to carry out. They should be a continuous flowing discussion based on questions and answers. The interviewer must be well informed in the subject area in order to compose pertinent questions as and when required. The respondent must be encouraged to talk about the appropriate issues whilst the interviewer listens, identifies the important issues and writes comprehensive notes without breaking the dialogue. It may be possible to seek the interviewee's approval to tape-record the interview.

Unstructured interviews are appropriate for searching for information that may be useful within a very broad area, but it is difficult to record answers in a structured way, so the analysis of the data can be problematic.

Preparation

Before embarking on an interview, it is essential to be well prepared. The interview is often the only chance you will have to pose your questions and get the infor-

RESEARCHING AND OBTAINING INFORMATION

mation needed. The interviewee(s) will probably be giving up valuable time for the interview and will not appreciate ill-prepared, rambling questions. Prior to the interview:

- Determine the objectives.
- Determine the information you require.
- Formulate your questions.
- Arrange them in a logical sequence.
- Confirm the date, time and place with the interviewee(s).
- Find out how much time will be available for the interview. Bear this in mind in your planning. It is also useful to prepare the interviewee(s) for the interview – if appropriate, write a letter to confirm the details and explain the objective in broad terms. This can save time on the day.

For the interview:

- Dress in an appropriate manner.
- If necessary, ensure you have some form of identification to verify who you are.
- Arrive on time. If you are late, the interviewee(s) may become irritated and not have sufficient time to answer your questions fully.
- Obtain necessary permissions if you are intending to conduct surveys on private property, e.g. on a supermarket forecourt.

Avoid using outdoor sites that are noisy or open to adverse weather conditions – no one will want to stop and answer questions if they are going to get drenched in the process.

Beginning the interview

Always introduce yourself and explain the purpose and objectives of the interview before you start asking questions. This helps to establish rapport and set the interviewee at ease. Be friendly and smile. Confirm the time that each interviewee has available and establish any rules of confidentiality that may apply. Outline the structure of the interview and confirm that this is agreeable to the interviewee. If it is not, you may need to do some negotiation.

You should ask permission to take notes on the answers to your questions. Sometimes it is easier to record the interview and transcribe it later. If this is your plan, you must request permission to record the interview, though some interviewees will not allow this. However, note that the presence of a microphone may inhibit the answers that the interviewee gives.

Once the preliminaries are over, progress to the main part of the interview in a clear and professional manner.

Conducting the interview procedures

When trying to gather information using an interview, always be polite and courteous but tactful and persuasive. Use a soft but audible tone of voice, speaking slowly and deliberately so that you can be understood easily. Sympathise if they say they are very busy and have little time, and express your gratitude for their time.

Figure 9.3 **Strategy for eliciting information from an interview**

LISTEN → REFLECT → SUMMARISE

Be precise in asking the questions, keep your objectives in mind and do not digress or ramble. Sequence the questions in a logical order so that they flow naturally. The questions should move from simple to complex. Do not confront the interviewee with an early and sudden request for personal information. Try to keep the questions open-ended and avoid closed questions that invoke a yes/no answer. You need to encourage the interviewee to provide full answers to your questions.

You must try to maintain the interest of the respondent, particularly if it is a lengthy interview. If you appear uninterested, you cannot expect your interviewee to be interested. Use active listening skills and non-verbal communication to encourage the interviewee to provide good answers. Prompt the interviewee as necessary by saying 'Yes, and ...', 'Go on ...', etc., and use non-verbal prompts such as head nods, smiles and raised eyebrows.

Suggestions for conducting an interview

- Allow the interviewee time to think; do not be tempted to break the silence. However, if it becomes obvious that the interviewee does not understand the question, be prepared to reframe it.
- Avoid the temptation to do all the talking – you are there to interview, not to present your views.
- Avoid asking leading questions and beware of introducing bias in the response by indicating your own feelings or leading the respondent.
- Never suggest answers, but remain neutral.
- Do not become agitated by the response or attitude of the respondent, but remain calm – control your body language signals, trying not to show your reaction to an answer.
- Take care in noting down the responses given, recording the answers legibly.
- Summarise occasionally – this will help the respondent and provides a check for you to ensure the answers given have been understood.
- Be prepared to be flexible – if the original plan for the interview disintegrates, do not panic, but try to get the best out of the situation.

RESEARCHING AND OBTAINING INFORMATION

Closing the interview

To draw the interview to a close, summarise the ground that has been covered. Ask the interviewee if they wish to pose any questions to you, and answer them. If appropriate, explain the next stages of the research and arrange any future communication that may be required. Before leaving, be sure to thank the respondent for their time and participation.

After the interview

When the interview is over, write up the notes as soon as possible while they are still fresh in your mind. Send a letter to the interviewee thanking them for their time and trouble.

Although interviews can be expensive in both time and money, they can eliminate the problems of a low response rate and incorrect completion of questionnaires. They also have the advantage that an interviewer can note down any observations they make. For example, it may be appropriate to know about the respondent's reactions, home, appearance, etc. These data would not be available from a postal questionnaire.

When interviewing, be wary of providing direction and guidance to the respondent beyond that provided by the interview schedule. Also, you should attempt to prompt and probe each respondent in the same way. It is easy, without realising it, to approach a respondent positively, or negatively, because of subconscious factors. This leads to one of the most common problems with interviews – the introduction of interviewer bias.

Exercise 9.7

Gathering data by questionnaire or interview

Assess each situation described below and decide which would be the better method of gathering data (postal questionnaire or interview):

(a) You need to be sure that a particular person answers the questions.
(b) The respondents are all over Yorkshire, Humberside and Lincolnshire.
(c) You need to be sure of a particular structure for your sample.
(d) The questions you need to ask are complex and require detailed explanation.
(e) The questions are of a personal nature.
(f) Time is an important factor in completing the data collection.
(g) The questions require a spontaneous response.

Observation

Gathering primary data through observation involves listening to people and observing their behaviour. Observation may also be used if you are collecting data about events. For example, when researchers collect data about the traffic using a particular road, they observe what actually happens. It would be difficult to collect data about traffic in any other way. However, there are some situations that would prove impossible to observe – for example, observing what people would do if they won the national lottery.

An advantage of observation as a method of collecting data is that there is less chance of collecting incorrect data through respondents misinterpreting the questions. However, you need to be accurate and diligent in your observation. Observation can be a useful way of checking for bias after gathering data by survey methods – do the respondents actually do what they say they do?

As an observer, you may fully participate in what you are observing, although sometimes this may be inappropriate and you should remain completely detached. Each of these approaches is problematic. If, for example, you are a full participant observing a situation, you could become so immersed in it that you are unable to be objective and become biased. On the other hand, if you observe but do not participate, you may miss much of the richness of the situation.

Although observation can be inexpensive to carry out, there are some situations where it could prove costly – for example, it may not be very efficient to follow a manager around all day to observe how they spend their time.

When carrying out observation, it is important to remember that the act of observing may cause the person(s) being observed to change their behaviour. The results therefore will not provide a picture of the normal situation. It is sometimes possible to overcome this by using concealed means: for example, hidden cameras in supermarkets to observe the effectiveness of a display. However, it is important to remember that if people are involved in the observation exercise, you must get their consent beforehand. These are ethical issues that must be considered at the outset of the research.

A drawback of this method of data collection is that it does not enable you to probe into the underlying reasons why someone or something behaves in the way it is observed. For example, a traffic census will determine the number of cars passing a particular junction, but not why they pass.

Exercise 9.8

Collecting data by observation
Identify the problems and advantages of collecting data using observation.

Experimentation

Many people think of experiments in a laboratory setting, with people in white coats surrounded by test tubes, chemicals, samples, etc. Others view experiments as simply trying something different to see whether the outcome improves: for example, planting vegetables earlier than usual in the year to see if a better crop results, or painting a room a different colour to see if the ambience improves. Both of these are examples of experiments. It is not what is done but the way it is done that qualifies something as an experiment.

Experiments may be designed to:

- answer such questions as 'What if . . .' – for example, *'What* will happen to sales *if* we change the wrapper on a product?'
- measure a particular attribute, such as the speed with which a car can take a bend in the road without rolling over
- test out a hypothesis – for example, you may believe that students prefer beer X to beer Y and an experiment may be set up to determine if this presumption is correct.

Experiments involve the researcher in constructing situations so that the conditions are controlled and the variables may be manipulated. This will allow any causal relationships to be evaluated, i.e. whether the change in one variable causes a change in another. The methods of carrying out experiments are beyond the scope of this text. If you choose to collect data in this way, it would be advisable to refer to textbooks covering research methods in more detail.

> ### Exercise 9.9
> #### Gathering data through experiments
> Provide examples of instances when it would be appropriate to gather data through experiments. Identify the problems and advantages of gathering data in this way.

Whichever way you decide is the most appropriate to collect the data required, it is important to remember that the respondents have a right to refuse to take part in the data collection, unless of course they are required to provide the data by law, as in the UK ten-year national census. Do not assume that everyone will respond to a request for data. You need to make provision for non-responses.

→ Analysis of data

Once the data have been collected, they must be analysed in some way in order to make sense of them. The analysis will depend on the type of data that you have collected. Some data will lend themselves to quantitative analysis, whereas other data will be inappropriate for this and require a qualitative treatment.

A number of different computer software packages are available, which will provide an analysis of the data: for example, Minitab, SPSS and Snap. If you decide to use one of these, ensure that you know at an early stage in what format the package will expect the data to be input. This will be a factor in the design of your data collection.

A detailed look at the analysis of data is beyond the scope of this book. Texts that include quantitative and qualitative data analysis should be consulted.

> ### Activity 9.6
> #### Gathering data
> The local theatre is considering the production of a series of plays by modern aspiring authors. They intend to cover six during the year, each play being staged on four consecutive Thursday evenings. Nothing like this has been tried in the city before, but the theatre management is anxious to try new things and wishes to establish potential levels of demand.
>
> You have been asked to conduct research to determine whether or not this will be a worthwhile venture.
>
> (a) Explain how you would select a suitable sample.
> (b) Which sampling method would you choose? Give reasons for your choice (and any assumptions you make).
> (c) How would you collect the data your require?

Summary

This chapter has outlined:
- that information, both primary and secondary, is a vital resource for every student
- the wide range of sources of secondary data available, including electronic sources
- the importance of determining the purpose for which the information is required and being adept at using key words and phrases, and search terms
- the need to check information and sources for reliability and validity
- if primary research is required, the importance of planning carefully in order to ensure that the data collection method used is appropriate and yields data that are reliable, valid and unbiased.

RESEARCHING AND OBTAINING INFORMATION

→ Answers to exercises

9.1
Key words/phrases: information, value of information, decision behaviour

Related terms/synonyms: decision making, decision-making style, data, worth, problem solving, etc.

9.2
Further examples of scholarly journals include *Long Range Planning* and *British Journal of Industrial Relations*.

Further examples of substantive journals include *Personnel Management* and *Management Today*.

Further examples of popular magazines include *Good Housekeeping* and *Hello Magazine*.

9.3
The answers to these questions may be found in:
(a) *Monthly Digest of Statistics*
(b) *Monthly Digest of Statistics*
(c) *Social Trends*
(d) *Social Trends*
(e) *Social Trends*
(f) *Annual Abstract of Statistics*

9.4
(a) Systematic – for example, every tenth person leaving the resource centre.
(b) Obtain a list of residents from the local library, number them and use random number tables to select the sample, *or* stratify the population according to how close each member lives to the proposed site.
(c) Obtain a list of the halls of residence; take a sample from each in proportion to the number of residents in each.
(d) Obtain the age profile of the employees and sample according to the number in each age range.

9.5
(a) This may mean different things to different people. 'Use the library' is a very general term. Are you interested in which library facility is used – books, journals, computer-based facilities, reading rooms, etc? This question may be better structured with a list of the library facilities you are interested in and a series of pre-defined statements about usage, e.g. once a week.
(b) 'Garden' means different things to different people – the question needs to be more specific and if necessary define what is meant by a garden.
(c) This question puts pressure on the respondents to know the answer, as the only choice is Yes or No. Add a further choice of Don't know.
(d) This question is prestige loaded – respondents may answer falsely, i.e. that they are going on holiday, for status reasons.
(e) This question contains an emotive word – troublemaker. It is also a generalisation.
(f) This question uses complex language, which may confuse the respondent. Reword the question using simple language that all respondents will easily understand.
(g) This is a leading question. Use a pre-defined response (scaling or semantic differential).

9.6
Advantages include: reasonably cheap and easy to administer, allows data collection from a geographically spread population, respondents' answers are not affected by interviewer bias.

Disadvantages include: low response rate, respondents who return questionnaires may be untypical of the population, question design is crucial as the respondent is unable to ask for clarification, responses are not spontaneous.

9.7
(a) Interview
(b) Postal questionnaire
(c) Interview
(d) Interview
(e) Interview
(f) Personally administered questionnaire
(g) Telephone questionnaire

9.8
Problems include setting it up, bias resulting from the observed knowing they are being observed, can be time-consuming and expensive, often unable to determine underlying reasons.

Advantages include getting information about things that could not be asked via a questionnaire or interview (e.g. behaviour, environment), gathering information about actual events rather than relying on someone's account, not liable to misinterpretation by respondents.

9.9
Examples could include new product testing, determining people's reactions or actions, etc.

10 Group and team-working skills

> **Learning outcomes**
>
> After studying this chapter, you should be able to:
> - summarise the major features of group work
> - describe the main characteristics of a group
> - identify a range of factors which influence groups
> - specify a number of group processes
> - contrast groups and teams
> - participate in group work with increased self-assurance.

→ Introduction

During university or college life, working as part of a group and submitting group work that will be assessed towards your qualification is common. This may require group presentations or the compilation of group reports. Having to work closely with others may not be something you are used to at the moment, although at university or college it may become an everyday experience. This is a reflection of organisational life, as employees have to rely on others to provide them with information in order to be able to carry out their duties. The overwhelming reason for the use of groups in organisations is that they improve performance, and that is why it is necessary to understand the intricacies of group work.

Some students do not like certain aspects of group work. Occasionally, for example, frustration occurs because less effective group members are diluting individual effort. Alternatively, uncomfortable peer pressure may be exerted to make individual group members work harder or meet deadlines, etc. It is important to come to terms with group work as groups are a fact of student life. A greater knowledge and understanding of how groups operate will enable you to be more effective as a group member. This chapter will provide an insight into what happens when people get together to work in groups. As well as being a fact of student life, groups are the 'building blocks' of organisations. Organisations require group working in project groups or teams to undertake tasks. It is also likely that you will have to work in groups at university or college to complete assessments for the course. Whilst the focus of this chapter is to enable you to become a more effective group member during your studies, the information is equally relevant for all group work.

→ Why should students know about group dynamics?

See Activity 10.1 HOW TO BE A GOOD LISTENER in the Online Study Guide.

At times in university or college life you will experience the joys and benefits of group work as well as some of the frustrations. You will undoubtedly experience *group synergy* at some time during your course. Group synergy is when the output of the group effort is more than the sum of the individual inputs. An example of this is team sports when each person contributes his or her individual skill towards the team effort, which is greater than the sum of each individual's efforts. A particularly good illustration of this is when the 'underdog' team wins against all the odds – they win because they strive as a team and they are able to achieve much more than either they or their opponents expect.

A group has to deal with a number of issues when it is first formed and during its lifetime while it performs the tasks it has been set up to complete. The group will have to allocate tasks to individual members. The size of the group will have an influence on the behaviour and feelings of individuals. Some students prefer to work in small groups while others prefer the security of a larger group. The behaviour of individual student members will influence and affect the way the group interacts and develops. It will also determine who plays which role in the group. The patterns of behaviour that develop and the roles allocated will in turn reinforce or inhibit the behaviour of other students who participate in the group's activities, or who join the group at a later date.

Power relationships within and between groups influence who does what for whom. Some students will attempt to lead a particular group or manipulate the group into doing what they want. Status relationships are important in determining a person's standing in particular groups. Some students may defer to a particular group member because he or she has access to particular information or expert knowledge. An understanding of these relationships can help you to deal with interpersonal dynamics in group situations.

The cohesiveness evident within a group is an important factor in influencing the level of group effort and performance. When working in groups at university or college, the group will need to utilise group cohesiveness productively, but it is essential to avoid the negative aspects of too much cohesiveness.

It is possible to become a more effective group member if you understand the diverse factors that influence groups. The various aspects of group work will be explored in more detail in this chapter.

> **Remember...**
> Some of your assessments may involve group work.

> **Stop and think**
> - How many groups do you participate in?
> - What are the differences and similarities between them?
> - What do you like/dislike about each group?
> - What are the goals of each of the groups?
> - Is each group successful in achieving its goals?
> - How could each group improve the way it operates?

→ Small group dynamics

Group dynamics is the name given to the way that a group deals with the factors that affect it from within itself, such as the interactions of the student members and how the group grows and develops over time. These aspects of groups can be quite difficult to identify and analyse. However, there are some aspects of a group that can be identified easily and a number of these are summarised in Figure 10.1. For example, a group will have a number of members, some form of structure, a purpose or goal, and other relatively fixed factors such as the times when it meets. It will also have a task to complete: for example, to produce a product or provide a service over a period of time. In university or college this is likely to be an assessment. A group will change over time through development and interaction as well as reacting to the situational pressures faced. In addition, the group will need to deal with how the members interact together. This interaction is called *process* or *dynamics* and some assessments may require reflection about, and analysis of, this aspect of group work.

All group work consists of both task and process elements. Frequently, student attention is focused on the task and the process issues are neglected. However, the group will

Figure 10.1 Factors that affect groups

PART 1   DEVELOPING STUDY SKILLS

always be affected by the ways that the student members work together. Group process or dynamics is frequently ignored, even though it can be the major cause of ineffective group working. It is important, therefore, for students to learn to be sensitive to the aspects of group process so that any difficulties that occur can be dealt with effectively. Leadership struggles, conflict, competition, participation, cooperation and group atmosphere are all factors that affect the group's ability to perform. An awareness of the factors and an ability to diagnose and deal with them will enable you to become a more effective group member.

Knowledge of small group dynamics will lead to an understanding of the interactions with other students when working together as a group because predictable patterns of behaviour usually develop. A few areas to be aware of are:

- how the group interacts and influences individual members
- the ways in which the group influences the individual
- the relationships between groups
- the group's interactions with the larger organisation.

Students who have an understanding of what happens when people meet in groups increase their influence in any groups of which they are members.

> **Remember...**
> Understanding group processes increases your influence in groups.

Group goals

See Activity 10.2 SELF ESTEEM QUIZ in the Online Study Guide.

All groups have goals to achieve. The goals may be the product or output from the group, though sub-goals could be to enjoy meeting and make friends. These goals form the basis of interactions out of which certain types of behaviour are likely to emerge. The goals of student groups will be to complete assessments and probably to get on well together. In some instances, as part of the assessment it may be a requirement to analyse the relationships between the various students in a group. It may be necessary to compare the way a group works using a particular group model and to discuss the efficiency and effectiveness of the group as it completes the set task.

Stop and think   ○ Do your assessments require the analysis of group relationships?

Organisation or structure

This applies to certain aspects of group work, such as procedures; rules; particular tasks for individual students; the way the group operates in making decisions; and who reports to whom. Some type of group structure will arise spontaneously because most students feel more comfortable given a framework within which to work. There will be some informal aspects of structure, perhaps a sharing of leadership, and others that will be agreed upon by the group members. As the group develops, certain patterns of behaviour and relationships will occur. Some of these are not formally agreed, but are shared psychologically by the members of the group. Whether the group members are consciously aware of them or not, each student will be influenced by the patterns. In all groups these patterns of behaviour are unwritten, informal guidelines that group members develop and accept in the majority of cases without realising it. These patterns of behaviour are called *norms*.

→ Development of norms

Norms always develop in groups and will control or inhibit the behaviour of individual members in a particular set of circumstances. They provide a framework for how group members should, ought to and must behave, and will usually operate without anyone writing them down or verbalising them in any way. The norms that emerge in student groups will be influenced by a number of factors such as the size of the group, the frequency of meetings and the environment in which the group operates. Norms may be known by all, known by only a few, or operating completely below the level of awareness of the various students who make up the group. They are also affected by the personalities of the individuals involved in the group, their experience, the ambiguities and demands faced and the problems to be solved.

Groups vary widely in the types of norm they develop. For example, a particular group may develop norms to encourage everyone to perform extremely diligently to produce high-quality work in pursuit of high grades. In another student group the norms may be completely the opposite and all group members may do as little work as possible with the consequence that some students actually fail. Within groups at university or college there will be a whole range of behaviours that are acceptable and a number that are unacceptable. In many cases, group members will not be aware of the norms operating and of the fact that these are exerting considerable influence on the behaviour of the majority of students in the group.

Activity 10.1

Group norms

The next time you work in a student group, look for answers to the following questions as they will give an indication of the types of norm that are operating. Make notes of your observations.

- Does the group avoid certain topics, such as absentees, lack of progress in achieving the set task, leader behaviour, etc?
- How is this avoidance achieved and maintained?
- Are there participation norms: for example does each person feel obliged to speak?
- Are some people not expected to contribute?
- Are questions restricted to innocuous subjects?
- Does the group expect a particular student to make all decisions or take control?

- Is it acceptable for some students to be late for meetings, but not others?
- Is conflict and disagreement avoided or encouraged?
- Are group members always polite to each other?
- Is a questioning or challenging approach encouraged?
- Are only positive or only negative feelings expressed?
- Are group members able to express their feelings?

Drawing on your observations, complete the following:

- Identify and write down the norms that operate.
- Which norms encourage certain types of behaviour?
- Which norms discourage or inhibit certain types of behaviour?
- Check out your conclusions with a student colleague to see if their perceptions match your own.
- How can you use this information in the future?

Norms always exist even if it is not possible to identify them, and these rules will influence the behaviour expected of the student members; those who do not conform to the norms will face sanctions or punishments from the group. Sanctions will vary from group to group and can include making fun of someone, ignoring them and, in extreme cases, threatening behaviour. However, it is possible to influence how the group operates: for example, by raising the issue of which norms are operating and in what ways they affect the functioning of the group.

Roles

Whenever people work together on a common goal, roles emerge and this will occur in student groups. Each individual group member will display particular behaviours that occur on a regular basis. These are the roles that group members play over time. Roles can be categorised as group task roles, group maintenance roles and self-seeking roles. (based on Benne and Sheats, 1948).

Group task roles

Some people spontaneously assume certain roles related to achieving the tasks or purposes of the group. Among roles of this type are initiator, contributor, information gatherer, opinion seeker, information giver, opinion giver, elaborator, coordinator, evaluator, critic, energiser, record keeper, proposer, summariser, ideas generator, opposer, clarifier, planner, organiser, goal-setter and timekeeper.

Typical behaviours displayed by students who adopt these roles are as follows.

Ideas generator

A student who adopts the ideas generator role will come up with plenty of new ideas, and will suggest new ways of doing things.

Information giver

An information giver will provide relevant facts, searching out information to assist the group in completing the set task.

Evaluator

The student who takes on the evaluator role will evaluate the ideas presented to the group and measure the progress that the group is making towards achieving the output required.

Coordinator

The coordinator will bring together ideas and suggestions and coordinate the activities of the group.

> **Remember...**
> When working in your student groups, it is important to think in terms of the functions that the roles are fulfilling rather than trying to be too precise about labelling the role.

Stop and think

Who is fulfilling the task role? Is someone:
- trying to make sure that the group is on target to complete the task?
- stopping the group going off at a tangent?
- summarising what has been done and listing what else needs to be done to complete the task?
- providing facts, ideas, feedback or alternative proposals to complete the task?
- organising the working areas satisfactorily?
- keeping records, sharing information, planning?

If someone, or several people, are performing these roles, they are adopting a group task role. When group members perform these roles, it will help the group complete the set task.

Group maintenance or process roles

Student groups need to beware of pursuing the task at the expense of maintaining relationships. If group maintenance is devalued or ignored, individual student members will focus on their own needs and lose sight of what the group has to achieve. This will increase misunderstandings and lead to discord and conflict that will in turn decrease the effectiveness of the group. There is a need to maintain the group through encouragement, respect and trust, and by valuing the contribution of each group member. Inevitably, some students in the group will develop and maintain the group, whilst other students will pursue the task unaware of maintenance issues, and yet others will fulfil their personal needs rather than meeting the needs of the group. Individuals will also adopt roles that fulfil the social and emotional relationships in the group. Some student members will support others with whom they agree, defend those under attack, and help other students to be heard – these are examples of group maintenance roles. Among roles of this type are encourager, harmoniser, compromiser, gatekeeper, mediator, standard setter, commentator, follower, carer, adviser, negotiator, facilitator, helper, peacemaker, supporter and teacher.

Group maintenance behaviours help the group members to get on with each other more effectively. The following provides advice about the behaviours to look out for in student groups when a group member is displaying a particular type of behaviour.

Gatekeeper

This group member will make sure that everybody has a fair opportunity to join in the discussions by specifically asking the quieter members of the group their views and limiting the contributions of the more vociferous ones. The student who adopts the gatekeeper role will open up channels of communication in the group and may prevent the group from being denied important or necessary information as well as unfounded criticism.

Compromiser

The compromiser will give ground on his or her point of view. They are usually prepared to acknowledge that the overall value of the argument put forward by other students will enable the group as a whole to achieve greater progress. A student who adopts this role will encourage compromise generally in the group.

Harmoniser

This group member will act as an intermediary when differences of opinion prevent the group from making progress. This student will reconcile viewpoints and attempt to deal with conflicts to ensure that the opponents reach an amicable solution.

Supporter and encourager

The student who is a supporter and encourager will invite contributions from other students and be warm, friendly and responsive. He or she will give credit and praise to others for their contribution and be helpful in encouraging newcomers or shy members to join in the discussions.

Self-seeking roles

Self-seeking roles are more likely to be an indicator of an individual student's personality. An individual may consistently try to dominate others in all groups that he or she joins. He or she may become the group humorist, aggressor, blocker, recognition seeker, avoider, dominator, politician, cynic, clown, game player, flirt, self-confessor or special-interest pleader. Typical behaviours displayed by group members who adopt self-seeking roles are as follows.

Aggressor

This group member will criticise other members of the group, argue with reasonable points put forward by others, and appear to be ready for a fight with anyone.

Dominator

This group member will try to control and/or take over the meeting, manipulate the group to his or her views and attempt to have disproportionate influence over the group's decisions. The student who adopts this role will typically try to dominate the group and prevent others from contributing fully.

Blocker

This group member will reject the views of other group members, raise insignificant points to delay or halt the proceedings, or waste time by raising unrelated issues. The student who adopts this role will present negative views and opinions about the task the group is pursuing as well as impeding the developing relationships within the group.

Recognition seeker

This group member will constantly boast about their achievements, point out their status or expertise, and introduce an apparently impressive solution to every problem. In many cases this solution is less impressive on closer inspection.

When working in groups, watch out for people adopting the roles outlined above. It will be possible to observe most of them over time. If all of them are not observed at university or college, be vigilant when in employment as they will appear sooner or later. You may be fortunate enough not to encounter an aggressor or a blocker during the course of your studies, but may face him or her across the table in a meeting with a manager when the stakes could be considerably higher.

If you let your imagination roam, there are many more roles to identify and you may wish to develop your own role categories – for example, watch out for the dolly bird, medallion man, seducer, superman, moaner, whistle-blower, con man or woman, lame duck and fixer.

Cohesiveness

If group members have similar interests and backgrounds, this will help to develop cohesion and could lead to an improvement in the performance of a group. The term *cohesiveness* is generally used to refer to the degree to which members desire to stay in the group and express agreement with the group's goals. Unlike the structure of the group and how it operates, which members can shape, cohesiveness is a product of interactions.

There are both advantages and disadvantages of cohesiveness.

Advantages of cohesiveness

A frequently encountered assumption about group working is that there is a link between high morale and output. Team sports are the most obvious example.

Camaraderie is regarded as an essential element in a winning team. In other words, cohesiveness is a desirable attribute for all groups to attain, as highly cohesive groups communicate and cooperate more, respond more to group influence, achieve goals more efficiently, and experience greater satisfaction from working in that group. Cohesiveness is also said to increase trust, confidence, self-esteem and acceptance among members, as well as commitment and loyalty to the group goals. The pressures that a cohesive group exerts on its members to conform give the group more influence over the individual. Very cohesive groups tend to meet important needs of the members. In fact, within groups individual behaviour is highly influenced by other group members. It is very difficult for an individual group member to hold out against the wishes of the group.

High cohesiveness is also identified with *group maturity*. As groups go through developmental stages, members have to complete tasks and deal with interpersonal relationships, and this facilitates increased maturity. So, as the group becomes more mature, cohesiveness also increases. It would be most unusual not to experience working in a cohesive group during studies at university or college. Look for indications of cohesiveness developing in student groups through such aspects as effective communication, friendships, confidence in the other students, feelings of responsibility to work hard and achieve good grades, few disagreements and general compliance with the wishes of the group. Unfortunately, it is not possible to prove that highly cohesive groups perform better than less cohesive groups, and there are a number of disadvantages of cohesiveness which all groups need to appreciate.

Disadvantages of cohesiveness

A student group may become highly cohesive under the pressure of doing the work required, developing friendships and conforming behaviour. Cohesiveness, however, may be detrimental if it removes conflict. If a group agrees about everything all the time, it may be missing important alternative perspectives, approaches or new ways of doing things. All groups should have a certain level of conflict in order to overcome the disadvantages of cohesiveness. Student groups also need to guard against too much similarity of the behaviour that brings increased cohesiveness as this can actually be counterproductive. The group can be blind to alternative approaches and may take inappropriate actions based on emotional factors, accepting too readily that it has the capabilities to perform. Instead of taking a questioning stance, the group may believe that it cannot be wrong and that therefore it is acceptable to cover up unethical behaviour, misconduct or rule breaking. If one of the members challenges this approach, actions are justified as being in the interests of the group and the individual student has to conform to what have become norms of the group. Some group members may act to prevent the group from receiving certain adverse information. In fact, it could be suggested that the group becomes almost obsessed with taking certain actions which negatively affect the overall output of the group. In the face of external and internal feedback that does not match with the prevailing view in the group, the student leaders will blame external factors for problems that arise or poor decisions made. Students may refuse to look at how the group functions and justify poor performance and output on factors beyond their control.

Cohesiveness is undoubtedly a desirable characteristic for student and other groups as it facilitates the development of the group through various phases. However, as student groups become more cohesive, it is important to guard against the disadvantages that increasing levels of cohesiveness bring.

→ Developmental stages of groups

Groups go through certain stages as they grow and develop, although not all groups go through each stage with the same speed or intensity. It is important to appreciate that student groups will certainly go through stages of development. These stages cannot be avoided, speeded up or ignored (see Figure 10.2).

> **Remember...**
> There will be times when the group is affected by pressures of deadlines, absence of an influential member, a traumatic experience, or a new member joining, and this will accelerate or inhibit development.

Bear in mind also that the group composition may be decided by the tutor and as a consequence some group members may not wish to be in the group at all. They may be hostile to the other group members and the set task. On the other hand, there will be occasions when the group will be self-selected – members choose to be in the group. In this case, group members will probably like each other, gain a great deal from group work and enjoy sharing the successes and difficulties encountered, but need to guard against too much cohesiveness. Interestingly, some self-selecting student groups that choose to work with friends come to regret their choices, especially if the friend turns out to be a freewheeler or does not deliver the work on time or to the required quality

Figure 10.2 **Stages of group development**

- Adjourning
- Performing
- Norming
- Storming
- Forming

standard. Often groups that are constructed by the tutor learn more than self-selecting groups.

It is difficult to be precise about the number of stages a group will go through, but there will be several. One of the most popular models of group development is that of Tuckman (1965), who identified four stages.

Stage 1 - Forming

At this stage the group members will be interested in getting to know each other. Individuals will not express strongly held views to avoid rejection. The tendency is to be polite and try to identify leadership and other roles. Group members will try to find out what behaviours are acceptable. At this stage the task is a secondary consideration.

Stage 2 - Storming

This stage is characterised by conflict. There may be disagreements over leadership and how to carry out the task and group goals. Group members will attempt to resist the influence of the group. Some group members will find the hostility difficult to cope with and withdraw from the tension generated in the group. The group cannot progress to the next stage until the conflict has been managed effectively.

Stage 3 - Norming

The guidelines and standards become accepted in this stage and cooperation and compromise are evident. Cooperation ensures that the group members plan the task, commit to the group goals and agree about levels of performance. Close relationships develop, promoting harmony, open communication and sharing of information. Group cohesiveness develops as members are mutually supportive, empathetic and concerned for others.

Stage 4 - Performing

At this stage the group completes the task effectively and efficiently. Individual roles are accepted and valued within the group structure as contributing towards performance. The focus is on solving problems and taking decisions to achieve group goals. The group's energy is directed towards completing the task rather than dealing with conflict.

In 1977, Tuckman with Jensen added a fifth stage to the model. The fifth stage does not apply to permanent groups, only to those that are put together temporarily to complete a time-constrained project.

Stage 5 - Adjourning

This stage is characterised by feelings of loss and parting as the group has completed the task and individuals go their separate ways. Individuals may have to deal with loss of friendships if the group is disbanded at the end of the project. The group may also have to deal with feelings of elation and fulfilment at completing the task, especially if the outcome is highly successful.

Moving from one stage to another

It is important to be aware that all groups go through various stages. The stages are developmental and, whilst it is possible to identify that a group is at a particular stage, it is not practical, or even perhaps desirable, to attempt to rush each of the stages. Indeed, it has been suggested that many groups do not develop to another stage until a 'trauma' is experienced. For example, the group can come under severe pressure to 'perform' and at that point moves to the next stage.

If several students have to work together on a particular task during one class period, then clearly the group will have to move through the stages very quickly. The group will need to stay very focused on the task to be completed. If the group gets stuck in the early stages of development, it will flounder and the task will remain unfinished. To move from stage 1 to 2 may simply require group members to abandon non-threatening topics and risk the possibility of conflict.

If, however, the group has to work together for a whole semester of about three or four months, or even the entire academic year, it may take a long time to go through stage 2. Conflict may be evident for a considerable period of time as students attempt to gain power for themselves or their subgroup. For the group to work together well and move to stage 3, some form of conflict resolution is necessary. This is likely to require the intervention of those students who adopt group maintenance roles such as mediator and peacemaker. If conflict and disagreements remain unresolved, the subgroups will continue to hinder efficiency and effectiveness. If the group is unable to overcome the friction and discord, it will have to struggle on in the knowledge that it is underperforming. The most important skills that are needed to enable groups to move from stage 2 to 3 are the ability to listen and the capacity and willingness to deal with the conflict evident in the group. When the group has dealt with the conflict, cohesion will develop during stage 3. Being able to reach a consensus among the students is necessary to facilitate the transition from stage 3 to 4.

See downloadable template 10.1 ASSESSING YOUR OWN GROUP AND TEAMWORK ACTIVITIES for your Personal Development Plan online.

Activity 10.2

Group stages of development

Think about a group at university or college in which you have begun to participate recently.

- Has the group reached stage 2 yet?
- Identify the stage of development that the group has reached by listing the behaviours that are displayed by the other students.
- What does the group need to do to be able to progress to the next stage?
- Has the group dealt with issues from previous stages? If not, what behaviours indicate that there are unresolved issues, and what does the group need to do to deal with these issues?
- How can you use this knowledge to improve your performance in groups?

PART 1   DEVELOPING STUDY SKILLS

→ How to know more about groups

When working in groups, look out for evidence of the following. It will provide a firm foundation for becoming an effective and influential group member.

Status

Status is another aspect that always exists in groups and affects how the members behave towards each other. Over a period of time, students will assign status to each other from highest to lowest. Higher status is usually based on factors such as the ability to solve problems, possess analytical skills or judge the motivation and capabilities of others. Higher status is also bestowed on a member who has specialist knowledge, interpersonal skills, credibility or experience that the group needs. Similarly, if a group member possesses any other skill or quality valued by the group, they will be considered to have a higher status than those who do not possess the skill. The degree to which a student conforms to the norms of the group will affect their status – high conformers generally have higher status, and low conformers have lower status.

Deviant group members

The other student members of the group will frequently reject 'deviant' group members – students who do not agree with the prevailing views, or prefer an atmosphere of conflict. The other group members will initially try to persuade the deviant student to their perspective. However, if the deviant student will not be persuaded, over time the group will communicate with them less and less. Ultimately, the deviant may find himself or

Figure 10.3 Factors that influence groups

herself completely ignored or even cast out of the group. However, groups need to be aware that it is necessary to have someone play the devil's advocate role that prevents the group becoming too cohesive. It is, therefore, not a good idea to cast out a deviant group member who performs a useful function. If someone seems to be being difficult and disagreeing with group members, they may actually be helping the group rather than hindering it.

Subgroups of members (cliques)

Subgroupings or cliques of larger groups frequently form during group work. These may consist of two or three members of the larger group who have particular shared interests, are fighting for the same cause or are like-minded individuals. Subgroups may sometimes be identified through seating arrangements: for example, if each group member sits in the same place every time the group meets, this can encourage the development of cliques or factions. It can be quite difficult to identify subgroups and an external observer can frequently identify subgroups more readily than the group members themselves.

Subgroups may not be apparent at the surface level of group working or may not influence the group greatly for most of the time. On other occasions, cliques may be very powerful and their influence could be positive or negative. For example, the subgroups may present creative and innovative ideas to the larger group. However, the subgroup may be antagonistic to the leader or another subgroup, and the in-fighting which takes place could have very negative consequences for the group, hindering progress towards goals.

> **Stop and think**
>
> When working in student groups, ask yourself the following questions:
> - are two or three members consistently agreeing and supporting each other?
> - are two or three members consistently opposing another subgroup?
> - is a subgroup treated as 'outsiders' by the remainder of the group?
> - who 'wins' when voting takes place?
> - what effect does it have on the subgroup?
> - does the subgroup distinguish itself in some way from the remainder of the group?
> - what effect does this have on the group?

Participation

Patterns of group participation can be very informative. If you are able to answer the following questions, you will be able to identify the communication patterns/flows in a group.

- Who talks to whom? Is everyone included in the discussion?
- Who interrupts whom? Is it always the same person who interrupts?
- Is the same person interrupted consistently?
- What effect does this have on their level of contribution?

- Who contributes a lot or a little? Are there any changes in levels of participation?
- How are silent group members treated? How is silence interpreted: as agreement, apathy, opposition?

Group ambience

Individuals may differ in the kind of ambience they like in a group. Most group members prefer a friendly and congenial ambience. Others prefer collaboration, and some enjoy provocation and challenge. Look for answers to the following questions to enable you to identify how the ambience of the group is maintained.

- Do group members conceal conflict or unpleasant feelings to maintain a falsely congenial ambience?
- Are group members hostile towards each other?
- Does one member challenge the views of the others?
- Are some group members deliberately antagonistic, contentious or provocative?
- Are people involved, interested, enthusiastic or apathetic?
- Does any group member introduce fun or humour into the group interaction?
- Is one group member (or more) nurturing or taking care of others?

Decision making

Some individuals in groups make autocratic decisions without considering the effects on the other members in the group. Others want all participants to engage in consensus decision making, where all participants can accept and support the decision made. Look for answers to the following questions to understand more about group decision making.

- How are decisions made – majority vote, consensus, pushed through by a minority, silence interpreted as agreement, no identifiable means?
- What happens to any group member who disagrees with the decision? Are they ignored, coerced or overruled?
- Does bargaining, negotiation or compromise occur? What are the effects on the group?
- Are autocratic, unilateral decisions made and imposed on others? How do those group members react?
- Is someone's proposal always ignored (or accepted)?
- What effect does this have on the group member?
- Does the group actually reach a decision? Is it implemented, ignored or overturned?

Leadership

There are different issues of leadership that a group will have to deal with. The officially appointed leader may, in fact, not lead the group, and an informal leader may emerge to control activities. There can be leadership struggles that influence group behaviour and atmosphere. Answers to the following questions will reveal a great deal about leadership in the group.

- How is the leader chosen – elected, proposed, imposed or volunteered in some other way?
- How does each group member feel about the leadership pattern – content, antagonistic, apathetic?
- Does the leader structure the discussions? Does the leader provide adequate control, dominate the discussions or allow them to ramble aimlessly?
- Is the leadership helpful or unhelpful in ensuring effectiveness and efficiency in the functioning of the group?

> **Remember...**
> Identify and analyse as much information as possible about how the group operates, as it can be put to very productive use.

Differences between groups and teams

What is the difference between groups and teams? At a basic level, two or more people working together, having the objective of completing a project or task, can be described as a group. A team is much more than this, as can be seen from Table 10.1. A team possesses extra qualities that a group does not have; sometimes these are indefinable, but in some way lead to improved performance, bordering on excellence. The team gels together through trust, honesty and commitment, and all members feel that their contribution and membership are essential to effective performance. Each team member feels valued and this leads to synergy, producing a combined output that is more than the sum of each individual's contributions. The team feels that performance is impaired if one or more members are missing and is dependent on each member to become a 'functioning whole'.

A sports team analogy is useful to clarify the difference between a group and a team: for example, if a player is sent off or absent because of injury or illness, the team gives a below-par performance. The team seeks to maximise attainment even at the expense of individual achievement, which will be sacrificed in pursuit of successful team performance.

A further aspect that differentiates teams from groups is emotions. Team members care for each other and feel a sense of belonging and responsibility which enables, encourages, enthuses, empowers and ennobles everyone. Emotional reactions are accepted and encouraged as fundamental and valuable elements of teamworking that are dealt with constructively, facilitating openness, honesty and integrity in team interactions.

An effective team therefore displays the following properties:

- Team members care for each other.
- Process/maintenance issues are dealt with.

Table 10.1 Differences between groups and teams

Group	Team
Group members work independently of each other.	The team recognises and utilises the interdependence of the members advantageously, accepting mutual accountability. 'Synergistic' outcomes occur, which means that the output from the team is more than the sum of the individual effort put into performance.
Group members focus on individual goals rather than those of the group.	There is a shared commitment to the goal(s) of the team through support, involvement, cooperation and the pursuit of excellence.
Instructions are given to the group by the leader.	Participation in the team task is through application of talent.
Conflict is divisive and distrust between members leads to a win-lose situation.	Risks conflict – it is considered as necessary and healthy and the trust between team members leads to a win-win situation.
Conflict is dealt with by the leader.	The team resolves conflict.
Subgroups are evident and communication is guarded.	Open, honest communication takes place – team members communicate effectively and appropriately, leading to the team members feeling a sense of belonging, caring and compassion for others.
Conformity is more important than positive results.	Positive outcomes are more important than conformity.
Decision making is by the leader.	Decision making is by consensus.
The group has variable commitment to implementing the decisions made.	The team is highly committed to implementing the decisions made.
The leader confronts an inadequate performer.	Team members confront each other if performance is inadequate – including that of the leader.
The leader determines the agenda.	The team determines the agenda.
The agenda is restricted to innocuous issues.	The agenda addresses core issues.
Meetings are to provide information and advice.	Meetings are used for problem solving and planning.

- Feelings are expressed freely with consideration and compassion.
- Team members are open and truthful with each other.
- Sophisticated communications are appropriate to the situation.
- There are no hidden agendas.
- There are high levels of trust, honesty and integrity between team members because strengths and weaknesses are known to all.

GROUP AND TEAM-WORKING SKILLS

- All ideas are listened to.
- There is strong commitment to the team through positive participation and involvement, ownership of actions and shared responsibility.
- Negotiations take place in a climate of influencing with integrity.
- Decision making is by consensus – not necessarily everyone agreeing with the decision wholeheartedly, but being able to go along with the decision without negative feelings.
- Conflict is acknowledged, worked through and dealt with by the whole team.

Stop and think
○ Are you working in a group or a team?

See Activity 10.4 GROUP SUCCESS in the Online Study Guide.

The perfect team will always produce excellent results, or so it is claimed, and therefore various models suggesting what makes a perfect team have been proposed. One of the most successful is the *team role theory* put forward by R. Meredith Belbin (1981) and outlined below.

→ Team role theory

Team working is a very significant aspect of working with other students and it is important to consider the composition of the team. Unfortunately, not all teams work well together or succeed at the set task, and this may occur at university or college. However, R. Meredith Belbin has researched and analysed effective team performance and suggests a team model of nine different roles. He says that if all team roles are evident this leads to effective and successful performance: in other words, the perfect team. It is not necessary for there to be nine team members, but all the roles must be undertaken by the team, so some team members may have two or three team roles that they adopt while the task is completed.

The nine team role descriptions are as follows.

The Coordinator

This person likes to organise, coordinate and control the way the team works. They guide the team by clarifying the situation and encouraging the members to achieve the set objectives. The Coordinator commands the respect of the team and inspires enthusiasm. They are a good communicator and are well liked by the team members. The Coordinator is self-controlled, calm and able to sum up the current situation for the team by providing balance.

The Shaper

The Shaper imposes a pattern on the discussion and encourages the team to action. The Shaper exudes drive and enthusiasm, and makes things happen. They have an aptitude for uniting disparate ideas and persuading other team members to follow them. The Shaper can be impulsive, arrogant and impatient, and is frequently intolerant of vague ideas. Their dynamic, dominant character interprets a lack of enthusiasm in others as an indication that they are difficult to manage or rebellious.

The Implementor

The Implementor is the person who turns concepts and plans into practicalities. They are hard workers who like clear objectives and direction. On the whole, the Implementor is inflexible and does not like untested and unproven ideas. They are conservative in outlook, efficient and sincere in their trust of the other team members. The Implementor is good at organising and displays a disciplined approach.

The Monitor Evaluator

The Monitor Evaluator analyses problems and evaluates ideas and suggestions. They prevent the group behaving hastily by bringing critical thinking and objective dispassionate analysis to proposals put forward by the team. The Monitor Evaluator is discerning, displays good judgement, is rarely wrong and is able to take a strategic view, although he or she can be less than tactful with the rest of the team members. Other team members consider the Monitor Evaluator to be aloof, unemotional and sober. However, the Monitor Evaluator prevents the team from taking excessive risks.

The Plant

The Plant is the ideas generator. Whilst the Plant will furnish many ideas and be imaginative, innovative and creative, the team will have to nourish these ideas and bring them to fruition. The Plant has a tendency to be impractical and can make careless mistakes. However, if criticised by others, he or she may take offence and sulk. This dominant, individualistic, unorthodox team member needs careful handling by the team.

The Resource Investigator

The Resource Investigator will explore opportunities for the team by developing contacts and negotiating with outsiders. They are likeable, enthusiastic, creative and innovative, excelling under pressure through improvisation. The Resource Investigator's gregarious extrovert personality manages relationships across the boundary of the team to other teams. When the team is not making progress, the Resource Investigator brings in new ideas from elsewhere. They can appear to be over-enthusiastic to other team members and occasionally do not deliver on promises made. However, they are able to escape criticism by using charm and good communication skills.

The Team Worker

The Team Worker improves communications between team members and fosters team spirit. They are very perceptive and trusting, and are able to pick up any hidden agendas in the team. The Team Worker promotes harmony, is diplomatic and a good communicator, but does not contribute a great deal to the team task. They can appear to be indecisive and are considered to be 'soft' by some team members. However, the Team Worker is missed most if they are absent, as they are the 'cement' that holds the team together.

The Completer

The Completer ensures that there is a sense of urgency within the team and that targets and deadlines are met. They are anxious and painstaking and worry about completing the task successfully. They are orderly and conscientious, planning activities in a painstaking, perfectionist way. The Completer is intolerant of the more casual members of the team, nagging them about the time passing, and this can lower the morale of some of the team members.

The Specialist

The Specialist is an addition to Belbin's original model. The Specialist contributes technical skills or specialist knowledge to the team task on a narrow front. They provide expertise and are single-minded in their approach, but dedicated to their specialist field. The Specialist is self-motivated, committed and professional in outlook.

> **Stop and think**
> - Which role do you think best fits you?
> - Can you identify your characteristics in the role descriptors?

See Activity 10.5 GROUP ROLES in the Online Study Guide.

Belbin argues that if the team is deficient in a team role, or is composed of too many of the same type of role, it will be less effective than it could be. So, for example, if a team is composed mainly of Team Workers, the team will have an enjoyable time, everyone will feel valued, communication will be good, conflict will be absent, but tough decisions will not be taken. If, on the other hand, the team has several Completers, there will be a feeling of urgency, clock-watching and planning to complete the task perfectly, and to be sure the task will be completed long before the deadline!

Belbin suggests that once the team is formed, performance and effectiveness can be improved by assigning tasks and responsibilities to team members according to their strongest team role. He also suggests that team members should be encouraged to utilise and draw on the team role strengths of others.

> **Remember...**
> Team members may take on more than one role.

Working in groups and teams at university or college

It is likely that working in groups and teams will be required frequently during a course of study at university or college. This may be informally, when choosing to work with others of one's own choice because it is pleasant to share ideas or they are like-minded individuals. On the other hand, it may be necessary to have to work in formal groups determined by the tutor. The output of either informal or formal groupings may be assessed: for example, through group reports, presentations or discussions. (See Chapters 14 and 16 for more information.)

Group discussions

During university or college courses it is likely that you will be expected to participate in group discussions in seminars. Many students fear to speak in a group situation because they feel that each comment should be novel, excellent or profound in order to be heard. Some students do not join in the discussion because they feel that their contribution will be seen as trivial and therefore might be ignored. Provided that any pre-reading specified by the tutor or course literature has been completed and understood, your comments are likely to be as relevant as those of any other group member present. In any case, it is less of a problem to find out that you have misunderstood something in a seminar than in an assessment. If you feel in any way intimidated about joining in a group discussion, try some of the following suggestions.

Suggestions for contributions to group discussions

- Say what you think the topic is about in your own words.
- If you think another student's contribution is accurate, add some information to it.
- To check that you understand, paraphrase in your own words what another student has said.
- Seek clarification from other group members or the tutor on points you do not understand.
- If another student's interpretation is different from your own, identify the ways in which it differs.
- Clarify how new material confirms, challenges or develops an earlier point.
- Provide and discuss illustrative examples from your own experience.

Suggestions for group work

For your groups to be effective and efficient:
- Clarify and agree the goal(s) to be achieved.
- Seek individual and team commitment to the goal(s).
- Determine what needs to be done to achieve the goal(s).
- Decide how this will be achieved – who will do what.
- Identify the planning requirements, how decisions will be made, how conflict will be resolved.
- Reach agreement about how to monitor performance.
- Resolve how the group will measure progress towards the goal(s).
- Identify the stage of development the group is at and devise strategies to move it to achieve the set task.
- Analyse whether the group has become a team and therefore more effective and efficient.
- Identify whether it is deficient in any of the roles that would improve performance.

GROUP AND TEAM-WORKING SKILLS

Activity 10.3

Groups and teams behaviour sheet

Compare your group/team against the behaviours listed in the table below. Where the answer is yes/no, give examples of the behaviour(s) that support your conclusions. Write in detail about your experience in the particular group/team you are describing in the spaces provided.

How can you use this knowledge and information to (a) be a more effective and efficient group member, and (b) ensure that the group becomes a team?

Norms	Provide examples
Does the group: 1 avoid certain topics, such as absentees, lack of progress in achieving the set task, leader behaviour, etc? 2 achieve and maintain this avoidance? 3 have participation norms, e.g. each person feels obliged to speak? 4 restrict questions to innocuous subjects? 5 expect a particular student to make all decisions? 6 accept that some students will be late for meetings, but not others? 7 avoid conflict and disagreement? 8 expect group members always to be polite to each other? 9 permit only positive feelings to be expressed? 10 allow group members to express their feelings?	
Task behaviours	**Provide examples**
Does anyone: 1 try to make sure that the group is on target to complete the task? 2 stop the group from going off at a tangent? 3 summarise what has been done and list what else needs to be done to complete the task? 4 provide facts, ideas, feedback or alternative proposals to complete the task? 5 judge whether it is completing the task effectively or efficiently? 6 organise the working area satisfactorily? 7 keep records, share information, plan?	
Group maintenance behaviours	**Provide examples**
Does anyone act as: 1 gatekeeper? 2 compromiser? 3 harmoniser? 4 mediator? 5 standard setter? 6 commentator? 7 follower? 8 carer?	

Group maintenance behaviours (cotd)	Provide examples
Does anyone act as: 9 adviser? 10 negotiator? 11 facilitator? 12 helper? 13 peace-maker? 14 teacher? 15 supporter and encourager? 16 aggressor? 17 dominator? 18 blocker? 19 recognition seeker? 20 any other role you can identify?	
Subgroups	**Provide examples**
Are: 1 subgroups or cliques developing, e.g. two or three members consistently agreeing and supporting each other, or opposing another subgroup? 2 some group members being treated as 'outsiders'? Do they constantly 'lose' when voting takes place? What effect does this have on them? 3 some group members leaning forward or backward in their chairs, or moving their chairs towards or away from the table? What effect does this have on the group?	
Stages of group development	**Provide examples**
Which stage of development is the group at: 1 Stage 1 – Forming? 2 Stage 2 – Storming? 3 Stage 3 – Norming? 4 Stage 4 – Performing? 5 Stage 5 – Adjourning? What behaviours are being displayed which lead you to this conclusion?	
Participation	**Provide examples**
Do individuals note: 1 'communication clusters'? 2 who talks to whom? 3 who interrupts whom? Was the person interrupting always the same person? Was the same person interrupted consistently? 4 who contributes a lot or a little? Were there any changes in participation? 5 whether efforts are made to involve everyone? 6 how silent group members are treated? How is silence interpreted? As agreement, apathy, opposition?	

Group atmosphere	Provide examples
Does the group: 1 conceal conflict or unpleasant feelings to maintain a falsely congenial atmosphere? 2 permit group members to be hostile towards each other? 3 ask someone to play 'devil's advocate'? 4 encourage individuals to be involved, interested and enthusiastic, or allow apathy to reign? 5 introduce fun or humour into the group interaction? 6 encourage nurturing behaviour?	
Decision making	*Provide examples*
How does the group: 1 make decisions? Majority vote, consensus, steam-rollered by a minority, silence interpreted as agreement, no identifiable means? 2 deal with any group member who disagrees with the decision (dissidents)? 3 bargain, negotiate or compromise? 4 impose autocratic, unilateral decision making on other group members – or is all decision making participative and democratic? 5 deal with the person whose proposal is always ignored (or accepted)? What effect does this have on the group member? 6 actually reach a decision?	
Leadership	*Provide examples*
Can the group identify: 1 how was the leader chosen? Elected, proposed, imposed, volunteered some other way? 2 how each group member feels about the leadership pattern? 3 whether the leader provides an adequate structure for discussions? 4 whether the leader dominates the discussions or allows them to ramble aimlessly? 5 if the leadership is helpful or unhelpful in ensuring effectiveness and efficiency in the functioning of the group?	
Is the team effective?	*Provide examples*
Can team members identify: 1 whether team members care for each other? 2 if process/maintenance issues dealt with? 3 whether feelings are expressed freely with consideration and compassion? 4 if team members are open and truthful with each other? 5 whether there are any hidden agendas?	

PART 1   DEVELOPING STUDY SKILLS

> See downloadable template 10.2 ASSESSING STUDENTS' GROUP AND TEAMWORK ACTIVITIES for your Personal Development Plan online.

Is the team effective?	Provide examples
Can team members identify: 6 if there are high levels of trust, honesty and integrity between team members because strengths and weaknesses are known to all? 7 if all ideas are listened to? 8 if there is a strong commitment to the team through positive participation and involvement, ownership of actions and shared responsibility? 9 whether negotiations take place in a climate of influencing with integrity? 10 if decision making is by consensus – not necessarily everyone agreeing with the decision wholeheartedly, but being able to go along with the decision without negative feelings? 11 whether conflict is acknowledged, worked through and dealt with by the whole team?	

→ Summary

This chapter has described:

- group dynamics – the factors that affect groups and teams
- goals, roles, norms, subgroups and status, and processes such as decision making, participation and ambience so that understanding can be enhanced
- the development stages that groups go through from forming to adjourning
- the difference between groups and teams
- team role theory, which it is claimed produces a highly effective team when all the roles are evident in a team.

11 Time management

> **Learning outcomes**
>
> After studying this chapter, you should be able to:
> - describe the essentials of time management
> - determine personal time wasters
> - identify how to manage time more effectively.

→ Introduction

Now that you have started out on a new phase of your life at university or college, there are a number of things that you should think about very carefully. You may, for example, find that for the first time you have to manage your own budget and do your own shopping, cooking, washing and ironing. In addition to dealing with these aspects of student life, you may also have to get used to family and friends not being around as frequently as they have been.

It can be a very liberating experience, being able to stay out all night and not worry about parental concern or anger on your return home. However, you may find it quite a shock not to have parents stocking up the fridge, freezer and cupboards with your favourite meals and snacks. Shopping trips, laundry visits and many other things that may have been taken for granted when you lived at home will need to be organised and scheduled.

You may also have to get used to living in different accommodation, possibly with strangers, adjusting to their habits and preferences, some of which may be completely different from your own. For example, they may have a very tidy bedroom with everything in its place, or wash up after every meal, and you are just the opposite; or vice versa – you are the saint and they apparently enjoy living in an untidy mess and wash up only when absolutely necessary. You may feel that other students adjust readily, are competent at shopping, washing and ironing, and appear to be fantastic cooks, whilst you struggle to open a can of beans. Take heart, many students have made spaghetti bolognese for their own evening meal, only to end up with a pan so full of spaghetti that it would almost feed the entire student residence!

In addition to all this, you have to attend lectures and tutorials at irregular hours and manage the remainder of the learning experience yourself (see Chapter 1 for more detailed information). Universities or colleges generally encourage students to become independent learners. What this means is that you will have to schedule your own learning outside your formally scheduled classes. It can be quite tempting at first not to organise yourself. The attraction of start-of-semester events, and the exhilaration and freedom of being in charge of your own budget, perhaps for the first time, are powerful incentives not to lock yourself in your study bedroom and schedule study time.

→ How to manage your time effectively

It is essential to find a balance between studying and social activities as early as possible into your course. There will be more studying than you have done before, and there will be opportunities for attending sports activities, concerts, nightclubs, parties, clubs and societies, and so on. You will have to make a conscious choice to balance the competing demands on your time in order to be successful. The way to achieve this is by managing your time effectively. It is not a good idea to study for all the time available to you; scheduling leisure and relaxation activities into your week is important. Similarly, do not go to so many parties and other social activities that you neglect your studies – that would be a route to disaster. If you schedule both study and leisure time you will be in an appropriate frame of mind for studying and you will be able to enjoy your leisure time with a clear conscience.

> **! Remember...**
> You have 168 hours in a week – spend it wisely, you cannot save it.

The Pareto principle

The nineteenth-century sociologist and economist, Vilfredo Pareto, identified the principle that has been named after him. He found that approximately 80% of Italian wealth was owned by 20% of the population and that this so-called 80:20 rule applied in many situations.

You can use the Pareto principle to improve your time management, as usually about 80% of your productive output will be derived from 20% of activities that you engage in. When you analyse your use of time, you should apply the 80:20 rule. It would not be very effective, for example, to spend a great deal of effort and energy trying to save time on the university or college study activities which take up 20% of your time but provide 80% of your output, such as assessments, seminar papers and reports. Divert your attention to the activities that take up 80% of your time but deliver only 20% of your output. By applying time management techniques, you can concentrate effort on these high-payoff activities. If you invest effort to bring about an improvement in this ratio, it is likely that this will lead to major progress in study habits.

TIME MANAGEMENT

> **Stop and think**
> - Which activities do you spend 80% of your time on that produce 20% of results?
> - Which activities take up 20% of your time but deliver 80% of your results?
> - What can you do about this?

Your body clock

See Activity 11.1 TIME IN OR TIME OUT? in the Online Study Guide.

You will be able to recognise times when you are energised and raring to go. At other times you may just want to sit down like a couch potato in front of the television and do nothing at all. You may be a 'night owl' and like to study into the middle of the night, or alternatively you may be an 'early bird' and prefer to get up very early in the morning to study. It is important to match your peak studying powers with the time available to study.

These peak times are called *circadian rhythms* and they govern the body's performance. These are the natural, biological rhythms of the body – your body clock – and they occur approximately every 24 hours. Taking advantage of the natural rhythms affecting the body by scheduling study during peak time will help you to maximise learning opportunities. It is possible to increase your output considerably simply by working with your circadian rhythms, without having to make major changes to your lifestyle by 'burning the midnight oil' or getting up before dawn breaks.

→ Essentials of time management

Everybody gets 168 hours in every week. No one gets any more, and no one gets any less. Time cannot be hoarded away for a binge, and neither can it be taken away if it has been used frivolously. We cannot go back in time and do something over again. We cannot 'save' time and spend more tomorrow because we are on holiday or meeting a favourite person. Whether you spend it well, or waste it, you will still get 168 hours next week to spend as you see fit.

Activity 11.1

Time allocation

- Think back over the last week and write down what you did and for how long on each day from Monday to Sunday.
- What did you find out?
- You cannot account for your 168 hours?
- Are there large chunks of time for which you are unable to say with any certainty what you did?
- Alternatively have you found out that you spend a great deal of time asleep, daydreaming, listening to music, etc.?

PART 1   DEVELOPING STUDY SKILLS

Prioritising your time

Are you able to say what you do with your 168 hours each week? Can you say with certainty which activities provide you with the most output and which take up most of your time but achieve little? Are you aware of your peak energy times and have you scheduled the most difficult activities for those times? Now that you have started at university or college, it is a good time to take a look at how you spend your time, because you will need to use it wisely in order to pass the assessments you have to complete before you obtain your qualification.

It is surprising that memory is such an unreliable guide to how time is spent. Many people would be unable to identify in detail what they do with their weekly 168 hours, but it is important to be able to ensure that enough time is available to complete your studies successfully. A useful starting point to find out what you currently do with your

Activity 11.2

Weekly time log

Copy out and use the following grid to keep your time log for the next week. Carry this time log with you and write down what you do as you do it. Each time you change to another activity, note down the time of the change. Also write down your feelings at each change of activity. For example, do you feel elated, exhausted, full of energy, lethargic, bored?

	Activity	Feelings
Monday		
07.00		
08.00		
09.00		
10.00		
11.00 and so on for 24 hours		
Tuesday		
07.00		
08.00		
09.00		
10.00 and so on for 24 hours		
Wednesday		
07.00		
08.00		
09.00		
10.00 (complete for 7 days - 24 hours per day)		

TIME MANAGEMENT

time is to keep a *time log* for seven days. This will allow you to identify how you use your 168 hours. Once you have completed your time log, it can then be used to manage your time.

Now look back at your weekly time log and identify

- *have to do*
- *ought to do* and
- *like to do* activities.

Tabulate each of your activities under these headings (see Activity 11.3).

The things that are *have to do* have the highest priority and are the critical items that must be done each week, such as attending lectures/tutorials, completing assessments, sleeping, eating and travelling. These activities are vital to success and have a high value in terms of achievement on a course of study.

Next consider *ought to do* items. These are not such a high priority and are less essential items that do not have critical deadlines but which contribute to moderately important goals. These activities may include preparation for *have to do* items such as research for assessments. Other *ought to do* items, like a phone call to a relative, can usually be put off until the weekend.

Finally, consider *like to do* items. These are lower priority and contribute to relatively unimportant goals. They may be fun and exciting, but can be postponed, or even avoided altogether, unless scheduled specifically as relaxation or other leisure activities.

> See downloadable template 11.1 PERSONAL TIME MANAGEMENT CHART for your Personal Development Plan online.

Activity 11.3

Prioritising activities

Which activities can you postpone, reschedule or abandon in order to create more time for study?

Have to do	Ought to do	Like to do

> See Activity 11.2 SETTING PRIORITIES in the Online Study Guide.

In your time log you will have captured the main areas in your life. Some of these will be responsibilities that you have chosen, such as your course, for which you have to produce results. Others will be important to your well-being, such as relaxation, and these need to be included in your time schedule. At this stage it is useful to spend some time clarifying which areas of your life have the highest priority and which have a lower priority. In this way you can make space in your week for your studies. You could draw a chart which will give you a visual representation of your current activities, such as study, sleep, relaxation, seeing parents, eating, plus any others that you have identified (see Figure 11.1).

Figure 11.1 Estimated use of time for a typical student

- Working 12%
- Eating 4%
- Travelling 6%
- Relaxing 9%
- Socialising 9%
- Studying 27%
- Sleeping 33%

Now that you have prioritised your activities into *have to do*, *ought to do*, and *like to do* things, you will be able to manage your time more effectively. Each day draw up a 'To do' list. Identify the *have*, *ought* and *like to do* activities and rank them in order of importance. This will enable you to organise your activities, which in turn will reduce stress.

There is no excuse for not doing a *have to do* item. Obviously, however, priorities change over time, and when you receive a piece of work to complete which is to be assessed, it might be an *ought to do* for the first two weeks. For the last two weeks before the submission date it becomes a *have to do*, so that you can hand it in by the deadline. Unfortunately, time is often spent doing things that are *like to do* items at the expense of things that are difficult, even though these difficult tasks may be the critical ones. (See the section on the Pareto principle for more information.)

Everyone needs to find a balance between the various competing demands on their time. At university or college you will have to decide how much time to spend studying, engaging in paid employment, and being with friends and family. You will also have to decide what to do with the time which is uncommitted – how much to use for leisure, hobbies, etc. It is necessary to include some leisure activities and time for hobbies, whether these are vigorous exercise or sedentary, such as reading, fishing, meditating or watching television. These types of activity can be helpful in reducing stress levels by refreshing the mind, body or spirit. Whatever you decide, make sure that these leisure activities are pleasurable.

At times of transition, such as starting a new course at university or college, the key areas of life can easily get out of balance. It is important that you manage your time well to make sure that sufficient time is given to the essentials. If you feel stressed about not having enough time, stop and ask yourself, 'Why am I doing this right now?' Your answer to this question will help you to decide what activities to focus on. It will help you to make choices about what you want to do and, whilst deciding on the priorities in your life may be hard and even occasionally painful, it must be confronted.

Keeping a healthy balance between the various demands on your time whilst you are at university or college is essential, as it will enable you to maintain a positive attitude and approach. To help keep this balance, plan to do things every day that will help measurably to achieve your study goals.

TIME MANAGEMENT

> **! Remember...**
> Make sure that you do one thing every day that you find enjoyable and also do something every day which balances university or college life with private life: for example, hobbies, family, relaxation or sport.

As you start out on your university or college course, think very carefully about how to schedule time to enable you to achieve extra study time when necessary. Clearly you will have to use your judgement to decide what to do and always consider what the most productive use of time is at that moment. If you are doing something that is not satisfying and you are not achieving your goals, then stop doing it. At university or college a full-time course requires about 40 or more hours each week. In order to make the time available to study, you might prefer to schedule a 9 a.m. to 5 p.m. Monday to Friday timetable for yourself, leaving the evenings and weekends free to pursue other activities. Alternatively, a morning person may prefer to schedule some study time very early in the morning when everyone else is asleep and complete the remainder at university or college in timetabled classes.

When you schedule time for activities that have a fixed deadline – for example completing an essay assessment or examinations – make sure that you make allowances for the unexpected, such as emergencies. For example, unavoidable events such as accidents, sickness and interruptions may disrupt studies. Other urgent tasks which temporarily become more important than the assessment, and breakdown of equipment such as personal computer, printer, etc., can interfere with the plans of even the most organised student. Usually work proceeds without a hitch and assessments are completed with plenty of time to spare. Occasionally problems do arise, but with careful planning it is still possible to complete the work in time to meet the deadline. Be particularly meticulous when scheduling and planning revision time for examinations (see Chapter 18 for more details).

Whatever approach is chosen, there is a need to find sufficient time to study. Effective study needs a lot of time and in usable 'chunks', not in five minutes here and there. For the next few years you will need to be adept at creating plenty of time for study activities in order to be successful on your course.

See Activity 11.3 YOUR TYPICAL DAY in the Online Study Guide.

Activity 11.4

Time inventory

Now draw up a weekly time inventory in which you specifically schedule your study targets for your university or college course.

- Schedule all your classes, such as lectures, seminars and tutorials.
- Estimate and schedule the time needed to study each subject or part of your course. Include this in your inventory, especially independent or directed study time.
- Allow time for review of lecture/tutorial material.
- Schedule extra time in the weeks before an assessment is due to be handed in.

PART 1   DEVELOPING STUDY SKILLS

- Plan revision time for exams towards the end of the semester or term.
- Allow some unscheduled time for emergencies such as sickness, accidents or equipment breakdown.
- Schedule discretionary study activities at your peak energy times, i.e. those that you control, such as preparation for seminars or tutorials, reading for essays, etc.

In addition to the above, schedule all your other *have to do* activities such as shopping, travelling to and from university or college, sleeping, going to the bank, dentist, etc.

In the remaining time you can schedule the most important of your *ought to do* activities. Finally, you should leave some time for your *like to do* activities, such as relaxation or leisure pursuits.

Review your weekly time log and analyse it to see if any patterns emerge.

Identify your peak time - your best time to study - by drawing your performance curve on the following diagram. If you are most energetic at 10.00 a.m. mark 100 at that time, and if your energy starts to dip soon after lunch indicate where you think your energy level is then. Your energy may plummet at about 4.00 or 5.00 p.m. in which case you should mark a 0 at that time. Then draw your personal energy/performance curve.

Energy or performance cycle

[Graph with y-axis showing 0%, 50%, 100% and x-axis showing 0.00 hrs, 12.00 hrs, 24.00 hrs]

> See downloadable template 11.2 ASSESSING THE WAY YOU WORK for your Personal Development Plan online.

You can now use this information to schedule your university/college work. Schedule routine tasks when your energy cycle is low, and difficult or intellectually demanding tasks when your energy cycle is high.

Stop and think

Have you:
- ○ included all your scheduled university/college activities?
- ○ scheduled sufficient time for independent and directed study?
- ○ scheduled enough time to be able to meet colleague students to complete group work?
- ○ taken account of your body clock?
- ○ planned for emergencies and unexpected eventualities?
- ○ included revision?
- ○ been realistic with your estimates/scheduling?

Time wasters

It is a feature of being human to waste time – everyone does it to some extent. The important thing is to recognise when you are relaxing in order to recharge your batteries and when you are daydreaming to avoid getting down to your studies.

Self-inflicted time wasters

Procrastination

Everyone puts off doing tasks that are boring, difficult, laborious or disagreeable. If you are a student who puts off until later what you could do now, you should consider ways to deal with it, such as making sure you set a deadline – and then stick to it. Use prompts so you cannot 'forget' to do something – write reminders for yourself on 'Post-it' notes and stick them up on the kitchen cupboards, fridge door, television screen and any mirror that you use regularly. Promise yourself a reward when you have completed the task. Ensure that the reward is linked to successful completion of the task, as this will provide encouragement and a record of success. If the task seems overwhelming or daunting and this puts you off starting work, divide it up into smaller parts, as this will make it more manageable. Remember that with all tasks, difficult or easy, the sooner you get under way, the sooner you will complete the work.

Perfectionism

It is easy to get so engrossed in trying to do something perfectly that there is no time left for other important tasks. Once you have spent a reasonable amount of time on a task, ask yourself what the likely impact will be if you spend further time trying to improve what you have already done.

Self-discipline

Having committed yourself to a course of study, it is essential to maintain the resolve to carry it through to success. Everyone has to complete work that at times may not be enjoyable, or seems too difficult, but perseverance is usually the answer.

Worrying

It is easy from time to time to become overwhelmed by the amount of study necessary to complete a course, but it is much better to use energy productively doing as much as possible, rather than being overwhelmed by worry. Avoid spending time worrying about assessments. If you divide the task into smaller, more manageable 'chunks' and keep yourself busy planning, organising and doing the research, there will be no time or need to worry because you will have finished the task.

Personal disorganisation

Are you disorganised, untidy, unable to find things on your desk or in your room? Make yourself tidy up – at the very least, every night put away your books and study items, pens, pencils, calculators, notebooks and files. Remain focused on one task at a time and make sure that it is completed before starting something new. At the first sign of an interruption, do not break off from what you are doing, leaving it unfinished.

PART 1   DEVELOPING STUDY SKILLS

Overcommitment

See Activity 11.4 TIME WASTERS in the Online Study Guide.

If you are unable to say 'no', then now is the time to be selfish. Remind yourself that you want to complete this course successfully – this is your passport to a rewarding future. Saying 'no' to a friend asking you to go out for a drink need not offend them. Offer an alternative: for example, tell them that you are busy just now, but would like to go to the club/theatre at the weekend.

Lack of priorities

If you have not prioritised the demands on your time, you may try to do too many things at once, be unable to concentrate on the important tasks and be tempted to spend too much time on trivialities. Complete weekly *have*, *ought* and *like to do* lists. Prioritise your activities with these lists. Draw up a daily 'To do' list.

External time wasters

Telephone

If you are busy, ask the person to ring back; offer to ring them when you are free; get someone else to answer the phone and take a message; or use an answering machine.

Visitors

Be polite, but firm. Tell student colleagues that you are busy, but could meet them at some other time.

Intrusions

Close the door; do not answer the telephone.

Television

It is very easy to be tempted to watch more television than you intended. If you are a fan of a particular 'soap', do not be lured into watching the remaining programmes for the evening.

Travelling

Use this time productively. If you are travelling on public transport, use the time to read one of the course books or write notes, etc. Do not sit staring out of the window watching the world go by, or sit seething because the bus or train is running late.

Waiting

A lot of time is wasted waiting – for the dentist, tutor or other students. This need not be wasted time; take a book to read, review lecture notes, etc.

See downloadable template 11.3 DEALING WITH OBSTACLES for your Personal Development Plan online.

Coffee bar conversations

These may be enjoyable, but do not overdo it.

Crises

Most of us face several crises in our lives; some are beyond our control, but some are self-generated because we ignore critical deadlines.

TIME MANAGEMENT

Activity 11.5

Time wasters

1. Identify your self-inflicted time wasters.
2. Brainstorm what you could do to alleviate them.
3. Choose your three favourite solutions from your brainstormed list.
4. Write down what you think will be the consequences for yourself and others if you were to implement your solutions.
5. Try out one of your solutions, but observe what happens and review the effect of the changes you have implemented. If it works for you then continue with the changes; if it does not work, try something different from your list.
6. Regularly review the changes you have made to ensure that they are still effective. If they are, continue with your changes. If not, introduce some different ones.

Now carry out the same procedure for your external time wasters. What have you learned about your time management as a result of this activity?

> **Remember...**
> Good time management can improve self-confidence.

→ Personal benefits from effective time management

There are a number of personal benefits from managing your time effectively.

- You will be able to plan your life better, which will mean that you have more time to think and your thinking will be clearer.
- You will be better organised in both studies and other aspects of life, which will give you much more time for important university or college tasks – research, coursework and assessments – enabling you to produce more and better quality work.
- You are likely to be under less stress from unanticipated tasks and have scheduled quality time available for discretionary activities such as hobbies and socialising.
- You will have more self-confidence and fewer feelings of guilt, because you have identified your own beliefs and set your own priorities, and this in turn will enable you to experience and enjoy better interpersonal relationships.
- You will be more productive, enjoy your studies, be more in control of what you do, and have more quality time for leisure and relaxation, which will reduce stress.
- You will ultimately improve your career prospects because employers value effective and efficient employees.

See downloadable template 11.4 STUDENTS' TIME MANAGEMENT SKILLS for your Personal Development Plan online.

Suggestions for improving time management

- Decide what are the key aspects of your studies; ensure most of your time is spent on them; review this regularly.
- Set realistic goals for your studies and personal life; accept that you cannot do everything at once.
- Plan and schedule sufficient time for study.
- Put up reminders in your study/bedroom about your goals.
- Decide how much sleep you need and make sure that you get sufficient.
- Concentrate your effort and energies on one thing at a time.
- Plan each day carefully. At the start of each day, reflect on your 'To do' list; if items remain on it for too many days, reassess whether they are still important.
- Question everything you do. If you feel you should not be doing something, do not do it: for example, do not attend social occasions such as the theatre, pub or students' union events too frequently.
- Organise the most demanding tasks at your peak time.
- Allow time after presentations and assessments to evaluate what you have done.
- Fight procrastination – do it now if it is important.
- Do not spend time regretting failures – learn from your mistakes.
- Acquire good study habits – study at the same time each day.
- Prioritise what you need to do – do not overschedule your day.
- Think of time as a scarce resource; let other students know that your time is valuable, but without deterring them from communicating with you.
- Leave time in your day to reflect, think, plan and listen.
- Make time in your schedule for your hobbies, interests, activities and relaxation.

See Activity 11.5 TIME MANAGEMENT QUIZ in the Online Study Guide.

→ Summary

This chapter has outlined that:

- effective time management will be an important factor in the success of your studies
- time is an irreplaceable resource that requires activities to be planned, scheduled and organised
- a time log is a useful tool to analyse and prioritise *have to do*, *ought to do* and *like to do* activities, thus enabling decisions to be made about how best to use time
- 'peak time' can be scheduled to take advantage of natural body rhythms, which will improve effectiveness and efficiency
- major time wasters, both self-inflicted and external, can be identified so that their impact can be minimised

12 Managing stress

> **Learning outcomes**
> After studying this chapter, you should be able to:
> - identify the causes, symptoms and consequences of stress
> - cope better with and manage stress
> - increase your effectiveness and reduce stress.

Introduction

There are various definitions of stress, but basically it is how we as human beings react to the pressures we face in our everyday lives. Each person, whether a student, parent, tutor, police officer or politician, experiences a number of different and competing demands on them. These demands come from within the individual and from the situations that person has to operate in, and this is what causes stress. Stress levels fluctuate on a daily basis depending upon the pressures of the situation encountered. An individual may feel considerable stress, for example, if the train is delayed and he or she is late for an important event, such as an examination or a job interview.

Stress occurs when threatening or challenging situations are faced and the individual considers that there is an imbalance between the demands being made and his or her ability to deal with them. An individual may feel, for example, that he or she does not possess the mental resilience or intellectual ability to cope with particular circumstances. The majority of people are able to deal adequately with these demands most of the time, but it is necessary to be able to assess stress levels. If the pressures start to rise at an unacceptable pace, steps can be taken to alleviate the competing demands, particularly at times of change such as leaving home to start a university course.

In order to understand how to assess and deal with stress levels, it is first necessary to understand what happens to a person when a stressful situation is encountered. The reaction to pressure, tension and stress applies to students just the same as to people in all walks of life.

This chapter will help you to identify what stress is, the consequences and causes of stress, and how to manage stress.

PART 1   DEVELOPING STUDY SKILLS

→ What is stress?

The body is equipped with systems to deal with stress. These systems consist of automatic responses to stress, which produce sweating, an increase in blood pressure, faster heartbeats, rapid breathing, tense muscles and increased blood flow to the muscles. If a stressful situation is not dealt with adequately, the effects of not having used the energy available may be experienced over an extended period of time.

Your aim as a student should be to find the most appropriate level of stress for yourself in your particular circumstances, and to maintain it at the optimum level whilst adjusting to meet changing situations. This may sometimes mean increasing stress levels rather than reducing them because everyone varies enormously in the amount, intensity, type and duration of stress that can be coped with (see Figure 12.1).

Stress levels occur on a continuum from not having enough to do, through normal healthy levels of activity, to trying to do too much in too short a time. Some students do experience levels of stress that are too high, but others might be helped by increasing their level of stress by taking on more challenging work. For example, it may be necessary for you to sustain a high level of performance on your course, particularly during assessment periods such as examinations. At these times it will be necessary to maintain your level of performance under what may seem to be extreme levels of stress. However, do not fall into the trap of being self-indulgent and use high stress levels as an excuse to avoid working hard enough to be successful. Pay attention to your stress levels,

Figure 12.1 **Optimum stress levels**

250

MANAGING STRESS

and learn to relax when necessary, get more sleep, meditate, exercise or whatever it takes to lower excessive stress. Either too much or too little stress will affect you; whilst it is relatively straightforward to detect changes in stress levels, it is more difficult to do something about them.

> **Remember...**
> Manageable levels of stress are essential for normal body functioning.

→ Some consequences of stress

To put stress in perspective, it must be understood that it is essential for normal functioning of the body. Individuals need stimulation and challenge, in order to function. Each person needs stress, but not too much, or for too long.

Stress is an essential part of life and can be either positive or negative. It provides excitement, impetus and motivation as well as distress and anxiety. The human stress response occurs not only to threatening demands and situations but also to pleasant and joyous experiences. The body reacts to both extremes of stress. It is important to

Figure 12.2 The human stress curve

251

> See Activity 12.1a FIND YOUR INNER CALM 1 in the Online Study Guide.

understand that there is a distinction between *distress*, which is the destructive form, and *eustress* (Selye 1956), which occurs when feelings of elation, exhilaration and delight are experienced.

It is eustress that promotes alertness and helps you to meet everyday challenges and solve problems. If you are not sure what eustress is, think back to a situation when you were excited, such as the night before a holiday, Christmas or some other major event, and you could not sleep – this is the stress of eustress.

Up to a certain level stress is beneficial to performance, but beyond that level additional stress may affect performance and output which could result in a deterioration in achievements. This is called a *distress response* and is evident when the body overreacts to the situations faced. If something is particularly onerous or anxiety provoking, the body reacts accordingly. However, it is only if stress is intense over a considerable period of time that the effects can occasionally be harmful (see Figure 12.2).

> **Stop and think**
> - What examples of eustress can you identify from your own experience? How did these affect you?
> - What examples of negative stress can you identify from your own experience? How did you deal with them?

Causes of stress

There is never one single cause of stress. It is usual for stress to arise from a number of sources.

From within the individual

Stress can arise from:

- obligation towards other students
- perfectionism – an inability to accept that the work is acceptable
- inadequacy – even if this is unfounded
- inferiority – feeling that other students are more competent
- apprehension about the changes that student life will bring
- incompetence because this is a new subject that you are studying
- trying to meet expectations of others
- fear of failure because the course is very demanding
- unrealistic desires or beliefs, which cause anxiety
- inability to manage time effectively.

Personal and family relationships

Stress can result from:

- changing relationships with parents and relatives

Activity 12.1

Identifying your stressors

There are a number of origins of stress, some of which are listed in the table below. Using the scale provided, identify those that apply to you in your role as a student by placing a tick in the appropriate box. Add in additional ones that apply to you from those listed in the section on causes of stress.

Stressor	Disagree ⟵⟶ Agree				
	A lot	A little	Neutral	A little	A lot
Pressures imposed by oneself, especially expectations we place on ourselves					
Expectations of others					
Unable to manage time effectively					
Feelings of inadequacy					
Unfulfilled wants and desires					
Concern for family and friends					
Unsatisfying relationships					
Lifestyle out of balance – too much or too little study time, family and hobbies					
Academic pressure					
Being taken for granted					
Being physically unfit					
Ill-health					
Disorganisation					
Your physical environment – noise in study bedroom; weather (too hot/cold)					
Excessive demands					
Unclear career plans					
Financial pressures					

Read the section on managing stress to find out what you can do to reduce your stressors.

- family changes, such as pregnancy, birth, marriage, divorce or death
- peer pressures at university or college
- unsatisfactory relationships with other students or tutors
- problems with housemates
- building or ending intimate relationships.

Organisational factors

Stress can arise from:

- the demands of student life, such as independent learning
- having to perform beyond one's perceived abilities
- dealing with assessment
- balancing the needs of successfully completing the course with a social life
- having chosen the wrong course
- the need to undertake paid employment.

Cultural factors

Stress can result from:

- racial issues, such as racial discrimination
- religious concerns, such as ignorance of religious festivals
- gender issues, in the form of sexual harassment.

If you find that you experience a lack of interest in your studies, are unable to concentrate adequately or become restless, are unable to unwind, or have no time to relax, these are stress symptoms. Similarly, if you do not feel like socialising, argue frequently with other students, your parents and other relatives, have major disagreements with your close friends, or withdraw from your relationship with your girlfriend or boyfriend, you may be experiencing stress levels that need some attention. Certainly you should seek assistance if you generally feel unwell, lose your appetite, overeat or find that you increase your use of stimulants, such as alcohol or cigarettes, or start to use other drugs not prescribed by a doctor.

Levels of stress that stay high over a long period of time may cause a student to change considerably. He or she may change to being:

- an absentee rather than a regular attender in class
- habitually late instead of punctual
- lazy rather than industrious
- negative rather than possessing a positive attitude and behaviour
- antagonistic rather than cooperative.

Not only should you attempt to be aware of these symptoms in yourself, so that you can take steps to lessen them, but you should also try to be aware of other students who exhibit such symptoms. You may be able to help them reduce their stress levels until they are more manageable.

If you feel unduly stressed at university or college, it is important to seek help from one or more of the following:

See Activity 12.1b FIND YOUR INNER CALM 2 in the Online Study Guide.

- the student counselling service
- parents
- a doctor
- the university or college health centre, if there is one
- friends
- religious leader
- personal tutor or someone associated with the course whom you feel you can talk to.

→ Life events

It is said that important life events and changes, particularly when several occur close together, may produce a cumulative stress condition that makes the individual more vulnerable to illnesses. Holmes and Rahe (1967) have developed what they call the *Social Readjustment Rating Scale*, in which each life event is given a score. The total score is then compared against set levels to determine whether there is a high or low health risk. Table 12.1 is a version of the scale adapted for students.

Table 12.1 The rating scale for life events – student version

Event	Life change unit	Event	Life change unit
1 Death of a close family member	100	17 New girlfriend or boyfriend	38
2 Death of a close friend	73	18 Increased workload at university or college	37
3 Divorce of parents	65		
4 Prison sentence	63	19 Outstanding personal achievement	36
5 Severe personal injury or illness	63		
		20 First year in university or college	35
6 Marriage	58		
7 Sacked from job	50	21 Change in living conditions	31
8 Failure in an important module on your course	47	22 Major disagreement with lecturer/tutor	30
9 Change in health of close family member	45	23 Lower grades than expected	29
		24 Change in sleeping habits	29
10 Pregnancy (own or girlfriend's)	45	25 Change in social activities	29
		26 Change in eating habits	28
11 Sexual difficulties	44	27 Frequent car breakdowns	26
12 Serious quarrel with a close friend	40	28 Change in number of family get-togethers	26
13 Change in finances (better or worse)	39	29 Too many missed lectures/ seminars/tutorials	25
14 Change of academic subject (course)	39	30 Change of university or college	24
15 Gain of new brother or sister	39	31 Change of recreation	20
16 Difficulties with parents	39	32 Minor breaches of the law	20

Source: Adapted from Zimbardo *et al.* (1995); originally from Holmes and Rahe (1967).

PART 1   DEVELOPING STUDY SKILLS

> ### Activity 12.2
>
> ### Stress rating scale
>
> Complete the scale in Table 12.1 to find out your score. Assess yourself on whether each of the events identified has occurred in your life during the past year. You may wish to complete this activity each semester/term, as this will permit you to note any trends in your levels of stress. Add up your scores and mark your total on the line below:
>
> ```
> 0           150           300           450
> |------------|-------------|-------------|
> ```
>
> ### Interpreting your scores
>
> - If your score is 150 or less you are not experiencing a high level of change at the moment. The recent life event changes you have experienced will be well within your capabilities.
> - For scores between 150 and 300, the higher your score, the more likely you are to be feeling the pressure. If you scored close to 300, you have experienced a fairly high level of change during the period reviewed and you may wish to utilise stress-reducing techniques if you feel pressured.
> - For scores over 300, there have obviously been some major changes in your life during the review period. You need to pay particular attention to managing your stress levels.

Holmes and Rahe suggest that the score represents the degree of readjustment that a person has to make in their lives as a result of the change event. Note that the changes identified include pleasant as well as unpleasant events, as they all contribute to stress levels. Whether or not an event is stress producing will depend upon how it is experienced. What is troublesome for one student may not be a problem for another.

> ### Activity 12.3
>
> ### Diagnosing personal stressors
>
> 1. Using the information you have gained from completing the rating scale for life events and your stressors, reflect upon and write down those elements that you think are your causes of stress that need attention. Can you draw out or identify any themes? For example, in student life, some students may be continuously anxious about their grades, competences and skills. Others may be more worried by interpersonal relationships.
> 2. Note carefully how you respond to stressful situations. Identify and describe the behaviour that you display: for example, do you normally remove yourself to another location, become aggressive and argumentative, or more conforming and accommodating when you find yourself disagreeing with another student? Is your response the same or different if this person is a tutor/parent or other influential individual?
> 3. What influences the way you behave in this situation?
> 4. What other influences are there? For example, an individual might have a lot of power over you or you might have power over another individual.
> 5. Now read the section on managing stress and develop a strategy to deal with any excessive stress you are experiencing.

Stop and think
- What have you learned about your stressors from the activities?
- Is there anything that you need to do to reduce your current level of stress?

→ Managing stress

The stress response enables people to produce more energy when it is required to deal with a stressful situation. It helps you to meet personal deadlines and crises easily and confidently. However, it can interfere with the ability to cope if it lasts for too long and at too high a level. Each person experiences stress in their own unique way, so what for one student may be overwhelmingly stressful to another is something they enjoy. For example, as a student you may have to give a presentation by yourself in a lecture theatre to 50 or 60 colleagues. Student responses to this situation will vary on a continuum from enjoyment at being the centre of attention, to attempting to get through what is perceived to be an arduous ordeal. Because stress responses are specific to the individual student, there are no methods for preventing and reducing stress that are going to work for everyone. You should find the ones that work for you.

In understanding that stress largely comes from a mismatch between the individual and demanding situations, you can combat its effects by doing competently what is necessary at university or college by developing your skills and abilities. If you learn how to deal with conflict situations in a positive way, know if it is necessary to seek counselling or medical help, and are able to use your support network of family, friends and religious leaders, you will be able to manage your stress response effectively.

In order to control your stress response, it is necessary to be able to identify and understand your reactions to difficult situations, such as knowing what causes you stress in the academic and personal situations faced. You may have:

- left home for the first time
- moved from a village to a large city
- moved into a house with complete strangers
- become one of a large number of students rather than a well-liked and respected senior in school
- left a girlfriend or boyfriend in your home town.

It is not surprising that, whatever your personal circumstances, it will take a period of readjustment. You may feel very homesick for some time, or you may delight in the freedom from parental control and thoroughly enjoy the social side of university. It may well take you some time to readjust to your new life at university or college. However, it is possible to learn how to maximise your potential by using daily stress control techniques, and being aware of your personal energy patterns and working with them.

! Remember...
Responses to stress are different for each individual and different situations.

Coping mechanisms

The following are some of the coping mechanisms that many students, and others, use to deal with stress. Some coping mechanisms are more likely to bring definite benefits than others, and you need to attempt to deal with the stresses that you face in a positive way.

Avoidance

If you adopt this approach, you will avoid acknowledging, confronting or dealing with the problem by pushing it out of your mind. Alternatively, you may avoid dealing with the problem by withdrawing from the stressful situation, either physically or emotionally. If you find yourself avoiding the stressful situation, it would be useful to make an appointment with the student counselling service or talk with your family, friends, personal tutor, religious leader, etc. They will help you deal with the problem, especially if it is in relation to concerns about assessments, poor performance, financial worries etc.

Procrastination

You may attempt to lessen the problem without actually curing it, hoping that it will go away, by putting off until tomorrow what should be dealt with today. This is procrastination. Some actions chosen may be counterproductive in the longer term: for example, increased smoking, drinking and other drug use.

It is often better to deal with problems with the help of others – the old saying, 'A problem shared is a problem halved' is a truism. For some students there are advantages in being alone and having some privacy. The downside to that approach is the lack of social and emotional support as well as the loss of an alternative viewpoint. If you are experiencing severe stress, you should talk to the student counselling service, peers and friends, relatives, tutors and anyone else involved in the situation who may be able to help. No matter what the problem is which is causing stress, or the degree of seriousness, it is likely that the student counselling service and tutors have seen students who have experienced that particular type of issue before.

Clarify your personal beliefs

It is vital to clarify what is important in *your* life and then to follow your beliefs. Self-awareness, in terms of knowledge, skills, abilities, values and beliefs, is very important. This includes identifying clearly your expectations, goals and needs, so that you do what you want to do rather than responding to the 'oughts' and 'shoulds' in life, which come from other people. Your time at university or college is an exciting, significant and formative part of your life. You will look back on it years later as a period of personal growth and change of some magnitude. As a consequence, it is essential that you are pursuing your own expectations, goals and needs because this will ensure that you are firmly committed to a successful outcome for your studies. If you go to university or college because you thought it was the right thing to do, your friends were going, or your parents wanted or expected you to go, then you are unlikely to enjoy yourself as much as you could and it is doubtful that you will achieve your true potential.

Keep fit and healthy

Everyone is able to cope with stress better if they are physically fit and take regular exercise. Jogging, walking, swimming, aerobics or any kind of vigorous exercise will not only invigorate and energise you physically, it will revitalise you mentally. Universities and colleges generally have excellent sports facilities, such as a gym, swimming pool and playing fields, that you can use to improve or maintain your fitness. If they are not available at university or college, some facilities are usually available in nearby towns and cities.

In order to ensure that you remain physically healthy, it is necessary to be aware of the three main elements that contribute to a healthy body and a healthy mind: exercise, diet and rest. It is important to ensure that you get sufficient exercise and rest and that you eat a balanced diet.

Exercise

This is probably one of the best physical stress reduction techniques. One of the keys to maintaining physical fitness is to take regular exercise (cycling, swimming, dancing, jogging or running, step aerobics, a workout in a gym) – any hard physical exercise for a minimum of half an hour which leaves you out of breath and sweating. This will improve fitness and relax tension, and making you physically tired will aid sleep. However, make sure that you take advice either from expert sports coaches at university or college or from a local health and fitness club before you launch into an exercise programme. If you have not been used to taking regular physical exercise, it is best to build up gradually as your fitness increases.

Diet

It is essential to eat a healthy diet. 'Junk food' is all right occasionally, but preserving a nutritional balance is important. You should avoid too much caffeine in coffee or soft drinks because it may cause irritability and insomnia. Eating sugar – for example, in chocolate or sweets – may give short bursts of energy, and can be a temporary solution that may prove useful for completing assessments such as examinations, but shortly afterwards there will be an energy drop. Also avoid eating too much salt and saturated fat such as butter, milk, cream and cheese. As part of an overall health and fitness strategy, eating a nutritious diet may help to lengthen the amount of time you are able to spend studying each day. There are many sources of help on diets, such as books, videos, DVDs, television programmes, a medical practice or a health centre. Many universities and colleges have a health centre that will normally provide advice and dietary guidance to students.

Rest

Another major factor that contributes to physical health is to get enough sleep. Most students need between six and eight hours' sleep each night, but some need more while others can manage with only a few hours. Listen to your body and if you are tired take more sleep. Alternatively, if you get up with a headache and feel listless, it is likely that you have not had enough sleep (unless, of course, over-indulgence in alcohol the night before is the culprit!).

PART 1   DEVELOPING STUDY SKILLS

Use relaxation techniques

There are many forms of relaxation and you should find one that suits you and your student lifestyle. Some examples are meditation, yoga, breathing exercises and progressive relaxation techniques. There are many books, videos and DVDs that will provide advice and guidance.

Take breaks to restore your energy

It is not a good idea to work for extended periods of time without a break. A five- to ten-minute break every hour is an essential requirement of effective study. If you have been working intensively for a while, get up, stretch and walk around for a few minutes. If you do not take short breaks during your study periods, you will find that your concentration lapses and you will study less effectively. When you have been working for a long time, trying to understand a particularly difficult chapter or an article requiring a great deal of mental energy, doing something completely different for a while will give your brain a rest.

As well as using your preferred relaxation method to restore your energy, you should learn to take 'time out' during the day. You may find yourself rushing between lectures, tutorials, group meetings and the library. If you take even a ten-second 'time out' at the beginning and end of each session, you will feel the benefit. A longer 'time out', say five minutes or so, will provide your mind and body with the chance to recuperate and will recharge your batteries. Use the longer 'time out' if you are kept waiting, if you are travelling or when you arrive home after your day at university or college.

Activity 12.4

Taking 'time out'

The following activity will help you to take a five-minute 'time out':

- Close your eyes, place your feet firmly on the floor, sit up straight and put your hands in your lap.
- Inhale slowly, taking a slow deep breath, then slowly breathe out.
- Pay particular attention to each part of your body. Imagine that each part is becoming relaxed. Make sure that you remain sitting up straight.
- Start with your head; work slowly down your face and jaw, throat and neck, before relaxing your shoulders and arms. Taking each arm in turn, work slowly down to your fingers and feel the stress leaving your fingertips.
- Then relax your chest, back, lower abdomen, legs and feet. Relax each leg in turn, working slowly down to your toes and feel the stress leaving through your toes.
- Inhale another very slow deep breath, then very slowly exhale.
- Stretch gently and open your eyes.

Having completed this activity, note how this has reduced your stress levels. How can you use this technique to help aid your learning?

MANAGING STRESS

Create and sustain a personal support system

See Activity 12.2 GOOD OR BAD ADVICE? in the Online Study Guide.

'People need people' is another saying which has a lot of truth in it. Whilst you are at university or college, you will need the support, companionship and friendship of people whom you can trust. They will be able to provide you with support at times when you need it. Long before you need to draw on your personal support system, identify and make a list of your friends and relatives whom you can turn to when you need to let off steam. At the same time, identify a person or persons whom you can talk to about your innermost thoughts, who will listen to you without judgement and who will respect and keep your confidences. How many people can you identify who will respect and challenge you if necessary? Who, from your student friends as well as your family, will nurture, support and console you in your times of need, when you are simply feeling a bit down, or if you have a major crisis?

However, it is important not to wallow in negative emotions: try to look forward and search for positive solutions. Do not forget to let your friends know that you will reciprocate when they need support. You should also make sure that you share your positive feelings as well. Your friends will be delighted to share your happy times, so, whilst you may want to talk with them when you are feeling sad or low, equally let them know when you are excited, elated or filled with the joy of living.

Use positive thinking to reduce stress

If your lack of confidence is a contributor to your stress levels, you can overcome this by using positive thinking. It is possible to conquer negative thoughts by using *positive affirmations* – these are positive statements that you say aloud to yourself. Some examples of positive affirmations are 'I will do this'; 'I deserve to do this'; 'I can achieve my qualification'; 'I am in control of my life'. If you believe that you can achieve your qualification, you will commit yourself to the hard work necessary to make it happen. Make notices of these affirmations and stick them up where you can see them regularly, on the mirror, in the kitchen, above your bed, etc. Repeat them frequently and this will give a boost to your confidence when necessary.

> **Stop and think**
> ○ How can you use positive thinking to lower your stress levels?

> ### Suggestions for managing stress – general
> - Reflect on and review your obligations periodically. Make sure that they are still right for you. If they are not, change them.
> - Try out new experiences. Allow yourself to delight in the experience of different foods, different places, new hobbies and new things.
> - Remind yourself to maintain positive thoughts.
> - Find ways to relax, and use relaxation or meditation techniques.
> - Keep a sensible diet and sensible sleep habits.
> - Engage in regular vigorous physical exercise.

> See Activity 12.3 STRESS MANAGEMENT in the Online Study Guide.

- Look after yourself by keeping the company of people you like and enjoy.
- Accept responsibility for your life and feelings. If necessary, take steps to change or curtail stressful relationships.
- Take some time outs each day in which you maintain your privacy, personal freedoms and space, i.e. enjoy your own company, play your favourite music, indulge yourself.
- If worries build up, talk to a friend or someone you can trust.
- Avoid extreme reactions by developing a thick skin.

Specific stress associated with being a student

As has already been mentioned, stress is a fact of life. Many students experience increased levels of stress when they move away from home for the first time. This is perfectly natural. Dealing with budgeting, shopping, laundry and personal relationships as well as academic demands is difficult for some students. If you experience difficulties, talk with your classmates and find out what they do. If you continue to experience levels of stress that are unacceptable, talk with your parents, doctor, religious leader or the student counselling service if one is available. If the university or college has a student counselling service, it will normally be able to offer all kinds of advice about finance, personal problems, course-related issues, exam anxiety, etc. Similarly, if the university or college has a health centre, advice about health-related matters such as diet, relaxation or stopping smoking is likely to be available. However, there are particular stressful situations which you may experience for the first time when you are a student. These are frequently associated with assessment, such as examinations.

Examination anxiety

Examination nerves are perfectly natural and most students experience them at some stage in their academic lives. (See Chapter 18 for a more detailed discussion of different types of examinations.) Accept the fact that you will feel nervous and possibly have butterflies in your stomach before an examination – in fact this is likely to drive you on to an improved performance. Learn to use the nervous energy created prior to an examination to stimulate your performance. Passing examinations is a skill that can be learned. As long as you have done appropriate coursework and use the following technique, you will be able to be successful with examinations – even if you have had difficulties in the past. The following will help you deal with and reduce examination stress:

- Arrive at the examination room early with a watch and everything necessary to complete the examination.
- Maintain a positive attitude.
- Decide to do your best.
- Do not blame yourself for what you do not know.
- Do not worry about your knowledge or ability, the behaviour of other students, the number of questions, or even short memory lapses. These can be self-limiting beliefs.

- Concentrate on the examination.
- For the first few minutes, read the instructions carefully and concentrate on getting an overview of the examination. This will calm your nerves.
- Pay close attention to one question at a time. This kind of concentration will help to reduce anxiety. Focus on the questions, not on how well you are doing.
- Relax. If you are too nervous to think or read carefully, try to slow down physically.
- Change your mood by taking three or four slow, deep breaths, breathe normally for 30 seconds between each breath and then start to work.

If the stress becomes intolerable before the examination and you experience sleeplessness, are unable to concentrate on your revision or feel excessive tenseness, talk with the university or college counselling service. They will be able to provide some help. It is possible for the counselling service gradually to introduce you to the examination situation, so that it becomes less stressful. Many universities and colleges set up 'mock' examination situations, so that you will be able to experience examination conditions in a supportive environment. If you find examinations very stressful, you should take advantage of the opportunity to undergo a mock examination or test. If you practise, you will find that examinations become less of a problem. Eventually you will be able to acquire the skill and use the techniques to deal with examinations successfully.

Most universities and colleges keep past examination papers in the library, or faculty office, or make them available to students in some way. If you suffer unduly from examination nerves, get copies of previous examination papers and attempt the various questions in the time stated. It is then possible to check answers against textbooks and notes. Practice produces proficiency in the skills needed to pass examinations. Providing you have done the necessary reading and revision, the skills necessary to pass examinations can be learned, just like any others. It takes time, patience and perseverance.

See downloadable template 12.1 DEALING WITH STRESSFUL SITUATIONS for your Personal Development Plan online.

Suggestions for dealing with course-related stresses

- Set realistic goals for yourself.
- Do not overwhelm yourself by considering your entire workload at a particular time.
- Set realistic goals for yourself, using SMART objectives (Specific, Measurable, Achievable, Realistic, Time constrained).
- Divide course/module tasks into smaller elements that you can cope with.
- Identify milestones, so that you can reward yourself when you reach them successfully.
- Do things one at a time.
- Schedule your reading and assessed work.
- Prioritise the tasks that you must complete.
- Do not leave things until the last minute.
- Talk with other students, as this will help you to realise that you are not the only one feeling this way.
- If necessary, seek professional help from your health centre, tutor, financial or personal counsellor.

Manage your time

Being a successful university or college student will probably demand a more careful and effective use of your time than you have needed to achieve before, otherwise your stress levels will increase. If your stress is caused by poor time management and this means that you achieve less than your potential, you should attempt to manage your time more effectively.

You will be timetabled for a certain number of classroom hours every week. You will need to schedule the remainder of the time to ensure that the preparatory work necessary is completed to meet deadlines. It is likely that you will need to spend in the region of 40 hours per week studying and this time needs to be planned and incorporated into a study timetable. You may have found that school scheduled your study time for you, but this is unlikely to happen at university or college. Class contact time with your tutor may be minimal – possibly in the region of 10 hours a week or less. However, for each class contact hour it is likely that you will be expected to complete about 4 hours per week independent or directed study, so that you are doing 30–40 hours' study each week for the duration of your modules. You will be expected to read and complete assessments either individually or with a group of other students, and this needs thought and planning. It will require careful time management or you may find yourself (and possibly others) in an extremely stressful situation just before the deadline for submission of the assessment because you have not planned and completed the work.

It is a good idea to think of study as a job. It will require a lot of dedication, motivation and commitment to be successful. But, of course, like all jobs, studying can be carried out either effectively and efficiently, or ineffectively and inefficiently. The way to improve study habits is to manage time effectively. As this is a very important aspect of study, it forms the basis of a separate chapter (see Chapter 11).

Summary

This chapter has outlined that:

- stress affects everyone, particularly students
- stress comes from a range of sources and is largely under an individual's control
- whilst there are optimum levels of stress, too much is unpleasant and may inhibit performance
- there are causes and consequences of stress and ways to manage it
- stress management techniques can be used to deal with stresses of student life
- to help to overcome the effects of stress at university or college, it is necessary to be proactive by managing time better, engaging in exercise, using relaxation techniques and talking with family, friends and others as necessary.

Part 2 DEVELOPING ASSESSMENT SKILLS

- 13 CASE STUDIES
- 14 PRESENTATIONS
- 15 ESSAY WRITING
- 16 REPORT WRITING
- 17 WRITING DISSERTATIONS OR RESEARCH PROJECTS
- 18 EXAMINATIONS

This book is accompanied by a Premium Companion Website at **www.pearsoned.co.uk/payne** containing:

- an Online Study Guide with additional topic coverage
- interactive exercises and activities
- downloadable templates for your Personal Development Plan or Portfolio.

To access these resources simply register using the pin code on the access card that came with this book.

Introduction to Part 2

As a student, some of the work you do will be in the form of assessments. This is inevitable – you and your tutors must be able to measure your progress towards achieving the learning outcomes for the subjects you study. Assessments may occur during the module/course (often referred to as in-course) or at the end of a stage (term, semester, year). Assessments are not just a chore to get through so that your tutor can assess your performance, but a crucial part of the learning process. They enable you to assess your own understanding of a topic and explore sources of information. They provide an opportunity for you to demonstrate knowledge and skills by allowing you to articulate your learning, thoughts and ideas in an organised and coherent way which your tutors and others will understand.

The assessments you do will vary in degree of importance. Some may be non-contributory (*formative*) whereas others will be major activities and count towards the overall assessment of your qualification (*summative*). The marks gained from non-contributory assessments do not determine your overall grade of qualification, but they need to be passed to progress from one level to the next. Some students put little effort into these, just enough to pass and progress to the next level; *but* remember that courses are generally progressive, i.e. success in modules depends on knowledge and skills gained in earlier modules. Therefore, you must put as much effort into the earlier modules to be able to perform well in the later stages.

Assessments often require you to examine something in detail and you may need to find additional resources (books, articles, videos, etc.) to help you. Occasionally you may have to go and gather information from other people. Chapter 9 provides advice on gathering information for your assessments.

Assessments may take a variety of forms – essays, reports, case studies, examinations, etc. Some may require you to answer a series of questions demanding concise answers. These will require you to develop your ability to express yourself succinctly as well as accurately. Others may form the basis of a tutorial and you may be asked to lead a tutorial discussion, or present your findings to your tutorial or seminar group. Some assessments will require you to present your ideas in written form (essays, reports, projects, dissertations, discussion papers, etc.), whilst others may require practical work, or presentation of your work orally and even, occasionally, audio-visually.

→ Learning opportunity

In order to get the best out of assessments, ensure that you are clear about what the aims of each assessment are. Many assessments are designed with a number of different aims – to introduce you to an issue that is central to a topic area, to give you practice in the methodologies of the discipline, to diagnose your ability to write clearly and logically, present your views orally, etc. Think carefully about what you hope to achieve from completing the piece of work. Treat each assessment as an opportunity to learn by identifying the aspect of your learning on which you wish to focus, and the skills you wish to improve or acquire.

Sometimes your purpose will conflict with what is expected of you. For example, you may have to complete a piece of work on a topic that holds little interest for you at the outset, or have to produce it in a format that you feel is not the most appropriate. It is sometimes possible to ask the tutor if you can change the topic or format. However, assessments are usually constructed as part of an overall plan to ensure that you cover all the required aspects of the module (and course), and it may not be possible to change them.

> **Remember...**
> Give your assessments originality – most tutors prefer a well-researched and well-argued fresh approach rather than a reiteration of familiar textbooks or their lectures and handouts, which may lead to inadvertent plagiarism.

→ Expectations

Before starting the assessment, ensure that you are clear about what you have to do and the intellectual skills you need to demonstrate. This will vary at each level of your course – as you progress through each level, you are expected to build on your abilities in organising and expressing ideas and information.

Benjamin Bloom (1956) developed a classification of levels of intellectual behaviour important in learning. Many courses are designed to encourage students to develop their intellectual behaviour at each of these levels, with students in the final stages expected to display evidence of the higher levels. Table 1 shows the levels of intellectual behaviour in ascending order of complexity.

In the final stages of a course, it is unlikely that high marks will be gained by displaying the lower levels of behaviour (describing, explaining, summarising) – assessments at this level require analysis, discrimination and critical evaluation of the material.

Table 1 Levels of intellectual behaviour

Level	Behaviour	Examples of verbs used in assessments
Foundation stage Knowledge	Emphasis at this level is on memorisation, recognition and recall of a wide range of material from specific facts to complete theories. At this level, you are required to be able to bring to mind the appropriate information or recall a procedure or series of steps to solve a problem. You may not understand why you are following the procedure, but you are aware that by following it you can solve the problem or get the correct answer.	Define, describe, find, list, measure, memorise, name, present, recognise, recount, relate, select
Comprehension	This level involves grasping the meaning of material – the information must be understood. This may be demonstrated by explaining the ideas and concepts in your own words, putting them in context and indicating their importance. You should be able to predict the consequences and effects of the concepts you have learned.	Clarify, contrast, discuss, explain, express, formulate, identify, illustrate, indicate, judge, justify, review
Intermediate stage Application	At this level you must be able to transfer what you have learned (ideas, methods, concepts, etc.) to new situations. You should be able to select the appropriate material or procedure and apply it correctly.	Apply, assess, choose, demonstrate, employ, explain, practise, predict, show, use
Analysis	This level requires an understanding of both the content and the structural form of the material. The material is broken down into its constituent parts so that the relationships between the parts and the organising principles of its structure may be understood.	Analyse, compare, conclude, contrast, criticise, debate, differentiate, examine, justify, question, resolve
Advanced stage Synthesis	This is the most creative of the intellectual levels with the emphasis on the formulation of new patterns and structures. It requires an ability to create new ideas or procedures by reconfiguring the constituent parts and including additional elements to form a new whole.	Argue, combine, construct, create, derive, design, develop, discuss, formulate, synthesise, generalise, organise, propose, redefine, restate, summarise
Evaluation	At this level you should be able to judge the value of material presented to you using the criteria given or determining your own criteria on which to base your judgement.	Appraise, assess, choose, criticise, critique, defend, discriminate, estimate, evaluate, judge, rate, review support

Source: Inspired by Benjamin Bloom (1956).

→ Assessment criteria

Assessments are usually accompanied by a set of assessment criteria. These provide details of what your tutors will be looking for when they mark your assessments. It is important that you spend some time familiarising yourself with the assessment criteria and ensuring that you understand them. Before submitting any assessment take the opportunity to reflect on your work and how what you have done meets the assessment criteria.

→ Presentation of assessments

When completing assessments, ensure that any particular criteria about presentation identified by the tutor are adhered to – for example, is there a specified word length, should written assessments be word processed and presented with double or single line spacing, and how long should the oral presentation be? Valuable marks may be lost if you do not keep to the specifications or present the assessment in the required format.

→ Deadlines

Whatever the format, the secret of a good assessment is good planning. It is desirable to start doing this well before the date on which you need to hand work in, so that you have plenty of time to think things over before the assessment is due to be submitted. It is a good idea to aim to complete an assessment at least a week in advance of the submission date. You can then read it through a day or two before submission, which will allow time for any revisions you think necessary to be made. It also allows for any unforeseen eventualities.

Some universities and colleges will impose penalties for work that is submitted late. It is therefore important that you submit assessments by the due date to avoid losing valuable marks. In addition, if you fall behind in your studies, it can be very difficult to catch up, and often everything tends to suffer on the domino principle – if one falls over, then the rest fall over!

If things get out of hand and you find you are unable to meet the deadline, then you may be able to request an extension to the submission date (though some institutions will not allow this). To request an extension, you must have a good reason. It is unacceptable to present 'not being able to organise yourself' as an excuse – time management, organisation and planning are all part of the learning process. Most tutors will recognise that circumstances may arise that are outside the control of a student, making it impossible to complete work to the deadlines. In such cases, tutors will generally be sympathetic when negotiating extensions.

If you are unable to gain an extension or complete the work on time, then it is often better to submit a poor piece of work, perhaps staying up all night in order to complete it rather than not submit anything. A low-quality piece of work is likely to gain some marks, whereas a non-submission will earn a zero. Submitting a low-quality piece of work rather than nothing at all may also stand in your favour in the future if you should happen to be a borderline pass/fail case. If you have not submitted work, the tutors and/or examiners will not be impressed with your efforts and may therefore be less sympathetic to your case.

Above all, it is important to begin working on assessments as soon as possible. Do not fall into the trap of leaving them until just before the deadline.

→ Group assessments

For some assessments, you may be required to work as part of a team with other students. This not only means you can tackle more demanding questions, but it is also an opportunity to develop your skills of working with others. Chapter 10 provides more detailed information about working in groups.

Any assessment that requires research takes time and usually takes longer than initial estimates. A group project will almost certainly take longer, as there are often additional problems such as coordination and managing conflict. A common issue arising with group work is that some people are working harder than others. This may cause resentment and/or an imbalance in the finished product. It is essential that a group assessment is planned for completion well before the deadline in order to include a safety margin for time to resolve any difficulties.

Suggested stages for completing a group assessment

1 *Prepare a schedule.* Determine (and agree) the timetable for completion of the assessment. The group may also wish to identify a leader at this stage. It may be appropriate to specify who is responsible for doing what at this stage.

2 *Initial research.* At this stage, the whole group should do some preliminary reading, particularly if the topic is unfamiliar. An outline of the main points to be tackled for the project then needs to be agreed by the group. This will provide some indication of how the project may be divided up. This may be completed at the first meeting of the group if sufficient is known about the subject area.

3 *Allocation of tasks.* Allocate the members of the group to the different parts of the project – if there are sufficient members, two or more could work together as a subgroup.

4 *General approach.* Decide on the general approach to be taken by the group. A problem can arise if the different members or subgroups take different approaches – for example, if a few members argue for the inclusion of a particular aspect and the rest argue against. It is a good idea to deal with this in the preliminary stages.

5 *Complete the tasks.* At this stage, each member or subgroup can read and prepare their part of the project. It is useful to hold regular meetings of the group so that progress and problems can be discussed and resolved.

6 *Write the draft.* A small inner circle of two or three members should write the full draft assessment, combining the parts submitted by all group members or subgroups. This may require rewriting and editing in order to match writing styles, etc. It is important that the final product is seamless and does not appear as a number of different bits hastily put together. An introduction, conclusion and summary will also need to be compiled.

7 *Discuss the draft.* The whole group meets to discuss the draft and agree to it. This is important, as the people writing the draft may have misinterpreted something or made compromises.

8 *Prepare the final submission.* Write the final report or prepare the oral presentation, paying attention to any assessment criteria. If an oral presentation is required, the group must decide who is to speak. Sometimes it is a requirement for each member to speak – if so, ensure that the presentation does not appear to be disjointed. (Chapter 14 provides useful suggestions to help you give effective group presentations.)

Common problems encountered in working on group assessments

Leadership

Sometimes the person selected as leader may prove inadequate. Although difficult, the group must try to discuss the situation openly and, if necessary, nominate someone else as leader. This needs careful consideration, as it will undoubtedly generate ill-will and the replaced leader may subsequently not contribute to the best of their ability.

Free-riders

Often one or two free-riders may appear within the group. They will do little or no work and leave everything to the rest of the members, although the group may share equally in the final mark. This can cause resentment and ill-will within the group. If free-riders appear, the group should arrange a meeting to discuss this and see if the situation can be resolved. Sometimes there may be good reasons for members not taking their full share – for example, health or personal problems. In these cases, the group needs to offer support and perhaps renegotiate the allocation of tasks. In extreme cases it may be necessary to speak with your tutor to resolve the situation.

If you are unable to resolve the situation, console yourself with the fact that free-riders disadvantage themselves in the end – they learn far less.

Peer assessment

Sometimes tutors will allow students to allocate marks amongst group members rather than accept an equal sharing of the final marks. This will help to combat the free-rider problem. However, the process of trying to achieve an equitable distribution can become very complicated. Keep the process of allocation as simple as possible and ensure that every member of the group knows and understands the process and agrees to abide by it.

→ Feedback

When assessments are returned with a mark or grade and tutor feedback, do not just file them away. It is important to read the comments made by the tutor and learn from them. The feedback provided may give you an indication of what you need to do to improve your grade or mark in future assessments. Compare your feedback comments with those of other students; they may have comments giving guidance in different aspects. Sometimes you may have the chance to ask the tutor for more detailed feedback – this is a good opportunity to learn how to improve your assessment skills. However, it is important to prepare for a feedback session and determine beforehand the questions you wish to ask. Some tutors may provide group feedback sessions – these can be very useful, as many different aspects of the assessment may be covered.

The following chapters of this book provide more detail and advice on the different forms of assessment you may encounter during your course of study.

Checklist: Things to consider before completing assessments (excluding examinations)

- Have you identified the main topic areas covered by the assessment? ☐
- Have you identified which skills the assessment is designed to develop and/or assess? ☐
- Do you know what form the assessment is required to take? ☐
- Do you know the deadline for submission of the assessment? ☐
- Do you understand the criteria by which the assessment submission will be judged? ☐

Checklist: Things to consider before submitting your assessments (excluding examinations)

- Does your submission address the topic/s required? ☐
- How does your submission meet the assessment criteria? ☐
- Does the assessment meet all specific criteria about the form of assessment (e.g. word limit)? ☐
- Have you met the deadline? ☐

13 Case studies

> **Learning outcomes**
>
> After studying this chapter, you should be able to:
> - use a framework for the successful analysis of case studies
> - systematically analyse the information given in a case study
> - recognise the problems/issues within a case study and devise solutions
> - evaluate the solutions generated to make sound recommendations.

→ Introduction

A case study is a means of learning whereby you must actively participate using your skills and knowledge to analyse problem situations and make recommendations for their solution. A case study can bridge the gap between classroom theory and business experience by simulating a realistic situation (some may be based on fact). This enables students to practise problem-solving and decision-making skills in a low-risk, non-threatening environment without making expensive 'real' mistakes.

Working on a case study provides you with the opportunity to practise and strengthen your skills in analysing situations, identifying problems, deciding priorities and appraising possible courses of action. You are able to apply theories you have learned to a realistic situation, which results in deeper learning that can be applied more readily to real-life problems. This will give you confidence in your ability to cope with the ambiguities and uncertainties that you will encounter in the world of work.

Case studies are often applied to organisational situations, although they could relate to a particular situation facing an individual, group, community or nation. In reality, problem situations very rarely fall into rigid subject areas but will require a multidisciplinary approach. Similarly, case studies require you to take a holistic view, and in any one situation you may be called upon to apply any part of your knowledge and use any of your skills. It is important to remember that it is the application of theoretical concepts and techniques to the analysis and evaluation of situations that is vital in successful case study preparation. You need to apply the knowledge and experience you have acquired, and techniques, concepts and skills that are appropriate, in determining solution(s) to the problem(s) presented.

Case studies are usually paper based, although they may be presented on audio-visual media. They vary in content and length – some may be short (mini cases) and give a brief summary of a situation, while others may be quite lengthy, giving a detailed account of a complex situation incorporating many different aspects, such as finance, personnel and strategy. Whether long or short, complex or simple, single or multi-issue, there is no doubt that you will feel that the information given is imperfect and incomplete. This simulates the real world – rarely do we have complete and perfect information on which to base a decision, but must face uncertainty and make the best decision using the information available to us.

Many students feel apprehensive when faced with a case study. Case studies can be quite demanding because of their unstructured nature, the analysis required, and a feeling of uncertainty caused by an apparent lack of sufficient information. Whatever the length and complexity of the case study, the process of analysis will be similar. The aim of this chapter is to provide a framework to help you to analyse case studies successfully.

The use of case studies

Case studies provide a valuable learning experience and will enable the tutor to assess your ability to diagnose problems and use problem-solving and decision-making skills to determine, present, justify and defend recommended courses of action.

There are a number of different ways in which a tutor may introduce and use a case study.

Class discussion

The tutor may issue a case study to the whole group and ask everyone to study it prior to the next meeting, when a group discussion will take place around the case study. In this instance you should familiarise yourself with, and prepare answers for, the case study so that you are able to participate fully in the discussion. Group discussion of case studies is a valuable learning process, requiring the use of interpersonal skills as well as case skills. Full participation in the discussion can be challenging but rewarding. Use the opportunity to practise:

- presenting your view
- listening to other perspectives presented by your classmates
- challenging others' opinions and interpretations
- defending your ideas
- handling criticism from others.

See Chapter 10 for more information on group discussion.

Alternatively, the tutor may issue a case study within a class and expect discussion straight away – there is no time to prepare answers but you are expected to 'think on your feet'. This reflects business situations where problems arise without warning and solutions need to be found immediately.

Discussions on case material may be done on an individual basis or the tutor may split the class into smaller groups and ask each group either to work on the whole case study or to tackle different aspects of the case and report back to the full class. Working on a case study in this way provides an opportunity to practise your listening and group working skills.

See Activity 13.1 CASE STUDIES QUIZ in the Online Study Guide.

Assessment

A case study is often used as a basis for assessment. Sometimes a case may be distributed and you are asked to prepare an analysis to be presented either in written form (e.g. report) or orally for assessment at a later date. A case study may also be used as the basis for an examination. The case study may be 'seen' although the questions are not known. In this situation, the case material is distributed a number of days or weeks prior to the examination in order that it may be digested and some initial analysis carried out. Sometimes it may be permissible to take rough notes or an annotated copy of the case study into the examination room. On other occasions you may not be allowed to take any workings in with you.

Sometimes the case study is not distributed beforehand, but is distributed at the beginning of the examination. If the case study is not seen before the examination, time may be given at the beginning (designated as reading time) specifically for the case study to be read. Writing is not allowed until this time has elapsed.

Stop and think
○ What are you allowed to take into the examination room?

Whatever the format, the answers to case studies are individual – there will be no one correct answer. The solutions offered, the criteria for evaluating them and the final recommendations will vary from one person to the next depending on that person's experience, knowledge and opinions. It is therefore essential that you are able to present your findings clearly and convincingly.

Remember...
There is usually no right answer – ensure the solutions you present are justified.

→ Framework for case study analysis

The key to success in case study analysis is to work logically through a number of steps. The following guidelines refer to case studies on organisations but may be applied to other case studies.

PART 2   DEVELOPING ASSESSMENT SKILLS

1 Familiarise yourself with the case material

Read the case study quickly to gain an overview of the situation presented. Do not stop to re-read anything; just try to get the general picture. No analysis should be started at this stage. Do not be tempted to start solving problems that you think exist before you have thoroughly analysed the information given.

Sometimes only part of the information may be given out, with the rest available on request. This is used to develop the skill of asking questions. A tutor is unlikely to respond to the general question, 'Is there any more information?' However, it may be wise to ask for specific information if you feel it would be useful.

> **Stop and think**
> ○ What further information do you need?

2 Read the instructions

Read the instructions carefully and ensure you understand what you are required to do. For example:

- Do you have to look at the whole case or only certain aspects of it?
- Are you expected to assume a particular role? If so, be clear about what capacity you are acting in (adviser, employee, external consultant, trainee manager, etc.). The answers, and the way you present them, should reflect this role.
- How are your findings to be presented? You may be asked to prepare either an oral or a written presentation of your answers; if a written presentation is required, check if it should be in a particular format (e.g. a report).

Figure 13.1 Framework for case study analysis

Case familiarisation
↓
Examine the information
↓
Define the problem(s)
↓
Determine the causes
↓
Generate solutions
↓
Evaluate solutions
↓
Make recommendations

Sometimes the instructions may be implied or hidden within the case study. For example, 'The managing director has asked you to find out ...' would imply that you should take the role of 'expert'.

3 Read the questions

If the case study includes questions to be answered, read them carefully. These are the questions that must be answered. If marks are assigned to questions, consider how the marks are distributed between questions. This will give an indication of the relative importance of each question and, particularly in an examination, the amount of time it is advisable to spend on answering each one. For example, if a question is allocated 50% of the marks, then it is a good idea to spend 50% of the time available answering it!

> **Remember...**
> Answer the questions set. Avoid the temptation to create and answer your own questions!

After gaining an overview of the case study situation and a thorough understanding of the questions and their context, it is advisable to leave the case study for a while, providing you are not in an examination, returning to it some time later to do a more detailed analysis. This allows you to digest the information.

> **Remember...**
> Read the case.
> Read the instructions.
> Read the questions.

4 Analyse the information

Read the case study again, slowly, and consider the information and how it may be used. Aim to gain understanding and an awareness of the decisions to be made together with anything that may influence them, such as constraints and resources.

Suggestions to help you analyse the information

- As you read through the case study, make notes in the margin as they occur to you, noting any points of theory that may be helpful.
- Underline or highlight key points and phrases in the case which provide clues as to how the situation or problem is developing.
- Identify any underlying themes and determine how they may fit with the question posed.
- It can be useful to use a letter or number system to indicate areas that are interrelated.

The information contained in a case study is not always in an order conducive to logical analysis. This reflects life in organisations. If the information is not presented logically, it is worth spending some time putting the information into some sort of order or structure to make the analysis easier.

Some case studies may include numerical data. It is important to spend some time ensuring that you understand these data. For example, how were the figures arrived at? What do they mean? If financial data are presented, analyse them carefully.

The following questions, where appropriate, may be used to highlight information that can help you to understand the background to the situation presented in the case study.

The organisation

- What business is the organisation in?
- What business does the organisation want to be in?
- What facilities does the organisation have?
- What are the core skills of the organisation?
- Are the core skills the ones required for the business that the organisation wants to be in?
- What is the financial situation of the organisation?
- Are there any areas of conflict or potential conflict within the organisation?
- What is the predominant management style of the organisation?
- What is the formal structure of the organisation?
- How is information communicated within the organisation?
- Is there a strong informal organisation underlying the formal structure?
- What are the main systems within the organisation?
- What are the problems, if any, with the systems?

The characters

- Who are the main characters involved in the case study?
- What are their responsibilities, characteristics, attitudes and relationships to other characters? An extended form of organisation chart may be used to record this information.

The situation

- How has the situation developed over time?
  – What were the antecedent conditions?
  – Identify the stages of development or sequence of events.
  – Can a trend be detected?
- What are the underlying themes and issues?
- How critical is the situation? Does it require preventative or corrective action?
- What is the extent of the problem? Does it affect the whole organisation or just part(s) of it?
- Are there any underlying or long-standing issues?

CASE STUDIES

The context

See Activity 13.2 APPROACHING CASE STUDIES in the Online Study Guide.

Look at the context of the decisions to be made:

- Are the issues international, national, regional, local?
- Are there any constraints?
- What resources are available?
- What are the politics of the organisation?
- Are there any government policies that are pertinent to the situation?

> **Remember...**
> For factually based case studies, make a note of any specific dates given. These may give clues to incidents such as a period of high unemployment, industrial conflict or high interest rates, etc.

Some of the information within the case study will be highly relevant and some hardly relevant at all. The information must be analysed in order to try to determine what is relevant and what is not. The ability to pick out relevant information while discarding that which confuses the issues is a key skill.

One approach is to identify what are the facts and what are opinions or conjecture about the situation. This will help you to judge the validity of the information given. When deciding about the possible options, consider how much the information given can be relied upon. Never assume that the information provided is 'pure'; it will inevitably have been presented from a particular point of view and will have been filtered or possibly distorted.

Facts

Establish the facts of the situation. The facts of the case are objective and relate to actual happenings or events rather than being based on a mere statement of belief or opinion.

Deductions (deductive inference)

Use your powers of reasoning to deduce things from the facts presented. Deductions are conclusions that have their foundations in facts; they are deduced from what is known to be true or valid and are therefore certain.

Example

    Fact 1:   Anyone under the age of 18 is legally a minor.

    Fact 2:   Legally, minors cannot be sued.

    Deduction/conclusion: If you are under the age of 18, you cannot be sued.

The last statement (*conclusion*) is deduced from the other two factual statements (*premises*) and therefore can be made with certainty. Both premises are based on certain truths therefore the deduction is reliable (*sound argument*).

Inferences

It is necessary to use your powers of judgement to decide the validity of inferences. Inferences are based on facts, but they are someone's interpretation of those facts or evidence. Therefore they may contain elements of generalisations and assumptions, and might be speculations, which are not reliable information.

Example

Premise:	Everyone loves a winner.
Premise:	Peter is a winner.
Conclusion/inference:	Everyone loves Peter.

The last statement (*conclusion*) is inferred from the previous statements (*premises*). The argument is not sound but is logically strong. It is not necessarily true that everyone loves a winner; this is a generalisation and, as you do not know Peter, you cannot be sure he is a winner.

Opinions (attitudes, feelings, beliefs)

Opinions are frequently presented as if they are facts and can be seen to be true by the layperson. However, opinions are subjective, based on judgement and estimation, and therefore need to be treated with caution. If opinions are stated, you must decide how valid the opinion is, as this will have an influence on your subsequent decision making.

Opinion-based arguments are difficult to resolve as they are subjective, and arguably any one person's view is as good as the next. For example, the statement 'Manchester United is the best football team' is an opinion. Some people would argue that this statement is not correct and would offer their own ideas as to which football team is the best. It is impossible to arrive at an objective factual truth about this, as it is subjective, depending on beliefs and attitudes. However, an informed opinion generally holds more weight. For example, the view of a football expert would hold more weight than that of the average person in the street. Of course, if the coach of Manchester United offered the 'expert opinion' then this could be said to be a biased opinion!

In organisations, 'experts' in a field are expected to have experience and knowledge in that area and their opinions would therefore have influence. However, as with the example above, it would be necessary to evaluate them on the basis of how 'biased' they might be.

Whilst you need to treat opinions with caution, you should not discount them altogether, as people's opinions will influence their actions.

Table 13.1 Example table to record information

Statement	Fact or opinion?
Sales were down by 15% in the last quarter.	Fact (if supported with figures)
The sales director indicated the sales person did not appear to have the ability …	Informed opinion
The sales manager indicated that good sales people are born, not made.	Informed opinion but may be biased

Examine the material presented in a case study and identify which are informed and which are uninformed opinions, which are plausible, and which may be put down to prejudice or bias. A useful activity is to construct a table (see Table 13.1) in which you can record the information given and identify the facts and opinions within the case.

There are, of course, some pieces of information that are not easy to categorise in this way, but it may help to focus thinking on the information provided in the case study.

> ### Activity 13.1
>
> #### Categorising information
>
> Categorise the following statements. Where the classification is not clear-cut, make notes as to why this is the case.
>
> (a) The chairperson believed that the basic products had a growth rate only the same as the economy.
> (b) The company has over 110,000 employees worldwide.
> (c) The firm is a clear leader in its field with a correspondingly high profit record.
> (d) According to the IT manager, everyone should have a computer on their desk; this would make them more efficient.
> (e) The manager believed that the way forward was through investment in research and development.

See Activity 13.3 OPINIONS OR FACTS? in the Online Study Guide.

Numerical data are often thought to be representative of the facts and are frequently accepted without question. If financial data are presented in a case study, question how these data were arrived at. If this is not possible, it may be necessary to make some assumptions. State clearly any assumptions you make, in order to help the reader follow your reasoning.

> **Remember...**
> Clearly state any assumptions you make.

5 Define the problems

The next stage is to identify the problems and determine how it arose. Problems generally arise where things have changed in a situation, where there is a gap between what is and what should be, or if an expected level of performance is not being achieved.

What are the key indicators?

Identify the key indicators that show that a problem exists. Examples of such indicators are productivity rates, market share, customer complaints, employee turnover, financial indicators, etc.

The terminology used may also provide clues to the problems. For example, 'continued to disregard warnings', 'was not happy', 'showed concern', etc., may indicate some long-standing problems. Phrases such as 'ordered', 'supposed to be', 'had not realised', 'was unhappy' or 'private discussions' may indicate problems of relationships or management style.

What are the real problems/issues?

List the problems you have identified and determine which are the most important of those listed. Ensure that you are certain what the real problems are that underlie an issue. You need to distinguish carefully between symptoms and underlying causes. It is important to establish the root causes of the problems so that your answers deal with these rather than identifying and treating the symptoms. Are those problems you have listed the real ones or are they just symptoms of other more deep-rooted problems? Remember Pareto's principle (the 80:20 rule), which may apply to the situation – although many variables may be at work, often only a vital few are problematic (see Chapter 11 for more information on Pareto's principle).

> **Stop and think**   ○ Is the issue a symptom or a cause?

Are any of the problems/issues connected?

Consider whether any of the problems are connected – how complex is the situation? Draw a diagram indicating the relationships between the problems identified. This will help to detect the critical issues that are at the root of the problems.

If your analysis is sound and the problems are precisely defined, this will provide a firm foundation for deciding what can be done to resolve them. If problems are not defined correctly, a solution may be offered that alleviates the problems but does not resolve them.

In trying to understand the problems, use the theoretical concepts you have studied on your course to provide a framework for the analysis. This will help to provide focus.

6 Determine the causes

See Activity 13.4 EVALUATING PROBLEMS in the Online Study Guide.

Problems cannot be considered solved unless their causes have been isolated and dealt with effectively. To establish the root causes of the problems, you will need to sift through the information provided. This can be made easier if you look for links and relationships between pieces of information.

The fishbone diagram (cause and effect diagram)

This is a method of analysing problems and separating causes from effects. To construct a cause and effect or fishbone diagram:

1 Write the effect on the right-hand side of a piece of paper – be precise and give examples. For example, 'poor working conditions' is rather broad. It is better to be more specific and identify (in this example) the nature of the poor working conditions (e.g. cramped office layout).

2 Draw in the main ribs of the fish and write in the headings of the main problem areas. Most problem situations in organisations may be covered with six headings: people, environment, methods, plant, equipment, materials. Not all the headings will

Figure 13.2 The fishbone diagram

[Fishbone diagram with ribs labelled People, Environment, Methods (top) and Plant, Equipment, Materials (bottom), pointing to EFFECT.]

be relevant for all cases. Include only the ribs that are relevant to the case you are analysing.

3 Generate a list of causes that relate to the problem and write them against the appropriate headings.
4 Indicate the linkages between the different causes.
5 Think about the ideas for a while.
6 Analyse the whole diagram – most problems will have a few essential issues that need solutions.

7 Generate solutions

This is the creative aspect of the process. Once the root causes of the problems have been identified, alternative approaches to solve them will need to be created and developed. The first stage in determining solutions is to identify the objectives. The objectives may have been set within the case study or you may have to determine them for yourself. If you have to determine them, consider what you feel the situation should be in the future before you prescribe the means of getting there.

In setting objectives, it is helpful to identify the aspects that can be changed and those that cannot but must be accepted. It is important to prioritise your objectives in terms of what *must* be done and what is *desirable*. You may also need to consider the time frame of the solutions you suggest – long term, medium term and/or short term.

The objectives you set will determine the type of action required:

- *Corrective action*: this should lead to the eventual elimination of the problem.
- *Holding action*: this does not provide a permanent answer to the problem but is a short-term solution to keep the system and/or the people functioning. Eventually further action will need to be taken.
- *Minimising, adaptive*: if the problem really cannot be resolved then action should be taken to minimise its effects.

Consider whether the situation presented in the case study can be equated to a real-life situation. Has anything like this happened in an organisation with which you are familiar? If so, how was the problem dealt with? This may provide a starting point.

Brainstorming is a technique that could be used here to generate alternative solutions. After you have brainstormed ideas, refined them and identified some workable alternatives, make a list of the solutions generated.

> **Remember...**
> Brainstorm alternative solutions – you never know, a zany idea may turn out to have some merit on further consideration!

8 Evaluate solutions

From the list of alternative solutions identified, you need to decide which course(s) of action you are going to recommend. These should be the ones that will best fit with the objectives set. In order to make recommendations, first analyse and evaluate each of the alternative solutions. For each solution, predict the outcome(s) of implementing it, using both qualitative (reasoning) and quantitative supporting criteria. This will form the basis of your choice.

For each option, consider the following:

- What is the organisation's likely future environment in which the solutions will be operating?
- Will it work? Why or why not?
- How will it be implemented? All at once or in stages?
- Resources: what resources are needed or available?
    – Staff: who will be involved? Are they capable? Do they have the skills?
    – Who or what might block or hinder?
    – Money: how much will it cost? Where can savings or payoffs be found?
    – Time: how long will it take to implement? When should it be implemented?
- What action will be taken?
- What impact will the solution have on the organisation and/or the environment?
- What benefits will be gained from implementing the solution?
- What could go wrong?

Always consider the 'do nothing' solution and the consequences of following this course of action – sometimes it may be better to leave well alone.

A table may be constructed (see Table 13.2) to help your analysis and focus thinking when deciding which solution(s) to recommend.

Generally, the preferred alternative will be the one that is likely to produce the largest excess of positive aspects over unfavourable negative ones. If the aspects can be specified in monetary terms then a cost–benefit analysis may be used.

> **Remember...**
> Always consider both the positives and the negatives.

CASE STUDIES

Table 13.2 Analysis of solutions

Option/solution	Predicted outcome or impact	Positive aspects or benefits	Negative aspects or costs
Example: Training programme for machine operatives	Increased production levels, fewer defective products, etc.	Increase in morale, increase in skill level of workforce, improved product quality, etc.	Disruption to production, costs of training programme, etc.
Use of contractor/ outside body	Completed quicker as they may be more focused	Buying experience in	More expensive. Upset to staff as opportunities have been taken away

9 Make recommendations

Because there is unlikely to be a single best solution to the problems within a case study, the justification for the chosen recommendations is extremely important. The case presented should convince the reader or marker that it is the correct course of action based on the analysis of the material. Indicate how the solution achieves the objectives, the expected benefits or positive aspects and the costs or negative aspects of implementing the recommended solution.

The course(s) of action recommended should be specific, avoiding broad generalisations. Present well-supported, constructive arguments based on the selection and application of appropriate concepts and techniques.

Suggestions for the recommendations you make

Recommendations should be:

- feasible within the resource constraints
- imaginative but realistic
- pragmatic
- specific
- prioritised with respect to the problem outlined
- defensible and justifiable courses of action
- lucid, convincing and persuasive
- based on sound evidence.

In presenting your recommendations, remember to explain the what, why, when, how, where and who:

- *What* exactly are you recommending? Be specific. Clearly indicate the resources that will be required to implement the solution, new ones that need to be acquired and also current ones that will be utilised (e.g. equipment, staff training and facilities).

PART 2   DEVELOPING ASSESSMENT SKILLS

Figure 13.3   Presenting recommendations

- *What* are you recommending?
- *Who* will be involved in implementing the recommendations?
- *Why* are you making these recommendations?
- Recommendations
- *Where* will the recommendations be implemented?
- *When* should the recommendations be implemented?
- *How* should solutions be implemented?

> See downloadable template 13.1 ASSESSING GROUP WORK SKILLS for your Personal Development Plan online.

- *Why* – outline the reasoning leading to the recommendations.
- *When* – indicate the timescale you are recommending for implementing the solution(s). Should there be a trial run or a pilot scheme to see if it will work before the full recommendations are implemented? This may be advisable if radical change is being proposed.
- *How* – give a clear indication of how the solution should be implemented.
- *Where* – indicate precisely the parameters of any changes. For example, is the whole organisation involved or only specific parts?
- *Who* – indicate the responsibilities of any personnel involved in the solution.

When recommending solutions and looking at their implementation, it is worth considering the implications of change. Most solutions to cases will involve change of one kind or another and this will produce feelings of unrest and even conflict within an organisation. Demonstrate an awareness of the difficulties aroused by change situations and offer solutions as to how they may be handled successfully.

Suggestions for successful case study analysis

- Follow instructions and answer the questions given.
- Examine the facts as they are, not as they should be, not as they are said to be, and certainly not as you would like them to be.
- Identify the real problem(s) or issue(s) – resist the temptation to focus on symptoms.
- Separate the strategic issues from the operational basics.
- Look for cause and effect.
- Identify who owns the problem.
- Examine all the possible alternatives.
- Present a realistic, resourced implementation plan.
- Indicate any assumptions made.
- Recommend specific courses of action.
- Avoid hasty judgement.
- Solutions based on fact and supported by theory are more powerful and more likely to be accepted than those based on assumptions, beliefs or inferences.

Remember...
There is usually no right answer – your answers must persuade the reader that your solution is the best one.

→ Presentation of answers

When the analysis of the case material has been completed, the issues identified and the possible solutions evaluated, you need to turn your attention to the presentation of your findings in the appropriate format. Case studies simulate realistic situations and the answers presented should follow business conventions unless otherwise requested. If a report is required then the answers should be presented in a conventional report format. If an oral presentation is required, prepare yourself to give a professional presentation (see Chapters 14 and 16).

Do not underestimate the importance of presentation. Marks can be gained or lost by the quality and style of the presentation. Spend time on the presentation of your work; otherwise, no matter how brilliant your analysis and solutions, your work will be undervalued. Good presentation enhances the value of your work.

Note any constraints, such as a word or time limit, and keep within them. Written answers should generally be more structured and detailed than answers presented orally. Oral presentations may allow questions from the audience or requests for clarification of particular issues. This is not possible with a written submission. Keep answers simple and structured to help the reader or marker to follow your line of thought. If you have to present the answers orally, be prepared to defend your perspective and answer questions about your analysis and recommendations.

PART 2   DEVELOPING ASSESSMENT SKILLS

> **Remember...**
> Only interpretation, analysis and reasoned proposals will gain marks.

See downloadable template 13.2 FEEDBACK ON GROUP WORK SKILLS for your Personal Development Plan online.

Suggestions for presenting answers for case studies

- Spend time on the presentation of your answers, ensuring the style/format is appropriate for the context.
- Don't waffle – keep to the point. Avoid the temptation to pad out your answer with an extended general introduction. No credit will be given for this and there may be a word limit (or a limited amount of time for an oral presentation).
- Answer the questions posed, not the questions you think should have been asked. The content of your answers should reflect the questions set.
- Don't just describe the problem – provide solutions.
- Support solutions with fact or theory.
- Avoid reproducing or reworking the information provided in the case study. Extract the relevant bits to support the points and assertions made.
- Do not include observations that do not relate directly to the questions set.
- Clearly state any assumptions you make. Making assumptions is acceptable as long as they are reasonable and within the context of the case.
- Keep it simple and structured.

→ Summary

This chapter suggests:

- a framework that provides a systematic approach to analysing the information in a case study
- case studies require time to be spent on understanding the information contained within the case study in order to recognise and define the real problems
- the instructions need to be read carefully so that answers are appropriate to the context
- the information within the case study needs to be carefully analysed, in order to prepare and evaluate solutions to the problems identified, and appropriate recommendations made
- answers should be presented in an appropriate format, ensuring that the assessment criteria are met.

14 Presentations

> **Learning outcomes**
>
> After studying this chapter, you should be able to:
> - identify the main purposes of presentations
> - outline the major elements of a presentation
> - create, select and use the most appropriate visual aids
> - structure a presentation
> - deliver an effective presentation with confidence.

→ Introduction

Whilst at university or college you will certainly have to give presentations as part of your course. Some of them will be assessed and others will be formative in nature, which will help you to meet the assessment requirements later. Both assessed and non-assessed presentations may have to be given within the first few weeks of the start of your course. You may also choose to be involved with the students' union, societies and voluntary work, and these may require you to speak to groups of people. You will also find that subsequent to higher education many people in the business world have to give presentations as part of their job role.

What you should remember is that most of us are not born with a natural aptitude to give presentations. Most of us find it quite stressful at first, even managers and politicians, many of whom receive specialist coaching so that they are able to speak effectively. Many UK politicians, for example, when they are first elected to parliament are far from being effective presenters, but they all have to go through the nerve-wracking process of giving their maiden speech in the House of Commons. For many of them this takes place late at night with only a few other members of parliament in the chamber, so that the experience is not too intimidating. By the time a member of parliament reaches the front benches, either in government or in opposition, they have developed their presentation skills so that they normally excel at giving prepared speeches.

The majority of us may not wish to emulate members of parliament in many ways, but to be able to deliver presentations of the technical calibre some of them achieve is something we too can learn. It is, of course, necessary to practise presentations in order to become proficient. Those people in public life who have made an enormous impact with their presentations have usually spent many hours practising and rehearsing to improve their oral presentation skills. They normally also practise non-verbal signals to add emphasis appropriately – a smile, a nod or a sweeping gesture with their arm. There are some people in public life who will not give an impromptu presentation, speech or comment; they need the security of time to practise. The same is true of television presenters. The most natural and spontaneous-looking presentations are often the product of hours of practice and rehearsal.

It is a good idea to take every opportunity to speak in front of others while on a university or college course. It is quite normal to feel considerable trepidation at first, fearing that you will forget what you want to say, or that others will think that your comments are irrelevant. You may not even wish to contribute at all because you feel embarrassed about speaking in public. Console yourself with the knowledge that those people who appear supremely confident may be shaking like jellies inside and, even if they are not, they probably did in the past. Many of us feel nervous of speaking in public, but the aim of this chapter is to help you to develop the techniques of giving effective presentations and to enable nervousness to be overcome.

Purposes of presentations

At university or college there are formal, assessed presentations which will involve the tutor(s), possibly external business people, and sometimes colleague students marking performance against agreed criteria. In addition, there are informal presentations that are formative in nature and therefore are not assessed towards the qualification. Every opportunity should be taken to give informal non-assessed presentations because the feedback received from the audience will help to develop presentation skills.

Presentations are concerned with communicating a message to groups of people. As with other communication processes, presentations are used for the purposes of:

- giving information – for example, in business and education
- instruction – also used in business and educational settings
- persuading – used in business, education, politics and the media
- entertaining – used in the media and the performing arts.

On your course you may have to give presentations of all four types, but it may be that all of the elements are contained in a single presentation. Clearly the presentation will be designed to have a particular focus and this will influence, and be influenced by, a number of factors, such as:

- the material used in the presentation
- the breadth and depth of the topic
- the audience size

Figure 14.1 The process of presenting

```
Presenter → Message (Visual aids, voice, body language) → Audience
Audience → Feedback (Interest, attention, body language) → Presenter
```

- the layout of the presentation space
- the duration of the presentation
- the desired result.

Obviously a course may specify some of the factors: for instance, there may be an allocation of 20 minutes to give the presentation to a small group of about six people. This may permit audience participation in the presentation. Alternatively, there may be a requirement to give a group presentation to a large audience, which lasts one hour and necessitates standing at a lectern and using overhead transparencies or slides. This would mean that there was little prospect of involving the audience.

What must be borne in mind is that the message has to be communicated to the audience in the time available. This is represented visually in Figure 14.1.

→ Preparation

There are a number of questions to consider before starting research on a presentation. Try to answer the questions in the checklist before you begin.

It is essential to prepare carefully for a presentation and it is critical to be familiar with the subject. Think for a moment about sports people. They prepare for matches and races through dedicated practice or training. Preparing to give a presentation is little different from a student point of view.

PART 2   DEVELOPING ASSESSMENT SKILLS

> **Checklist: preparing for a presentation**
>
> What is the purpose of the presentation? To give information, persuade, etc? ☐
> What objectives have to be met? Is the presentation assessed, formative etc? ☐
> Who is the audience? What needs do they have? What knowledge does the audience bring to the presentation? ☐
> What is the length of the presentation. How can the time available be organised to make the best use of it? ☐
> Is the presentation to be instructive or interactive? Is it necessary to plan for audience questions or only delivery of the presentation? ☐
> Will visual aids and/or handouts be used? If visual aids are to be used, are overhead projectors, flip chart holders, computers, etc. available? ☐

Stop and think
- Are you preparing adequately?
- Do you know the subject in detail?
- Have you done enough research?
- Have you practiced many times?
- Are you ready?

There is little worse than a presenter who has not prepared fully or is unfamiliar with the subject. This person appears confused and disorganised, and has little worthwhile to say to the audience. Similarly, if the presenter reads *verbatim* (word for word) from a script, all spontaneity will be lost and the attention of the audience will probably not be captured.

> **! Remember...**
> Preparation is critical for a presentation.

→ Structure

The structure of the presentation needs to be coherent and logical. In order to ensure that this is the case, ask yourself why you are giving the presentation in the first place. What message or information needs to be given to the audience? When these questions have been answered it will be possible to focus on the essential aspects. Your presentation should be organised clearly and logically, and should contain at least the following:

Figure 14.2 **Presentation structure**

```
Introduction ──► development ──► conclusion
```

- Conclude with overview
- Summarise important points
- Provide evidence and examples
- Develop key points logically
- State objectives
- Subject in context

- An introduction – this should set the subject in context and state the objectives or outcomes.
- Several key points that are developed logically – evidence and examples should be provided to support key points and/or claims.
- A summary of the important points for the audience – possibly concluding with an overview of the presentation (see Figure 14.2).

→ Approach

The approach taken is very important in that it can either enhance a presentation or be distracting for the audience, in which case they will remember little of the content. When you are giving a presentation ensure that you:

- Rehearse your presentation in front of others to assess their reaction and to receive feedback from them. This also gives you an indication of the time it will take to deliver the presentation.
- Radiate confidence and speak with clarity and conviction.
- Appear enthusiastic, natural and sincere, but not over the top as this will put people off and they may not listen to the points being made. Frequently it is not what is said to an audience but how it is said that is remembered.
- Use short sentences – avoid long, complex and convoluted sentences.
- Avoid vagueness and ambiguity by being specific. For example, do not use phrases such as 'I conducted many interviews'; say 'I conducted 55 interviews'. Vague terms such as the following should not be used: 'they say that', 'almost every', 'some', 'about the size of', 'probably', 'that sort of thing', 'a large deputation'. These types of phrase communicate nothing to the audience.

> ### Suggestions for content of presentations
>
> All topics can be made interesting and stimulating with application and dedication. Take the following suggestions into account when preparing or presenting a talk:
>
> - Make the purpose of the presentation clear to the audience at the outset. What is the message that you are trying to get across?
> - Tailor the presentation to the audience. Make sure that you have thought carefully about the audience, and that you know their needs and the subject matter.
> - Consider how much the audience can absorb in the time allocated. The attention span of the listeners may be quite short, especially if numerical data are being presented. Do not overwhelm the audience with information.
> - Be specific and relevant. Do not wander off the main topic by spending too much time on anecdotes. Avoid the use of humour unless it is relevant. The audience may not share your sense of humour. This could mean that your presentation is not well received.
> - Develop a reasoned and compelling presentation.
> - Pause briefly after important points; this non-verbal marker will provide emphasis.
> - Use emphasis to help the audience isolate the main issues. Verbal markers such as 'There are five important points to remember about . . .' will alert the listeners to look for and remember the five points.
> - Define technical terms. Do not assume that because you understand a technical term your audience will share your understanding. Unless a technical term is explained, the listeners may think it is jargon.
> - Sequence points carefully. If content is presented in the wrong order, it may be ignored or misunderstood by the audience. It can be difficult to decide the sequencing of important points in presentations. For example, which is more effective – to present things chronologically, in the order in which they happened? Familiar to unfamiliar? Order of importance? Simple to complex? Known to unknown? Cause/effect/solution? Any of these may work, and from your knowledge of the audience you will need to decide which approach to take in each particular case.

→ The presentation

Before delivering a presentation, familiarise yourself with the room in which it is to take place. A visit to the room will enable you to identify the facilities available and be one fewer unknown factor to be nervous about. Ensure the layout of the room is to your liking – if not, change it by moving the furniture around. You may wish to have your audience sitting in rows if you are delivering a lecture, or a semi-circle or a 'u' shape to encourage communication. You may have to give your presentation in a lecture theatre where the furniture is fixed. Always be aware of the opportunities and limitations of the room in which you have to give the presentation and this will avoid a nasty surprise on the day.

Check also that the equipment needed is available in the room and that it works. It is no good planning to give a presentation using PowerPoint to project the images onto a screen, if the audience then has to sit in the dark because there is no natural light in the room. In some rooms the lighting is such that it is either all on or all off. In this instance, if the lighting is on, the audience would not be able to see and read the projected images. With the lights off, the images would be clear, but the audience would not be able to take any notes. Also check the room at the time of day when the presentation is to take place and in different weather conditions. A sunny day in a room without blinds can make a presentation projected on to a screen impossible to see.

Checklist: assessing the teaching room

Seating arrangements: 'U', circle, semi-circle, row? ☐
Lighting: is it adequate/versatile? ☐
Equipment:
Whiteboard? ☐
Pens? ☐
Overhead projector? ☐
Flip chart and holder? ☐
Lectern? ☐
Table? ☐
Microphone? ☐
Heating and ventilation: is the room warm enough and well ventilated? ☐

Timing

Ensure that you rehearse the presentation. If a specific time limit is allocated and this is exceeded, you may not be able to make all the relevant points. Similarly, if you do not use all the time available, the opportunity is missed to make a comprehensive presentation, and as a consequence, if it is assessed, the mark may be lower than might have been achieved with practice. If the presentation is too short, it may be that insufficient research has been carried out. When rehearsing the presentation, take a careful note of your speed of delivery. If it is too fast, the audience will not be able to keep up with what you are saying. On the other hand, if it is too slow, the audience will be bored or their attention will wander and the presentation may exceed the time limit.

When giving an assessed presentation, it is better not to allow interruptions from the audience. This will permit more control of the time allocation and questions can be taken at the end. If a questioner interrupts, politely tell him or her that all questions will be taken at the end of the presentation – or better still, at the outset, tell the audience that there will be time for questions at the end. If interruptions are allowed in the form of questions, it may not be possible to complete the presentation within the time limit. It is far better to complete the content and run out of time for questions, than to allow questions and not complete the presentation.

Body language

It is possible to use body language to enhance a presentation by using natural and spontaneous body movements and facial expressions (see also Chapter 5).

- Eye contact is very important. Make sure that intermittent eye contact is made with different people in the audience when speaking. Range your eyes over the audience; do not look at only one person, the ceiling or your notes all of the time. It is very easy to become fixated on one person who smiles briefly at the beginning. Do not be beguiled by such a person; make sure that the presentation is addressed to different parts of the room. Looking at the audience will allow you to assess the level of interest as well as audience understanding through their facial expressions, head nods and posture. Initially it may appear that there is no feedback from the audience, but do not be intimidated by what appears to be a lack of expression on people's faces. This means that they are concentrating on the presentation.

- Distracting mannerisms should be avoided when presenting. Do not gesticulate wildly, fidget, rock backwards and forwards, fiddle with your hair, play with a belt buckle or brooch, shuffle papers or notes, etc. If the presentation is rehearsed in front of a full-length mirror, you will be able to identify any personal mannerisms. Ask yourself whether you find the same mannerisms irritating or distracting from tutors when they are presenting lectures. If you are distracted by a tutor's mannerisms, your audience is likely to find them just as distracting or irritating from you. You will have noticed that, depending on the particular presentation, some presenters walk around, moving a pace or two from the lectern or the table. It is a good idea to stand up for the whole presentation, as it enables you to breathe deeply. Watch carefully what your tutors do, then decide which style and format you prefer and which is the most effective and then attempt to copy it. You may feel a little awkward at first, but persevere and it will become more natural with practice.

- Some gestures, however, are not distracting and can aid understanding by providing emphasis, communicating enthusiasm and indicating distance or nearness. Point to the overhead projector slides or posters, etc., as this draws the audience attention away from you, for a few seconds at least. However, do not turn away from the audience as they will not hear what you have to say. You should avoid speaking at the projected image on screen as the audience will only see the back of your head. It is acceptable to check that the image is visible, especially if you are using OHP acetates, but advisable to have aides-memoires on a table or lectern so that you face the audience when you speak.

- If several people are giving the presentation, look interested whilst the other presenters are speaking. You can guarantee that if you yawn and look bored whilst another student is speaking, the audience will feel the same way. Help each other during the presentation by providing support, particularly with visual aids. Nod your head to affirm important points that the other presenters are making. Try to smile where appropriate, as this will put you and your audience at ease. However, do not giggle or laugh nervously, especially if someone makes a mistake, as this will put him or her off and undermine the presentation.

- Personal appearance sends non-verbal signals to the audience. It is important to dress appropriately for a business presentation, especially if it is assessed. Smart clothes, clean shoes and neat appearance all send appropriate messages to the audience.

- At the end of the presentation it is a good idea to use non-verbal signals to indicate that the presentation is concluded. Thank the audience for listening, if appropriate. Collect your papers and slides together and switch off the projector or computer.

> **Stop and think**
> ○ Are you able to keep eye contact?
> ○ Do you have any distracting mannerisms?
> ○ Can you use gestures to emphasise a point?
> ○ Are you dressed appropriately?
> ○ Are you able to smile appropriately to put yourself and your audience at ease?

Speaking

When you are presenting, speak clearly, precisely and not too hurriedly. Speak with conviction, confidence and enthusiasm, as this will generate interest in the audience. Accents are acceptable as long as the audience is able to understand what is said, but do not mumble.

- Colloquialisms, jargon, slang and dialect should be avoided unless they are relevant to the content of the presentation.

- Avoid too many 'ums', 'you knows', 'I means', 'ers' and 'OKs'. Cut out all words that add nothing to the meaning: for example, change 'at this moment in time' to 'now'.

- Avoid using the same words too frequently – one sign of nervousness is using a particular word over and over again. Try to be aware of the audience response. If you do use a word too often, it should be possible to identify the audience reaction to its overuse. From then on, it is a good idea to try to avoid using that word.

- Keep your head up when you speak. If your head is down reading from your notes, your voice will be less distinct and the audience could miss important points. When a student presenter reads *verbatim* (word for word) from comprehensive notes, their voice lacks variety in terms of volume, pitch, speed, rhythm and inflection. You should try to avoid reading from notes.

- The majority of inexperienced presenters speak too fast. When presenters are nervous the tendency is to speed up, so try to avoid this through practice and make an effort to slow down. If anyone actually asks a presenter to slow down, you can be certain he or she needs to speak much more slowly. Again, audience reaction through non-verbal communication or body language should alert the presenter to the fact that he or she is going too fast. As a general rule, when speaking to a large audience, delivery should be slower.

- Vary the speed, pitch and tone of your voice when giving a presentation. If you speak in a monotone, your presentation will be dull and boring to the audience. Try to alter your voice, raising or lowering it to provide emphasis. If you pause, speed

> See Activity 14.1 PRACTICALITIES OF PRESENTATIONS in the Online Study Guide.

up or slow down the delivery and change the volume of your voice, this will make the presentation much more interesting to listen to. Project your voice so that everyone in the audience can hear what is said, but do not shout as this will hurt your vocal chords. Practise speaking into a tape recorder, as this will enable you to assess the degree of intonation in your voice. You will be able to determine whether you are distinct and precise in speech, and decide whether your voice is loud enough. From the recording you will be able to assess whether your speed is appropriate. Be careful not to strain your voice. It is all too easy to speak from the throat instead of breathing deeply and speaking from the chest. Taking a few deep breaths before starting a presentation will also calm your nerves. Finally, make sure that your voice does not drop at the end of a sentence, because the audience will not be able to hear the presentation if your voice falls away every few seconds. If you do this, you will find that the audience becomes bored and starts to move around restlessly, which will become distracting and may increase your nervousness.

> **Stop and think**
> - Are you using meaningless words?
> - Do you repeat the same words frequently?
> - Do you speak clearly?
> - Do you look at your audience?
> - Are you speaking at an appropriate pace?
> - Are you varying the speech, pitch and tone of your voice?
> - Can your voice be heard by everyone in the room?

Activity 14.1

Practise presentation

In the privacy of your own room, practise giving a short presentation of about five minutes on your favourite topic. Stand in front of a mirror and tape record or video your presentation. Check your body language and speaking voice.

Draw up an action plan of how to improve your presentation skills.

Notes

It is important when planning your presentation to decide what you will use as aides-memoires. Do not be tempted to give a presentation without any memory prompts. It is all too easy to stray from the topic, or miss important points by losing the sequence. Unless you possess an extremely good memory, it is advisable to use some method as a memory aid, such as prompt cards or notes pages from PowerPoint. Avoid using all capital letters as this will make your notes difficult to read. It is much better to use upper- and lower-case letters in a clear font that is fairly large.

The following are a few examples of what may be used as aides-memoires.

Mind maps

Some presenters use mind maps – see Chapter 6 for further information.

Prompt cards

Many presenters use prompt cards. These are small cards, approximately 7.5cm × 2.5cm, on which the presenter makes short notes that serve as memory prompts. If this method is chosen, do not be tempted to write the presentation out in full on the cards, but use a few words, a phrase or short sentence that serves as a reminder about a particular topic. It is important either to number the cards or to fasten them together with a treasury tag or string. If there are several loose cards and the presenter drops them in his or her nervousness, it may not be possible to sort them quickly during the presentation.

> **Remember...**
> Prompts will aid memory but do not write your presentation word for word.

A4 paper

See Activity 14.2 USING STAGES in the Online Study Guide.

Some student presenters write their presentation *verbatim* (word for word) on A4 paper and read it out. This is not advised, as you should be more familiar with the material to be presented. A lecturer or tutor would not be impressed by this approach because in most instances all spontaneity is lost and keeping audience interest proves difficult. In addition, many students who do this hold the A4 paper in front of them to read from, and any tremor or shake in the hands is amplified to the end of the paper. This indicates clearly to the lecturer or audience that the presenter is nervous. However, you should not worry too much about being a little nervous. It is said that all good performers suffer from nerves – just try not to display them to the audience.

→ Visual aids

Visual aids can improve a presentation enormously, and maximum use should be made of them. They are a very powerful way of getting the message across to the audience, but do not forget that a visual aid is simply a tool to enable you to create an impact. Different types of visual aid include overhead projector slides or transparencies, flip charts, whiteboards, videos, slide projectors, handouts and other props and objects. It is, however, a good idea to avoid using too many different types of visual aid in the same presentation. Do not let the presentation be dominated by superb slides or props, otherwise the succession of overhead projector slides, objects, charts, videos and handouts can bewilder the audience. The audience might be so entertained by the technical brilliance of the visual aids that they completely miss the message.

PowerPoint is increasingly used for presentations, and makes it very easy to create professional and impressive projected slides. However, the use of such software may make slides too technically detailed and as a consequence difficult to understand. Ensure that the quality and quantity of the visual aids that are used enhance the presentation. When overhead projector slides are produced using PowerPoint, they should reflect your proficiency at producing materials with the use of graphics packages (see Chapter 8)

> **Remember...**
> Whatever visual aids are used, the message should be straightforward, to the point and clear enough for the audience to be able to understand it.

Overhead projector slides or transparencies

You will almost certainly have to use overhead projector slides during your time at university or college. The overhead projector slide is a very versatile visual aid that can be used to support a presentation. If a presentation of 15 or 20 minutes' duration is required, it would be advisable to use overhead projector slides. Even for short presentations the overhead projector slide is very useful. In any presentation, slides can provide the presenter with all the cues and memory prompts necessary and other aides-memoires may not be needed.

Overhead projector slides are clear plastic sheets that can be written on with special pens. It is also possible to photocopy from an overhead transparency master or to print slides on a laser or ink-jet printer.

There are several types of overhead projector slide – those that can be:

- produced through a photocopier
- printed on a laser printer
- printed on an ink-jet printer
- written on.

The overhead projector slides that can be put through the photocopier or printer are much more expensive to buy than the write-on ones. The write-on overhead projector slides require special pens that are available in two types: non-permanent, which can be washed off the slide so it can be recycled; and permanent, which need a solvent to remove the ink. Invariably it is necessary to make alterations when creating slides, so if you decide to use the permanent pens, it is a good idea to purchase some of the solvent to remove the ink. For example, the writing, diagram or graph may be too small when projected, or you may make a mistake and need to make changes.

Before buying any overhead projector slide pens, try some out in a stationers to see which is preferred. Choose pens that enable you to write large enough so that the text can be read from the back of the room. Highlighting pens for projection film are also available, so slides photocopied in black may have a touch of colour added.

Producing overhead projector slides

The checklist on p. 304 will enable you to create effective overhead slides as visual aids, although many of the points are equally valid for whiteboards and flip charts.

Consider how to convert words into pictures, such as graphs, diagrams and illustrations. Most of people can absorb information much better if it is in pictures or symbols, and importantly they will remember more of it after the presentation (see Figure 14.3). Use diagrams to present complex concepts. It is sensible to use overlays to build up

Figure 14.3 Different types of graphical display

complex models. By adding an overlay it is possible to add to, or increase the complexity of, the model or diagram. Never try to describe a diagram without a visual aid, as this is likely to confuse the audience rather than get the message across.

Never present figures orally

Do not present a page full of numbers or lists of figures on a slide. A pie chart, histogram or picture graph will be much more effective and keep the audience interested, as well as providing variety. Make sure that any graphs used are simple and easy to understand. Explain what the axes represent and tell the audience what any boxes, arrows, symbols or signs mean. (See Chapter 7 for guidance on data presentation.)

Do not be tempted to put too much on to an overhead projector slide

This is one of the most frequent errors made when preparing overhead slides. Ensure that slides are kept simple and clear. Include about four points under one heading and consider whether the audience can quickly and readily take in what is on the slide. Try to confine each slide to one concept or a limited subject area. It is much better to use a series of slides to explain a complex topic rather than trying to squeeze everything onto the one slide. If too much detail is included, the audience will find it difficult to take in and it may cause confusion.

Use a large font

Title font should be about 44 points and bullet points about 28 points. Background colour should be light and font colour should be dark. The font should be clear and easy to read from a distance, such as Arial. Be careful to ensure that what looks good on a laptop or desktop also looks good when projected on screen. There is nothing worse than having what looks to be an excellent presentation on screen, only to find that when it is projected on an overhead projector, the audience cannot read the text.

Never use type size of 10 or 12 points. This is the size of type on a typewritten page and is not suitable for overhead slides. Your audience will not be able to read what is on the slide and they will lose attention very quickly. This also applies to flip charts and whiteboards. Everything on a flip chart and a whiteboard needs to be in large letters so that those sitting at the back of the room can read what has been written. The same applies to graphs, charts and maps – make them as big as practicable to ensure that they are easily read by those people sitting furthest away from the image.

Organise the material into sections

Examples of this are: chronologically from first to last; simple to complex; advantages and disadvantages; assets and liabilities; good and bad. Use bullet points or short phrases – do not use whole sentences. Bullet points, bold, italics or some other method can be used to highlight key words. If slides are handwritten, use a clear print. It is a good idea to use a lined A4 writing pad to rest on, so that when a new slide is placed on it, it is easy to write in straight lines by using the lines on the paper as a guide. Do not use all upper-case letters (capitals) as this is distracting for the audience.

Avoid punctuation as far as possible

When seen from a distance, slashes can look like letters, e.g. yes/no and exclamation marks (!) may look like a 'one' or the letter 'ell' when projected. Awkward line breaks, such as 'carpet' divided by a hyphen into car- and pet, could mislead the audience who may think that words or phrases are being used that do not make sense. Splitting of words onto separate lines in this way should generally be avoided wherever possible.

What is said in the presentation should confirm or elaborate the slide

It is desirable to amplify what is on the slide, but do not be tempted to talk about a different topic. Presenters who do this will cause consternation because the audience will not know whether to concentrate on the slide or to listen to what is being said. They cannot do both and may lose interest in the presentation.

Prepare overhead slides in advance of a presentation

Think carefully about what to include on your slide(s) and use colour, if possible, as this retains audience attention. Choose colours carefully: for example, avoid yellow or orange, which can be difficult to see. If you make a mistake or change your mind when preparing a slide before a presentation, it is a straightforward task to make a new slide. An attempt to draw slides *during* a presentation could bring disaster. Drawing a normal distribution curve or a graph may be simple well in advance of a presentation, but under pressure a steady hand might desert the presenter as it is not easy to draw the beautiful bell curve intended.

> **Checklist:**
>
> Do your presentations include figures?
> What is the most appropriate method to present these?
> Do your slides have impact?
> Do your slides appear crowded?
> Will the audience be able to read the text (particularly those people furthest away)?
> Is the material organised logically?
> Have you avoided punctuation that could be confusing?

PRESENTATIONS

Activity 14.2

Producing graphical overhead projector slides

Go to the library and look in the local and national newspapers and business journals to identify how figures are presented graphically. Find some lists of figures and draw up your own graphs on A4 paper/slides.

Produce slides containing graphics to display the most important points you made in your five-minute presentation about your favourite topic (Activity 14.1 in this chapter).

Suggestions for projecting slides

- *Keep the slide on the overhead projector for longer than you feel is necessary.* You are familiar with the content of the slide, and are talking through and developing it, but the audience will have to consider what you have included, assess it, and in some instances may wish to write down the essential details. It is a fundamental error to change slides too quickly. This will lead to the audience becoming restless and losing interest because they are unable to follow the presentation. Once the audience have lost interest, it is very difficult to arouse and captivate them again. Do not make the mistake of leaving the slide on the projector too long as this can divert attention away from what is being said. Remove slides from the overhead projector and switch it off when you have finished talking about that particular aspect of the presentation, as this will avoid the audience being distracted from the content of the presentation.
- *Number the slides in some way so they are easy to sequence.* Certain types of slide have a paper strip down one edge that can be written on. Alternatively, write a number in the bottom corner of each slide, or stick on an adhesive label on which to write the number. If the slides are dropped, it is then easy to sort them into sequence again. It is possible that during the presentation the slides will stick against each other as if they are glued together, but if dropped you can be sure they will scatter all over the floor!
- *Have a photocopy of the slide in front of you.* This will enable you to look directly at the audience and will help you as an aides-memoire. You could write extra points on your photocopy that will help with the presentation and remind you of additional material to be presented. This might eliminate the need for prompt cards. During the presentation do not spend most of the talk looking backwards at the projected image. This will make your voice indistinct and the audience will have to put up with the view of the back of your head.
- *Cover the majority of the slide with a piece of paper.* Move the paper slowly to progressively reveal information on the slide and this will focus the attention of the audience on the point you are making. This technique also maintains audience interest as they are kept in suspense about what is to be revealed next. It requires practice, however, as it is easy for the paper to fall off the projector when the bottom of the slide is reached. This problem can be overcome either by weighing down the paper with a pen or ruler, or by moving the slide forward on the platen. For small sections that are to be progressively revealed, it is useful to use Post-it stickers to cover certain words or parts of a diagram until it is necessary to reveal

them. The use of progressive disclosure prevents the audience from reading on ahead and then looking expectantly for more, or being bored because the presenter is taking longer than they would like over a certain point. An inexperienced presenter is likely to be encouraged to go faster and faster by these types of audience behaviour, resulting in the presentation being over in a fraction of the time it should have taken.

- *If you wish to show a complex model or diagram to the audience.* Use PowerPoint or make several slides and overlay them progressively one on top of the other. If you use slides, bear in mind that it might be quite difficult to align all of them, but it is possible to attach the overlays at the edges with clear sticky tape. The clear sticky tape acts like a hinge and permits each overlay to be folded into position when it is needed.

Stop and think

For the last presentation you gave, did you:
- ○ keep slides on projector for longer than might seem necessary?
- ○ number the slides?
- ○ have a copy of the slide in front of you?
- ○ reveal the points on the slide progressively?
- ○ use overlays or PowerPoint for complex diagrams?

Suggestions for using the overhead projector

PRESENTATIONS

- Check that the overhead projector is in the room and that it is in working order.
- Make sure that all the audience will be able to see and read from the image.
- Locate the on/off switch – there is nothing worse than having to search around in front of the audience to find the switch.
- Locate the focus knob and focus the image until it is sharp.
- Move the projector, if necessary, so that the image fills the whole screen.
- Make sure that the platen glass is clean, free from fingerprints, dust and other marks.
- Adjust the projector so that the image projected is square and does not look like a keystone (see Figure 14.4). You may find that the screen can be moved or that you need to move the projector.
- Practise putting slides on the overhead projector. Place them on the platen (glass screen) the right way up and the right way round. What you see in front of you is the image that will be projected. Make sure that all of the material on the overhead slide can be seen when it is projected. Some slides are larger than the usable area of the platen and care should be taken so that the audience can see the entire image.
- Do not obscure the image by standing in the line of sight of the audience or by getting in the way of the projected image. You will find that the light is blinding and the audience will be able to see only a large black shadow on the screen.

Figure 14.4 Projection techniques to avoid

Whiteboards

It is possible to use a whiteboard as well as, or instead of, overhead slides. The drawback to using a whiteboard is that it is necessary to write in front of everyone. It is still essential to prepare diagrams, graphs and bullet points, but it is not possible to utilise the same level of complexity that is available with overhead transparencies or PowerPoint. Whiteboards also need special non-permanent markers, which are different from the overhead projector pens. It is a good idea to ensure that you have your own and a whiteboard eraser, or that they are available in the presentation room.

Bear in mind that, whilst drawing or writing on the whiteboard, you will be facing away from the audience. If you wish to continue talking to the audience at the same time as writing on the board, ensure that your voice is clear and projected sufficiently for everyone to hear.

Before the start time for your presentation, check that the whiteboard is clean and that any writing on the board has not been done in a permanent pen. If it has, you will need to find some way to clean the board. As with overhead projector slides, write and draw much larger than usual. In advance of the presentation, practise writing on the board, as most inexperienced presenters tend to be unable to keep writing in a straight line. Consider also that the audience will be able to write or draw as quickly as you, so it is best to restrict yourself to an outline of your presentation or a few bullet points and then talk about each one. Make sure that there is enough space on the board for the points to be made, or valuable time will be wasted cleaning off what has been written.

Flip charts

Flip charts are a simple and effective means of providing visual information in small group situations. A flip chart is a large drawing pad containing several sheets of paper (A1 size – 59cm × 81cm). The flip chart is attached to a support bar and clamped by the top edge to a flip chart holder. The pages can then be 'flipped' backwards or forwards during a presentation.

Flip charts have certain advantages over whiteboards, in that some diagrams and graphs can be prepared in advance of the presentation. An outline of the presentation can be written up on the flip chart in advance, possibly using bullet points to talk through. If you wish to impress your audience with your ability to draw diagrams straight onto the flip chart, you can draw a faint outline in pencil. The pencil lines and anything else that is written faintly as memory prompts on the flip chart paper will not be visible to the audience.

If a flip chart is to be used, it will also be necessary to have a flip chart holder, unless the flip chart sheets are taped to the wall or whiteboard. As before, practise using the flip chart paper and holder. It is easier to write and draw the presentation flip chart sheets beforehand. However, it may be necessary to leave one blank page between each of the diagrams, charts or lists, because sometimes the paper is thin enough for the writing to show through from the sheet below.

Some flip charts are perforated towards the top of the sheet, and when presenting it may be best to tear off each sheet as the presentation progresses. Other flip charts are not perforated and it is necessary to fold the sheet back over the top of the flip chart holder. It is a good idea to have a couple of spring pegs or a spring bag closer which can be fastened on to the sheet that has been talked through, because used sheets have a nasty habit of sliding back over the flip chart holder. This can prove very entertaining for the audience, but very frustrating for the presenter.

Handouts

It may be a requirement to provide a handout for your audience at the beginning or end of your presentation, summarising the main points. If so, bear in mind that if it is given out at the beginning of the presentation, the audience may spend the time reading it,

See Activity 14.3 PRESENTATION TECHNIQUES in the Online Study Guide.

which can be distracting. The handout could be provided as pre-reading or at the end of the presentation. If, however, you have been asked to give a more comprehensive handout to the lecturer as part of the presentation, you should ensure that you comply with this requirement. Some presenters provide copies of transparency slides as a handout to the audience with space for notes.

Questions

Some assessed presentations require a question and answer session at the end of the presentation. If this is the case, then you must ensure that it occurs. However, if your presentation is not assessed, it is necessary to weigh up the pros and cons of leaving time at the end for questions.

It can be quite difficult to encourage some audiences to ask questions. If the presentation has been instructive in nature, then members of the audience may not ask questions for fear of displaying their ignorance or 'looking a fool'. However, questions often open up the topic and allow for a wider discussion to take place. The audience can display its understanding of the topic, or the presenter can correct any misunderstandings and if necessary clarify anything that the audience is unclear about.

If you do decide to leave time for a question and answer session, and there are few, if any, questions from the audience, it is a good idea to have one or two questions that you pose for the audience. The advantage of this is that you should be able to answer your own questions! This will probably encourage the audience to join in the discussion and they are then more likely to ask questions of their own. Normally in assessed presentations, students are unlikely to ask hostile questions. There is usually an atmosphere of mutual support, although if you do get a hostile questioner, avoid getting into an argument with them (see suggestions for how to deal with hostile questions).

If other students are required to ask questions as part of the assessment for both themselves and the presenters, you will need to be extremely familiar with the presentation material. Students who are being assessed on the questions they ask tend to ask very incisive and difficult questions, and your ability to answer them may improve your mark considerably.

Suggestions for answering hostile questions

- Be polite and respectful.
- Listen attentively.
- If necessary restate your point clearly.
- Answer the questioner with questions.
- Try to broaden the discussion to include others.
- Offer to discuss details at the end of the presentation.
- Try to anticipate questions and rehearse answers, but in the face of hostility be assertive not aggressive.
- Do not be drawn into an argument.
- Remember, it may be that the hostile questioner is the only one who disagrees with the point(s) being made.

Table 14.1 Criteria used to evaluate presentations

Presentation evaluation sheet		Good ←――――――――→ Poor				
Name(s):		5	4	3	2	1
Preparation	Familiarity with material Knowledge of subject matter					
Content and structure	Introduction Logical development Appropriateness of arguments Conclusion Summary Completeness					
Timing	Well executed Within time limit Appropriate use of time					
Visual aids	Adequacy Appropriateness Clarity Use of colour Impact					
Delivery *Verbal*	Intonation and emphasis Audibility Speed and pace Fluency Enunciation Vocabulary					
Non-verbal	Dress Posture Mannerisms Gestures Eye contact Confidence					
Overall effectiveness	Impact Audience response					
Response to questions	Ability to cope with questions Quality of answers given					

Comments overall: (*Tutor will delete those that do not apply*)

An excellent presentation. Very well structured, all relevant theoretical approaches included and no major omissions. Excellent presentation skills.

A good presentation. Well structured with appropriate content. Most of the theoretical approaches included, though some omissions. Presenters possess good presentation skills.

A satisfactory presentation. Some weaknesses in structure and content. Some theoretical approaches included, but with significant omissions. Presenters possess adequate presentation skills.

An inadequate presentation. Major weakness in structure and content. Some theoretical approaches considered, but major omissions. Presenters' presentation skills unsatisfactory.

Areas for improvement

PRESENTATIONS

→ Assessed presentations

During a university or college course, students are frequently required to give assessed presentations. Table 14.1 provides examples of some of the items that are commonly included in an evaluation sheet for presentations.

Activity 14.3

Analysis of a professional presenter

1 Watch a prominent politician giving a speech.
2 Observe a lecturer when you consider has good presentation skills, giving a lecture.
3 Study carefully the main presenter in a news bulletin.

Make detailed notes about the following:

(a) How does each presenter structure the information?
(b) What factors make the presentation interesting and easy to listen to?
(c) What makes one presentation clear, whilst another seems muddled and boring?
(d) How does the presenter make valuable points?
(e) How are facts, opinions and conclusions presented?
(f) How are emotive phrases and evasive arguments used?
(g) List the similarities and differences that you can identify. From your list, draw out those aspects that you think make an effective presentation. Compare your list with the presentation evaluation sheet in Table 14.1. Now create an action plan for your next presentation.

See downloadable template 14.1 ASSESSING PRESENTATION for your Personal Development Plan online.

Suggestions for the essential ingredients of a good presentation

- Organise and prepare your ideas.
- Present them to the audience in a clear and logical order.
- Use straightforward, clearly stated themes.
- Utilise effective visual aids.
- Rehearse frequently.
- Deliver with a confident manner.

If your presentation is pitched at the appropriate level for your audience, you cannot fail to be successful.

→ Creating a presentation using PowerPoint

When you are a competent presenter, you may wish to use PowerPoint to improve a presentation and give it more impact. PowerPoint and other software packages generate very professional visual images. It is a good idea to become familiar with the latest versions of presentation software as each has its advantages and disadvantages. However, whilst presentation software can provide the tools to create a superb presentation, it can also create the worst presentation imaginable. As with all presentations, one of the most important aspects is planning. You need to be sure what will work and what will not. It is possible to incorporate special effects such as animation and music or other sounds into the presentation, but the rule is to use them sparingly. (See also Chapter 8)

All the 'rules' of giving a presentation apply just as much to one using PowerPoint. Videos, music, speeches, etc. may be used to enhance a presentation, but beware of technical brilliance which can beguile the audience, so that the fundamental message of the presentation is missed.

> **Remember...**
> Sounds and animation can be annoying to the audience if overused.

Consistent style

It is a good idea to use a master slide, which determines the fonts on each slide, background colour, borders or bullet points. This will provide a consistent look throughout the presentation.

PowerPoint has a range of professionally designed templates which can be used as they are or modified to the presenter's preference. The colours on the templates are co-ordinated, and if you change fonts or colours you should ensure that any modification enhances rather than detracts from the presentation. Some colours do not match at all well with the background: for example, a black background and red or royal blue text. There are a number of text styles that can be used to give the slides impact and it is possible to arrange the text in pre-determined ways. Avoid having too much text on each

> **Remember...**
> Keep it simple. Avoid having too much information on each slide.

Stop and think
- Is the background dark and font light (for electronic presentations)?
- Is the font clear?
- Does the background colour complement the font colour used?
- Is the title a large enough font (44 point)?
- Are the bullets a minimum of 28 point font?
- Are the bullets animated appropriately?
- Do your slides have impact?
- If using images, are the colours appropriate?
- Have you rehearsed?

slide, as it will look cluttered. Think very carefully about the font colour and size. The pre-designed templates make use of colour and clear fonts, but before you finalise your choice it is a good idea to rehearse and take a good look at the projected image.

PowerPoint additionally provides the opportunity to produce speaker notes and handouts containing the bullet points for the audience. It is also possible to use the slide miniatures as aides-memoires.

The presentation software packages will not make you into a superb presenter, but with plenty of effort, organisation and planning they will automate many tasks that have to be carried out manually with overhead projector slides. You can, for example, use the AutoContent Wizard, which will take you through the procedure of creating various types of presentation. The use of software packages allows the presenter to concentrate on the content of the presentation rather than physically changing the slides one at a time, at best revealing each point sequentially.

Presentations using software packages can look very professional. However, care must be taken to ensure that the content is comprehensive; otherwise the presentation will be mostly electronic wizardry and little substance. A tutor will not be impressed by a presentation that comprises mainly packaging and neglects to include consideration of the content required by the course.

Delivery

It is possible to time the display when using software for the presentation. However, if there is any delay by the presenter, audience or some other interruption, this can cause problems because the presentation will continue at the pre-determined timings. It is probably better for the presenter to control the presentation using the mouse. This provides for much more flexibility: for example, varying the rate at which the pages are shown can control the speed of the presentation.

Suggestions for using animations on slides

- Do not have too many bullet points on each slide.
- Ensure that bullet points on text appear from the same direction.
- Avoid titles or text appearing as single letters.
- Use sounds sparingly and only to add appropriate emphasis.
- Do not have too many pictures/images on the slide.
- Keep any movie clips to a short extract.
- Build slides logically.
- Practise and rehearse the animation to ensure that it adds to rather than detracts from the presentation.

Presentations can be given a really professional look by presenting graphs in a very effective way: for example, data columns can be added by clicking the mouse button, or if a pie chart is used, slices can be added one at a time. This will capture the attention of the audience and focus it on important aspects of the presentation. The presenter can also verbally emphasise the most important aspects of the presentation as the slide is being built.

Transitions

Transitions can be used to change from one slide to the next, but it is essential to make sure that the same transition is used between each section of the presentation. A fade transition between slides can be quite effective, but do not slow the transition down too much for dramatic effect, as this may divert attention from the presentation message.

Keyboard shortcuts

Use the following keyboard shortcuts to save time during a presentation:

- **N** or the **arrow down key** will take the presentation to the next slide or to the next point if you have animated the slide. The space bar or left mouse button can be used to achieve the same result.
- **P** or the **arrow up key** will take the presentation to the previous slide, or to the previous point on animated slides.
- **Number** and **return key** will go to the numbered slide.
- **W** or **comma (,)** will replace the current slide with a white screen.
- **B** or **full stop (.)** will replace the current slide with a black screen.
- **Right click on the mouse** will bring up the pop-up menu (see below).
- **Control P**, changes pointer to pen.
- **Control A** changes pointer to arrow.
- **Control H** hides pointer and button.
- **'A' or '='** shows/hides arrow pointer.
- **Esc** ends slide show.

Mouse commands

In PowerPoint the right mouse button can be used in a similar way to keyboard shortcuts, although the audience will be able to see the commands on screen and the options differ slightly: for example, **Next** (next slide), **Previous** (previous slide), **Go** (via the slide navigator to the numbered slide), **Pointer** options (the cursor or a pen will appear on screen). Only the black screen option is available via the mouse commands.

> **Suggestions** for producing effective electronic presentations
>
> Aim for clarity.
>
> - Choose a consistent template.
> - Use master slides.
> - Plan and organise your presentation by using the outline view.
> - Practise using the slide show when you think your presentation is complete.
> - Keep it simple; do not wander from the topic and do not use very complex slides.
> - Do not use too many text styles.
> - Do not overuse transition techniques such as videos, music and sounds.
> - Check that the equipment works beforehand.
> - Check the compatibility of software on the machine.

PRESENTATIONS

Group presentations

Group presentations require very careful planning and rehearsal to ensure that each individual displays the required skills and that collaboration takes place. It will be necessary to plan each person's contribution, how these will be sequenced and how the handovers will be managed. Whether the presenters use an overhead projector or presentation software, all the slides should use the same template and fonts to ensure coherence and consistency.

Rehearsal is very important, as group members need to know who is to speak next and each speaker should be introduced to the audience. The group must decide in advance where each person will sit or stand when not presenting, and how the slides will be handled – will this be by the person presenting or one of the other group members? The group should also have a strategy to deal with a situation where a presenter talks beyond their allocated time or stops abruptly, unable to continue. During rehearsal the group should provide feedback to individual group members so that the performance of all members on the day is as accomplished and proficient as possible. It is essential for those providing feedback to be tactful and diplomatic, and for those receiving feedback to be receptive and mature, so that the overall performance is improved for all.

> **Stop and think**
>
> Has the group:
> ○ decided who will say what?
> ○ practised handovers?
> ○ created professional-looking slides?
> ○ agreed responsibility for slides?
> ○ ensured the time allocation is met?
> ○ decided what group members will do while not presenting?

> **Remember...**
> Always look interested in what other group members have to say.

Suggestions for group presentations

At university or college you may have to give group presentations that will be assessed. The following provides some specific pointers for group presentations to enable a group to give a competent performance, bearing in mind the other factors outlined in the chapter.

- At the start of the presentation, introduce the presenters – name badges are a good idea.
- Plan to have as few changeovers as possible, but include everyone, if that is required.

315

- Be supportive to other students whilst they are presenting.
- Ensure handovers are well practised – introduce the next presenter.
- Look interested and use positive non-verbal communication.
- Work as a team.
- Practise together so that the presentation is coherent, polished and well executed.
- Have a plan of action in case one of the presenters takes too long.
- Develop a plan of action in case one of the presenters 'dries up'.
- Provide each other with assistance when using visual aids.
- Have a contingency plan in case someone is unexpectedly absent.
- Use a standard format for overhead projector slides.
- Ensure that the presentation is structured.
- Practise delivery so that the presentation is completed within the time limit.
- If mechanical or electronic props are to be used, make sure that they are in working order.

If you have yet to give your first presentation, it is often useful to observe and listen to as many others as possible, identifying their strengths and weaknesses, what works and what does not work. Identify what makes some presentations better than others. Watch television presenters on news or current affairs programmes. They are usually very good. However, remember that they spend most of the day practising and have either completed a course in journalism or someone writing the script for them, as well as having the advantage of an auto-cue. By watching and listening to others giving presentations, you will gather a lot of ideas to help you with your own. Try out those ideas that work and avoid those that do not. When you are in an audience listening to a presentation, try to identify what the audience liked and found useful. Use those techniques in your own presentations.

Summary

This chapter has outlined:

- the purposes of presentations, including the need to consider how to get the message across to the audience
- the need for a structured approach, using appropriate content, timing, body language and speaking skills, as well as some form of memory prompt
- the different types of visual aid that can be used in a presentation and their appropriateness
- the need to practise the basic techniques for using an overhead projector
- how computer software can be used effectively to generate visual aids for presentations, including the need to use master slides and a consistent style.

15 Essay writing

> **Learning outcomes**
>
> After studying this chapter, you should be able to:
> - prepare, plan and write an essay
> - analyse and understand the requirements of an essay
> - gather and organise material for inclusion in an essay
> - construct an essay plan
> - present an essay in a clearly structured form.

→ Introduction

During your course of study, you may be asked to write an essay about a particular topic. Few people, especially students, write essays for pleasure. Essays are usually written as part of coursework (or examinations) to enable the tutor to assess your understanding and appreciation of a topic. This will require you to research the topic thoroughly in order to formulate your ideas before writing the essay.

An academic essay is not just an ordered presentation of relevant information about the topic, but is an argument (*thesis*) for which you should adopt a particular stance and in support of which you present evidence. The objective when writing an essay is to convince your reader that your particular standpoint is valid by presenting reasoned argument, based on evidence from authoritative sources.

The art of good essay writing lies in having something interesting to say and saying it clearly, concisely and with conviction. Writing an essay can be an arduous and time-consuming task to tackle, but when you are able to write essays with confidence, other types of assessment will seem relatively easy. If you have not had much experience (or success) with essay writing in the past, sitting down to write the first one at college or university can seem a daunting experience, but there are really only five basic stages in producing a good essay:

1 Analyse the essay title.
2 Find and organise the relevant material, making appropriate notes.

3 Make a plan.

4 Produce a rough draft.

5 Write the essay.

Each of these stages will be explored in a little more detail in the following sections. This will help you to understand why each stage is necessary.

> **Activity 15.1**
>
> **Identifying difficulties**
>
> If you have written an essay before, list any difficulties that you have already experienced with writing essays.

→ Analysing the essay title

Sometimes you may be given a list of topics or titles from which you may select the one(s) you are going to tackle. Before making your choice, read all the titles carefully and consider the following:

- *Your interest in the topic*. There is little point in writing an essay on a topic in which you have no interest (unless, of course, none of the titles holds any interest for you, but you have to complete one).
- *Your understanding of the topic area and the title itself*. Choose one that you have some understanding of, rather than something new and unfamiliar. This will help to save time.
- *The resources that are available*. You need to be sure that the information required is easily accessible in the time available.

If the subject of the essay is new to you, read about the topic to gain some understanding before beginning to plan the essay or make notes for it. Understanding the topic before writing about it is crucial for you to be able to select appropriate material for inclusion or to develop logical arguments around the material.

Once you have chosen the essay title, examine the title of the essay again and consider its meaning carefully. The essay title should be interpreted as literally as possible. It will have been very carefully thought out and phrased to be as clear as possible.

Content (what is the essay about?)

A useful starting point is to break the question up phrase by phrase, word by word if necessary, and highlight (by underlining or making a list) all of the *key words* or phrases. The key words indicate the subject matter to be dealt with in the essay. A dictionary or thesaurus can be helpful for definitions of the key words or concepts, but be careful not to lose the context of the words. It is not a good idea to go off at a tangent when learning to write good essays. When you are an experienced essay writer, you may be able to justify taking a novel or idiosyncratic approach, and this may lead to very high marks.

Table 15.1 Common instructional words and their definitions

Instructional word	Meaning
Account for	Give reasons for; provide evidence to support (do not confuse with 'give an account of', which is asking for a description)
Analyse	Break down into the component parts and explain how they relate to each other
Appraise	Assess; evaluate; find the value of
Assess	Estimate the importance or value of; judge
Compare	Examine similarities and differences – perhaps reach a conclusion about which is preferable
Consider	Take into account; weigh up the advantages/disadvantages
Contrast	Examine the differences between and provide explanations
Criticise	Give your judgement about the merit or demerit of theories or opinions or about the truth or falsehood of facts; support your judgement by a discussion of evidence or reasoning involved
Define	Give the precise meaning of a word or phrase. In some cases it may be necessary or desirable to examine different possible or often-used definitions
Demonstrate	Prove with examples; show
Describe	Give a detailed account; provide the main characteristics
Differentiate	Explain the difference; distinguish between
Discuss	Investigate and/or examine in detail; sift the arguments and debate; give reasons for and against; examine the implications
Distinguish between	Describe the important aspects, pointing out pros and cons
Evaluate	Appraise the merit or worth of something; judge the impact, importance or success of; include your personal opinion and evidence to support your evaluation
Examine	Investigate, scrutinise and question all the evidence
Explain	Provide details about how something happens/ed; give clear reasons for; account for
Identify	Ascertain the main feature(s) of
Illustrate	Make clear by the use of concrete examples from a range of sources. Use a figure or diagram to explain or clarify
Indicate	Show; point out; verify
Interpret	Expound the meaning of; make clear and explicit, usually giving your own judgement
Judge	Form an opinion; conclude
Justify	Show adequate grounds for decisions or conclusions; answer the main objections likely to be made to them; make a case for a particular perspective; provide evidence
Outline	Describe the main features, or general principles, of a subject, omitting minor details and emphasising structure and arrangement
Refute	Disprove a statement or argument
Relate	Show how things are connected to each other, and to what extent they are alike or affect each other
Review	Make a survey of, examining the subject carefully
State	Set down the main points; present in a brief, clear form
Summarise	Give a concise account of the main points of a matter, avoiding unnecessary details and examples
Trace	Indicate the development of events or progress of a subject in clear stages

However, until you have acquired advanced essay-writing skills, it is safer to take a fairly conventional approach.

A useful technique is to put the essay title in a circle in the middle of a piece of paper and extend lines out as you think about the title and ideas come to you (a mind map). Some people may prefer to do this in a linear form as a list – choose the method that is best for you. (Chapter 6 provides advice about mind maps.)

Approach (what does the title ask you to do?)

The approach to be taken is indicated by the *instructional* (or directive) word(s) in the essay title, such as 'contrast' 'assess' and 'discuss'. These words reveal how the subject matter should be dealt with. Table 15.1 shows some common instructional words and their definitions.

It is important at this stage that you have a thorough understanding of the essay title. You could compare your understanding with that of a friend to check that you have not misunderstood anything. If there is confusion, ask your tutor for clarification.

Once you have some idea of the scope of the essay, you can establish the main argument (or thesis).

Stop and think
- Do you understand the essay title?
- What are the key words in the essay title?
- How do these relate to the subject matter?
- What initial areas for researching do they suggest?

See Activity 15.1 FORMAL LANGUAGE in the Online Study Guide.

Exercise 15.1

Key and instructional words

Read the following essay title:

Discuss the proposition that government organisations are subject to more rigorous control and accountability than private organisations.

(a) List the key words.

(b) Outline the approach you would take in completing the essay, paying particular attention to the instructional word(s).

Finding your material

After analysing the essay title:

- Highlight the main points and draw up some subheadings. Always keep these in mind.
- Quickly jot down what you know about the question – this will help your

ESSAY WRITING

subconscious mind to start working on the topic. It may also provide some 'leads' to follow.

- Search initially for information that will provide an overview or a general introduction to the topic, particularly if the topic is new to you. Check if you have already been given any useful sources, such as references supplied by the tutor or module outline, or references and bibliographies in the recommended textbooks.

The most time-consuming part of essay writing is finding and organising relevant material to be included in the essay. Time management is important – make sure you allow sufficient time to read widely about the topic. To find information relating to the topic you will probably need to carry out a search (see Chapter 9). Make a note of the source of any information you intend to use (e.g. the page number, author and title of a book, and the title, author and location of an article). This will be useful when constructing the bibliography for the essay. (See Chapter 9 for information on constructing a bibliography.)

Suggestions when collecting information

- Always keep the essay title in mind.
- Avoid collecting information which, whilst interesting, is irrelevant to the essay. Many students who have difficulty in writing essays introduce information that they are unable to relate to the title. Information is included because they know it rather than know how to use it.
- Use up-to-date material from recent journals and quality newspapers where appropriate. This can add a touch of originality and freshness to the essay, thus helping it to stand out and be more interesting, particularly if a tutor may be marking many essays on the same topic.
- Always make a note of the source of any information, so that you can reference it correctly in your essay.

Organising the material once you have found it can be very difficult. The more ideas you have, the more material you find and the harder this stage becomes. You can have so much material that you feel overwhelmed, and making the decision what to leave out becomes a problem. All the material gathered needs to be worked through in a systematic and purposeful manner. Review it all and determine which parts are relevant to the essay and which are not. This is a time-consuming and very important stage of preparing an essay. Think about the topic over several days and allow your ideas to develop.

Remember...
Your essays cannot be well thought out if everything is left until the last minute, even if you have collected together the relevant material.

Reflect carefully on the information you find before deciding to include it in your essay. This should enable you to formulate the theme or argument that will permeate the essay. The analysis and the way in which you synthesise and present the arguments are your original contribution to the essay.

PART 2   DEVELOPING ASSESSMENT SKILLS

Once you have most of your material organised and in note form, you can start to plan the essay.

> **Stop and think**
> - What are the main arguments in the sources?
> - Do the various sources agree?
> - What are the major differences in the sources?

→ Making an essay plan or outline

The next stage is to construct an essay plan. You may have developed an outline as you have gathered information, but only when you feel you have all the material needed should the plan be written down in a firm and committed manner. However, the plan should never be so rigid that you cannot move away from the original outline – you may have a new idea which means a reorganisation of the material.

Planning is an important part of writing the essay, as it helps to:

- establish your main argument (thesis)
- organise the main ideas and important details into a logical order
- distinguish the main points from the supporting points
- reduce the risk of omitting some important fact
- make the writing of the essay much easier
- make your writing more fluent.

Review your notes to identify the main themes, and separate your rough notes into natural groups that support the different points to be made. You can then consider each of these groups in turn and decide the most logical order in which to put the different elements. When you have worked through each group, you will be in a good position to prepare a rough outline of how your essay will be organised or structured. Try sorting the groups a few times, altering the composition, until a coherent structure begins to emerge.

It is at this planning stage that you need to take into account any word limit set. You may be able to narrow the topic by taking out some of the groups, if you feel that they are not vital in supporting your argument and you may exceed the word limit.

Unfortunately, there are no set rules for what a good essay plan should look like. In many cases it will depend on the particular essay and the style that suits you best. The important thing to remember is that the essay plan should indicate at a glance exactly how you are going to approach the essay and itemise the information you consider relevant.

> **Suggestions** for planning an essay
>
> - Decide the stance you intend to adopt with regard to the topic.
> - Decide on the main points.
> - Put them in the most logical order – the points should follow a sequence that enables the reader to see how one point connects to the next.
> - Set alongside the main points all the supporting evidence, examples, data or illustrations that will be used to substantiate them. The essay will not carry conviction unless the reader believes what is written – this will be achieved by good supporting evidence.

Possible formats for an essay plan

There are a number of different formats that may be used for an essay plan. Three popular ones are outlined below.

Mind maps

Some people use mind maps as a visual plan for an essay. Mind maps can help you to discover the more surprising relationships between the points to be made. After constructing a mind map, a logical plan can then be developed.

Lists

A plan could take the form of a list of headings with all the relevant points itemised under those headings. You could divide the essay into paragraphs and briefly state the content of each one from the beginning to the end of the essay.

Flow charts

A flow chart could be constructed, highlighting the main themes and concepts, and showing how all the points relate to each other using those themes as a link.

Choose whichever method works for you and facilitates your own style of writing essays. The plan is there for you to work from and serves as a constant reminder of what you need to include.

> **Checklist:** what to look for after constructing the essay plan
>
> - Is there a theme running through your essay? ☐
> - Is there a logical progression? ☐
> - Are the linkages obvious? ☐
> - Is there sufficient relevant information to answer the question? ☐
> - Is there any irrelevant information? ☐
> - Is the balance/emphasis correct? ☐
> - Is there any repetition? ☐
> - Does it answer the question? ☐

Producing a rough draft

Once you have a plan, you are ready to begin writing the essay. A rough draft is a first attempt at writing the complete essay. It is important to consider how to express yourself – always aim for an appropriate academic style. Remember that an essay is a one-sided conversation. The reader is unable to ask for clarification, so it is important that the essay is presented so that someone else can easily understand it, follow it logically and know how the writer reached their conclusion. Producing a draft is a valuable process because you can begin to see what works and what does not, what satisfies you and what does not, before you totally commit yourself. If possible, ask another person to read through your draft to see if it makes sense to them.

Do not rush into writing the essay. You need to get into the mood to write, otherwise it will be a struggle to find the words to express yourself. It is important that there are no distractions to interrupt your thoughts and writing, so ensure that all the materials you need are present before starting to write.

> **Stop and think**
> ○ Do you have everything you need to write the essay?

Many people find it difficult to write the first words – even established authors can have this problem. A way of overcoming this is to start with 'Once upon a time . . .' This can help to get the words flowing, but it is essential that these words be changed before the essay is completed! Do not fall into the trap of writing the equivalent of a 'fairy story'. An essay is an academic piece of work and should be researched, referenced and written as such.

Although a rough draft is valuable, on occasions there may not be time to write one. In this case, there is all the more reason to plan the essay very thoroughly. However, do not be tempted to write only a final draft and submit it. This is a sure way to achieve less than you could do with sufficient planning, research, writing, reflection and modification.

The following checklist indicates things you should look for after producing the rough draft for an essay.

See Activity 15.2 PRACTISE FORMAL LANGUAGE in the Online Study Guide.

> **Checklist: what to look for after producing the rough draft of an essay**
>
> Is the emphasis correct? ☐
> Do some sections need expanding or contracting? ☐
> Are quotations, examples and other illustrative material used in a way that strengthens the arguments presented? ☐
> Does the essay flow? ☐
> Are there any unsupported personal views and opinions? ☐

> **Remember...**
> Leave enough time before the submission date to reflect on the rough draft and make any alterations you feel are beneficial.

→ Writing the essay

An essay falls into three major parts: introduction, main body and conclusion.

Introduction

A good introduction should set the scene, making it clear what you think the problem or question is, how you are going to approach it and how the essay will develop. It should contain some comment on the topic of the essay – perhaps definitions are needed, or some explanation of what you understand by the title. This section should also state the main issues involved and indicate which aspects of the topic you intend dealing with, and why. The introduction provides the reader with a preview of the stages through which the essay will develop. It usually does not need to be more than a paragraph.

Above all, it is essential that the introduction arouses the reader's interest and gives them reason to continue reading. Spend some time thinking about the first sentence of your essay – it is important that you gain the attention of the reader and make them interested in what you have to say.

Main body

The main body of the essay provides the opportunity to build up explanations and arguments with ideas, opinions and facts. Key points should be presented in a logical order and the linkages between them made explicit. It is vital that the key points are supported by relevant examples and any evidence gathered.

The logic of the paragraphs should reflect the logic of the plan prepared earlier. Each paragraph should raise a central issue, aspect or idea, and include evidence to support it. Ensure that each paragraph has unity and links naturally with the preceding and following paragraphs. Two paragraphs may be on different ideas but linked by that difference: for example, cause and effect, positive and negative aspects of one argument, or a before and after situation. The transition from paragraph to paragraph can often present some difficulty, but it is essential to maintain continuity and to give verbal signposts to your reader showing how you are moving on. This can be achieved by the use of linking words and phrases (see Table 15.2).

PART 2 — DEVELOPING ASSESSMENT SKILLS

Table 15.2 Common linking words and phrases

Linking word or phrase	Indicating
but, however, on the other hand, yet, nevertheless, on the contrary	contrast
for example, that is, for instance, in this case	illustration
similarly, moreover, furthermore, in addition, also	extension
therefore, consequently, as a result, thus	conclusion
then, after that, ultimately	the next step

In writing the main body of the essay, ensure that it provides a balanced view and that all aspects are given adequate coverage and supporting evidence.

See Chapter 5 for more linking (transition) words and phrases.

> **Checklist: writing the main body of an essay**
>
> Are key points supported by relevant examples? ☐
> Have you made the linkages between key points explicit? ☐
> Are the points made in a logical order? ☐
> Does it present a balanced view? ☐

Conclusion

When writing the conclusion to the essay, always refer back to the title. The conclusion should show the reader how the discussion in the essay has answered the question or arrived at a point of view.

The conclusion may not involve you in deciding whether or not you support or agree with the topic or concept you have written about, but may simply be a summary of the arguments. However, if the essay requires you to form a conclusion, summarise the main evidence in support of your view, making it clear what conclusions or implications follow from this. Ensure that the arguments presented throughout the essay are consistent with the conclusion.

The conclusion should provide a sense of having reached the end. Both you and the reader should feel that you have arrived somewhere at the end of the essay. It may also be appropriate to suggest to the reader areas worthy of further consideration.

The conclusion is normally about the same length as, or shorter than, the introduction. The introduction and conclusion should agree with each other and must never be contradictory. Avoid the temptation to repeat the introduction – the conclusion should indicate that you have progressed. The conclusion should not introduce new material, but should evolve from the main body of the essay.

Make sure you consider the following points when writing the conclusion for an essay.

> **Checklist: writing the conclusion for an essay**
>
> Have you referred back to the title of the essay? ☐
> Are the arguments presented consistent with the conclusion? ☐
> Do the introduction and conclusion agree? ☐
> Have you avoided introducing new material? ☐

Other points to remember

Subheadings

These tend to split up an essay into separate sections and make it more difficult for the various points to be presented in an integrated way. A good essay is a continuous piece of prose. For the same reason, try to avoid the use of lists in an essay. For example, rather than 'There are three relevant points to consider here: 1, 2, 3, ...', use whole sentences and paragraphs and say, 'There are three relevant points to consider here. The first of these is that ... Secondly ... Finally there is the fact that ...'

Diagrams or pictures

These may help to get the point across and provide a focus for the discussion. However, like lists, they disrupt the flow of an essay and tend to break it up into sections so that the connections are lost. Thus they should be used only when considered essential to aid the reader's understanding.

Abbreviations

These may be used as long as they are spelt out in full the first time. Similarly, words or phrases that are not in common usage, such as technical terms, should be defined the first time they are used.

References

See Activity 15.3 USING REFERENCES in the Online Study Guide.

If a piece of work completed by someone else or an idea or theory developed by another person is referred to, make it evident that it is not your own original view. This is done by putting the person's name and the date their work was published in the sentence, e.g. Coyle (2004). At the end of the essay, the bibliography should contain a list of all the work referred to, including author, date and title of the book or article where the piece of work can be found. See Chapter 9 for advice on referencing and bibliographies.

Plagiarism

Avoid presenting other people's words or ideas as your own. Plagiarism or using other authors' words or ideas without acknowledgement is not permitted. When making notes from passages in books and articles, put them into your own words; never be tempted to copy them verbatim (word for word), as you could subsequently inadvertently plagiarise, and this could have very serious consequences. Most universities and colleges have strict rules and procedures for dealing with plagiarism.

> **Remember...**
> All work you present during your course of study should be correctly referenced.

Quotations

See Activity 15.4 WRITING A REFERENCE LIST/BIBLIOGRAPHY in the Online Study Guide.

These should be used sparingly. They should support the points or arguments and must be directly relevant to the topic, not used for their own sake. Only use those phrases or sections that are so telling that no paraphrase of the author's idea will be as effective. If you use direct quotations, use quotation marks and acknowledge the author (name and date). The precise source of the quotation should be referenced either in a footnote or in the bibliography. For example:

> 'Education is what survives when what has been learnt has been forgotten.'*
> Skinner (1964)

Stop and think
- Have you referenced your work correctly?
- Have you used the Harvard method of referencing?

Word limit

See Activity 15.5 PRACTISE WRITING A REFERENCE LIST in the Online Study Guide.

Many of the essays you write will have word limits, i.e. a maximum number of words that should not be exceeded. If so, it is important not to exceed this. Sometimes you may be asked to write an essay with no word limit. This creates a problem of knowing how much to write and when to stop. There is no clear answer to this, as it depends on the particular approach you decide to adopt when answering the question. Deciding when to stop is part of the learning process and a skill that needs to be developed. It is your decision when to draw the line – a useful exercise is to formulate an explanation of why you stopped where you did.

→ Reviewing the essay

After completing the first draft of the essay, read it through in order to reflect on what is written. Try and do this as though reading it for the first time. This will be easier if you wait for at least a day or two, or preferably a week, after completing the first draft because you will be able to approach it more dispassionately. Reading the essay aloud is a good way to be sure that the language is not awkward and that it flows well.

When reviewing an essay, use the following questions as a guide.

---

*B. F. Skinner, *New Scientist*, 21 May 1964, 'Education in 1984'.

ESSAY WRITING

Checklist: reviewing an essay

Coherence
Does it make sense to you? ☐
Will it make sense to the reader? ☐
Is it coherent? ☐

Omissions
Have you included everything necessary? ☐
Are points missed or glossed over? ☐

Logic
Is the material sequenced logically? ☐

Relevance
Is all the content relevant? ☐
Have you included unnecessary padding? ☐

Balance
Is the emphasis correct? ☐
Do some sections need expanding or contracting? ☐

Flow
Does the essay flow? ☐
Are there any repetitions or ambiguities? ☐
Are there any spelling, punctuation or grammatical errors? ☐

Supporting evidence
Is there sufficient supporting evidence to uphold the arguments, views and opinions presented? ☐
Have you avoided any unsupported personal views and opinions? ☐

Illustrations
Will they aid understanding? ☐
Are they labelled correctly? ☐

Quotations
Are quotations referenced adequately? ☐
Are quotations, examples and other illustrative material used in a way that strengthens the arguments presented? ☐

Application
Have you answered the question? ☐

Sources
Are all sources referenced correctly throughout the essay? ☐
Is the bibliography complete? ☐

PART 2   DEVELOPING ASSESSMENT SKILLS

→ Common criticisms of essays

Table 15.3 indicates some of the common criticisms of essays and suggests some remedies to overcome these.

Table 15.3 Common criticisms of essays and their remedies

Criticism	Remedy
Too long or unfocused	Limit your essay plan to what can be included in the word limit. Prune irrelevant information. Keep to the point. Keep referring back to the title.
Too short or lacks sufficient content	Pay more attention to the explanations needed to get your points across. Use more examples. Do more research. Broaden the topic area.
Poor structure, badly organised, rambling	Practise doing essay plans, ensuring logical structure. Check for repetition and unnecessary padding.
Lacks fluency, poor style or presentation	Link your points/paragraphs. Check spelling and grammar. Leave time to review the essay before submitting it for marking.
Unbalanced answer	Check that your answer is not heavily weighted in one direction but gives a well-balanced, fair and objective evaluation of the subject.
Reaching conclusions without good evidence	Ensure you present the evidence for any conclusions you draw – believing it is the case is not sufficient; you must prove it.
Answer too personal	Avoid writing in the first person; use the third person. Do not express your own personal view unless the question specifically asks for it.
Poor conclusion	Ensure you have concluded the essay and indicated how you have answered the question. Do not introduce new information.
Poor introduction	Check you have introduced the topic area and explained to the reader what you are going to do.
Inclusion of irrelevant information	Ensure you understand the question and what it requires you to do. Ensure you answer the question and are not just giving the information you know and are comfortable with.
Boring, lacks originality	Alter your writing style; try and include something novel or take an innovative approach.
Too descriptive	Be more critical and evaluative of the information you have found. Provide a theoretical framework and use your knowledge, experience and examples to support what you are saying.

Table 15.3 continued

Criticism	Remedy
Little evidence of background reading	Do more research, widen your reading material.
Atheoretical	Provide more discussion of theoretical approaches.
Taking a chronological approach	If the subject has a historical dimension, beware of taking the easy approach and explaining what happened in the order it happened. Analyse the events and show why they occurred, etc., rather than describing them.
Failure to answer the question	Ensure correct interpretation of the question – look at the instructional words. Keep referring back to the title whilst writing the essay.

→ Writing essays under examination conditions

When writing essays under examination conditions, similar stages to those outlined above may be followed, although you are obviously unable to leave the examination room to do any research. Examine all the essay titles carefully and select the one(s) you feel most confident about answering. Do not choose a title because you see a topic you recognise and have revised – it is important that you are able to answer the question being asked about the topic.

For more details on essays under examination conditions, see Chapter 18.

Suggestions for writing essays under examination conditions

- Identify the essay you are going to attempt first.
- List the *key words* in the title and identify the *instructional* words.
- Jot down ideas as they come to you.
- Prepare a plan for the essay. Ensure this is legible so that, if you run out of time, the tutor can look at the plan and see how you intended to progress.
- Begin to write the essay. Ensure that you stay within the time you have allocated for the question; it is easy to get carried away when writing an essay.
- If you run out of time, jot down some headings to give an indication of how you would have completed the essay.

Activity 15.2

Dealing with the difficulties of essay writing

Look at the list of problems you identified in Activity 15.1. Devise a strategy that will help you to overcome these problems.

PART 2   DEVELOPING ASSESSMENT SKILLS

Figure 15.1 Elements of a good essay

A good essay
- Shows understanding of relevant ideas, theories and concepts
- Shows evidence of wide reading/research of the topic
- Critical and evaluative approach
- Planning and preparation
- Logical development
- Sources, etc., acknowledged correctly and in a conventional format
- Focuses on the topic
- Supporting evidence provided for the arguments presented
- Answers the question
- Clear, coherent and convincing arguments or analysis

→ Summary

See downloadable template 15.1 MONITORING ESSAY WRITING SKILLS for your Personal Development Plan online.

This chapter has outlined that:

- a good essay requires planning and preparation, which take time
- before starting the essay it is necessary to have a full understanding of the title of the essay and the instructional words that indicate how the topic should be treated
- wide reading and research of the topic area are required
- planning and reflection before writing will pay dividends later
- it is always advisable to write a rough draft before writing the final version of an essay
- after writing an essay it is important to read and review it, checking for things such as logical development, grammar, etc.

→ Answer to exercise

15.1
(a) Key words: organisations, government, private organisations, control, accountability.
    Other key words that might be appropriate: markets, competition, audit, public sector, government funding, profit/loss.
(b) Outline of one approach:
    Examine what government organisations are.
    Define public sector.
    Define private sector.
    Examine and define control and accountability aspects within those organisations.
    Present evidence (examples) providing reasons to support and/or refute the proposition argued in the essay.
    Conclude.

16 Report writing

> **Learning outcomes**
>
> After studying this chapter, you should be able to:
> - plan the stages and use of time in preparing a report
> - use a recognised and logical report structure
> - include information appropriate to the purpose of the report
> - construct an effective report.

→ Introduction

Whilst studying at university or college you may be asked to present information for an assessment in a report format. The construction of a report for an assessment allows you to practise presenting information in a format that is very relevant to many forms of employment. Whereas essays tend to be academic and theoretically based, reports are often more action oriented and generally have a wider scope. Report writing will involve using skills of application – applying what has been learned to a particular situation, rather than investigating and discussing theory.

Reports are commonly used for communication within an organisation to present facts or findings about a particular situation for a specific audience. When you join an organisation, it may have its own house style to which all reports are expected to conform. Tutors may also favour a particular style that they require students to adopt.

It is not easy to generalise about reports, as they may take many different forms depending on their purpose and for whom they are written. Whatever the purpose or style of a report, it is crucial that it is objective, accurate and concise, but sufficiently comprehensive for the reader to understand the issues. A well-written report can be a powerful means of persuasion and obtaining agreement or cooperation. Thus, an ability to write effective reports is an important and valuable skill for all students to acquire.

This chapter aims to provide advice on the compilation of reports. The secret of successful report writing is to approach it systematically and present material in a simple, clear and logical way. The preparation of a report divides logically into four stages – preliminary, preparation, writing and review.

PART 2   DEVELOPING ASSESSMENT SKILLS

Figure 16.1 Stages of report writing

Preliminary → Preparation → Writing → Review

→ Preliminary stage

Before beginning the report, it is important to be clear in your own mind exactly what you have been asked to do. Consider the following.

Objective (why is the report being written?)

The purpose behind the report will influence the way you approach it. A report may be written for a number of different reasons:

- To *provide information*. This may be a straightforward statement of facts or an explanation of events or findings. Examples include an accident report for an organisation's health and safety records; a company's annual report, in which the company's position is summarised for its shareholders and employees, an explanation of a new procedure or a summary of a conference, etc.
- To *make a request*. This type of report aims to persuade or motivate the reader into action – for example, a request to purchase a new piece of equipment, make a donation to a worthy cause, or accept a new procedure.
- To *influence decision making*. An example is a proposal to launch a new product or enter a new market.
- To *solve a problem*. The results of an investigation into a problem are presented within the report and one or more solutions offered based on the findings.

These reasons are not mutually exclusive. You may have to write reports as part of your assessment and they will usually be written from one of the perspectives outlined above. This may involve you adopting a particular role: for example, consultant, manager or trainee. It is important that, before writing a report, you understand from which perspective the report is to be approached and what role, if any, you are to assume. Failure to adopt a particular approach may lose valuable marks.

> **Stop and think**
> - Why is the report being written?
> - From which perspective will you approach the report?

Content (what is the principal subject matter?)

It is important to identify the major subject matter or focus of the report and the themes and issues that will need to be included. This will be helpful when collecting the material and evidence required for the report.

The facts of two different reports may be identical, but the purpose of the report will determine how these facts are presented. For example, pressure groups for and against a bypass around a village may have the same 'facts', but would choose to emphasise different aspects in order to persuade their audience.

Audience (who is the intended reader?)

Remember that the report is being written for the benefit of someone else. To be successful it should be directed to the particular requirements, needs and interests of the reader. Consider who will be reading the report – tutor/lecturer, executives, experts or the ordinary person in the street.

- *What does the reader know about the subject area?* It is important to ensure that you communicate at a level appropriate to the reader and offer enough explanation. If you overestimate their expertise, you may blind them with science, but, on the other hand, if you underestimate it, you may well bore them. As a student, it will be fairly safe to assume that the tutor for whom you are writing the report will be knowledgeable about the subject area.

- *What does the reader want/need to know?* Awareness of this will help you to prepare your case accordingly.

- *What are the reader's opinions of the subject of the report?* Does the reader think the subject is important, and are they likely to support or oppose the recommendations? This may influence how you present your final report.

- *What are the reader's preferences?* Is there a particular format or style they prefer? Do they like to see tables and charts, pictures or statistics? How much detail do they want? You need to tailor the final presentation of the report according to your reader's preferences.

Constraints (what are the limitations?)

What resources are available to you in terms of time (ensure you are certain of the date the report is required), money and information? Is there sufficient published material available to provide the evidence needed? If not, you may need to consider primary sources of information (see Chapter 9).

The answers to these questions will enable you to write the *terms of reference* for your report.

Terms of reference

The *terms of reference* (sometimes called *objectives*) define the scope of the report and indicate how you intend to achieve the aim. They outline the aspects to be considered and indicate the limitations to be observed. It is essential to write feasible terms of reference, as they form the basis of the report, and at university or college you may be graded on whether or not you achieve the terms of reference. If you have any doubts at this stage, seek clarification from your tutor or the person requesting the report. Only when you have determined the terms of reference can you begin to start collecting the data for your report.

Stop and think
- What are the audience needs for your report?
- What has already been written about the topic area?
- What are the terms of reference for your report?

Checklist: the preliminary stage of report writing

Why is the report being written?
What role, if any, do you need to adopt?
What is the subject matter?
Who is your target audience for the report?
What will the reader already know about the subject area?
What does the reader need to know?
What are your reader's opinions of the subject of the report?
How will the principal reader expect the report to be presented?
What, if any, are the limitations to the preparation of the report?

→ Preparation stage

Information gathering

The next stage is to collect the information you need – see Chapter 9 for a more comprehensive approach to gathering the necessary data to complete the report.

What information do you require?

Begin by jotting down your ideas on what could be included in the report – a mind map is a useful tool for this (see Chapter 6). Circle the related ideas and sort them into groups or topics – this will give you an idea of the material you need to collect. Gathering information is very time consuming; only collect material that is relevant to what you are trying to do. Keep focused by continually referring to the terms of reference.

Where from?

Alongside each of the groups or topics identified, list the possible sources of information for it. The sources you need to use will vary depending on the nature of the report.

When collecting information from secondary sources such as books and journals, it is important to note the sources precisely, so that you can refer to them again if necessary. They should also be included in the bibliography. If the collection of primary data is necessary, a section should be included in the report on how this was done (methodology/procedure), unless this is specifically not required. The factual basis of many reports you write will rely mainly, if not entirely, on your own data collection. The reliability of the report depends upon the accurate and honest handling of this data.

Suggestions for the collection of data

- Check the accuracy of the facts.
- Separate facts from opinions and assertions – and assess the merits of these.
- Separate facts from inferences – assess if inferences have a sound base.
- Select information carefully:
  - collect only relevant material;
  - do not exclude relevant information in the interests of brevity.

How much information?

It is difficult to determine how much information is required to write the report. One important rule is that anything irrelevant must be rejected – it may be interesting, but if it does not help to achieve the aim of the report, it is using valuable space and the tutor will not award marks for irrelevancies.

Time may be a factor in how much information is collected, but ensure that sufficient information is provided to allow a complete case to be presented to the reader.

Organisation of material

Once all the material has been gathered, you need to plan carefully the structure of the report. As with any assessment, it is worth spending time in careful planning. This will make the task of writing much easier and will be thoroughly justified by the quality of the final report.

Most subjects can be broken down into major and minor aspects. This is extremely important in report writing, as it helps you to prioritise the material and sort it into manageable sections.

Suggestions for organising material

- List the major points that you wish to make.
- Break these down into smaller or subsidiary points, each with an appropriate heading.
- Under each heading, list the facts, ideas, etc. that logically fit under each heading.
- Alongside these, note the information that will be used to support them.
- Mark the least important points, i.e. ones that the reader may find irrelevant. These will probably be rejected.
- Reread the list to check it is complete. Compare it to the terms of reference, as this will help you to keep focused.
- Once your list is complete, arrange the points in a logical sequence that will enable you to achieve the purpose and lead the reader to the same conclusion as your own.

Following these steps will provide a clear and well-organised structure for the report. It will also help to determine which information should be presented in the main body and which should go in the appendices.

Remember...
Inclusion of unnecessary material will distract the reader.

Writing the report

A lengthy report is usually broken down into a number of sections which are standard, recognised parts of a report. The report should be *presented* in the order set out below but may be *written* in a different order. For example, although the summary is one of the first sections to be presented in the report, it would probably be written last.

Title page

The title page is used to identify the report and should contain the following information:

- Title of the report
- Author's name
- Date
- Distribution list, if there is one

It is a good idea to keep the layout simple and not to overcrowd the page.

Contents page

The contents page lists the main sections, subsections (if any) and appendices, indicating their page numbers. It can be useful to construct the contents page before beginning to write, as this provides an outline for the report. Most word-processing packages now offer a facility that enables you to construct the contents page automatically.

A list of tables and figures (if used) is usually shown separately.

Summary or abstract

The summary or abstract is a very important part of the report. It provides a brief outline of the major themes or issues covered in the report, so that the reader can gain an appreciation of the whole picture without having to read the full report. The reader may then decide to read the recommendations and only refer to the detail of the report for further information where necessary. The summary must therefore be capable of standing as a complete, accurate and comprehensible item, independent of the main body of the report.

The summary or abstract should contain an overview of the following information:

- the purpose and scope of the report
- background information to set the scene
- what has been done and how
- the main findings
- conclusion
- recommendations (if necessary).

It is no easy task to write this section, so be certain to leave sufficient time to do this.

Introduction

The introduction should provide a broad, general view of the report, indicating what will be covered and why the report was necessary. It should present sufficient background information to enable the reader to understand the context of the report and provide the motivation for them to continue to read.

The best way to tackle the introduction is to be very obvious and state in the first sentence what the report is about. The introduction should supply details about the following:

- *Context*. Provide an indication of the subject of the report, a brief general background and/or history surrounding the report, and who requested it (if relevant). Only sufficient information is needed to enable the reader to understand and follow the report.
- *Purpose*. The aim of the report should be quite clearly and briefly articulated.
- *Scope*. The terms of reference should be stated, including the limitations of the report.
- *Procedure/method*. Outline briefly the methods used to gather the information. Sometimes this section appears as a separate section with its own major headings (see below).

Procedure/method

Some reports require a section detailing the method(s) used to gather the information contained in the report. In order for the report to have credibility, the reader must be convinced that the data and information on which the report is based are reliable and valid. This section of the report therefore aims to establish this. It is an opportunity for you to explain which sources of information (books, articles, etc.) were consulted and which methods of investigation (survey, observation, experimentation) were used.

If you experienced difficulties in gathering some of the information, which meant that you were unable to investigate certain aspects, this should be explained in this section. The reader is then able to understand why these aspects were not explored or facts were not given or verified.

The procedure/method section should lead logically to the next section, the main body, which will present the information gathered from each source.

Findings

This section provides the detailed facts and findings of the report and indicates how they were arrived at and the inferences to be drawn from them. It is also important to remember that this section provides the foundation for your conclusions and recommendations. If the report is required to address appropriate academic theory then this section should also contain an analysis of the theory on which the findings of the report are to be based.

There is no specific format for this section, but the facts should be built into a logical and consistent case. Think very carefully about the most logical sequence in which to present the material – always refer back to the terms of reference for the report, as this will prevent you from straying from the topic under scrutiny.

It is helpful to the reader if the main body of the report is divided into major sections which group facts or ideas together under subheadings or numbered points. This creates a logical and persuasive structure and guides the reader smoothly through the report until they reach the point at which the conclusions can be revealed. If there are lengthy sections in this part of the report, it is easier if a brief summary and conclusion is provided at the end of each section. The next section can then restate these and move forward.

This section should be as concise as possible, containing only the essential detail. Any detailed supporting material that may detract the reader from the central theme should be relegated to the appendices.

Suggestions for writing the main body of the report

- Develop ideas logically and as fully as possible (with one main topic or idea per paragraph).
- Consider the different aspects of the problem but keep an appropriate balance – do not develop one section to the exclusion of others.
- Your reasoning should be clear to the reader.
- Explain and justify the points made, presenting supporting evidence where appropriate.
- Keep focused by constantly referring to the terms of reference.

REPORT WRITING

Figure 16.2 Conclusions

Star diagram with "CONCLUSIONS" in the centre, and the five points labelled: Consistent, Clear, Considered, Coherent, Concise.

Conclusions

The material presented in the main body of the report should lead the reader logically to the conclusions. The purpose of the conclusions is to summarise the main findings and offer some evaluation and/or opinion of them. The conclusions (see Figure 16.2) should be:

- *Clear* – use simple and direct language. If a number of points are to be made, they should be set out as separate paragraphs with references made back to the main body by page number and paragraph if necessary.
- *Concise* – stick to the point, do not ramble.
- *Consistent* with what has gone before (do *not* introduce any new material at this stage).
- *Considered* – thought through, not superficial suggestions.
- *Coherent* – arguments, themes and issues developed logically.

See Activity 16.2 PRACTISE SUMMARISING in the Online Study Guide.

If the previous parts of the report have been clearly and logically constructed, the conclusions will follow naturally from them. In turn, the conclusions should lead logically to the recommendations (if these are required).

The conclusions are written after the main body of the report has been completed and are the test of a well-written report. They should be brief and the order of presentation should correspond with that of your actual report.

Recommendations

It is not always essential to provide recommendations; this will depend on the terms of reference for the report. If recommendations are required, they should indicate the action needed in order to achieve the aim of the report and follow naturally from, and be based solely on, the material presented in the conclusions. Do not introduce any new issues or arguments that have not been dealt with in the main body of the report or the conclusions.

Figure 16.3 Presenting recommendations

```
                    Direct              Convincing

Itemised – set out                                      Sound – founded
in separate                                             upon clearly stated
paragraphs              Recommendations                 facts and rational
which may be                                            arguments
numbered for
ease of reference

        Fully considered      Concise      Fulfil the requirements
        including the                      of the terms of
        consequences                       reference
```

Recommendations are important and influential factors in affecting future action and decision making, so careful thought should be given to them. However, it is important to remember that recommendations are only *advisory* – the decision whether or not to act upon them will be taken by the reader. The tone you use is therefore important – try not to alienate the reader by ordering or threatening, but rather advise, suggest, recommend or urge. This is more effective. For example:

not: The bonus scheme must be introduced immediately.

but: The board should consider the introduction of the bonus scheme as a matter of urgency.

A good report will carry the reader along by the argument, so that by the time they reach the end they will need no further convincing.

References

Whenever you draw from other writers' ideas, provide the reference – an indication of which particular piece of their writing you are drawing from. It is important to use an accepted convention when acknowledging other people's work (for example, the Harvard system) so that the reader may easily identify the item that is being referred to. The Harvard system of citation is simple to use – it requires you to mention only the author and year of publication within the text. The reader may then find a full description of the work that you have cited by referring to the bibliography at the end of your report. For example:

The work of Handy (1993) suggests that . . .

The reader may then turn to the bibliography to determine which of Handy's works is being referred to. It is vitally important that any sources used should be acknowledged and quotations should be attributed correctly to avoid problems with plagiarism.

REPORT WRITING

> See Activity 16.1 SECTIONS OF A REPORT in the Online Study Guide.

Activity 16.1

Referencing

Check with your tutor or librarian which referencing conventions are used in your university or college – it may be a requirement to use footnotes.

Bibliography

Always provide a bibliography. The bibliography provides a list of materials that have been consulted as a basis for the report and will therefore provide evidence on the validity of the information presented.

The bibliography should enable the reader to follow up a reference made within the main body of the work. It is therefore important that the first two elements of the reference (author and date) form the link between the text and the bibliography. Table 16.1 indicates the order in which information should be presented for items appearing in the bibliography.

It is also important that if information has been retrieved from non-printed sources, these are also adequately referenced. For example, electronic journal articles retrieved from the World Wide Web should be referenced in the same way as printed articles, but include an availability statement and the date they were accessed.

Table 16.1 Constructing a bibliography

1 Printed sources		
Books	*Journal articles*	*Newspaper articles*
Author(s), editor(s) or the institution responsible (indicate editors by ed.)	Author	Author
(Year of publication)	(Year of publication)	(Year of publication)
Title: Subtitle	Title of article	Title of article
Series and individual volume number	*Title of journal*	*Newspaper*
Edition (if not the first)	Volume and part number, month or season, page numbers of the article	Date article published
Place of publication		
Publisher	Note: Electronic journal articles from the Internet should be referenced in the same way as a printed article, but include an availability statement, i.e. Available from: <http://www...> [Accessed ...]	
Example:	*Example:*	*Example:*
Kotler, P., and Armstrong, G. (2004) *Principles of Marketing*. 10th edition, Upper Saddle River, NJ: Pearson Education.	Capaldi, N. (2005) Corporate social responsibility and the bottom line. *International Journal of Social Economics*, Vol. 32, issue 5, pp. 408-23.	Skapinker, M. (2005) Be cheered: the workplace bully has a soft underbelly. *Financial Times*, 23 March, p. 12.

343

Table 16.1 **continued**

2 Audio-visual sources		
Videos	*On-line images*	*World Wide Web documents*
Programme title	Title (or description)	Author/editor
(Year)	Year	Year
Series title	[online image]	Title
Series number	Available from <www address>	Internet
Place of publication	Filename, including extension	Edition
Publisher	[Date accessed]	Place of publication
Date of transmission/issue		Publisher (if available)
		Available from: <www address>
[Medium: Format]		[Accessed date]
Example:	*Example:*	*Example:*
How to stop them leaving: Talent management: (2004) London: Video Arts [Video: VHS]	The Vase of Cornflowers (1959) [online image]. Available from: <http://www.virtualdali.com/59VaseofCornflowers.html>, [Accessed 24 June 2005].	Gundry, J., and Slater, S. (2005) *Flexible Working: Can Home Workers And Their Managers Make It Work?*, [Internet], Available from: <www.knowab.co.uk/wbwflexwork.html>, [Accessed 11 August 2005].

An example bibliography is shown below:

> Campbell, D., Stonehouse, G., and Houston B. (2004) *Business Strategy*. 2nd edition, Oxford: Elsevier Butterworth-Heinemann.
>
> Cannon, H., and Schwaiger, M. (2005) The role of company reputation in business simulations. *Simulation and Gaming*. Vol. 36, no. 2, pp. 188-202.
>
> McKenna. R., and Martin-Smith, B. (2005) Decision making as a simplification process: new conceptual perspectives. *Management Decisions*. Vol. 43, no. 6, June 2005, pp. 821-36(16) [Internet]. Available from: <http://hermia.emeraldinsight.com/vl=19779020/cl=40/fm=html/nw=1/rpsv/cgi-bin/linker?ini=connect&infobike=/mcb/001/2005/00000043/00000006/art00003&infomagic=f7465b9b3ad6be338fab990680f0a60e>, [Accessed 17 August 2005].

Activity 16.2

Bibliography

Check with your tutor or librarian what the conventions are in your university or college.

Select a range of material for a topic you are studying and compile a bibliography according to the convention.

Check with your tutor or librarian that your bibliography is presented correctly.

Appendices

Appendices contain any supplementary material that is needed to support the report but is not essential to the main findings. If they were included in the findings of the report, they would disrupt the flow and detract from the facts and arguments being presented.

For easy reference, appendices should be grouped appropriately and annotated with letters or numbers consecutively as they are mentioned in the main text, e.g. Appendix A1, A2, Appendix B1, B2, B3, etc. It is not a good idea to have too many and those included should be referred to within the main body of the report. Appendices should be presented on the same paper size as the rest of the report. Sometimes the appendices count towards the word limit for the report – check this with your tutor.

Glossary

See Activity 16.3 FINDING THE MISTAKES in the Online Study Guide.

If technical terms have been used in the construction of the report, you may need to provide an explanation of these terms in a glossary. A glossary provides definitions of terms or acronyms that are technical or difficult because they are specific to the topic area. Glossaries are particularly helpful if the readers include non-experts in the subject area as well as experts.

Acknowledgements

The acknowledgements provide an opportunity to thank the people who have helped in the preparation of the report by providing information or resources. The acknowledgements may be presented either at the beginning or at the end of the report.

Presentation

There are a number of different conventions that may be used when compiling reports. If the report is constructed using word-processing software, you may find that the software contains a report-formatting element. Key aspects of report formatting are outlined below, but remember that different organisations, including your university or college, may use, and insist on, their own house style. Check with your tutor to determine if there are any specific rules of presentation that you must follow.

Appearance and layout

However you decide to present your report, it is important to be consistent in the presentation – for example, in the use of underlining and italics, bullet points, font size, line spacing and margins.

Page numbering

Pages of a report are usually numbered consecutively except for the title page. The position of the page numbers (top, bottom, centre, right) should be consistent throughout the report. Appendices are numbered separately on each page.

Figure 16.4 An example of a report structure

```
Report on the ..............................................................
1.0   Summary
2.0   Introduction
3.0   Method
         3.1   Limitations
4.0   ..............................................................
         4.1
         4.2
               4.2.1
               4.2.2
         4.3
5.0   ..............................................................
6.0   Conclusions
7.0   Recommendations
Bibliography
Appendix A ..............................................................
Appendix B ..............................................................
```

Headings

These provide a framework within which to construct a well-organised report and act as signposts to the reader. A report could be written without headings, but it would be confusing and thus difficult to read. However, too many headings may interrupt the flow of the text and also make the report difficult to read. It is interesting to note that readers often ignore the headings when reading the text and thus you should treat them as separate from the text and not as part of the structure.

Subheadings

If used, these should be appropriate to the material, guiding the reader through the main sections and providing an immediate outline for reference purposes.

Paragraphs

The first word of the paragraph usually begins at the margin and is not indented. There is no optimum length of paragraph. A paragraph should contain related material and may have to be quite long. However, bear in mind that if paragraphs are too long, the reader may lose the sense before reaching the end. If paragraphs are too short, this may lead to an abrupt style and appearance, and disrupt the reading flow. Single-sentence paragraphs should be avoided.

A new paragraph is usually indicated by additional line spacing. Additional line spacing may also be used above and below each main and group heading to keep it clear of the text. Sub-paragraphs may be used to break up the flow of a very long paragraph

REPORT WRITING

or tabulate a number of items or points. If sub-paragraphs are used in the report, they should be indented.

Some reports are written using a classification system for ease of reference. Classification systems use a system of headlines, number or letter sequences and margins to indicate each section or subsection, whose relative importance is indicated by:

- the size of headline
- its number or letter
- the position on the paper.

All classification must be consistent.

Abbreviations

These can be an irritation to the reader if they are unfamiliar with them. The first time an abbreviation is used it should be spelt out in full, with the abbreviation shown in brackets immediately afterwards, e.g. Bachelor of Arts (BA), Institute of Directors (IOD). Future reference to the term may then be shown as an abbreviation. Ensure that any use of abbreviations is consistent.

Graphs, tables, charts

Consider using tables, graphs and bar charts for clarification, not for decoration. They should be used to aid comprehension, provide reinforcement and help the reader to understand relationships. Remember, a picture is said to be worth a thousand words!

Style of writing

See Activity 16.4 PUTTING IT ALL TOGETHER in the Online Study Guide.

The language and style must be appropriate to the reader and the aim of the report. A report is a formal document and thus you should avoid the use of colloquialisms. Reports should be written in the third person – only use 'I' in an eyewitness report. Try to express yourself in a style that is clear, carries conviction and arouses interest in the reader.

It is a natural tendency to put in additional adjectives, qualifying phrases and explanatory sentences to avoid any misunderstanding, but this is merely padding and slows the reader down so that impact may be lost. The draft report should be pruned ruthlessly to cut out the inessential.

→ Review

The secret of success in reviewing the completed report, as in writing, is to be systematic. Read the report, not once but several times. Each time you read the report, concentrate on a different aspect – for example, logic, expression, punctuation and grammar (prune out ambiguities, pompous words, spelling and grammatical errors). This list is not exhaustive – there may be other aspects depending on the requirements of the report.

PART 2　　DEVELOPING ASSESSMENT SKILLS

Activity 16.3

Reviewing reports

Find a published report in your library. Assess it according to the checklist in Table 16.2. What are the major omissions?

Table 16.2 Questions to ask when reviewing a report

Title page	*Are all the details required present and correct?*
Contents page	Is the list complete and correct?
	Is there a list of tables and charts?
	Are the appendices listed in order and with a page reference?
Summary	Is this understandable on its own if the reader does not wish to read the whole report?
	Is it as concise as possible without any major omissions?
	Is it accurate?
Introduction	Is the background as brief as possible whilst providing sufficient information so that the reader understands the context?
	Are the terms of reference clearly stated?
	Does it motivate the reader to read the whole of the report?
Procedure/method	Is the method used for gathering the information appropriate?
	Does this section enable the reader to establish the validity of the material?
Main body	Are the findings presented in a logical order?
	Does the text flow naturally?
	Is the language clear and precise?
	Are the facts and figures accurate?
	Are opinions and assertions supported?
	Is the material presented balanced?
	Is each main point well supported?
	Is the content relevant to the terms of reference?
	Are all the main aspects covered in sufficient depth?
	Is all the work correctly referenced?
Conclusions	Do these flow naturally from the main body?
	Has any new information been introduced?
	Are all the conclusions supported?
	Do the conclusions reflect a sound analysis of the material?
Recommendations	Is each recommendation listed in an order corresponding to the conclusions?
	Is it clear what action is required?
	Are they relevant to the terms of reference?
	Are they appropriate and practical?
	Do they fulfil the aim of the report?

REPORT WRITING

See downloadable template 16.1 EVALUATING A REPORT for your Personal Development Plan online.

Table 16.2 continued

Title page	Are all the details required present and correct?
Appendices	Are there any omissions?
	Are they in the correct order and numbered accordingly?
Bibliography	Are there any omissions?
	Is this accurate?
	Is it presented in the correct format?
References	Are there any omissions?
	Can the reader trace the references from the information given?
Glossary	Do all the technical terms used appear?
	Are the terms explained in a way that a non-expert may understand?
Presentation	Is it clearly written and well laid out?
	Does it meet the needs of the reader?
	Are the grammar, punctuation and spelling correct?

→ Types of report

Reports may be written for a variety of purposes. Table 16.3 lists some guidelines for compiling reports for different situations.

Table 16.3 Guidelines for compiling reports

Purpose of report	Guidelines
Providing information (good news)	Be direct and present the main idea first.
	Present all the relevant information.
Providing information (bad news)	Present neutral or positive information first to provide a buffer. When presenting the bad news, provide any reasoning behind it.
	Avoid using jargon but be logical and clear so that there can be no misunderstanding.
	Try to be optimistic in concluding, offering a lesser alternative if this is appropriate.
Persuasive request	Get the reader's attention immediately.
	Present the strongest motivator first.
	Explain the advantages of accepting the proposal to the reader.
	Detail the action you want to see and when.
	If possible, offer some sort of incentive.

> See downloadable template 16.2 FEEDBACK ON WRITTEN REPORTS for your Personal Development Plan online.

Table 16.3 continued

Purpose of report	Guidelines
Proposal	Provide an outline of the current situation.
	Give a reasoned account of the steps leading to the proposal.
	Outline the advantages and disadvantages of the proposal.
Problem solving	Define the problem clearly and concisely.
	Provide a clear analysis of the problem.
	Indicate the consequences of not addressing the problem.
	Give the possible solutions to the problem.
	Indicate how you are going to evaluate the solutions presented.
	Provide recommendations for dealing with the problem.

Group reports

Sometimes an assessment may involve the completion of a group report. One way of approaching this is for each member of the group to look at a different aspect and thus complete a separate section. If this is the case, care must be taken that the finished product is presented as a coherent piece of work, in both content and style. This can take some time, so ensure that there is enough time to do it properly.

In completing a group report, it is essential to hold regular meetings of the group so that progress can be monitored and any problems discussed.

Activity 16.4

Writing reports

1 Identify and examine a problem on campus (e.g. registration, lack of computer facilities) and prepare a report for the appropriate administrator recommending an effective response to the situation.

2 Prepare a report for the university about the cost of studying at university. Outline the methodology used to gather the information about the major expenses that students have to meet, draw conclusions and make recommendations as to how students may reduce their expenses.

→ Summary

This chapter has explained that:

- writing effective reports is a lengthy process, requiring careful planning and perseverance
- Many organisations have a particular 'house' style, which you may be required to use when constructing a report – if not, it is important to ensure that all the aspects required are covered
- effective reports achieve their purpose, conveying their message authoritatively and convincingly with material presented objectively, accurately and logically
- any opinions or assertions should be supported with facts and any irrelevant material omitted
- reports should be concise but complete and comprehensible.

17 Writing dissertations or research projects

> **Learning outcomes**
> After studying this chapter, you should be able to:
> - understand the requirements of selecting a research topic
> - define a research question
> - understand the requirements of a dissertation
> - transfer report-writing skills to the presentation of research in a dissertation.

→ Introduction

Many honours degree courses require students to complete a dissertation or research project as part of the final assessment for the degree. A dissertation is a major piece of individual work involving in-depth research about a topic with the end product being a formal report (and in some instances a presentation). Research projects and dissertations often form part of the assessment at later stages in a course, as they require the use of the higher-level cognitive skills of analysis, synthesis and evaluation.

Most of the assessments you will undertake are prescriptive in terms of the topic studied. Dissertations and research projects generally allow greater freedom in what may be done to satisfy the assessment requirements, offering the possibility of choosing an area of particular interest to you within the scope of the course you are studying. Many students feel liberated at the idea of selecting a topic for themselves and relish the opportunity of exploring something of great interest to them. Others will approach the task with trepidation, feeling wary of embarking on a task without the appropriate detail normally provided by tutors. Doing a dissertation means that, instead of knowledge and information being presented and following a prescribed route for answering questions, you are thrust into an active role of managing an investigation into a topic area. This means researching and discovering things for yourself. You will have to set your own targets and parameters, pose your own central research question and decide on the appropriate sources of information to support the research. Dissertations are very time consuming and require a great deal of commitment, but if everything goes to plan they can create a high level of motivation and provide a great sense of achievement on completion of the work.

Many universities or colleges will issue guidelines for the completion of dissertations for the course you are studying. Obtain a copy of these as soon as you can and read them thoroughly so that you are aware from the beginning what is expected of you. It may also be possible to borrow copies of previous dissertations submitted for your course – they are sometimes available for reference in the library. Studying these will help you to get a picture of what you have to produce.

The philosophy underpinning a dissertation is that how you carry out the research (process) is of equal (or possibly greater) importance as the final product. Thus, an understanding of appropriate methodological and analytical techniques is important. There are now many good textbooks available that cover dissertations and the research process in depth. This chapter provides an overview and indicates what may be required of you whilst undertaking such a task.

> **Remember...**
> The research process is as important as the final product.

See Activity 17.1 STAGES OF A DISSERTATION in the Online Study Guide.

Activity 17.1

Dissertation requirements for the course

Many courses provide guidelines for completing dissertations. Obtain a copy of dissertation guidelines for your course (if available) and complete the following:

1 What are the limitations, if any, to your choice of topic?
2 Is primary research a requirement?
3 What is the word limit?
4 What is the date of submission?
5 Are there any intermediate submission dates (e.g. research proposal, literature review) and, if so, what and when are they?
6 Are there specific requirements for presentation?
   - Font type and size
   - Double/single line spacing
   - Margins
   - Binding
   - Number of copies required for submission
7 How are marks allocated for the dissertation (if available)?
8 What support is offered (e.g. individual or group tutorials, etc.)?

Selection of a topic

If you are able to choose the topic for your dissertation, you will need to consider this carefully. Start thinking about it as early as possible – keep notes on interesting ideas that you think of during your studies which you can then reflect on as possible research topics. If you are struggling to find a suitable topic, there are a number of possible sources of ideas:

- Visit the library and read the current journals and quality newspapers. These are a good source of topical issues and developments that may provide an idea for your research.
- Look at the end of chapters or articles that you find interesting to see if the author has recommended further research in a particular area.
- Look into an organisation, business or industrial sector in which you have employment experience – perhaps you became aware of a particular problem that the organisation was facing, or recognised that the industry needed to develop in a particular way. Examples such as these can provide a suitable basis for research.
- Consult copies of dissertations completed in previous years – many universities or colleges make these available. The titles or abstracts may suggest something that could be researched further. However, if you do get an idea from a previous dissertation, ensure that your research is sufficiently different from the original and do not be tempted to plagiarise. This is a very serious offence.
- Some universities and colleges may issue a list of staff research interests that may be of interest to you and worth considering for your research. If so, it may be helpful to discuss it with the member of staff concerned.

Considerations in choosing a topic

See downloadable template 17.1 PLANNING A DISSERTATION for your Personal Development Plan online.

Some students may have difficulty choosing from the wide variety of topics they are interested in, whilst others may struggle to come to terms with the freedom of selecting their own topic. Highlighted below are some of the issues that must be considered when making the final choice for your dissertation.

Interest

It is important that you choose something that you are interested in and that will maintain your interest until the work is completed.

Philosophy/requirements of the course

The topic you choose should enable you to satisfy the requirements and reflect the philosophy of the course on which you are studying. For example, if you are studying on a business course it may be inappropriate to complete a dissertation about the history of the Roman Empire.

The chosen topic should have sufficient theoretical grounding and secondary sources for a literature review to be carried out. This will form the basis for any primary research you may be required to conduct.

If your course requirements for the dissertation state that your investigation must include primary research, then the topic you choose should allow for this. This is an important consideration – you need to be certain that the collection of the primary data required is possible, given the resource constraints under which you will be working. Gathering primary data can be a very time-consuming and expensive activity.

Ability/experience

The topic should provide scope for you to demonstrate your abilities to the full but not be so complex that you are unable to complete it successfully. Consider what you know already and avoid any topic or area you find difficult. Try to choose something that will complement your strengths and abilities.

Resources

Choose a topic that it is possible to research within the limited resources available to you:

- *Time*. Dissertations are very time consuming. It is therefore important that you think carefully about the time required to do the research and the time available. Read Chapter 11 for tips on how to improve time management skills.
- *Information (both primary and secondary)*. Consider the library resources that are readily accessible to you – there is little point attempting a dissertation on the banking system of eastern Malaysia if the library you regularly use has very little or no information about this. To complete such a topic satisfactorily, you will need to be absolutely certain that you have access to information from other sources. Primary data can be very difficult to gather and may require the cooperation of people and organisations external to the university or college. You may need to seek permission to collect the data you need.
- *Money*. Not many student budgets will accommodate a trip to a distant destination to carry out a detailed investigation. Be realistic in your estimation of the costs of travel, postage and telephone calls, etc., needed to collect the information required for the topic you are considering.
- *Support*. What support mechanisms are available to you in completing the research? Some universities and colleges are unable to guarantee that a dissertation tutor will have specific knowledge in the area you are researching. However, tutors will normally have knowledge and experience of the research process. If you are basing your research within an organisation, it is vital that you have its support. Often students have good ideas but they involve the collection of data that are confidential and/or sensitive. It is imperative that permission be obtained from the host organisation for the collection and publication of confidential and sensitive data.

Moral/ethical considerations

Reflect on any moral or ethical issues surrounding any research that you are proposing to do. Do not attempt to do anything that is likely to bring you or your university or college into disrepute, and ensure that, if you promise confidentiality to any of your sources, you are able to respect that promise. You should also avoid any research that will cause damage to the environment or involves breaking the law. The university or college may have specific guidelines covering this area.

Activity 17.2

Ethical considerations

Many universities and colleges now issue guidelines on ethics for dissertations and research projects. Obtain a copy of your institution's guidelines (and those for your course if available). Before finalising your topic area, read the guidelines and assess how they may affect your research.

Stop and think
- Does your university or college have an ethical policy relating to research?
- What are the ethical aspects of the research you are proposing to do?
- Do you need to protect confidentiality?

Life of the topic

It is important that the topic you choose will be 'live' for the duration of the work. Often students choose extremely topical issues that are or have been important in recent times. After six months, the general interest may decline and thus data become inaccessible.

Start thinking about the topic as early as possible. Decide a provisional area of interest, review the relevant literature, and produce a scheme or model of the issues involved (see Chapter 15).

Activity 17.3

Identifying suitable topics for research

Identify two topic areas you are interested in investigating for a dissertation. Using the considerations highlighted above and the checklist below, determine the issues surrounding each of the topics you have identified.

Checklist: determining the suitability of the topic chosen

Question	
What is your interest in the topic chosen?	☐
Does the topic provide sufficient scope for you to meet the requirements of your course?	☐
Will the topic allow you to demonstrate your strengths?	☐
Does the university/college library have appropriate information – or can you obtain the information required from other libraries/sources?	☐
Is it possible to collect the appropriate primary data to support the research, if required?	☐
Is it possible to complete the research in the time you have available?	☐
Is it possible to complete the research within your financial budget?	☐
If the research is based on a specific organisation or industry, do you have the support of the appropriate people? Note: organisation/industry personnel change – be sure that you are not reliant on a single individual!	☐
Do you have the support of your tutors to do the research?	☐
Will the topic area remain 'live' until the research has been completed?	☐

→ Defining the research question and objective

Once the topic area has been determined, it will be necessary to refine the research area by defining a research question that will provide a focus and thus avoid the dissertation becoming a mere collection of facts. The research question must be clearly, precisely and unambiguously stated. Students often find that this is the most difficult thing to do, but, once done, everything else can easily fall into place.

It is easy for a project or dissertation to become overly descriptive. In order to avoid this, try to think of a genuine question. You can then analyse the facts and evidence you gather to determine and support the answer to this question.

See Activity 17.2 DEFINING THE RESEARCH QUESTION AND OBJECTIVE in the Online Study Guide.

Activity 17.4

Determining the research question

Identify a suitable topic area for a dissertation and define an appropriate research question and objective for it.

Feasibility

Once a topic has been identified, some preliminary work needs to be carried out to determine the feasibility of completing the research. This will also help to refine the research area. An initial library search using any key words you have identified for the topic will identify sources and provide an indication of what is readily available that may be of help.

At this stage, the methods to be used to collect the data required need to be identified. Careful consideration needs to be given to the different research methods that may be adopted in order to choose the one that will enable the collection of reliable and valid data in support of the research (see Chapter 9).

Checklist: the feasibility of a research topic

- Is the topic too broad or narrow an area to work with? ☐
- Is there a clearly defined research question? ☐
- Is there sufficient secondary information easily accessible to you? ☐
- Will there be sufficient theoretical content? ☐
- Will the collection of primary data be possible (if this is a requirement)? ☐
- Are there likely to be problems of confidentiality of data? ☐
- Does the topic require the consideration and collation of too much data? ☐
- Will it involve statistical analysis work (and problems) which are insurmountable? ☐
- Can it be completed in the timescale available? ☐
- Has it been done before (some universities and colleges do not allow the same topic to be researched within a certain time frame)? ☐
- Do you have the skills necessary to do justice to the work? ☐

Beware of under-focus (ideas not specific enough to form the basis of a good dissertation) at this stage, i.e. you may find that the topic selected is too broad and must therefore be redefined. One of the most common criticisms of initial ideas for student projects and dissertations is that the topic is too broad and lacks sufficient focus. This may result in the final submission providing a descriptive overview rather than an in-depth analysis of the problem or situation.

Beware also of having a single-minded aim of pursuing a particular topic whatever happens. If the feasibility study indicates that there will be problems collecting and analysing the data, or it is not possible to gain permission from the organisation you were hoping to research, do not pursue the idea. Time will be better spent searching for a new topic area.

The initial thinking phase for projects and dissertations is very time consuming. However, it is important to get the research area precisely defined before going too far with the research process.

Research proposal

See Activity 17.3 MAKING A RESEARCH PROPOSAL AND OUTLINE in the Online Study Guide.

You may have to submit a proposal or outline for your project or dissertation. A proposal ensures that everyone connected with the research is perfectly clear about and in agreement with the aim of the research, what is going to be done and how it is going to be done. The research proposal or outline should be agreed with your tutor (and employer or sponsor if necessary) before *any* in-depth research is begun. The proposal clearly states the aim of the research, the terms of reference (the steps required to achieve the aim) and the proposed methods of investigation, and gives an indication of an initial bibliography.

Below is a general guide to what to include in a research proposal. Your course may have specific requirements for the research proposal, so check the regulations to see exactly what is required.

Introduction/background

The introduction should aim to provide a person who has no previous knowledge of the topic with sufficient background information to understand why the research is being undertaken.

Research aim

The research project or dissertation should have only one aim. This should be stated in a clear, concise and accurate way, indicating the focus of the research and what you hope to achieve. A reader should be left in no doubt as to what you are aiming to do after reading this section of the proposal. Producing such a statement seems to be a very difficult exercise for some students, yet it is crucial to good research that a correctly formulated aim is achieved. Beware of including the word 'and' as this may conceal a multiple aim.

Figure 17.1 Refining the research

```
Topic area  ──────────▶  Leadership/motivation
    │                           │
    ▼                           ▼
Research     ──────────▶  Does leadership style affect motivation?
question                        │
    │                           ▼
    ▼
Research     ──────────▶  To determine if the style of leadership in an
objective                 organisation affects the motivation of its
                          employees
```

Terms of reference (objectives)

This is a listing, in logical sequence, of the tasks that will have to be completed in order to achieve the aim. They indicate the data that are required to complete the research. You need to be quite precise in articulating the terms of reference – state exactly what is going to be done in sequence.

Some suggested terms of reference for the research objective identified in Figure 17.1 are:

- to review the different styles of leadership
- to define motivation
- to identify the factors affecting motivation
- to identify the relationship between style of leadership and motivation
- to determine if the style of leadership affects motivation in an organisation.

> **Remember...**
> You may be assessed on how well you have achieved the terms of reference in your dissertation, so ensure that they are achievable.

Activity 17.5

Constructing the terms of reference

For the research objective you defined in the previous activity, determine the terms of reference that would be appropriate in achieving the objective.

Method

See Activity 17.4 DECIDING ON RESEARCH METHODS in the Online Study Guide.

This section outlines how you propose to achieve the aim and the reasons why a particular method was chosen. Sufficient information must be included to enable the reader to determine the validity of the proposed method and the probable degree of accuracy. This section of the proposal may be subdivided into research design and data collection.

Research design

The research design indicates the general way in which it is intended to carry out the research. Does it involve both primary and secondary research? If primary research is involved, how will this be done – interviews, questionnaires, etc.?

The research design should also state where the research will be conducted and why. For example, is it necessary to gather data from a single organisation, a cross-section of organisations, the general public, etc? The research population from within this also needs to be identified. If you are researching within an organisation, it is necessary to specify which population, from within that organisation, will be used and why. For example, a number of different populations may be identified from within a university – students, academic staff, administrative staff, managers, trade unions, etc. Many of these populations may be subdivided further (e.g. students – full time, part time, etc.). The population you intend to use for your investigation needs to be defined as precisely as possible.

> **Stop and think**
> - What is the population for the research topic you are considering?
> - How might it be subdivided?

Data collection

This section should provide a more detailed account of the data required, how they will be collected and any problems anticipated with doing this, such as confidentiality.

- Identify what you intend to achieve from the *secondary* research and highlight the major sources that will be consulted. Indicate which areas the secondary information will support and/or resolve, e.g. theory, background to the organisation or industry, etc.

- Identify the *primary* data that are required and why. Provide more detail about how the data will be collected, including any sampling techniques to be used. For example, if it is intended to interview people, explain how the interviews are to be conducted, what the interviews are intended to achieve, who will be interviewed, how the sample will be constructed, etc. (see Chapter 9).

You should also provide an explanation of how you intend to analyse the data you collect and how this will relate back to the aim of your research.

Bibliography

At this stage, the bibliography is an indication of the sources you intend to use and the books, journals, etc., already consulted in the selection of the topic and preparation of the proposal (see Chapter 9).

Planning

Some universities or colleges may also require a section on planning to be included within the proposal. If so, you will need to include details about the timescale involved and the resources required. Be careful not to underestimate the requirements: completing a dissertation takes time and money.

Conducting the research

Doing the research for a dissertation is a lengthy process and requires plenty of perseverance, energy and commitment. Do not underestimate the time it will take to gather the data – for example, sending out postal questionnaires and waiting for responses may take several weeks.

Once the topic and aim of the research have been determined, a thorough search and review of the available literature should be conducted. This will help to increase and refine your knowledge of the issues and themes that will inform the primary research. Any research should always start with a review of secondary sources.

See Chapter 9 for more advice on doing the research.

Writing up the research

Many students find writing up their research a daunting and difficult task. Writing up the research requires a deep understanding of the topic, which will enable you to explain and present your research in such a way that the reader is able easily to understand and follow the arguments and discussions. The dissertation must incorporate the appropriate elements as set down in the university or college guidelines. Writing up the research will draw on your experience of writing reports, as the final format will reflect many features of a formal report. Refer to Chapter 16 for more detail on report writing.

Assessment criteria

This section provides an indication of some of the things markers may be looking for when reading a dissertation. However, you should check the course regulations for the specific marking criteria that will be applied to your dissertation.

> **Stop and think**
> ○ What are the marking criteria for your disseration?

Methodology

This will vary according to the type of dissertation you undertake. The methodology should give details of the method eventually used, a justification for using that particular method, and a discussion of the advantages and limitations of that approach. The final method used may differ from the one outlined in the proposal. If this is the case, you must explain the reasons within the methodology.

The marker may be looking for evidence of the following:

- a thorough discussion and justification of the research method(s) used
- an appropriate research method for the problem being investigated
- a well-defined research population
- a sampling method appropriate for the population
- sufficient information about the population and sampling methods used to determine the validity and reliability of the data collected
- identification and discussion of the limitations (if any) of the method used
- identification of data analysis techniques appropriate for the data.

Secondary research

The secondary research should indicate that a thorough literature search and/or review of the relevant theory has been undertaken. The marker may be looking for evidence of the following:

- consultation of a range of quality, contemporaneous sources
- no omissions of seminal texts or significant theorists in the area
- collection of information relevant to the terms of reference
- evidence of analysis and critique of the material rather than straightforward acceptance
- where generalisations have been made, are they based on adequate observations?
- are any assumptions explicit?
- correctly referenced sources
- correctly attributed and appropriate quotations where necessary.

Primary research

If primary research is required, the marker may be looking for evidence of the following:

- collection of data relevant to the terms of reference
- collection of data in an appropriate manner and from an appropriate sample
- recognition of the limitations of the data and that they have been dealt with in an appropriate manner
- the correct application of appropriate data analysis techniques
- an analysis and evaluation of the findings rather than a description
- an explicit relationship between the primary and secondary research.

Suggestions for the successful completion of a dissertation or research project

- A sound logical structure should permeate the dissertation.
- Arguments should be lucid and to the point.
- The evidence offered in support of an argument or case should be clearly stated.
- Make clear what use is made of the research undertaken and what it shows.
- Be critically evaluative of the concepts, theories or models considered in light of the data collected.
- Provide continuity by making adequate linkages between the chapters/sections - this may be aided by the use of brief introductions and summaries for each chapter/section.
- Use tables, graphs, charts, etc., where appropriate to enhance presentation of the data.
- Give due recognition to the limitations of the research findings.
- Be rigorous in the development and analysis of the material.
- If the dissertation is based on an organisation, ensure that it meets the academic requirements and do not let the organisation drive the dissertation.

Management of the dissertation or research project

The dissertation draws on your abilities to cope as an independent learner. In completing this form of assessment successfully, you will have to decide what you want to know, determine how you are going to find it out, and set your own targets and deadlines. Most universities and colleges will operate some form of supervision, but this will largely be to monitor the process – the management and completion of the final product is up to you.

Supervision

You may be allocated an academic tutor to supervise your dissertation. This may involve you in a different type of relationship with a tutor than you have experienced before. There may be opportunities to have one-to-one discussions with the tutor/supervisor, whom you have previously encountered only in a classroom situation. It is important to work out a friendly but professional working relationship with your supervisor – find out what they expect from you and work with them to decide what support you may need. Discuss how often you need to meet and if possible work out a schedule with deadlines for particular parts of the work to be completed. Remember that the supervisor is there to guide and advise you, particularly on the process. They are not going to do the research or write the dissertation for you.

Universities or colleges will probably have some guidelines with regard to the supervision of dissertations, but generally supervisors will expect you to:

- work independently – seeking help elsewhere as well as from the supervisor

- attend meetings regularly (and promptly) to keep them informed of your progress
- be prepared for your meetings
- follow their advice
- be committed and enthusiastic.

You may expect your supervisor to:

- be supportive
- be constructively critical
- give you appropriate quality time
- exert influence if necessary on your behalf.

However, remember that it is your dissertation and you are responsible for the final quality of the work you submit, even if it is awarded a poor mark.

→ Summary

This chapter has outlined that:

- the completion of research projects or dissertations is very time consuming and requires planning and dedication
- time spent at the outset to ensure that the research topic meets all the required criteria is time well spent and may save time and effort in later stages
- a course may have specific requirements and it is important to ensure that these are met
- it is essential to understand the criteria by which the dissertation or research project will be assessed.

18 Examinations

> **Learning outcomes**
> After studying this chapter, you should be able to:
> - organise, plan and prepare effectively for different forms of examination
> - develop efficient and effective strategies for revision
> - work effectively in an examination
> - devise strategies to overcome problems you may encounter with examinations.

Introduction

The final assessment of some of the modules you study at university or college may be an examination. Most students will have done examinations in some form before entering higher education – either mainly theoretical examinations, such as GCSEs and A levels, or practical examinations, such as music, dance or driving (though this now includes a theoretical test as well). Just as practical examinations in music measure the skill of playing a particular musical instrument, theoretical examinations are a measure by which knowledge, skills and ability to think may be measured.

Examinations are generally held at the end of a study period, pulling together everything that has been studied during the course or module and encouraging consolidation of what has been learned. Passing examinations demonstrates not only the acquisition of a certain level of knowledge and/or skill, but also the ability to apply oneself to a job of work – in this case, studying. However, it is important to remember that passing examinations is not the be all and end all of life.

Many students think of examinations and feel anxious, which can mean that they do not perform as well as they could. It is important to think of examinations as challenging and positive experiences. Thinking positively will empower you to reach your capabilities, because beliefs create results. You must believe that you *can* do it (otherwise you will not commit yourself to do it), that you *deserve* to do it, and that it is *worth* the effort required.

Formulating abstract ideas and concepts into something that the memory can handle and use in the examination setting is a matter of application and practice. Just consider for a moment that between birth and five years, you learned to walk, carry out the social niceties of eating with cutlery, live with others, etc., and in addition to all that you learned an entire language. Mastering the techniques to pass examinations by comparison is a small feat.

The better prepared you are for examinations, the less stressful the experience. Unfortunately, examinations do not just measure knowledge and skills in an academic discipline, but they also measure the ability to take examinations. This chapter provides a guide to some of the skills and techniques you may find helpful in improving your ability to take and successfully pass examinations. They will not help unless you know and understand the material on which you are being examined, but they may help to prevent the unnecessary loss of marks.

→ Why examinations?

Examinations provide you (and others) with an indication of your progress in a particular skill or academic discipline. They can highlight any problems of understanding or skill deficiency that may need to be rectified before continuing to the next stage of study.

Some examinations are required by law to indicate that a particular level of competence has been achieved. For example, no one is allowed to hold a full driving licence in the UK unless they have passed both the theoretical and practical parts of the driving test. Some professions, such as law, accountancy and medicine, cannot be practised unless the appropriate professional examinations have been passed.

Examinations at university or college are likely to be a different experience from those you may have taken at school. At school you may have been provided with revision sheets, completed mock examinations, etc., but in higher education you are expected to take responsibility for your own learning and preparation for examinations. In addition, examinations at this level are more likely to test whether or not you can apply the knowledge gained rather than simply ask for a regurgitation of facts.

See Activity 18.1 FROM 'EXAM HELL' TO 'EXAM HEAVEN' in the Online Study Guide.

Activity 18.1

Benefits gained from examinations

Make a list of three different examinations/tests you have taken during your life (not necessarily examinations that you have passed).

(a) Why did you take these examinations/tests?

(b) What benefits have you gained from having taken these examinations?

(c) How can you use this knowledge to improve your performance in examinations/tests in the future?

Preparing for examinations

In order to give yourself the best possible chance of completing an examination successfully, it is important to be fully prepared and know what to expect. This will help to reduce anxiety and avoid panic attacks in the examination room. It is important to be prepared, not just intellectually, but also emotionally and physically.

Emotional preparation

It is very easy for stress to take over as the examination approaches. Try to keep calm and relaxed. Read Chapter 12 and develop a strategy to control any anxiety you might experience. Many universities and colleges have student counselling services. If the stress and anxiety become unbearable and you are unable to cope, talk to your tutor and/or the student counsellor.

There may be times when, because of circumstances beyond your control, you are unable to perform to your best ability or even take the examination. If you have a problem that you believe will hinder your performance, ensure that your tutor is informed as soon as possible and before the examination. Never miss an examination if you can possibly help it – this can cause problems later on, particularly if you have other assessments to complete.

Physical preparation

It is important that you eat regular well-balanced meals, exercise and get a good night's sleep, particularly the night before the examination. This will ensure you are in good physical shape on the day. Beware of overdosing on caffeine in coffee or soft drinks for stimulation – this may cause you to lose sleep and thus impair your concentration and performance during the examination.

If you have a disability that will affect your performance, make sure that this is registered well before the examination so that any special arrangements may be made to accommodate you. For example, students experiencing dyslexia may be allowed extra reading and writing time in an examination.

Arrangements for the examination

It is essential that you are aware of the exact format of the examination well in advance of commencing revision, as the preparation required will be dependent upon the type of examination. Examinations will vary in length (time) and the number of questions to be answered. Some examinations contain compulsory questions with no choice, others may allow a completely free choice, and some may offer a combination of compulsory questions and choice.

Stop and think
- Do you know all the details and arrangements for the examinations you are going to take?
- How many examinations do you have?

PART 2   DEVELOPING ASSESSMENT SKILLS

As soon as you know that you will be assessed by examination, find out the answers to the questions in Table 18.1 for each examination you have to take.

Table 18.1 **Examination format**

Module/subject:		
When is the examination: Date? Time?		
How long will it last?		
Where will it be held?		
What type of examination will it be?		
Which part(s) of the syllabus or course will it cover?		
Written	*Oral*	*Practical*
Open or closed book?	Can I take notes with me?	Open or closed book?
If open book, what materials can I take with me?		If open book, what materials can I take with me?
Is it a *seen* exam paper?	Will I know the questions that will be asked beforehand?	Do I know the nature of the tasks to be performed?
How many questions?	How many questions?	How many tasks will I have to do?
What type of questions will there be?	How many examiners will be present?	How many examiners will be present?
Are there any compulsory questions?	What role will the examiners take?	Do I have a choice in what I can do?
How much choice will there be?	Are questions based on a written submission?	What will the examiners be looking for? Which skills are being tested?
Do all questions carry equal marks?	Do all questions carry equal marks?	Do all aspects carry equal marks?
Do I need any material for the examination (e.g. case study, seen questions, calculator)?		*What equipment will be provided? Do I have to provide any additional equipment?*

→ Revision

Examination preparation should be a continuous process, starting from the day of any new course or module of study. Revision should not normally be used to learn new material or develop new skills. It is simply reviewing material that you already understand and improving the skills you have previously acquired. If there are substantial parts of the course that you have not understood, it may be better to omit them altogether rather than confuse your revision by attempting to learn new ideas, concepts and skills.

Many students regard revision as something to be done in the last couple of weeks before the examination – this is cramming and is not advisable. It is far better to plan revision systematically throughout the course as an integral part of your study programme. Reviewing material regularly counteracts the rate of loss of recall in the future.

There is no easy answer to how much revision or practice is required. It depends on you, your learning style and how much work and review you have done during the course or module.

> **Remember...**
> It is easier to remember something if it is reviewed within 24 hours of hearing it.

Suggestions to make your revision easier

- Start your revision early, well before the examination period.
- Follow up queries about a topic as and when they arise during the course.
- Do not use revision to learn new material or develop new skills.
- Systematically plan revision throughout the course, not just before the examination.

Make a plan

When you start revising, work out a timetable for yourself. Planning what needs to be done and setting manageable targets will help to reduce any energy-sapping panic attacks (see Table 18.2).

To develop a timetable, draw a grid encompassing the 168 hours in a week. You will probably need to do this for a number of weeks leading up to the examination period. Block out all the times when revision is impossible, ensuring that you include all activities you need or want to continue. Only you can decide which social, domestic or work activities are to be abandoned until after the examinations. Giving up going to the pub for a few weeks will seem worthwhile once the examination is passed! As the examination draws closer, aim to increase the amount of time spent on revision during each week. Never attempt to study 24 hours a day – this rarely works and your efficiency and capacity to retain material will rapidly decrease.

See downloadable template 18.1 ORGANISING YOUR REVISION TIMETABLE for your Personal Development Plan online.

PART 2 DEVELOPING ASSESSMENT SKILLS

Chapter 11 provides some useful tips on how to improve your skills in managing your time. At each stage:

- Identify what you *have to do*, apart from revision.
- Stop doing things that you *like to do*, but which are not essential.
- Review other things that you *ought to do* and decide whether they really are essential, or can be put off for a few weeks.

By completing a timetable, you will be able to identify potential times when revision is possible and when it is not, such as when you are asleep. Once potential revision times have been identified, schedule your actual revision time.

Some universities and colleges give reading weeks before examination periods. This usually means that formal classes are cancelled so that students may use the time for revising. If there is a reading week, use the time wisely and plan what you are going to do.

Table 18.2 Example of a revision timetable

See downloadable template 18.2 REVISION CHART for your Personal Development Plan online.

Day/time	00-9 a.m.	9-10 a.m.	10-11 a.m.	11-12 a.m.	etc.	9-10 p.m.
Monday	Sleep					
Tuesday	and		Revision			Pub
Wednesday	travel	Revision	Jogging	Revision		Job
Thursday	to		Revision			Job
Friday	university			Revision		Job
Saturday	Sleep			Visit home		Theatre
Sunday	Sleep	Job	Revision	Job		

> **Stop and think** ○ Which activities wil you give up to allow more time for revision?

Activity 18.2

Future benefits

If you have difficulty in motivating yourself to find time for revision, take a few minutes to consider the following questions:

- What benefits will passing this examination bring to you?
- In view of these benefits, make a list of what are you prepared to give up in order to increase your chances of passing the examination(s).

When you have a revision timetable:

- *Systematically organise yourself.* Bear in mind your natural body clock. Some people are 'night owls' and like to revise into the middle of the night, whilst others are 'early birds' and prefer to get up the moment dawn breaks. Whichever is the best time for you to revise, schedule the bulk of revision at that time to maximise your learning opportunities. Decide which topic to revise in each block of time. Be realistic – two hours per week per module or subject will not be enough!

- *Give yourself a break!* Schedule breaks for meals, snacks and refreshments. Do not force yourself to study beyond your normal limits of concentration – if you can concentrate for only 10 or 20 minutes at a time, study for only that period of time and then take a short break. Give your brain a rest; think about anything but revising: play music, walk in the garden or round the house or apartment, and return refreshed to your revision. This will help your concentration to return.
- *Reward yourself.* Most people respond to the possibility of a reward, so set targets and reward yourself when you achieve them – for example, watch your favourite television programme, treat yourself to a chocolate biscuit, etc. But make sure you achieve the target first; the reward should be contingent upon reaching the target.
- *Make yourself comfortable.* It is important to find a comfortable place to revise where the general ambience is conducive to studying. The place you choose should be quiet and well lit and have good ventilation. Try not to choose somewhere that you associate with doing other things because this may distract you.
- *Have everything you need.* Ensure that all the things you will need are close to hand so that you do not have to break your concentration to get something.
- *Keep focused.* Whilst revising, do not allow yourself to be distracted. Ask your friends and family not to interrupt. It is a good idea to ignore the telephone, knocks at the door, etc. Put up a sign on your door indicating that you do not want to be interrupted. Try to avoid letting your thoughts wander until it is time for your five-minute break.
- *Remain calm.* Do not try to revise while you are unsettled or distressed by events in your personal life. Trying to study under these conditions will hinder your concentration and hence cause more distress. Take some time out to resolve the problems.

> **Remember...**
> Regular, short study periods are more productive than lengthy single sessions.

Suggestions for preparing for examinations

- Be prepared emotionally, physically and intellectually.
- Try to maintain a reasonably regular schedule of revising, eating, sleeping and relaxing.
- Do not cram; start revising early.
- Be reasonable and realistic about the demands you place on yourself.
- Reward yourself for achieving targets.

Written examinations

Written examinations generally test theoretical knowledge and cognitive skills. When a module or course is assessed by written examination, it is essential to find out details about the examination as early as possible. This information will provide valuable insights into how to prepare for the examination.

Written examinations may be either *closed book* or *open book*. A closed book examination is the traditional form of examination where candidates are not allowed to take any reference material into the examination room. In contrast, for an open-book examination material can be taken into the examination room – this may be notes, textbooks or both. It is important to establish the rules about the material that is allowed into the examination before any preparation or revision is commenced, as this will influence the work required.

It can be tempting to think that not much revision is necessary for open-book examinations. However, this is not the case. Preparation and revision are vital – there will not be sufficient time during the examination for continual reference to notes and books, and certainly not enough time to investigate new topics.

The type of questions and answers in written examinations will vary depending on what is to be tested.

Types of written examination

Objective tests

Objective tests consist of a series of questions that have only one pre-determined correct answer. Subjectivity is removed and marking is thus objective. They may be used when it is important to test knowledge and understanding of the whole syllabus of a course, and may therefore form part or all of the assessment in the earlier stages to spot gaps in basic knowledge, competences or prerequisite knowledge.

Many objective tests are designed to test an ability to recognise and recall information, or to translate data from one form to another (for example, the interpretation of graphical data), or to solve problems. However, they may also be designed to make use of high-level critical reasoning skills to determine the correct answer.

The types of question found in objective tests are explained in Table 18.3 and Figure 18.2.

> **Stop and think**
> - How many of your examinations are multi-choice?
> - Do the multi-choice questions in your examination carry penalties for incorrect answers?
> - Have you practised with previous multi-choice question papers?

Short answers

Short answer questions usually include an instruction word indicating what is required, e.g. list, name, define, explain, describe (see Chapter 15 for more information about instruction words). Sometimes the parameters for answering are given within the ques-

Table 18.3 Common types of question used in objective tests

Type of question	Explanation
Multi-choice questions	These questions consist of two parts: the stem (statement/question) and a list of alternative answers (distracters) from which you select the correct one. They may be *single completion* (one choice is correct) or *multiple completion* (more than one of the choices offered is correct). Some multi-choice questions have penalties for wrong answers. If a wrong answer incurs a penalty, answer only those questions for which you know the correct answers. If there is no penalty for a wrong answer and you do not know the answer, then guess. There is a 1 in 4 or 5 chance of picking the correct answer. *Note*: The first example in Figure 18.1 is a factually based question whereas the second example involves some reasoning. (However, if you did not know that the capital of France was Paris, this question could also involve reasoning.)
True-false questions	These consist of a statement which you must decide whether or not is true. Circling the appropriate word or crossing out the incorrect answer indicates your decision.
Matching item questions	This type of question contains a list of items and a series of statements or items. To answer the question, each listed item must be matched with the statement it best represents.
Completion questions	These require the insertion of one or more words to complete an incomplete sentence or phrase correctly. Diagrams, formulae or calculations may also be used in this type of question.
Assertion-reason questions	These consist of two statements (assertion and reason). You must first decide the truth or falsity of the two statements independently. Then, if both are true, decide whether the reason is a correct explanation of the assertion.

tion, e.g. 'Describe in not more than 20 words ...'; if so, ensure that you do not exceed the word limit.

Figure 18.1 Example of short answer question

> Explain, in not more than 20 words, what is meant by the term Fixed Costs.

Essays

Examinations requiring essay answers generally aim to test a few areas of a syllabus in depth. Questions are open-ended and test for an ability to be both selective and fluent in the handling of ideas when working under a time constraint. See Chapter 15 for further details about essays.

Case study examinations

See Chapter 13 for detailed information about case studies.

PART 2 DEVELOPING ASSESSMENT SKILLS

Figure 18.2 **Examples of different types of examination question**

Multi-choice questions

The capital of France is:
- A. Lyons
- B. Brussels
- C. Paris
- D. Vienna

If cricket becomes more popular than tennis there will be:
- A. A shortage of tennis racquets
- B. An increase in the price of tennis racquets
- C. A fall in the price of cricket bats
- D. An increase in the production of cricket bats
- E. A surplus of cricket bats

True-false question

Computer hardware represents the programs that cause data to be manipulated.
TRUE / FALSE

Matching item question

Match each of the collective nouns in the first column with the appropriate animals in the second column.

Shoal	Crows
Murder	Lions
Skulk	Fish
Pride	Owls
Parliament	Foxes

Completion question

_____ planning is carried out by senior levels of management in organisations.

Assertion-reason question

Decide whether:
a. both assertion and reason are right statements and the reason is the correct explanation.
b. both assertion and reason are right statements, but the reason is not the correct explanation.
c. the assertion is true and the reason is a false statement.
d. the assertion is false, and the reason is a true statement.
e. both are false statements.

Assertion	Reason
A normal demand curve slopes downwards from left to right.	An elastic demand implies a high sensitivity of quantity changes to price changes.

Examinations involving calculations

Some examinations may contain, or are completely composed of, questions requiring calculations, perhaps with an explanation of the answer, a term or the assumptions made when doing the calculation. Often, in this type of examination, marks are given not only for the correct answer but also for the method used. It is therefore important to show how you arrive at your answer – even if you have an incorrect final answer, you may gain marks for method.

It is important to leave some time at the end of the examination to check your answers. If time is short, at least skim your answers to ensure they are of the right magnitude and you have not, for example, inadvertently misplaced a decimal point!

> **Remember...**
> Take a calculator. Mobile phones are not generally allowed in the examination room.

Preparing for written examinations

What to revise

It is important to be organised when revising. Reading your notes from beginning to end is very inefficient and you will also probably find it boring. It is more effective to break the material down into manageable sections and think strategically – which sections do you need to revise? There are various sources that may be used for guidance on this.

- *Revision list.* The tutor may provide a revision list indicating the topics to revise. This is a good place to start.
- *Module outline.* This will help in identifying the major topic areas. Choose topics you are interested in; this will provide motivation. However, do not concentrate on these topics at the expense of others which may be more important.
- *Previous examination papers.* These will provide an idea about the topics that have been examined in the past but, remember, the tutors will not necessarily include them again this time! Avoid question spotting, as this can lead to problems – if you restrict revision to a number of topics that were previously included on the examination paper and this year one or two are not, your chances of passing may be greatly reduced.
- *Tutor.* Ask the tutor what to anticipate. He or she can only refuse to divulge the information! Pay particular attention to points the tutor emphasises during the classes immediately prior to the examination.

Revision techniques

Although revising largely involves going over previously prepared notes, it does not mean just passively reading them. Try to make revision active by using and manipulating the information, looking at different ways of dealing with the material collected. This will make it more effective and interesting, keeping your mind alert. The following activities will help to keep your revision active:

Reorganise your notes

You may find that the notes taken during the course are too lengthy for final revision. Revision could therefore be partly based on making new, condensed notes that integrate those taken in lectures, from texts and other sources. This process is an active form of learning and results in a final brief form of materials for further revision.

By the time the examinations are imminent, you should be able to encapsulate each topic on a postcard, or even down to 5–10 words. These words are used as 'triggers' which in the examination room will enable you to recall sufficient detail to be able to answer whatever question the examiner asks.

Another way of reorganising notes is to draw pictures or diagrams of the topic. A bit of artistic flair will provide a distinctive visual framework that you may find easier to recall than textual information.

Talk about the subject

Discussing the subject with someone or explaining it to them forces you to articulate the ideas and concepts in your own words. Being able to explain something is the only way to be sure that you fully understand it.

Become the examiner

Put yourself in the role of the examiner and generate a list of questions that you would ask if you were setting the examination paper. Look at the syllabus content and identify the main topic areas. Consider how the topics relate to one another – are there any themes emerging? Think of questions that may be asked around these themes. Write outline answers for the questions you generate.

Test yourself at regular intervals during your revision

One way of doing this is to create 'flash' cards with terms, lists, important facts, etc., on one side and the answers on the other. Carry them with you and use pockets of spare time (e.g. on the bus/train, waiting in queues) to test yourself.

Use every opportunity to revise

It is important to use every opportunity you can to revise material. For example, recite what you have learnt whilst doing other things, such as cooking, cleaning or showering, or record your notes on a tape and listen to them on a personal tape player/recorder as you do other things.

Practise what you will have to do in the examination

It is useful, for all types of written examination, to practise answering the types of question you are expecting in the actual examination. Often copies of past examination papers are available in the university or college library or from tutors. These can be instructive in familiarising you with the type of question, the structure and format of the examination and so on. Try writing model answers to questions and ask a friend or family member to check whether, in their opinion, you have answered the questions adequately.

Check how much time was taken to write the answer, and note how much time is available to answer the question in the examination. If, for example, you have taken four or five hours to answer a question for which half an hour would be allocated in the exam, this is a good indication that you will need to be much more familiar with the material, and able to write a full and appropriate answer more quickly.

Before the day of the examination, it is a good idea to practise answering at least one question in the time allocated in the exam, without the aid of your notes or books. This will demonstrate how quickly time passes in the examination room. Check your completed answer by referring to your notes. Be honest with yourself: if you have missed out major elements that should have been included, you need to do some more revision.

> **Stop and think**
> ○ Which topics do you need to revise in preparation for your examination?
> ○ How can you revise more effectively?
> ○ Have you checked past examination papers?
> ○ Have you practised writing answers in the time available?

Open-book examinations

Open-book examinations require a particular revision strategy. It is easy to be lured into a false sense of security because you are able to take materials into the examination. However, it is important that you prepare for open-book examinations by:

- Familiarising yourself with one or two key textbooks which you intend to take to the examination. You could make mind maps to summarise the key concepts in each chapter.
- Familiarising yourself with your notes and organising them in such a way that you can easily find your way around them.
- Indexing your notes to save valuable time during the examination.

> **Remember...**
> Be careful not to plagiarise in open-book examinations – ensure that any sentences, etc., taken from books are in quotation marks and correctly referenced.

If you have never done open-book examinations, it is good practice to attempt a previous examination paper, just to experience how long it takes to look things up in books under examination conditions. It is easy to underestimate the time required to locate information in books.

Sometimes you may be allowed to take one or two pages of prepared notes into an examination. In this case, do not be tempted to write answers to questions you think may come up – this is likely to be a waste of time unless you know the precise wording of the questions. Use the pages to summarise key points, including a few relevant quotations.

> **Suggestions for a revision strategy**
> - Make your revision active.
> - Keep revision sessions as pure revision.
> - Practise answering questions.

Objective tests

It is important to review concepts and examples as well as facts. Look through your notes and textbooks and actively seek the sort of material that can be answered objectively

Short answers
Review your notes and appropriate textbooks. Make a list of the important terms and their definitions. Think of examples or illustrations of each term so that, if required in the examination, you can provide examples quickly and accurately.

Essay questions
Review any essays you have written during the module. It may be a good idea to swap copies of essays with other students, particularly if their essays cover different topics; but choose whom you do this with carefully.

Select a number of topics that seem central to the module, think up possible essay titles in these areas and write an outline for each of these. Write as many essays as possible using the outlines, giving yourself only as much time for each as will be available in the examination. Review the practice essays, paying attention to those that could be improved.

Quantitative questions
Review your notes and textbooks, listing formulae and concepts. Look for fundamental problem types. Use worked examples in your textbook and notes for practice – cover up the solution, work out the answer and then check to see if your answers match the solutions given. If you have difficulties with some, try others of a similar nature until you are proficient in the techniques required.

Often examinations involving calculations are open book – if so, index your notes so that things can be found quickly, and copy important formulae on to a single sheet of paper for quick reference in the examination.

For all examinations, aim to gain an understanding of the material you are revising. Students who are able to demonstrate a deep understanding of the concepts and issues raised in the examination question write the best answers.

Do not be too disheartened if you make mistakes or are unable fully to complete past examination papers. Investigate where you went wrong and return to your notes to find the correct answers or information.

> **Remember...**
> We learn far more from our mistakes than we do from our successes.

The day before the examination

It is fairly certain that you are going to feel some anxiety about examinations. This is only natural. Remember that a little anxiety can help to sharpen your senses and therefore help to stimulate your brain. If you are overconfident, you may well miss something.

Being well prepared and knowing what to expect will help to reduce unnecessary stress and anxiety. You should have noted the correct dates, times and locations of each examination when the examination timetable became available. However, check again carefully with your student colleagues that you have the correct date, time and place, and that you know exactly where the examination is to take place. Sometimes examinations are scheduled in locations other than the usual teaching accommodation, so double check. It might be necessary to allow extra travelling time. If there is any confusion, check again with the university or college administrators.

> **Stop and think**
> ○ When is the examination?
> ○ What time does the examination start>
> ○ Where is the examination?

The night before the examination, make sure that you have everything you may need ready to take with you. Set your alarm clock to go off early, so you can get ready unhurriedly, and, if you are inclined to oversleep, ask several of your friends or family to telephone or knock on your door to check that you are awake.

Do not revise new material the night before, but build up confidence by reinforcing what you do know, rather than worrying yourself by discovering what you do not know.

Checklist: what you need for the examination

- Pens ☐
- Pencils ☐
- Eraser ☐
- Correction fluid (if allowed) ☐
- Highlighter pens/coloured pens ☐
- Ruler ☐
- Calculator (and spare batteries) - check the type of calculator you are allowed to use, since often programmable calculators are not allowed. *Mobile telephones are usually not allowed in the examination room (or must be switched off).* ☐
- Mathematical instruments (if necessary) ☐
- Books/notes - for open-book examinations ☐
- Case study (if appropriate) ☐
- Student identity card - many colleges and universities now require that you present some form of proof of identity when taking examinations. ☐

The day of the examination

Prepare yourself by thinking positively. Remind yourself why you are doing the examination and the benefits of passing. Boost your confidence by reminding yourself that you are well prepared and going to do well. Keep calm. You will be able to think more clearly the less stress you are experiencing. Avoid last minute stress by:

- not studying in the hour or so before an exam
- arriving at the examination room early to avoid last-minute pressure

- avoiding talking to other students about the subject or discussing possible questions, particularly with those whom you know are worriers – examination nerves are contagious and unproductive.

The examination

When candidates are allowed into the examination room:

- Quickly find a place to sit – some universities and colleges will allocate candidates to specific desks; others will allow candidates to select places for themselves. If you have a choice, choose a place with adequate light and ventilation, and away from the distractions of other candidates.
- Ensure that you can see a clock if you do not have your own watch. If you are unable to see a clock, ask the invigilator if the clock may be repositioned, or move to another seat.
- Lay out everything you need on the desk or table.
- Listen carefully to the invigilator's instructions.
- Write your name and student number on the front of the examination booklet.
- Do not start until you are told to do so.

Often universities and colleges hold examinations for hundreds of candidates in one room. Do not be overawed by the number of people in the room, but concentrate on organising yourself and focusing on the task to be completed.

The examination paper

When the examination actually starts, *pause* and take several slow, deep breaths to relax. Many candidates lose marks because they rush at the paper. If necessary sit on your hands, so that you avoid the temptation to pick up your pen and write. Read the instructions carefully, paying particular attention to the number of questions to be answered. If you do not understand the instructions, do not be afraid to ask the examiners for clarification.

Plan your time, remembering to allocate time at the end to review what you have done. Divide the time by the number of questions you have to answer, but bear in mind the weighting given to the questions. This is particularly important if the paper contains a mixture of questions such as multi-choice and essays. So, if question 1 has a weighting of 50%, spend 50% of the time on it, and if questions 2 and 3 have a weighting of 25% each, spend 25% of the time on each of them. Do not be tempted to spend 'an extra five minutes' on an answer, but stop when your allocated time is up.

> **Remember...**
> It is much easier to get the first 50% of any marks available for a question than the rest.

It is important that you answer the correct number of questions in an examination. If you are asked to answer four questions, answer four questions, not three, two or even

EXAMINATIONS

one! Do not answer more questions than are required – the examiner will normally only mark the required number of answers.

Consider the following example of three hypothetical students sitting an examination. The examination paper asks the student to answer four questions and 100 marks are available (25% or 25 marks for each question). The pass mark is 40%.

- Student 1 answers four questions and gains 12.5 for each answer, giving $4 \times 12.5 = 50\%$, and the student passes comfortably.
- Student 2 answers 3 questions and gains 12.5 for each answer, giving $3 \times 12.5 = 37.5\%$, and the student is referred or failed.
- Student 3 answers two questions and gains 18 for each answer, giving $2 \times 18 = 36\%$, and this student too is referred or failed.

It is therefore better to answer four questions reasonably well, rather than two questions excellently. By adopting this strategy, the probability of passing the exam is increased.

See Activity 18.2 EXAM INSTRUCTIONS TEST in the Online Study Guide.

> **Remember...**
> Do not be afraid to ask the examiner if anything on the paper is unclear.

Your answers

When sitting examinations (except objective tests), read the question paper thoroughly. Ensure you understand what each question requires. If there are ambiguities or typographical errors that do not make sense, ask the examiners for clarification of the wording of the questions. If there is a choice of questions, put a line through the questions you feel unable to attempt and put a mark against those you can definitely do. Write down anything that immediately comes to mind about a question, such as key words and concepts – this will help to unclutter your mind.

Tackle the questions that you find easiest first, leaving the more doubtful ones until later. This will boost confidence, reduce anxiety and facilitate clear thinking. It may also gain you some time for the harder questions!

Objective tests

Check the instructions to see if there is a penalty for incorrect answers. If there is no penalty then take an intelligent guess at the questions for which you do not know the answer. You cannot score marks if you do not answer, but you may be lucky and guess correctly.

Work through each question one by one, reading it carefully before answering. Skip any questions you are unable to do, marking them with an X so that you can return to them later.

If the questions attract different marks, allow more time for those of higher value, but work quickly, allocating time according to the question weighting. Leave sufficient time at the end to review your answers and return to consider those marked with an X.

Multi-choice questions

Cover up the answers to multi-choice questions, anticipate the correct answer and then look for it in the list of choices. Ensure you read all the choices for the answer before making a selection. It can be tempting, if you think the answer is A, not to read the other choices and skip to the next question. There may be a more appropriate answer in B, C or D.

If you are not sure about the answer, cross out the choices that you know are definitely wrong. Mark the question with a ? and return to it at the end. If one of the choices is 'All of the above' it is often, but not always, correct. If you are sure that two or three of the options are correct, then 'All of the above' is a distinct possibility.

Do not pay any attention to how many As, Bs, Cs, etc., you have already selected. Always choose the 'best' answer – this is often the answer that uses a word or phrase specific to the module, and when in doubt guess (unless there is a penalty for a wrong answer!). Your first choice is usually correct, so avoid the temptation to change answers unless you are absolutely certain about the correction.

See Activity 18.3 WHAT DOES THE QUESTION MEAN? in the Online Study Guide.

True-false questions

Check the instructions to determine whether you have to explain your answer. The following provides general guidelines for formulating answers.

- Absolute terms (never, always, only, necessary, must, entirely, no, none, every, etc.) are rarely true, whereas relative terms (often, seldom, sometimes, perhaps, generally, ordinarily, frequently, etc.) make more modest claims that are more likely to reflect reality and are thus often true.

- Be careful with questions containing the word 'and' – all the statements or phrases within the question have to be true to answer true. For those questions with 'or', only one of the statements or phrases would have to be true to give a true answer.

- Beware of negatives (no, not, etc.) within a question, as they can be confusing. Try underlining the negative words and reading the sentence excluding them. If this sentence is true then the answer is *false* and vice versa.

Matching questions

Look at the first item in the first list. Read *all* the items in the second list before selecting the appropriate one. Match the items you know are definitely correct – this will reduce the number of options for those you are not sure about. Make sure all the items have been matched before moving on to the next question.

Short answers

It is useful to start by defining all the terms in the question. Relate the terms to the general ideas presented during the module and add supporting examples if possible. Be sure to write enough but make certain to limit the answers to the parameters given – if you are asked to answer in fewer than 20 words, make sure that is what you do. Write the answer in simple concise sentences including as much information as possible – this is usually more important than style.

Use common sense to make a guess if you are not sure of the correct answer. This may gain valuable marks – if you do not answer, you will not get any marks!

Quantitative examinations

If the examination is not open book, jot down all the formulae, definitions, etc., that you are trying to remember as soon as the examination starts. This will help to clear your mind and boost your confidence if you have remembered the correct formulae.

Examine all the questions and note anything that comes into your mind and is appropriate to the question. Identify those problems you definitely know how to do straight away and those you expect to have to think about. Start with the questions you find easiest, since this will boost your confidence and reduce any anxiety. Plan the time carefully, ensuring that you leave sufficient time to look over the answers thoroughly at the end – it is easy to make a mistake when working under pressure.

Once you have decided on the method of solution for a problem, follow it through carefully, checking each step for consistency. Evaluate your solutions at each stage. Do the answers fit? Are they of the right magnitude compared to the information given in the question? It is very easy to add extra zeros, miss zeros or omit decimal points in an examination. If you use a calculator, take time to ensure you press the right buttons; it is very easy to miskey a number when you are working under pressure.

Work quickly and carefully, showing your workings – if an answer is incorrect, the examiner may give some credit if they can see how the problem was approached. Clearly write each step of the solution and keep checking as you are working. If you are stuck, move on to the next question and return to the problem one later. If you run out of time, indicate the solution or formulae that would have been used for the remaining question(s), since this may earn some valuable extra marks.

Leave sufficient time at the end of the examination to check your answers for obvious errors and ensure that you do not inadvertently miss parts of a question.

Essay questions

Essay questions test the ability to present appropriate information and relate ideas. It is important that the information included is accurate, but it is also vital that the examiner can follow the logic of the arguments and ideas presented.

Read all the questions carefully, crossing out those you cannot or do not want to do (if you have a choice). When reading the questions, note any specific points as they occur to you. Choose the questions for which you feel best prepared. Once you have decided on one, do not change your mind.

Analyse the question, looking for the instruction words. For example, if the question asks for an evaluation of a particular theory, few marks will be awarded for describing the theory. Underline the instruction words in the question and circle the main terms and concepts. Check the chapter on essay writing for more information on instruction words.

Plan your answer. Do not be tempted to start writing the answer immediately, even if everyone else is writing furiously. Take a few minutes to plan each answer, and jot down notes, quotations, examples, etc., either in the answer book or on spare paper. Identify them as notes, and rule a line through them when you have finished with them. Plan a logical structure, identifying the related elements in the question and separating the general issues from the supporting detail and examples. Check that your outline answers the question set and adjust it if necessary.

Write the answer. Once you have planned the answer, start writing. Begin the essay with a strong first statement that will indicate to the marker the main idea of the essay. Use the first paragraph to outline a plan for the essay, introducing the main ideas. Each

See downloadable template 18.5 PLANNING YOUR ANSWER for your Personal Development Plan online.

Figure 18.3 Strategy for completing essay questions

> READ the QUESTION
>
> ⬇
>
> PLAN the ANSWER
>
> ⬇
>
> WRITE the WORDS

idea should then be explained and developed in subsequent paragraphs. Try not to confuse issues by discussing more than one main point within a paragraph, but use transitions such as 'therefore' and 'nevertheless' to connect the paragraphs. See Chapter 5 for more transition words.

Structure your answer by selecting the important facts, developing them in a chronological sequence as required by the question, and linking them to appropriate theories or theorists. This will provide the foundations of a good answer. Include as many specific references (names, dates, direct quotations) as possible in support of the points made. Take time to write a strong conclusion that summarises the main ideas in the essay.

> **Remember...**
> In the examination, you will be able to use only part of what you have revised, so you need to select carefully from your memory.

If you have to do more than one essay question in the examination, leave plenty of space between your answers. Thus, if you finish a question, or the paper, early, you can return and add to an answer.

Take time at the end to review your answers and check for any obvious errors in figures, dates, spelling, grammar, etc.

See Activity 18.4 ANSWERING THE QUESTION in the Online Study Guide.

> **Remember...**
> Examinations are about understanding, rather than what you can remember.

> **Suggestions** for completing essay questions in examinations
>
> - Do not waffle: be direct and *answer the question*.
> - Make yourself clear.
> - Be persuasive.
> - Ensure that the points you make are backed up with evidence.
> - Structure the answer – make several points and develop them logically and progressively.
> - Select the most important information to include in your answer.
> - Write legibly.
> - *Answer the question*.
>
> This last point may seem obvious, but it is surprising how many students do not answer the question set by the examiner.

Towards the end of the examination

Use the last few minutes of the examination to read your answers and correct any obvious errors. Make any changes you think are important, but do not substantially change your answers without a good reason.

Do not leave the examination early. It is natural to want to leave as soon as you have finished, but it is wise to use any spare time to keep reviewing and checking your answers. Once you have left the examination room, you will not be able to re-enter if you suddenly remember something!

If you are running out of time, complete the remaining question(s) in note form or indicate the method of solution you would have used. This may gain valuable marks. It is particularly important that you present a legible essay plan for the last essay question in an examination. If you do not have the time to complete the essay fully, the essay plan will indicate how you intended to progress and thus may be awarded marks by the examiner.

Make sure you hand in all your answer sheets to the invigilators, ensuring that your name or student number is clearly visible on every piece of paper submitted and that each answer is clearly marked with the appropriate question number.

After the examination

On leaving the examination, it can be tempting to stand and discuss the answers to the questions and commiserate with other students, but this is a mistake. The examination is over and there is no point in worrying about what you did or did not do. Discussion may only make you feel depressed or angry. If you have another examination to do, this will not help or put you in the right frame of mind. Instead of dwelling on the last examination, look forward to the next, or, if they are all over, go out and celebrate!

> **Remember…**
> Post-mortems of examinations are depressing!

PART 2   DEVELOPING ASSESSMENT SKILLS

How to do well in examinations

An unhappy marker is not usually a generous marker, so you should aim to make your script examiner friendly.

- Use blue or black ink; do not annoy the markers and make their life difficult by using red or green as the main colour. Markers may be marking hundreds of scripts and they will not want to struggle with colours that are not easy on the eye.
- Write legibly.
- Do not waste time by copying out the whole question, but make sure the examiner knows which question is being answered.
- Clearly indicate the question number at the beginning of your answer – if you write question 1 and answer question 2, you may get no marks.
- Plan your answers; do not ramble.
- Answer the question and keep to the point.
- Write concisely and coherently, but not in note form (unless this is required).
- Avoid prescriptive words like 'should' and 'ought' – the marker may not agree.
- Use critical analysis and argument – markers generally like to see an analytical approach rather than description (unless the question specifically asks you to describe).
- Use diagrams where appropriate.
- Avoid making comments about the paper, such as 'This is an unfair question . . .' This is unlikely to impress the examiner.

Suggestions for completing written examinations successfully

- Read the instructions carefully.
- Note the marks that are assigned to each question and allocate the time accordingly.
- Read all the questions carefully.
- Work on the questions one at a time.
- Plan your answers – make brief concise notes for each essay question. This is useful if you run out of time, as the marker can see from the plan what you intended to include and may give marks for this.
- Stay in control.
- If you have a problem with a question, leave it and try another. Return to the unfinished one later if there is time.
- Leave some time at the end to review your answers.
- Check you have answered the questions asked and not the questions you wanted to be asked.
- Check your answers are accurate (calculations, spelling, grammar, facts).
- Check your answers are complete (all the information required has been included).
- Check you have answered the correct number of questions.

EXAMINATIONS

Activity 18.3

Avoiding examination failure

Listed below are some of the common contributors to examination failure. Consider each and determine a way of avoiding these pitfalls.

Problem	Remedy
Long first answer, other answers short	
Failing to answer the question set	
Using revision time to try and master new material	
Panic/anxiety	
Running out of time	
Format of the questions was unexpected	
No practice exam questions attempted prior to the exam	
Too little revision	
Cramming	
Failing to interpret a term correctly	
Misreading or misunderstanding the question	
Misreading or misunderstanding the instructions	
Unable to answer the required number of questions	
Using the wrong formulae	
Attributing the wrong theorist to a theory/theories	
Answers are anecdotal rather than theoretical	

→ Oral examinations (*viva voce*)

An oral examination (sometimes referred to as a *viva voce*) is used to test candidates' ability to articulate answers to questions on a topic studied in depth. The candidate may be asked to express opinions on a topic and the answers given should convince the examiners of your expertise and understanding in this area.

Oral examinations may be used as a supplement to a project, dissertation or thesis and the candidate must answer questions on the research work that has been completed. This provides the candidate with an opportunity to enhance their written submission by expanding on various areas. Oral examinations are also used to satisfy the examiners that a written submission represents the examinee's individual effort (or collaborative effort if the written submission is by a group).

Often this form of examination will involve more than one examiner and possibly an external examiner (someone from outside the university or college).

PART 2   DEVELOPING ASSESSMENT SKILLS

> **Stop and think**
>
> For oral examinations:
> - How many examiners will be present?
> - What roles are they likely to adopt?

Preparing for oral examinations

If the oral is to be based on a written submission (which may have been submitted some weeks earlier), refresh your memory and read a copy of the document a number of times to familiarise yourself with the material. Be critical and assess the strengths and weaknesses of your submission – these are usually the areas on which the examiners will pose questions. You need to be prepared to answer the criticisms and exploit the strengths.

Discuss and debate the topic with other students or, if possible, rehearse with someone taking the role of examiner. This will give you the opportunity to practise articulating your answers.

Read Chapter 14 to get ideas on how to present information orally.

The examination

Take a deep breath before entering the examination room and enter with a confident smile on your face. Listen carefully to any introduction or instructions the examiner(s) may give, asking for clarification if there is anything you do not understand or did not hear. Do not be afraid to politely request the examiner(s) to speak up; it is important that you hear the questions clearly.

Answer the questions openly and honestly, maintaining eye contact with the person posing the question. Do not be aggressive, waffle or try to bluff – admit your shortcomings if necessary. Make your answers concise but complete and do not ramble. If you do not understand the question, ask for clarification from the examiners. Take time to consider your answer before speaking so that, when ready, you can respond with confidence.

At the end of the examination, the examiners may ask if there is anything you wish to add. Think carefully about this and put forward anything that you think is important but has not been highlighted by the examiners.

→ Practical examinations

This form of examination is common where it is vital that particular practical skills as well as cognitive skills are acquired. We would not want a surgeon to operate on us if we were not sure that they had the skills to do this – hence a surgeon's training would involve some practical examinations. Practical examinations are often used for scientific and technical subjects such as physics, engineering, cooking and botany, or performance arts such as dance, theatre and music.

Preparing for practical examinations

If possible, rehearse the techniques and/or routines as many times as you can before the actual examination. Pay particular attention to timing and how long it takes to complete the different tasks. In the examination, they may take longer because of nerves or some unplanned eventualities. Consider the possible problems you may encounter and work out strategies for coping with them if they should occur during the examination. Pay particular attention to checking which equipment will be available to you in the examination room and determine whether you need to provide some of your own.

The examination

Arrive in good time so that you can prepare the equipment needed. When the examination begins, do not panic but work calmly through the procedures rehearsed, paying attention to health and safety procedures where appropriate. If things do not go as planned, do not panic, but keep calm and adopt another procedure or strategy.

> **Activity 18.4**
>
> **Review of examination technique**
> Consider the last time that you sat an examination and answer the following:
>
> - Did you use your time well?
> - What was asked that you did not expect?
> - Which part of the examination did you find most difficult?
> - Were the examination questions more from readings or from lecture/tutorial material?
> - What should you do differently to improve your performance in preparing for the next examination?

→ What to do if you fail an examination

It is important to remember that life goes on even if you fail (or are referred in) an examination. Try to keep a sense of perspective – all is not lost. Remember that there are plenty of examples of people who are successful in life having only few, if any, academic qualifications.

Most universities or colleges will allow students to attempt the examination again (resit), but check your course regulations for specific details.

> **Stop and think**
>
> ○ Does the examination have to be retaken before you can progress to the next stage of studying?
> ○ Does the resit examination have to be taken within a certain time frame? How many times may you attempt the examination?
> ○ What is the maximum mark you can be awarded for a resit examination?

If you have failed (or been referred in) an examination, it is useful to contact the tutor to discuss the options available to you. If possible, ask to look at your examination script or ask your tutor for feedback on your performance.

Analyse your own performance – to what extent was your examination preparation and technique to blame? If you can understand what went wrong in previous examinations, it will highlight where improvements need to be made in preparation for future examinations.

→ Cheating

It can be tempting, especially when you are under extreme pressure, to try to help yourself by devising strategies to enable you to take unauthorised material into the examination room. This is cheating and most institutions regard this as a serious offence. Other forms of gaining unfair advantage include talking to another candidate during the examination and copying another candidate's answers. Do not try to gain unfair advantage – it is not worth the risk and the potential loss is great.

And finally, when the examinations are over, treat yourself and go and celebrate. There is no point in worrying about the result – this is now in the hands of the examiners!

Figure 18.4 **Strategy for examinations**

> PLAN
> PREPARE
> PRACTISE
> BE POSITIVE
> but
> DON'T PANIC
> or
> PLAGIARISE

→ Summary

This chapter has explained that:

- most courses at university or college will involve some assessment in the form of examinations
- when studying for examinations it is important to think positively and spend time planning on how to approach the examination – this will help to relieve many anxieties
- planning and preparing for examinations does not include just the intellectual aspects; it is also necessary to be prepared emotionally and physically in order to perform well
- knowing the format of the examination enables appropriate revision to be undertaken
- it is necessary to remain calm in the period before and during the examination
- it is important to understand and answer the questions that are asked or perform the procedures required in the examination.

This book is accompanied by a Premium Companion Website at **www.pearsoned.co.uk/payne** containing:

- An online study guide
- Interactive exercises and activities
- Downloadable templates for your Personal Development Plan or Portfolio.
- Additional information on more transferable skills:
  - Meetings
  - Influencing and negotiating
  - Leadership
  - Interviewing
  - Project Management
  - Problem Solving
  - Creativity

Bibliography

Belbin, R. M. (1981) *Management Teams: Why They Succeed and Fail*. Oxford: Butterworth-Heinemann.

Bell, J. (2005) *Doing your Research Project: A Guide for First Time Researchers in Education, Health and Social Science*. 4th edition, Milton Keynes: Open University Press.

Benne, K. and Sheats, P. (1948) Functional roles of group members. *Journal of Social Issues*, Vol. 1(4), pp. 41–9.

Bloom, B. S. (1956) *Taxonomy of Educational Objectives*. New York: David McKay Co. Inc.

Boud, D., Keogh, R. and Walker, D. (1985) *Reflection: Turning Experience into Learning*. London: Kogan Page.

Faust, B. and Faust, M. (2002) *Pitch Yourself*. Harlow: Pearson Education.

Harvey, L., Locke, W. and Morey A. (2002) *Enhancing Employability, Recognising Diversity*. Universities UK and CSU.

Holmes, T. H. and Rahe, R. H. (1967) The Social Readjustment Rating Scale. *Journal of Psychosomatic Research*. Vol. 11, no. 2, pp. 213–18.

Honey, P. and Mumford, A. (2000) *The Learning Style Questionnaire*. Cambridge: Peter Honey Publications.

Kolb, D. (1984) *Experiential Learning: Experience as the Source of Learning and Development*. Englewood Cliffs, NJ: Prentice Hall.

Lock, R. (1996) *Student Activities for Taking Charge of your Career Direction and Job Search*. 3rd edition, CA: Brooks/Cole Publishing.

Lock, R. D. (2000) *Taking Charge of Your Career Direction*. 4th edition, London: Wadsworth.

Mehrabian, A. (1970) *Tactics of Social Influence*. New York: Prentice Hall.

Pease, A. (1981) *Body Language*. London: Sheldon Press.

Saunders, M. and Lewis, P. (2003) *Research Methods for Business Students*. London: Financial Times Prentice Hall.

Schön, D. (1983) *The Reflective Practitioner: How Professionals Think in Action*. Aldershot: Arena.

Selye, H. (1956) *The Stress of Life*. New York: McGraw-Hill.

Swetnam, D. (2000) *Writing your Dissertation*. 3rd edition, Oxford: How To Books.

Tuckman, B. (1965) Developmental sequence in small groups. *Psychology Bulletin*. Vol. 63, pp. 384–99.

Tuckman, B. and Jensen, M. (1977) Stages of small group development. *Group and Organizational Studies*. Vol. 2, pp. 419–27

Zimbardo, P. *et al* (1995) *Psychology: A European Text*. London: HarperCollins.

Web addresses

Quality Assurance Agency: www.qaa.ac.uk
Chartered Institute of Personnel and Development: www.cipd.co.uk
Chartered Management Institute: www.managers.org.uk

Index

80/20 principle 284
A4 paper 300
abbreviations 113–15, 171, 327, 347
ABI/INFORM 175
ability 355
abstract 13, 175, 176, 179, 339
accessibility 191
accommodator 17, 19
achievements 29, 61
acknowledgements 345
active voice 97
activist 20
adaptation 285
addresses online 184
adjourning 222
advanced stage 269
aggressor 219
aim of research 358
ambience 226
analysis 269
   of questions 383
annotation 104–5
answers
   presentation of 289–90
   short 372–3, 378, 382
   writing down 383–4
appearance 94
   of report 345–7
appendices 345
application 269, 329
   letter 64
applications software 151
approach, general 271
arithmetic mean 135–7
assessments 267, 273, 277

criteria 270, 361–2
   formative 267
   presentation 270
   summative 267
assimilator 17, 19
Association for Information Management 167
attitudes 282–3
audience (who is the intended reader) 335
audio–visual media 178
authority 188
authors 79, 171, 172
AutoContent Wizard 313
availability 191
averages 135
avoidance 258

background 358
   reading 72–3
balance 329
bar charts 126–8
behaviour sheet 233–6
Belbin, R.M. 229, 231
beliefs 282–3
bias 192
bibliography 80, 343–4, 360
blockages to learning 24–5
   overcoming 28–31
blocker 219
Bloom, B. 268–9
body
   clock 239
   language 298–9
bookmarking 184, 187
books 172

Boud, D. 45
breaks 260, 371
British National Bibliography 171
broken scale 131
budgets 355

calculations in examinations 373, 375
calmness 371
career
   objectives 58–9
   options 53–5
   see also employability; job
case studies 275–90
   answers, presentation of 289–90
   assessment 277
   causes, determination of 284–5
   class discussion 276–7
   examinations 373
   familiarisation with case material 278
   information analysis 279–83
   instructions, following 278–9
   problems defined 283–4
   questions, reading of 279
   recommendations 287–8
   solutions evaluation 286–7
   solutions generating 285–6
cause and effect diagram 284–5
CD-ROM 178–9
cell 157–8
Central Statistical Office 176
central tendency (averages) 135–9

INDEX

character formatting 156
characters 280
Chartered Institute of Personnel and Development 34
Chartered Management Institute 34
charts 347
cheating 390
circadian rhythms 239
class
  discussion 276–7
  frequency 124
classified catalogue 171
clichés 98
clip-art 161
cliques 225
coffee bar conversations 246
coherence 329
cohesiveness 219–21
college 231–6
  computing facilities 151
  learning 9–10
comfort 371
commitment 28
communication 90–102
  active or passive voice 97
  glossary 101
  interpersonal communication process 91–2
  non-verbal 92–4
  skills 38
  spelling 97
  style 99–101
  transitional words and phrases 97–9
  words that are often confused 95–6
  written 94–5
compact disc 150
completer 231
component parts 58–9
comprehension 269
compromiser 218
conclusions 341
conditions for learning 22–3
confidentiality 191
confusing words 95–6

constraints (limitations) 27, 335–6
content (principle subject matter) 79–80, 335
contents list 172
contents page 339
context 280, 339
continuous professional development 34
converger 17, 18
coordinator 217, 229
coping mechanisms 258–62
copyright date 172
corrective action 285
cover letters 63–5
crises 246
critical reading 75
critically evaluative reading 87–8
cues 111
cultural factors 254–5
currency 178, 185, 188
curriculum vitae 57–62
  component parts 58–61
  organisation 61–2
  positive self-description 58
  preparation 62

data:
  analysis 207
  presentation 134
  set 119
  see also primary data collection
deadlines 270–1
decision-making 41, 226, 334
deductions (deductive inference) 281
deep approach 71–2
delivery 313
dependent learning 11, 12
desktop 154
deviant group members 224–5
Dewey Decimal System 169–70
Dewey, M. 169
diagrams 327
diet 259

directories 153, 177
Directory of Information Sources 167
disc storage 149
discriminatory language 98–9
discussion 81–2, 232–6
disorganisation 245
dispersion measures 135, 139–41
dissertations or research projects 352–64
  conducting research 361
  course requirements 353
  defining research question and objective 357–8
  management 363–4
  research proposal 358–61
  topic selection 354–6
  writing up research 361–3
distress 252
diverger 17, 18
doing (concrete experience) 13, 15
dominator 219
drafts 272, 324–5
dragging 149
dynamics 213–15

e-mail 201
education 59–60
electronic media 178
elements (units of analysis) 119
Emerald Reviews 175
emotional preparation for examinations 367
employability 48–68
  career options 53–5
  cover letters 63–5
  curriculum vitae 57–62
  interviews 65–8
  job market, understanding of 55–6
  self-analysis 50–2
employee specifications 65
employers, targeting of 55–6
employment history 60
encourager 218

395

INDEX

essay writing 317–32, 373
  abbreviations 327
  common criticisms 330–1
  conclusion 326–7
  diagrams or pictures 327
  essay plan or outline 322–3
  essay title, analysis of 318–20
  finding material 320–2
  introduction 325
  main body 325–6
  plagiarism 327
  quotations 328
  references 327
  reviewing 328–9
  rough draft 324–5
  subheadings 327
  under examination conditions 331–2
  word limit 328
estimation 136
ethical considerations 191, 355–6
eustress 252
evaluation 269
evaluator 217
evidence 35–7
  sources of 35
  supporting 329
examination/examinations 365–91
  anxiety 262–3
  benefits of 366
  cheating 390
  closed book 372
  conditions 331–2
  failing and what to do 389–90
  open book 372, 377
  oral (*viva voce*) 387–8
  papers, previous 375
  practical 388–9
  preparation 367–9
  revision 369–71
  see also written examinations
Excel 157–60
exercise 259
expectations 268

experience 355
  concrete 13
  re-evaluation 45
  returning to 45
Experiential Learning Model 13
experimenting (active experimentation) 13, 16, 206–7
Extel 177
extrinsic values 50
eye contact 93, 298

facts 281–2
familiarisation with case material 278
family relationships 252, 254
feasibility of topic 357–8
feedback 273
feelings 45, 282–3
figure-based data 179
files 152–3, 184
findings 340
first person ('I') 98
fishbone diagram (cause and effect diagram) 284–5
fixations 83–4
flip charts 308
flow 329
  charts 323
focus 185, 371
font, large 303–4
formatting in Word 157
forming 222
forward 172
foundation stage 269
free text search 179
free-riders 272
freehand drawing 161
frequency distributions 124–6, 133
  grouped 124, 125, 141
full text 179

gatekeeper 218
gaze 93
generalisations 13
geographic designations 185

gestures 93, 298
glossary 101, 345
government publications and statistics 176–7
Government Statistical Service 176
graphical displays 303
Graphical User Interface 154
graphs 130–2, 347
group
  assessments 271–2
  discussion 113
  presentations 315–16
  reports 350
  see also group and team working skills
group and team working skills 40–1, 211–36
  ambience 226
  at university or college 231–6
  cohesiveness 219–21
  decision making 226
  developmental stages 221–3
  deviant group members 224–5
  group dynamics 212
  groups and teams, differences between 227–9
  leadership 226–7
  maturity 220
  norms, development of 215–16
  participation 225–6
  roles 216–19
  small group dynamics 213–15
  status 224
  subgroups of members (cliques) 225
  team role theory 229–31
Guide to Official Statistics 176

handouts 308–9
hard copy 150
hardware 148
harmoniser 218

INDEX

Harvard system of citation 342
Harvey, L. 49
have to do activities 241, 242, 246
headings 346
health 259
HERO (Higher Education and Research Opportunities) 183
highlighting 105
hindrances 30
histograms 130, 139
holding action 285
Holmes, T.H. 255–6
Honey, P. 19–20

ideas generator 216
illustrations 329
implementor 230
independent learning 10–12
independent variables 131
indexing 79, 172, 179
influencing factors and learning 20–8
  blockages to learning 24–5
  conditions for learning 22–3
  learning development plan 25–8
  memory 21–2
  rewards for learning 23–4
information:
  analysis 279–83
  basic 58
  categorising 283
  collection 321–2
  and data, working with 39–40
  essential 111
  gathering 336–7
  giver 217
  overload 186
  primary 355
  provision 334
  see also information, researching and obtaining of; information technology skills; secondary information

information, researching and obtaining of 163–210
  audio-visual media 178
  CD-ROM 178–9
  data analysis 207
  electronic media 178
  information evaluation 188
  internet 180–7
  microfilm/microfiche 178
  online databases 180
  primary data collection 191–207
  printed resources 172–8
  secondary information: when to stop collecting 189–90
  secondary information 180
  secondary sources 167–72
  systematic approach 164–6
information technology skills 147–62
  hardware 148
  input 148–9
  output 150
  presentation software – PowerPoint 161
  processing unit/memory 149
  software 150–1
  spreadsheet software – Excel 157–60
  storage devices 149–50
  Windows 154–5
  word-processing software – Word 155–7
  work, organisation of 152–3
input 148–9
instructional words and their definitions 319, 320
instructions, following 278–9
intellectual behaviour 269
interest in topic 318, 354
interests 50
interface 185
intermediate state 269
internet 180–7, 201
  information accessing 181
  information from 185–6
  web search techniques 186–7

World Wide Web 181–4
Internet Explorer 182
interpersonal communication process 91–2
interpersonal skills 38–9
interviews 65–8, 202
  beginning 203
  closing 205
  conducting 203–5
  data gathering 205
  end of 205
  structured 202
  unstructured 202
intrinsic values 50
introduction 80, 339, 358
intrusions 246

jargon 101
Jensen, M. 222
job
  aspirations 51
  market, understanding of 55–6
  search strategy 56
Jordan Report 177
journals 173–4

key indicators 283–4
key words and phrases 164–5, 318
keyboard 148
  shortcuts 314
knowledge 269, 335
Kolb, D. 13, 16–17, 19, 43
Kompass Register 177

layout of report 345–7
leadership 226–7, 272
learning
  cycle 15–16, 43
  development plan 25–8
  experiences 7
  opportunity 268
  tendency 13–14
  see also learning to learn
learning to learn 5–31
  dependent learning 12

INDEX

independent learning 10–12
learning experiences 7
lifelong learning 7–9
methods of learning 6
strengths, building on and overcoming blockages 28–31
university or college learning 9–10
see also influencing factors and learning; styles of learning
lectures 9
lectures and note taking 109–13
   after lecture 112
   before lecture 110
   during lecture 110–11
libraries 167–71
   catalogues 170–2
   lending 168
   reference 168
Library of Congress Classification System 170
life events 255–6
life of topic 356
lifeline 26
lifelong learning 7–9, 34
like to do activities 241, 242, 246
line graphs 130–2
lists 323
logic 329
lower class boundary 124

mannerisms, distracting 298
margins, use of 104
material, organisation of 337–8
materials, preparation of for job search 56
maturity and learning 12
means, comparison of 137
median 137–8
Mehrabian, A. 90
memory 21–2
menus 155
methodology 361–2
methods of learning 6
microfilm/microfiche 178

microprocessor 149
Microsoft 182
mind maps 107–8, 300, 323
minimisation 285
Mintel 177
mode 138–9
module outline 375
monitor evaluator 230
moral considerations 191, 355–6
mouse 148
Mumford, A. 19–20

Netscape Navigator 182
network directories 183
newspapers 176
non-verbal communication 92–4
norming 222
norms, development of 215–16
notes 103–17, 300–1
   abbreviations and symbols 113–15
   annotation 104–5
   keeping notes 115–17
   making notes from group discussion 113
   making notes from text 109
   making notes in lectures 109–13
   mind maps 107–8
   outline 107
   reasons for making 103–4
   reorganisation of 375–6
   sequential or linear 105, 106
   summary 105–6
numbers, working with 118–46
   bar charts 126–8
   central tendency (averages) 135–9
   dispersion or spread measures 139–41
   frequency distributions 124–6, 133
   histograms 130
   line graphs 130–2
   numerical data 119–20
   ogives 132, 133, 138

   percentages 121–2
   pictograms/pictographs 128–9
   pie charts 129–30
   rounding 120–1
   spreadsheet software 142
   tables 122–3
numerical data 119–20

objective tests 372, 377–8, 381
objectives
   and resources, consideration of 191–2, 334–5
   see also terms of reference
objectivity 188
observation 13, 205–6
ogives 132, 133, 138
omissions 329
online
   applications 65
   databases 180
open-ended class 126
opinions 282–3
oral (*viva voce*) examinations 387–8
organisation 280
   systematic 370–1
organisational factors 254
ought to do activities 241, 242, 246
output 150
overcommitment 246
overhead projector slides or transparencies 302–4

page
   formatting 156
   numbering 345
paragraphs 101, 346–7
   formatting 156
Pareto principle 238, 242
Pareto, V. 238
participation 225–6
passive voice 97
Pease, A. 90, 92
peer assessment 272
percentages 121–2

INDEX

perfectionism 245
performing 222
periodical indexes 175–6
periodicals 173–4
personal appearance 299
personal beliefs, clarification of 258
personal disorganisation 245
personal relationships 252, 254
personal skills 38–9
personal support system 261
personality 50
   traits 52
philosophy of course 354–5
physical preparation for examinations 367
pictograms/pictographs 128–9
pictures 327
pie charts 129–30
plagiarism 77, 327
planning 361, 369–70, 383
plant (ideas generator) 230
portfolio 32–47
   benefits 33–4
   compiling 35
   evidence 35–7
   reflection 41–7
   skills audit 37–41
positive thinking 29, 261
PowerPoint 161, 311–16
   delivery 313
   group presentations 315–16
   keyboard shortcuts 314
   mouse commands 314
   style, consistent 312–13
   transitions 314
practical examinations 388–9
pragmatist 20
preface 172
preparation 202–3, 367
presentations 291–316, 345–7
   approach 295–6
   assessed 311
   body language 298–9
   content 296
   practising 300
   preparation 293–4

purposes 292–3
questions 309–10
software 161
speaking 299–300
structure 294–5
teaching room, assessment of 297
timing 297
see also PowerPoint; visual aids
primary data collection 166, 191–207, 360
   data coverage 192–6
   experimentation 206–7
   objectives and resources, consideration of 191–2
   observation 205–6
   surveys 196–9
primary research 360, 362
printed resources 172–8
   abstracts 175, 176
   books 172
   directories 177
   government publications and statistics 176–7
   newspapers 176
   periodical indexes 175–6
   periodicals and journals 173–4
   problems associated with 178
   professional body publications 177
   special reports 177
priorities, lack of 246
problem solving 334
problems defined 283–4
procedure/method 339, 340
process 213
processing unit/memory 149
procrastination 245, 258
professional body publications 177
prompt cards 300
prospecting letter 64
prospective employer, identification of 56
publisher's comments 80

publisher's name 172
punctuation 100, 101
   avoidance 304

qualitative data 119
quality 185
Quality Assurance Agency 33
quantitative data 119
questionnaires 196
   administering 200
   data gathering 205
   design 196–9
   do's and don'ts 199
   personally administered 201–2
   postal/mail 200–4
   preparation 202
   problem questions 199
questions 76, 309–10
   closed 196
   dichotomous 196
   essay 378, 383–5
   filter 199
   matching 382
   multi-choice 381–2
   open-ended 196
   quantitative 378, 383
   reading of 279, 283
   scaling 198
   tick box 196
   true-false 382
   verbal 198
quotations 328, 329

Rahe, R.H. 255–6
Random Access Memory 149
range of values 140
ranking 198–9
Read Only Memory 149
'readers' 81
reading 76–7
   detailed 75
   flexibility 86–7
   questions 279, 383
   see also reading for study
reading for study 69–89
   background reading 72–3

INDEX

critically evaluative reading 87–8
detailed and critical reading 75
different approaches 71–2
discussion 81–2
'readers' 81
reasons for reading 70–1
scanning 74–5
selection of reading material 78–81
skimming 73–4
speed reading 82–7
SQ3R 75–8
summaries 81
techniques 78
recalling 77
reciting 77
recognition
   seeker 219
   span 83–5
recommendations 287–8, 341–2
references 327, 342–3
reflection 13, 41–7
reflector 20
regression (re-reading), avoidance of 85
relaxation techniques 260
relevance in essay review 329
reliability 188, 192
report writing 333–51
   acknowledgements 345
   appendices 345
   bibliography 343–4
   conclusions 341
   contents page 339
   findings 340
   glossary 345
   group reports 350
   introduction 339
   preliminary stage 334–6
   preparation stage 336–8
   presentation 345–7
   procedure/method 340
   recommendations 341–2
   references 342–3
   review 347–9

summary or abstract 339
title page 338
types 349–50
request making 334
research:
   initial 271
   population (target population) 192
   primary 360, 362
   projects *see* dissertations or research projects
   secondary 362
resource investigator 230
resources 318, 355
   see also printed resources
rest 259
review 77, 347–9
revision 369–71, 375
   list 375
   techniques 375–7
rewards 23–4, 30, 371
roles 216–19, 229–31
rounding 120–1

sampling 192–6
saving files 184
scanning 74–5, 78
schedule preparation 271
Schön, D. 45
search engines 182
secondary information 180, 355
   sources 166
   when to stop collecting 189–90
secondary research 362
secondary sources 167–72
sectioning material 304
security 185
selection of book 81
selectivity 111
self-analysis 50–2
self-discipline 245
self-management skills 52
Selye, H. 252
semantic differential 198
seminar 9
sensitivity 191

sentence length 101
shaper 229–30
shift key, use of 157
signals, non-verbal 299
situation and information analysis 280
size, absolute 122
size, relative 121–2
skills 61
   audit 37–41
   personal 38–9
   self-management 52
skimming 73–4, 78, 80–1
slang 98
Social Readjustment Rating Scale 255
soft copy 150
software 150–1
solutions:
   evaluation 286–7
   generating 285–6
SOSIG (SOcial Science Information Gateway) 183
sources 185, 329
   secondary 167–72
space 94
speaking 299–300
special reports 177
specialist 231
speculating (abstract conceptualisation) 13, 15–16
speed reading 82–7
spelling 97, 171, 186
spread measures 139–40
spreadsheet software 142, 157–60
SQ3R 75–8
   question 76
   reading 76–7
   recite or recall 77
   review 77
   survey 75–6
stages in learning 25
standard deviation 140–1
statistical data 179
status 224
storage devices 149–50

INDEX

storming 222
strengths, building on 28–31
stress management 249–73
   causes 252–5
   consequences of stress 251–2
   coping mechanisms 258–62
   definition of stress 250–1
   life events 255–6
   specific stress for students 262–3
   time management 264
student preference 13–14
style 99–101
   consistent 312–13
   of learning 12–20
      learning cycle 15–16
sub-directories 153
subgroups of members (cliques) 225
subheadings 327, 346
subject:
   index 171
   trees 183
submission, final, preparation of 272
summaries 81, 339
supervision 363–4
support 30, 355
supporter 218
surface approach 71
surveying a book 81
surveys 75–6, 196–9
SWOT analysis 42–4
symbols 113–15
synthesis 269
systems software 150–1

tables 122–3, 347
task:
   allocation 271
   completion 271
teaching room, assessment of 297
team:
   worker 230–1
   see also group and team working skills
technology, working with 40

telephone 201, 246
television 246
terminology 171
terms of reference (objectives) 336, 359
testing implications of concepts in new situations 13
text, selection of 156–7
themes, identification of 111
theorist 20
thinking (reflective observation) 13, 15
time 186, 297, 355
   accessing 186
   inventory 243–5
   see also time management
time management 237–48, 264
   body clock 239
   Pareto principle 238
   personal benefits 247–8
   prioritising 239–44
   time wasters 245–7
title 171
   bar 154
   of book 79
   page 172, 338
topic selection 354–6
touch 93
transitional words and phrases 97–9
transitions 314
travelling 246
Tuckman, B. 222
tutorial 9
tutors 375
two-or three-letter designations 185

underlining 104
understanding of topic area 318
Uniform Resource Locator 184, 187
university 231–6
   computing facilities 151
   learning 9–10
upper class boundary 124
user friendly 188

vagueness 99
validity 188, 192
values 50, 137
   range of 140
variable 119
   dependent 131
   independent 131
virtuous learning cycle 10
visitors 246
visual aids 301–9
   flip charts 308
   handouts 308–9
   overhead projector slides or transparencies 302–7
   whiteboards 307–8
vocabulary, extension of 85–6
vocalising, avoidance of 85
voice, active or passive 97

waiting 246
weekly time log 240–1
whiteboards 307–8
Windows 154–5
Word 155–7
word limit 328
word-processing software 155–7
work experience 60
work, organisation of 152–3
workbook 9
worksheet 157
workshop 9
World Wide Web 181–4
worrying 245
writing, style of 347
written communication 94–5
written examinations 372–87
   after examination 385
   answers 381–5
   day before examination 378–9
   day of examination 379–80
   examination paper 380–1
   how to do well 386–7
   preparation for 375–8
   types 372–5

Zimbardo, P. 255